# Career Counseling for Women

## Contemporary Topics in Vocational Psychology
W. Bruce Walsh and Samuel H. Osipow, Series Editors

Walsh/Osipow: Career Decision Making
Walsh/Osipow: Career Counseling for Women


A related volume published by Lawrence Erlbaum Associates:
Walsh/Osipow: Career Counseling (ISBN 0-8058-0266-5)

# Career Counseling for Women

Edited by
W. Bruce Walsh
Samuel H. Osipow
*The Ohio State University*

**LEA**
LAWRENCE ERLBAUM ASSOCIATES, PUBLISHERS
1994    Hillsdale, New Jersey                    Hove and London

Copyright © 1994 by Lawrence Erlbaum Associates, Inc.
   All rights reserved. No part of this book may be reproduced in
   any form, by photostat, microfilm, retrieval system, or any other
   means, without the prior written permission of the publisher.

Lawrence Erlbaum Associates, Inc., Publishers
365 Broadway
Hillsdale, New Jersey 07642

**Library of Congress Cataloging-in-Publication Data**

Career counseling for women / edited by W. Bruce Walsh & Samuel H.
   Osipow.
      p.     cm.
   Includes bibliographical references and index.
   ISBN 0-8058-1035-8 (c) / ISBN 0-8058-1401-9 (p)
   1. Vocational guidance for women.   I. Walsh, W. Bruce, 1936–
II. Osipow, Samuel H.
HF5382.6.C37   1993
331.7′02′082 – dc20                                          92-40288
                                                              CIP

Books published by Lawrence Erlbaum Associates are printed on acid-free paper, and their
bindings are chosen for strength and durability

Printed in the United States of America
10  9  8  7  6  5  4  3  2  1

Dedicated to
Anne Roe
1904–1991


Anne was a pioneer and a multifaceted, eminent scholar.
Through practice, example, and creativity she raised
awareness about the role of career in women's lives.

# Contents

# Introduction

W. Bruce Walsh
Samuel H. Osipow
*The Ohio State University*

Social trends since the late 1960s strongly indicate the significance of occupational pursuits in the plans and lives of women. As noted by Betz (chapter 1, this volume) most women will work outside the home and this work will play an increasingly important role in their lives. For example, the U.S. Bureau of Labor Statistics (1989) estimates that by the year 2000, the labor force will grow by 18%, an increase of 21 million workers. The Bureau further estimates that women and minorities will account for a large percentage of the growth. A significant question that needs to be asked is how counselors will help women prepare for making career choices in the future. The models, strategies, methods, and information on career counseling described and elaborated in this volume may help show the way.

This book presents nine significant topics focusing on career counseling for women: basic issues and concepts; career assessment; feminism and career counseling; gender and dual-career families; career counseling with ethnic minority women; career counseling for gifted women; women in the sciences and engineering; women in management; and counseling for career adjustment in the work environment.

Each chapter takes a distinctive approach to the career counseling needs of women. These range from a focus on feminist theory, issues related to career assessment, and the special needs of a broad range of women's diversity (e.g., minority status, the gifted, and special occupational factors).

Chapter 1 by Nancy Betz discusses basic issues and concepts in career counseling for women, and sets the stage for the more specifically focused chapters to follow. To do this, Betz outlines the unique issues that affect women's career development, versus that of men, especially the unique barriers to women that serve to restrict that development. The major barriers to and facilitators of women's career choices are discussed within the context of two assumptions. The first assumption is that women seek a variety of major sources of satisfaction in their lives. A second major assumption is that the fulfillment of individual potential for achievement is vitally important. Betz notes that although the roles of homemaker and mother are important and often very satisfying, they do not allow most women to fulfill their unique abilities and talents.

Within the context of these two assumptions, Betz discusses barriers to choice and facilitators that are the result of 25 years of research on women's career development. Barriers to choice are defined as variables leading to or related to the tendency to make gender stereotypic, traditionally female choices. Environmental barriers include gender role stereotypes, occupational stereotypes, gender bias in education, barriers in higher education, lack of role models, the null environment, gender-biased career counseling, and race discrimination. Individual barriers include family/career conflict, math avoidance, self-esteem, self-efficacy, and expectancies for success.

Facilitators to choice are defined as factors related to broadened career options, higher educational and career achievements, and greater success and satisfaction. Environmental facilitators include working mother, supportive father, highly educated parents, girls' schools or women's colleges, female models, proactive encouragement, androgynous upbringing, and work experience. Individual facilitators include late marriage or remaining single, no or few children, high self-esteem, strong academic self-concept, instrumentality, androgyny, pro-feminist attitudes. Finally, Betz notes that the concepts of barriers and facilitators have important implications for change because many of them are amenable to intervention, at either an individual or environmental level.

Gail Hackett and Susan Lonborg in chapter 2, "Career Assessment and Counseling for Women," primarily address the following question: How can career counselors approach assessment in their work with female clients in a way that facilitates confrontation and the surmounting of limits, rather than in a manner that perpetuates the status quo? In response to this question, the authors make a number of recommendations for career assessment with women. First, the authors indicate that counselors must be intimately familiar with the literature on the career psychology of women and with career assessment procedures. This includes the technical aspects of test construction and issues of bias in testing. Second, assessment in career counseling is argued to be best viewed as an integral component of intervention rather than as a discrete activity. In this context, career counselors need to examine the conceptual underpinnings of their approach to career counseling, being aware of the possibilities for bias. Third, in assessment, the career counselor needs to routinely view female clients within a social, cultural context, adopting some variant of gender aware counseling as described by Good, Gilbert, and Scher (1990), who suggest that effective counseling requires: (a) regarding conceptions of gender as integral aspects of counseling and mental health (to which Hackett and Lonborg would add career development); (b) considering client concerns within their societal context; (c) actively addressing gender injustices; (d) collaborative therapeutic relationships; and (e) respect for clients' freedom to choose. This recommendation further suggests the use of gender role analysis as an integral component of the career assessment process. A fourth recommendation notes that career counselors should routinely make use of qualitative alternatives to standardize testing such as vocational card sorts. Finally, Hackett and Lonborg recommend that counselors need to examine and work on their own gender-related issues continually if they are to be effectively and ethically responsible in delivering career services to women.

The feminism and career counseling chapter by Linda Brooks and Linda Forrest (chapter 3) overall presents the influence of feminism on the research and practice of career counseling. The first part of the chapter focuses on a research critique and feminists' recommendations for improving research practices of psychologists studying vocational behavior and career counseling. The second part of the chapter uses the four tenets of feminist therapy to make specific recommendations about the practice of career counseling with women, discussing each of the four common feminists' tenets as applied to career counseling. The first tenet suggests that the feminist career counselor approaches the assessment and diagnosis process with the attitude that social structures and societal prescriptions have molded and limited women's career development experiences and opportunities. Thus, the authors suggest that in addition to the usual appraisal process of identifying the clients' abilities, interests, work values, needs, personality characteristics, and educational background, the counselor also needs to assess the ways in which gender role issues have affected the client and created barriers to career development. The second principle that the personal is political, is a natural extension of the first feminist therapy tenet. A focus of the counseling interventions, then, is to help clients develop a political awareness of the ways in which the social structure has molded and limited them. Examples are restricted women's perceptions of occupational options and a focus on nurturing roles to the neglect of achieving roles. The third principle (the egalitarian relationship) advocates a client–counselor relationship characterized by equal worth. To implement this principle, Brooks and Forrest recommend that feminist career counselors work toward establishing the relationship as collaborative and facilitative rather than hierarchal, informing the client about the procedures and goals of counseling and the philosophy of the counselor, urging the client to give feedback to the counselor, and encouraging the client to shop for a counselor. The fourth feminist therapy tenet speaks to the goals of counseling. Brooks and Forrest note that one way of stating the overall goal of feminist counseling is that of empowering the client toward self-determination. Thus, counselors assist clients in gaining the skills, knowledge, and attitudes necessary to take control over her own life and to begin to influence others. Further, feminist career counselors believe that women should have the means or the skills to be financially independent. This means that they are economically as well as psychologically autonomous. Finally, Brooks and Forrest note that because it seems clear that most women will need to plan for and integrate multiple roles, life career-planning strategies can encourage women to engage in long-term planning and thereby exert some control over their future.

Chapter 4 by Gilbert, Hallett, and Eldridge on gender and dual-career families notes three assumptions that appear to be particularly important to dual-career family functioning and hence to career counseling in this area. The first of these assumptions is economic equality between women and men in general and more specifically between heterosexual spouses. The reality continues to be that women earn significantly less than men, are greatly underrepresented in nearly all professional areas, and experience significant attrition in male-dominated professions. Moreover, the authors note that the occupational distribution of women within the labor market has changed only slightly over time. Stated differently, women and men are still typically found in different occupations. The second assumption is a presumed compatibility of occupational and family systems. There is still considerable resistance to altering the structure of professional work and providing policies based on the assumption that both women and men, not just women, involve themselves in family work. A number of personal factors, relationship factors, and environmental societal factors that influence how couples combine occupational and family roles are discussed. The third assumption pertains to the partners themselves. It is presumed that spouses' self-concepts as women and men allow for the establishment of a relationship characterized by role-sharing and mutuality and by an interdependency free of the constraints of gender. Of crucial importance to the relationships between women and men is the assumption that,

under ideal circumstances, neither spouse would expect women to
accommodate to men's assumed superiority nor for men to have
authority over women. In this chapter, the authors first describe what
appears to be the case with regard to the three assumptions just
discussed and then use emerging gender perspectives to further describe and explain processes that may keep theory from becoming
reality. Factors influencing choices about occupations and family life are
considered from this broader gender perspective and followed by
discussions of choices, dilemmas, and sources of support characteristic
of dual-career families. Because the issues in career counseling with
regard to dual-career relationships differ in many respects for lesbian
and heterosexual women, separate sections of the chapter are at times
devoted to each.

Chapter 5 by Bingham and Ward, "Career Counseling With Ethnic
Minority Women," looks at issues relevant to providing career counseling services to African-American, Asian-American, Arab-American,
Latinas (American), and Native American women. The authors note
that it is not their intent to provide historical, anthropological, or
ethnographical information relevant to each ethnic group, but rather to
provide concepts the career counselor may use to gather information
more effectively about the client and how she views her opportunities in
the world of work. The authors note that the literature reveals at least
five areas that tend to affect the career development of racial/ethnic
minority women. These include information about the world of work;
familial involvement and approval; community influence, role models,
and language; impact of socialization; and impact of sexism and racism.
The actual steps for career counseling, the authors note, are really quite
straightforward and tend to be similar to those followed in any other
counseling relationship. Bingham and Ward have identified four steps
or phases: counselor preparation, exploration and assessment of client
variables, negotiation and working consensus, and intervention and
follow-up. These four steps are elaborately discussed, noting the need
for counselor skills and knowledge that embrace the concepts of
multicultural counseling.

Chapter 6 by Kerr and Maresh on career counseling for gifted women
examines giftedness of girls and women in terms of both general
intellectual ability and specific extraordinary talents. Kerr and Maresh's
review of the literature reveals a number of conclusions. First, it is noted
that the high aspirations and career fantasies of gifted girls do not
predict of their actual attainments. Second, decisions that bright women
make in early adolescence have long-term consequences for their adult
achievement and eventual life satisfaction. Third, good academic performance in high school and college may not be associated with

academic self-confidence, high social self-esteem, or high career aspirations. Fourth, the young adult and college years seem to be a critical time for gifted women, in which the college environment may have a permanent impact on the realization of these women's potential. Finally, what happens to gifted girls and women hardly seems to be career development, but rather a downward spiral as gifted women adjust their interests, aspirations, and achievements to fit their own perceived limitations in the absence of support from others to seek appropriate levels of achievement. Counselors working with gifted women must nurture their specific talents. Counselors must attend to issues of nurturing identity, assist in the discovery of a mentor, assist in arranging of specialized training and education, and prepare the young woman for sustained productivity in adulthood.

Thus, career interventions for gifted girls and women are very significant and may be categorized roughly into three levels of intervention. At the first level, girls are encouraged to explore careers in nontraditional fields such as engineering, computer science, and math no matter what their interests or values are. At the second level of intervention are the kinds of workshops that encourage gifted girls to raise their aspirations within occupations that are congruent with their personalities and needs. The third level of counseling interventions are more contemporary and value based in orientation. In summary, a comprehensive approach involving assessment, group counseling, and individual counseling, which takes into account the importance of roles and relationships as well as career goals is advocated. The focus of the special workshop is the search for meaning rather than the search for a job. Young women are encouraged to commit themselves to a deeply valued idea by pursuing an occupation that will permit the actualization of this value. In this way, important values are used to create career goals that take into account all aspects of women's needs and concerns.

The chapter by Betz (chapter 7) titled "Career Counseling for Women in the Sciences and Engineering" notes three critical points at which women are lost to the sciences: (a) the initial choice of careers in the sciences, engineering, and mathematics; (b) the transition from undergraduate degrees in the sciences to the pursuit and attainment of master's and PhD degrees; and (c) hostile climates for token women scientists in academia and elsewhere. Betz notes that women need to be encouraged to continue math and science coursework throughout high school and into the collegial years. Even if they do not end up choosing careers in science or engineering, math background is invaluable for most other career areas. In addition to encouraging continuation in math and science coursework, counselors need to interpret both ability and interest test scores advisedly, recalling the likely effects of experience deficits on scores. It is critical that counselors, when interpreting differential aptitude test scores, remember that gender role socialization shapes girls and boys differently. For example, girls are not encouraged to continue taking math, and may need more help in building confidence and reducing anxiety with respect to math. Furthermore, in interpreting vocational interest inventories, the use of same-gender norms and/or gender-balanced interest inventory scales allows counselors to be alert for areas in which the person has developed interests in spite of gender role socialization. Finally, Betz notes that counselors should keep track of the young women clients who declare science and engineering majors, inviting them to check in periodically so that encouragement and support can be provided. These students should be encouraged to participate in support groups for women science and engineering majors. In order to do this, counselors need to be aware of both local and national organizations providing support systems for women students and workers.

Chapter 8 by Russell focuses on women in management and begins with an elaborate discussion of external and internal barriers facing women managers. Russell notes that external barriers include discriminatory attitudes and gender role stereotypes and discriminatory practices in the workplace (e.g., biased treatment, unequal compensation, limited access to training and developmental opportunities, slower advancement and fewer promotion opportunities, backlash, and sexual harassment). Furthermore, women managers experience social isolation due to tokenism, having few female role models, little contact with subordinates, and limited access to mentoring relationships and informal networks. Internal barriers include the perception that they lack the necessary skills to be successful in management, that they will not be suited to the work, or that they will not have the self-confidence needed. They may think that they will be intimidated by men, that they will have to be competitive, or will have to outperform men. They may encounter a number of work–family issues and conflicts. In addition, Russell notes that women managers may have concerns over child-care issues, experience role conflict and overload, and perceive they have to sacrifice their careers for their marital or parental responsibilities. Overall, Russell notes women face tremendous social and peer pressure to select traditional careers. According to Russell, a variety of career counseling efforts are needed to assist women managers in dealing with these internal and external barriers. Some of these include career planning workshops and self-assessments, cognitive career counseling, and individual and group counseling. Concomitantly, organizations must adopt more innovative techniques and interventions to alter their structure to meet the needs of women managers. The future will continue to require change at both the individual level and organizational level to address the issues confronting women managers.

Chapter 9 by Fitzgerald and Rounds presents a framework for understanding women's work behavior within the general context of the theory of work adjustment (Dawis & Loftquist, 1984). The authors begin with a description of the theory, highlighting its strengths and the research it has generated, and then provide a critique from the perspective of the career psychology of women. An attempt is then made to demonstrate how the theory could potentially be expanded to account more adequately for women's vocational adjustment. The authors conclude with a discussion of practical ways in which an expanded formulation could be applied in counseling adult working women.

The final chapter by Harmon and Meara (chapter 10) discusses themes of the past and puzzles for the future in women's career counseling. They discuss some of the themes followed by some of the puzzles that they believe highlight essential conflicts that continue to impede women's achievement in the world of work. For example, the authors note that an underlying theme in the chapters seems to be that childrearing and family responsibilities are inevitably assigned to females. It is women who are mainly burdened by society's need to produce and socialize children. In reviewing puzzles that contribute to the lack of progress in the field of women's career counseling, Harmon and Meara note three areas of concern: puzzles related to social issues affecting clients, puzzles related to our own professional behavior, and the cognitive affective gap puzzle. Puzzles related to social issues affecting clients include gender relationships and the distribution of power, the definition of accomplishment in contemporary life, and the ambiguity of having it all. Puzzles related to professional behavior focus on individual help versus policymaking, and the unevenness of practice and science. Finally, Harmon and Meara discuss the cognitive affective gap, or the discrepancies between what makes cognitive sense and the affective reactions with respect to women's career development. The authors believe that progress toward equality and justice for women and men who work will be limited and marginal until the issues implicit in these puzzles are recognized and addressed.

The reader is encouraged to assess the degree to which the existing career counseling literature is valid for both women and men, as well as for women alone and men alone. Such analysis should lead to the specification of research that will reduce gaps in our knowledge about theory, data, and practice in career counseling for both women and men.

# REFERENCES

Dawis, R. V., & Loftquist, L. (1984). *A psychological theory of work adjustment.* Minneapolis, MN: University of Minnesota Press.

Good, G. E., Gilbert, L. A., & Scher, M. (1990). Gender aware therapy: A synthesis of feminist therapy and knowledge about gender. *Journal of Counseling and Development, 68,* 376–380.

U. S. Bureau of Labor Statistics. (1989). *Labor force statistics derived from the current population survey: A data book.* Washington, DC: Author.

# ❊ 1 ❊

# Basic Issues and Concepts in Career Counseling for Women

Nancy E. Betz
*Ohio State University*

Although the focus of this volume is on career counseling for women, a context for the need for such a volume should ideally precede discussion of specific aspects of counseling procedure and/or groups of women whose unique problems and issues are of concern to career counselors and psychologists. Accordingly, this chapter is designed to "set the stage" for the more specifically focused chapters to follow. It presumes a knowledge of basic career development theory and career counseling techniques, although readers who wish to enhance their knowledge of these areas may wish to consult Osipow's (1983) *Theories of Career Development*, Spokane's (1991) *Career Intervention*, and Brown and Brooks' (1990) *Career Counseling Techniques*, and the previous volumes in this series (Walsh & Osipow, 1986, 1988, 1990). Recent chapters by Richardson and Johnson (1984), Fitzgerald (1986), and a special issue of the *Career Development Quarterly* (Brooks & Haring-Hidore, 1988) also deal specifically with issues in the career counseling of women. For expanded discussions of research on women's career development, see Betz and Fitzgerald (1987) and Betz (in press).

In order, then, to set the stage for a volume on the career counseling of women, it is necessary to briefly outline the unique issues that affect women's career development, versus that of men, especially the unique barriers to women that have served to restrict that development. Only when career counselors and researchers understand the basic issues and problems in and barriers to women's career development, versus that of men, will they be able to adequately formulate both the objectives and the methods of career counseling with women and, more broadly, to

1

facilitate organizational and societal change capable of preventing problems before they occur.

## OVERVIEW OF ISSUES AND ASSUMPTIONS

Like many areas of psychology, attention to women in the field of career psychology is a relatively recent phenomenon. Women were essentially ignored for the first 50 or 60 years of the history of career psychology, because women were not viewed as pursuing careers. Everyone knew that although some women might "hold down jobs," as a temporary expedient until marriage, or permanently for those unlucky few who couldn't snare a man, the idea that women might want to choose and pursue careers was not considered until relatively recently.

In the mid-1960s, however, interest in women's career development began to grow, and the field has burgeoned since the late 1960s. The study of career development (men's as well as women's) can generally be divided into two major sections, corresponding to the two major phases of career behavior, that is, *career choice* and *career adjustment*. Career choice theory and research attempt to describe the nature and influences of the career choices people make. The most common choice points studied are the educational and career choices made by adolescents and young adults. Although some people do make initial career choices at later ages (e.g., reentry women), and others change their career direction once or more during their adult lives, the focus of theory and research has been on the initial choices made by young adults.

*Career adjustment*, on the other hand, is the term describing what happens to the individual after career entry. Two major dependent variables, success and satisfaction, have been used in the study of career adjustment (Crites, 1969; Dawis & Lofquist, 1984). Research and theory on career adjustment is what is generally also covered under the rubric "Women and Work" and encompassing such traditional topics as gender differences in job performance or success, satisfaction, and motivation, as well as such topics as discrimination, sexual harassment, dual-career issues, and the work–family interface.

### Importance of Careers to Women's Lives

Any discussion of a concept as basic as career development to the lives of women requires one to make certain assumptions. This chapter is based on several major assumptions, largely based on research findings. (Note that not all authors represented in this volume, not to mention all career psychology researchers, necessarily agree with these assumptions. Thus, although they are based largely on research findings, the author also takes sole responsibility for them.)

The first assumption is that women, like men, need a variety of major sources of satisfaction in their lives—as once stated by Freud (according to Erikson, 1950), the psychologically well-adjusted human being is able "to love and to work" effectively.

Both women and men need the satisfactions of interpersonal relationships, with family and/or friends, but also the satisfaction of achievement in the outside world. Osipow (1983), in his major treatise on theories of career development, stated that: "It is clear that working holds an important place both in society and in the lives of individuals" (p. vii). And as stated by Baruch and Barnett (1980):

> It is almost a cliche now for people who work long hours at demanding jobs, aware of what they are missing in terms of time with family, long talks with friends, concerts, all kinds of opportunities for leisure, to express the sentiment that "there is more to life than work." The problem is that life *without* productive work is terrible. We assume this for men in thinking about their unemployment and retirement, but we do not think about the situation of women in this way. (p. 244)

A second major assumption, fully elaborated in the next section, is that the fulfillment of individual potential for achievement is vitally important. Although the roles of homemaker and mother are important and often very satisfying, they do not allow most women to fulfill the development of their unique abilities and talents. These, rather, must be fulfilled through career pursuits or volunteer and avocational activities, just as they are in men. This is not to discount the importance of childrearing but only its insufficiency as a life-long answer to the issue of self-realization. Even if a woman spends a number of years creatively rearing children, these children inevitably grow up and begin their own lives, lives that must of necessity be increasingly independent from the parental home.

The evidence is very strong that homemakers who do not have other outlets for achievement and productivity are highly susceptible to psychological distress, particularly as children grow and leave home. For example, of the women in the Terman gifted sample, when followed up in their 60s (Sears & Barbie, 1977), the women who reported the highest levels of life satisfaction were the employed women. Least satisfied with their lives were those who'd been housewives all of their adult lives. The most psychologically disturbed women were those with exceptionally high IQs (above 170) who had not worked outside the home. It seems fairly clear that women with genius-level IQs who had not pursued meaningful careers outside the home have suffered psychological consequences for that failure.

More generally, there is strong evidence for the salutary effects of working outside the home on a women's psychological adjustment, regardless of her marital status. Bernard, in an analysis (1971) of the relationship between marital status and psychological health, concluded that the healthiest individuals were the married men and the single women, whereas married women were at particularly high risk for psychological distress. Further analysis of the relationships of marital status to mental health by Gove and Tudor (1973) and Radloff (1975), among others, led to similar conclusions.

However, it does not seem to be marriage per se that is detrimental to women's psychological adjustment, but rather the lack of meaningful paid employment. In the studies mentioned, the women who were not employed accounted for the surplus of psychological distress among the married women. Frederic Ilfeld (1977), in a large-scale study of households in the Chicago area, found that the women who were as psychologically healthy and free from symptoms of distress as the average man were those employed in high-prestige occupations. But both Ilfeld (1977) and Ferree (1976) found that even working-class employed women were happier and had higher self-esteem than their nonworking counterparts. Bart (1971), in a study of middle-aged women, found that employed women were much less susceptible to menopausal depression than were women who had concentrated all their attention on the home—women who were overidentified and overinvolved with children who had recently left home (leaving the "empty nest") were the most vulnerable to depression in middle age.

Given these assumptions, it is not surprising that I resist suggestions in the literature that marriage and childrearing, because they involve work at home, can by themselves constitute a legitimate "career" option. Although I accept the legitimacy of this as a lifestyle choice, it has been our premise (Betz & Fitzgerald, 1987) that such work does not constitute a legitimate "career" in the sense used by psychologists because this work (a) is unpaid and is also usually unaccompanied by such benefits as accumulation of retirement income; (b) has no opportunities for advancement; (c) has no training requirements or job security; and (d) would not be considered a legitimate career for a male (males who stay home are generally referred to as "unemployed").

Thus, this chapter is based on the assumption that women should pursue meaningful careers that allow them to fully utilize their individual abilities and talents. They, like men, should be able to "have it all," that is, both careers and families. Psychologists and others engaged in counseling with women, then, have a vital role to play in facilitating overall life satisfaction through a focus on career as well as personal development.

## Describing Women's Career Participation

In a disturbing study (Bingham & House, 1973), it was reported that career counselors were dismally uninformed concerning the facts of "women and work." To engage in career counseling knowing very little about "work" is a serious fault that, we hope, will be avoided by our readers. Such basic knowledge is the focus of the next sections.

Early in America's history, women worked long hours, not only in their homes but often in the fields of family farms (Matthews & Rodin, 1989). At the turn of the century, paid employment for women was the exception rather than the rule, and those women who did work outside the home did so only as preliminary to marriage and the bearing of children. The chief occupations held by women, were domestic service, factory work, and teaching. By the large, the only women working throughout adulthood were those "unfortunate" enough to be without a husband—the unlucky spinsters and the widowed. Thus, when the family life cycle began, the work cycle ended (Perun & DelVento-Bielby, 1981).

Although this pattern remained stable until about 1940, the World War II years were characterized by a large influx of women into the labor force to fill jobs vacated by servicemen. Views of women as the delicate sex were temporarily suspended when women were needed in such dangerous or physically demanding jobs as explosives manufacturing and construction. After the war, many of these women remained in the labor force, and over time their numbers have increased dramatically. In 1988, 56% of adult women, 54 million, were in the civilian labor force, constituting 45% of all workers (Green & Epstein, 1988). Of women in the prime working years of 25–64, 72% were in the labor force in 1988; by the year 2000 this figure is expected to be 81% (Green & Epstein, 1988). In the year 2000, we will have 66 million women in the U.S. labor force. Over half (55%) of currently married women work; 62% of mothers with children under 18 are now working, as are 54% of mothers with preschool children (Foster, Siegel, & Jacobs, 1988). Although about one third of working women are married and have husbands making adequate incomes, the other two thirds are women who are single, widowed, divorced, separated, or have husbands whose incomes are near or below poverty level (U.S. Department of Labor, 1988). Almost 22% of households with children are headed by single women (Bureau of the Census, 1989), and of those, 44.7% had incomes below the poverty level.

In summary, women whose adult lives will not include work outside the home are increasingly becoming the exception rather than the rule. As so well summarized by Hyde (1985), the fact that the majority of American women hold jobs outside the home is one of our country's best kept secrets: "The working woman, then, is not a variation from the norm, she *is* the norm" (p. 169).

Paralleling the greatly increased labor force participation of women is dramatic change in the *aspirations* of young women, with most young women now expressing a preference to combine career and family roles in their adult lives. The modal preferred and actual lifestyle in the 1990s and beyond is the "dual-career" or "working couple" lifestyle. Thus, evidence suggests that most college women want to "have it all"—career, marriage, and children—even though few are prepared for the realities of combining career and family (Catalyst, 1987).

In summary, trends over the past 25 years and recent data strongly suggest the importance of occupational pursuits in the plans and lives of women. It is clear that most women will work outside the home and that this work will play an increasingly important role in their lives. However, although the extent of women's labor force participation is approaching that of men, the nature of that participation continues to differ greatly from that of men, keeping working women economically disadvantaged, lower in status, and burdened with multiple role demands. The career and life choices that young women make continue to tend toward stereotypically female occupational fields and to represent lower levels of both educational and career achievement compared to equally able males. These problems are elaborated further.

## Problem: Continued Occupational Sex-Segregation

Although some occupational barriers have fallen, the U.S. work force is still sex-segregated—most occupations continue to be dominated by one sex or the other (Ferraro, 1984). The problem of women's low earning power is due to both sex-based wage discrimination and occupational sex-segregation (Ferraro, 1984), among other factors. Simply put, women get paid less than men for doing the same job, and the jobs that women tend to be concentrated in are by and large low status and low paying, with few or no opportunities for advancement. More specifically, even though women constitute 45% of the labor force, they continue to be concentrated in a small number of traditionally female jobs and professions (Matthews & Rodin, 1989). A majority of women workers are in "pink collar" jobs (Howe, 1977), especially clerical work, retail sales, the jobs of waitress and beautician, and housekeeping services (U.S. Department of Labor, 1988).

Women professionals are concentrated in professions of lower pay and status than the male-dominated professions, and women continue to be seriously underrepresented in many career fields, particularly those in mathematics, the sciences, and engineering, as well as the skilled trades (Dix, 1987; National Science Foundation, 1990). For example, the proportion of women entering schools of engineering increased from 5% in 1973 to 17% in 1983 but then began to go back down, to 15% in 1986 (Vetter, 1988). In 1985 women accounted for 87% of librarians and 95% of nurses but only 18% of lawyers and judges, 17% of doctors, 11% of architects, and 7% of engineers (U.S. Department of Labor Statistics, 1989).

Ehrhart and Sandler (1987) and Vetter and Babco (1986) documented the way in which the underrepresentation of women in traditionally male careers is mirrored in and, worse, perpetuated by their continued low college and graduate school enrollments in those fields. For example, even though women constituted 39%, 41%, 44%, and 27% of the 1983 bachelor's degrees in agriculture, business, mathematics, and physical sciences, respectively, their share of doctorates in those fields in 1983 was, respectively, 14%, 17%, 16%, and 14% (cf. Ehrhart & Sandler, 1987). On the other hand, women earned 95% of the BAs and 68% of the doctorates in home economics, 76% of the bachelor's degrees in education, and 83% of those in the allied medical fields of medical technology, physical and occupational therapy, and dental hygiene. And even though more women are now pursuing careers in some previously male-dominated fields such as business and law, their levels of pay and rates of advancement continue to lag behind those of comparably educated and experienced men (Dix, 1987; Moore, 1986).

Further, the career aspirations of young women and girls continue to focus on stereotypically female occupations. Recent evidence suggests that, in comparison to men, women continue to select occupations from a more restricted range of options (Hesse-Biber, 1985), see fewer occupations as suitable (Poole & Clooney, 1985), and choose occupations less consistent with their vocational interests (Knapp, Knapp, & Knapp-Lee, 1985). Although there does seem to be a small proportionate increase in the number of women pursuing nontraditional careers, the predominant pattern among women continues to suggest a limited and sex-stereotypic range of female occupational pursuits.

## Problem: Underutilization of Abilities

Related to women's concentration in traditionally female and frequently low-level occupations is the finding that, in contrast to men in general, women's intellectual capacities and talents are not reflected in their educational and occupational achievements; women's career aspirations and choices are frequently far lower in level than are the aspirations of males with comparable levels of ability (Fitzgerald & Crites, 1980).

The oldest and most pervasive model of career choice, the "matching" or trait-factor model, posits that people will be most successful and satisfied in careers that utilize their individual abilities, talents, and interests. This is, in essence, a model fostering the nurturance of individual differences in those characteristics relevant to educational and work pursuits, especially abilities and talents. It is a model valuing self-fulfillment and actualization. Within a model of this sort, a relationship between ability level and attained educational and occupational levels is not only expected but desirable for subsequent individual satisfaction and fulfillment.

Among men, the relationship of intellect to obtained educational and occupational level holds reasonably well (Tyler, 1978). Among women, however, the relationship begins to break down in adolescence, and by college age and beyond, for the majority of women, has broken down almost completely. Women fail to use their talents and abilities in educational and career pursuits, resulting in losses both to themselves and to a society that needs their talents.

Ironically, females start out as the higher achievers in comparison to males and as the children more likely to utilize their abilities in educational pursuits. Girls perform better academically than boys at all educational levels. Studies going back as far as 1929 have shown that girls obtain higher school grades than do boys beginning in elementary school and continuing through college (Hyde, 1985; Rosser, 1989). Among 1960 Project Talent seniors, 51% of the girls in comparison to 39% of the boys reported high school averages of mostly As and Bs (Carnegie Commission on Higher Education, 1973).

The school progress of girls is also superior to that of boys. Girls less frequently need to repeat a grade, and girls are more likely than boys to be accelerated and promoted (cf. Hyde, 1985). In college, women consistently receive higher grades than do men in major fields ranging from the humanities and social sciences to the sciences, engineering, and even mathematics (Rosser, 1989). Women's grade-point advantage ranges from one-half to one full grade point, depending on the major field.

In addition to obtaining higher school and college grades, women receive higher grades in relationship to their scholastic aptitude test scores and their high school grade-point averages (GPAs) than do men. Thus, the predicted college GPA would be higher for a given female than for a male with an equivalent record of test scores and high school grades (Rosser, 1989).

But women's strong academic performance has not been reflected in occupational achievements. One of the most striking examples of the waste of female intellectual talent comes from the longitudinal studies of gifted children of Terman, Merrill, and Oden. The sample, originally obtained in 1921–1922, consisted of 1,528 children having measured IQs equal to or greater than 135. Of the sample, 671 were girls and 847 were boys.

The follow-up study of the gifted group at middle age (Terman & Oden, 1959) indicated that, as expected, the great majority of men had achieved prominence in professional and managerial occupations. They had, by their mid forties, been exceptionally productive scientists, made extensive literary and artistic contributions, and become prominent lawyers, physicians, psychologists, and college professors. In contrast to the men, the women were primarily housewives or were employed in traditionally female occupations. About 50% of the women had been and continued to be full-time housewives. Of those who were working full-time, 21% were teachers in elementary or secondary schools, 8% were social workers, 20% were secretaries, and 8% were either librarians or nurses. Only 7% of those working were academicians, 5% were physicians, lawyers, or psychologists, 8% were executives, and 9% were writers, artists, or musicians. Two-thirds of the women with IQs equal to or greater than 170 (clearly genius level) were either housewives or office workers. Further, although the girls were judged the most artistically gifted as children, and the seven most talented writers were girls, all of the adult artists and writers were men (Terman & Oden, 1959).

Thus, ability and talent in gifted girls had almost no relationship to their achievements as women. At least seven talented writers, as well as unknown numbers of artists, musicians, psychologists, biologists, geneticists, and astronomers, were lost to the world. As stated in the report of the Carnegie Commission on Higher Education (1973), "The supply of human intelligence is limited, and the demand for it in society is even greater. The largest unused supply is found among women" (p. 27).

More recent studies continue to show the serious underutilization of female abilities. For example, Arnold (1987, 1989) reported the results of the Illinois Valedictorian project, a longitudinal study of the lives of 80 students, 46 women and 34 men, who graduated in 1981 as valedictorian or salutatorian of their Illinois high school classes. Results indicated that all but four (two male and two female) students finished college and, on the average, performed exceedingly well (mean GPAs of 3.6 and 3.5 for the women and the men, respectively).

Other than the nonsignificant difference in collegiate scholastic performance, gender differences began to emerge immediately after high school. Significant differences that emerged were a decline in the intellectual self-confidence of the women, a persistent concern among the women about combining career and family (with a consequent abandonment of medical school aspirations among six women), and striking gender differences in both the extent and level of planned labor force participation (Arnold & Denny, 1984, 1985). Two-thirds of the women valedictorians, but none of the men, planned to reduce or interrupt their labor force participation to accommodate child raising. In the most recent follow-up (Arnold, 1989), both male and female vale-dictorians were pursuing careers in the traditionally male areas of science, business, and the professions (law, medicine, academia), but a substantial proportion of women (but no men) were pursuing tradition-ally female "helping" professions and, in a few cases, nonprofessional or homeworker roles. Interestingly, differences in educational and career achievements among the men could be predicted by individual differ-ences in ability, motivation, job experience, and college prestige, while the only useful predictor among the women was career versus family priorities (Arnold, 1989).

Thus, the underutilization of female abilities in career pursuits re-mains a serious problem both for women themselves and for our society. Kerr's chapter in this volume focuses on career counseling for gifted women, a vitally important group, but underutilization of abilities is a serious general problem in women's career development.

## BARRIERS AND FACILITATORS

In summary, although women not only do but plan to work outside the home, they have been seriously disadvantaged in terms of their partic-ipation in the labor market, working at a largely lower level, lower paying, gender-stereotypic group of occupations that have not allowed them to fully utilize their abilities and talents. As counseling psycholo-gists committed to the concepts of individual self-actualization and a "matching model" of career development, we continue to be faced with a serious problem needing much better career counseling. Following awareness of the nature and extent of this problem, a next step in its solution involves the concepts of barriers to and facilitators of women's career development. Barriers to choice are variables/forces leading to or related to the tendency to make gender-stereotypic, traditionally female choices. Barriers to adjustment are forces that act to limit the employed woman's success and/or satisfaction (see the Fitzgerald chapter in this volume). Facilitators are factors related to broadened career options, higher educational and career achievements, and greater success and satisfaction.

One point concerning the barrier/facilitator distinction should be made: that is, a given factor can be both a barrier and a facilitator, depending on whether it is present or absent. For example, lack of female role models is a significant barrier to women's view of career options, and the presence of role models can be an important facilitator of career development. If we are considering methods of environmental enrichment/positive intervention, providing role models would be one important source of such enrichment.

In addition to the distinction between barriers and facilitators, it is useful to distinguish environmental barriers or facilitators from internal/ individual (often socialized) barriers or facilitators. For example, Farmer (1976) suggested six internal or self-concept barriers to women, including fear of success, sex-role orientation, risk-taking behavior, home-career conflict, and low academic self-esteem, and three environmental barriers, that is, discrimination, family socialization, and availability of resources, such as child care. Similarly, Harmon (1977) proposed that women's career development is affected by both internal/psychological and external/sociological constraints. This distinction is especially important when we wish to consider interventions — environmental barriers are best dealt with by societal change, including changes in laws and public policy, in organizational rules and regulations, and in our educational, religious, and family systems. Internal barriers, often originally the result of a sexist or stereotyped society (e.g., the internalized belief that girls can't do well in math), may be dealt with through direct reeducation or counseling.

Table 1.1 provides a summary of barriers to and facilitators of choice, categorized according to the environmental/individual distinction. This table summarizes the results of what is now about 25 years of research on women's career development (reviewed by Betz & Fitzgerald, 1987; Matlin, 1992; and others). A brief overview of these barriers and facilitators follows.

## Environmental Barriers

### Gender Role and Occupational Stereotypes

Certainly the first and most basic barrier to women's career development is societal stereotypes about both life and occupational roles. Early childhood socialization, reinforced by parents, teachers, religion, the media, etc., teaches girls to emphasize home and family pursuits, to expect to assume primary responsibility for childrearing, and to defer to

## TABLE 1.1
### Summary of Major Barriers to and Facilitators of
### Women's Career Choices

| Barriers | Facilitators |
|---|---|
| Environmental ||
| Gender-role stereotypes | Working mother |
| Occupational stereotypes | Supportive father |
| Gender bias in education | Highly educated parents |
| Barriers in higher education | Girls schools/women's colleges |
| Lack of role models | Female models |
| The null environment | Proactive encouragement |
| Gender-biased career counseling | Androgynous upbringing |
| Race discrimination | Work experience |
| Individual (Socialized) ||
| Family–career conflict | Late marriage or single |
| Math avoidance | No or few children |
| Low self-esteem | High self-esteem |
| Weak expectations of Self-efficacy | Strong academic self-concept |
|  | Instrumentality |
| Low expectancies for success | Androgyny |
|  | Profeminist attitudes |

the career priorities of their husbands. In terms of personality characteristics, men are expected to develop those associated with competency, instrumentality, and achievement, whereas women are to develop those comprising a "warmth-expressiveness" cluster, including
nurturance, sensitivity, warmth, and emotional expressiveness.

Related to sex-role stereotypes are occupational stereotypes, or normative views of the appropriateness of various occupations for males
and females. Although a number of studies have shown that occupational stereotypes are consistent and durable in adult populations
(Panek, Rush, & Greenwalt, 1977), the study of Shinar (1975) was a
classic in this area. Shinar asked college students to rate 129 occupations
as masculine, feminine, or neutral, using a 7-point rating scale where
*Masculine* was at the 1 point and *Feminine* was at the 7 point. The results
indicated that both male and female students consistently stereotyped
occupations as masculine or feminine. Mean ratings of masculinity/
femininity ranged from the most masculine-stereotypic job of miner,
which received a mean rating of 1.0 with no variability, to the occupations of receptionist (6.3), nurse (6.6), and manicurist (6.7). Other highly
masculine stereotypic occupations were highway maintenance worker
(1.2), heavy equipment operator (1.2), and U.S. Supreme Court justice
(1.3). Among the professions, district attorney (1.6), engineer (1.9),
federal judge (1.9), dentist (2.1), surgeon (2.2), physicist (2.3), veteri-
narian (2.7) and physician (2.7) were clearly masculine-stereotypic,

while nurse (6.6), head librarian (5.6), elementary school teacher (5.6), and dietician (5.3) were feminine typed. A recent study by White, Kruczek, Brown, and White (1989) essentially replicated the Shinar study.

Not only do adults stereotype occupations as appropriate for males or females, but children appear to learn these stereotypes very early. For example, Gettys and Cann (1981) found that children as young as 2 ½ were able to distinguish masculine and feminine occupations, and occupational stereotypes are consistently found in elementary school children (Gettys & Cann, 1981; Rosenthal & Chapman, 1982).

Further, children's occupational preferences tend to be consistent with the occupational stereotypes they hold. Both boys and girls tend to choose sex-typed occupations (MacKay & Miller, 1982). In MacKay and Miller's (1982) study, third- and fifth-grade boys most frequently chose the occupations of policemen, truck driver, pilot, and architect, while girls chose nurse, teacher, and stewardess. Zuckerman and Sayre (1982) found that the majority of middle-class girls aged 4 to 8 chose nurse or teacher. It is unfortunate indeed that occupational stereotypes have limited girls' perceived career options before they finish elementary school.

Findings of limited occupational preferences among children as young as first and second grades are consistent with Gottfredson's (1981) theory of circumscription and compromise in career choice. Gottfredson proposed that an individual's occupational aspirations become circumscribed within a range of acceptable sex-typed alternatives, and that this acceptable range is normally set by ages 6 to 8. Further, Gottfredson suggested that once set, the range of acceptable alternatives is extremely difficult to modify. Although the suggestion of such early constriction in choices is very difficult to accept, it does not seem to be inconsistent with the available research data on the occupational preferences of children.

### Barriers in the Educational System

The educational system has transmitted not only cognitive and social skills, but it has also been a major source of sex-role socialization, a source of messages concerning appropriate behaviors and roles for girls versus boys and women versus men. And, unfortunately, schools have long been communicating to children the same gender biases that characterize society as a whole; see, for example, Ehrhart and Sandler (1987), Hall and Sandler (1982), and Klein and Simonson (1984), among others, for more detailed discussions of the literature on sex discrimination in education.

For example, elementary school texts have portrayed stereotyped adult roles (Scott, 1981) and, possibly even more damaging in its effects on subsequent self-esteem and self-efficacy, differential capabilities, and personalities of boys and girls. One major difference may be summarized as "Boys do and girls watch." Boys are portrayed as active, resourceful, brave, creative, and as problem-solvers, whereas girls are portrayed as passive, helpless, and dull (Scott, 1981). Girls, through stupidity, get into rough spots from which boys rescue them. One children's book entitled I'm Glad I'm a Boy! I'm Glad I'm a Girl! taught such differences as "Boys invent things" and "Girls use what boys invent" (cf. Key, 1975, p. 56). And Margaret Mead's quote "Man is unsexed by failure, woman by success" (cf. Key, 1975) is being taught to children from the first school readers they use.

In addition to elementary school texts and readers, gender-biased content has been demonstrated to characterize texts in all substantive areas and from secondary school to higher education (e.g., Martin, 1982). Women continue to be portrayed primarily in domestic situations. They were absent from history, philosophy, art, and music and were treated in biased and stereotyped ways (when not ignored completely) in psychology, medicine, anthropology, and education (Howe, 1979).

As reviewed by many researchers (American Association of University Women, 1991; Sadker & Sadker, 1985, among others), there is also evidence that teachers themselves respond differently to boys and girls. Although much more research is needed to understand teachers' reactions under different conditions, some preliminary generalizations are that boys receive more attention, both positive and negative, from teachers; although they may receive more disapproval, they also receive more positive attention, encouragement, and approval (American Association of University Women, 1989).

### Barriers to Women in Higher Education

The enrollment and progress of women in higher education have long been impeded by sex discrimination, both overt and subtle. Examples of overt discriminatory admissions practices have included higher admissions requirements for female than male applicants, sex quotas for admission, discrimination in the award of financial aid, and age restrictions on enrollment that constitute inadvertant discrimination against women (Hall & Sandler, 1984). In terms of financial aid practices, men have traditionally received the bulk of financial aids and awards—obvious examples, include athletic scholarships, the GI Bill, and the Reserve Officers' Training Corps (ROTC), and many prestigious fellowships reserved for male applicants (e.g., until recently the Rhodes

Scholarship program), but the pattern has fit more general types of loans, fellowships, and graduate assistantships as well. The recent case concerning the differential award of the New York State Regent Scholarships to boys, based on somewhat higher combined Scholastic Aptitude Test scores (SATs), was shown to involve discrimination against women because women's GPAs in high school were higher and because women did better in college (GPA-wise) than did men with comparable SATs (Rosser, 1989). Thus, if criterion performance is truly the basis for scholarship awards, predominant use of SAT data is inappropriate and, of course, discriminatory.

In a related vein, the recent proposed policy decision of the trustees of the University of North Carolina to shift its admissions emphasis from high school grades (where girls are superior) to SATs (where boys are ahead), so that more men than women would be admitted ("Chapel Hill's Coeds," 1987), is equally discriminatory. Apparently there was concern on the part of the UNC trustees that rich alumni (presumably mostly male) would give more money if they thought they were giving it to young men rather than to young women.

Finally, overtly (as opposed to subtly) discriminatory faculty attitudes and practices include the sexual harassment of women students (see Fitzgerald et al., 1988; Fitzgerald, Weitzman, Gold, & Omerod, 1988). The significance and severity of the effects of sexual harassment on women students cannot be overestimated.

As serious and possibly even more pernicious because we can't address them through legislation are the effects on women of subtle forms of discrimination in higher education. Legislation attempts to address discriminatory treatment but it does not address the prejudices underlying the treatment—in our case, strong and ingrained prejudices against women students. The prejudices remain and, inevitably, exert themselves in ways outside the bounds of legislation. In other words, it is possible to legislate behavior change but far more difficult to bring about attitudinal change (Bernard, 1976). Jessie Bernard has long been writing about the nature and deleterious consequences of subtle forms of discrimination against women in higher education. Her descriptions of the "stag effect" and the "putdown" provided graphic and still useful characterizations of what really happens to women.

The "stag effect," as defined by Bernard, is a "complex of exclusionary customs, practices, attitudes, conventions, and other social forms which protect the male turf from the intrusion of women" (Bernard, 1976, p. 23). At its most blatant, the stag effect took the form of male-only clubs and professional societies and activities, for example, male-only business and faculty clubs, and the traditional golf game where major decisions are reached. As related to students, the stag effect is usually reflected in various means of avoiding and failing to encourage and support women students. In three important reports prepared under the auspices of the Project on the Status and Education of Women (Hall & Sandler, 1982, 1984; Ehrhart & Sandler, 1987), the nature and impact of differential treatment of women in the college classroom and the wider campus setting are discussed. Such negative treatments of women as being discouraged from classroom participation, discouraging the informal contact with faculty that is so essential to future professional development, and the undermining of self-confidence are particularly characteristic of male-dominated fields (Ehrhart & Sandler, 1987).

The putdown, of course, refers to behaviors that actively disparage, demean, insult, and unfairly criticize women (Bernard, 1976, 1988). Such behaviors include: (a) disparaging women's intellectual capabilities or professional potential; (b) using sexist humor; (c) advising women to lower their academic and career goals; (d) responding with surprise when women express demanding career goals; (e) not actively encouraging women to apply for fellowships, grants, and awards; and (f) focusing on marital and parental status as a potential barrier to the career development of women but as an advantage for men (a sign that he's stable, mature, and heterosexual) (Ehrhart & Sandler, 1987).

The especially important point is made (Association for Women in Science, 1984) that although individual events of this type may appear trivial when viewed in isolation, their effect is cumulative and more than the sum of the individual incidents. As stated by Pearson, Shavlik, and Touchton (1988): "The present record of higher education, in spite of some significant efforts, is not particularly good. Female students, on the whole, still experience a loss of personal and career confidence over the period they spend in higher education, even when they make very high grades. For men, the reverse is true." Bernard (1988) has characterized the effects of such continuing discrimination on women as the "inferiority curriculum," causing even the most capable women depression, frustration, and damaged self-esteem.

### Lack of Role Models

An additional barrier to women in education has been the lack of female role models throughout the educational system, beginning with elementary and secondary school. Elementary teachers are primarily female, but the principals and administrators are primarily male (currently 81%). High school teachers, although balanced by sex, teach in stereotypic subject matter areas—females predominate in the teaching of literature and the arts, and males predominate in the teaching of math and science (and, of course, the possible existence of a male high school home economics teacher or a female electronics teacher is difficult to imagine). Males also predominate in secondary as well as elementary school administration. Eccles (1987), in her model of the relationship of gender roles to achievement-related behaviors, suggests that the lack of role models for young women may have its most serious effect in reducing their "perceived field of options" (Eccles, 1987, pp. 141–142). As pointed out by Eccles, a reduced field of options will most certainly affect the subsequent career choice.

The situation is even worse in higher education, where there are even fewer female faculty members, so women students must rely on men, as well as the few women, to get the mentoring they need (Paludi & Fankell-Hauser, 1986; Weishaar, Green, & Craighead, 1981). Even though male professors can serve essential role modeling and mentoring functions for their female students, there is evidence that the relative lack of female faculty is a deterrent to women's educational and career pursuits, particularly in science and other pioneer fields (Ehrhart & Sandler, 1987). The facilitative effects of same-sex models and mentors were suggested by Tidball (1980, 1986), who reported that as the proportion of women faculty relative to the number of women students increases, so does the proportion of women high achievers in professional life.

*Higher Education for Women: The Null Environment.*   One of the most basic and most important concepts summarizing the difficulties faced by women in higher education is Jo Freeman's (1989) concept of the *null educational environment.* A null environment, as defined by Freeman (1989), is an environment that neither encourages nor discourages individuals—it simply ignores them. Its effect is to leave the individual at the mercy of whatever environmental or personal resources to which she or he has access. The effects of null environments on women were first postulated by Freeman following her study of students at the University of Chicago. In this study, students were asked to describe the sources and extent of environmental support they received for their educational and career goals. Although both male and female students reported being ignored by faculty, thus experiencing what Freeman called a null educational environment, male students reported more encouragement and support from others in their environments, for example, parents, friends, relatives, and significant others.

When added to the greater occurrence of negative messages regarding women's roles and, in particular, regarding women's pursuit of careers in fields traditionally dominated by men, the overall effect of the faculty's simply ignoring women students was a form of passive discrimination, of discrimination through failure to act. As stated by Freeman, "An academic situation that neither encourages nor discourages students of either sex is inherently discriminatory against women because it fails to take into account the differentiating external environments from which women and men students come," where external environments refer to differences in familial, peer, and societal support for career pursuits (Freeman, 1989, p. 221).

In other words, professors don't have to overtly discourage or discriminate against female students. Society has already placed countless negative marks on the female student's "ballot," so a passive approach, a laissez-faire attitude, will probably ensure her failure. Career-oriented female students, to survive, must do it without much support from their environments (see also Betz, 1989).

Thus, discrimination can result from errors of omission as well as of commission, and both have negative effects on females' progress and success in higher education. The critical aspect of this concept for educators, counselors, parents, etc. is that if we are not actively supporting and encouraging women we are, in effect, leaving them at the mercy of gender role and occupational stereotypes. Eccles (1987) also stated it well when she wrote: "Given the omnipresence of gender-role prescriptions regarding appropriate female life choices, there is little basis for females to develop non-traditional goals if their parents, peers, teachers, and counselors do not encourage them to consider these options" (p. 164). Failure to support her may not be an error of commission, like overt discrimination or sexual harassment, but it is an error of omission because its ultimate effects are the same, that is, limitations in her ability to fully develop and utilize her abilities and talents in educational and career pursuits.

### Gender-Biased Career Counseling

Studies done in the 1970s (summarized in Betz & Fitzgerald, 1987) strongly indicated that counselors may view and treat women in the same gender-stereotypic, limiting ways characteristic of society in general. Findings such as a lack of information and a tendency to steer women toward traditional roles and traditionally female careers and away from male-dominated careers were typical in early research. Although most practicing psychologists should now be aware that sexism and gender-role stereotyping are contrary to the policy of their professional organizations (e.g., the American Psychological Association [APA] and the American Counseling Association [ACA] etc.) and therefore should be less likely to report sexist attitudes to researchers, the existence of gender-biased attitudes toward career and lifestyle choices continues to be documented in research (see Fitzgerald, 1980; Fitzgerald & Cherpas, 1985; Robertson & Fitzgerald, 1990).

As discussed in the previous section on the null educational environment, a laissez-faire attitude on the part of counselors is bad enough, as it leaves women at the mercy of a sexist society. Even worse, though, are counselors who, instead of being part of the solution, are part of the problem by behaving in sexist ways.

A further problem, in addition to sexist career counselors, has been gender-restrictive vocational interest inventories and gender bias in aptitude testing (see the Hackett chapter on assessment issues and the Betz chapter on counseling women in the sciences, herein). Even a well-meaning counselor would do a disservice to a female client in using an interest inventory where, for example, 80% to 90% of female examinees were classified as "social." Thus, continuing vigilance and technical improvement must occur if we as a profession are not to be among the barriers to women's career development.

### Race/Ethnicity

A final and extremely important, although neglected, variable is race/ethnicity. Unfortunately, we know little about the role of race and/or ethnicity in women's career development, but it is safe to say that being a racial/ethnic minority serves as a barrier to career development but may also have facilitative aspects. Because Bingham's chapter deals extensively with counseling minority women, the following discussion is brief.

All racial/ethnic minority women are in a position of what has been referred to as "double jeopardy" (Beale, 1970), that is, discrimination because they are women added to discrimination because they are minorities. Thus, they are doubly at risk for discrimination and harassment in both the educational and occupational environments. Furthermore, because they are often not only token women but token minorities (Loo & Rolison, 1986; Zappert & Stansbury, 1984), the problems of isolation, loneliness, and heightened visibility faced by tokens more generally (Henry, 1985; Loo & Rolison, 1986) are exacerbated.

Although racial/ethnic minority women share the burden of double jeopardy, it is a mistake to assume homogeneity in the effects of minority status on career development, as each culture has its unique socialization pressures. For example, African-American women, in comparison to their Anglo counterparts, have expected to work part or all of their adult lives (e.g., Smith, 1982). Although the actual labor force participation rate among Anglo women is now catching up to that among African-American women (Almquist, 1989), the labor force participation rate among African-American women has traditionally been greater than that of Anglo women (Almquist, 1989). Although this greater labor force participation has not led to greater socioeconomic status for African-American women, it has led to a different "mindset" among young black women concerning adult roles—most African-American women have never had the luxury to conceive of a life as solely a homemaker and mother, but have always planned for economic self-sufficiency. Related to this is the fact that in our current interest in dual-career families and strategies of multiple role management we often overlook the potential wisdom of African-American women, who have always had to "manage multiple roles."

Hispanic and Asian-American women, like African-American women, suffer the disadvantages of being both a minority and a woman, and yet there are some vitally important differences in that these women are possibly even more subject to rigid and traditional sex-role norms and expectations than are either Anglo or African-American women (Arbona, 1990; Gonzales, 1988; Yang, 1991).

In terms of higher education, Hispanic women again face the barriers associated with double tokenism—isolation, lack of role models, a feeling that they carry the fate of their race on their shoulders, and overt and subtle discrimination (Espin, 1980; Vasquez, 1982; Zeff, 1982). In addition, perceptions among young Chicanas that Hispanic males will be threatened by their educational accomplishments and that college attainment will cause them to be seen as elitist by the larger Chicano community (Gonzales, 1988) further complicate the picture.

Native American women (see La Fromboise, 1988) face extreme difficulties—they are the least likely of any U.S. minority to either begin or complete college educations (Astin, 1982), and the effects on their attained occupational level are commensurate.

## Socialized Barriers

### Career-Family Conflict

Even though the majority of women now wish to pursue a career, the continued belief that they will need to be the primary homemaker and childraiser causes many young women to downscale their aspirations and accept lower levels of achievement. And regardless of the career decision a woman has made, the assumption that she is still primarily responsible for maintenance of a home and family, as well as her career, creates obstacles in the form of role overload and role conflict. In other words, at the same time that women pursue careers, 90% still expect to have two or more children (Russo & Denmark, 1984). Although traditionally the family cycle, when it occurred, was to supercede the work cycle in women's lives, it now most often occurs concurrently. For women, the major practical implication of these changes is that they are now expected to successfully handle two full-time jobs, that is, one outside the home and the other that of homemaker and mother (Scarr, Phillips, & McCartney, 1989).

One unfortunate implication of the perceived conflict between and overload caused by career and family priorities is that women for whom husband and children are a high priority tend to downscale their career aspirations, relative to other women and to men. (Men, of course, have not had to downscale their career aspirations in order to have a family.) The research of Arnold (1987, 1989) and Arnold and Denny (1984, 1985) following the lives of Illinois valedictorians and discussed earlier in this chapter provides a particularly vivid illustration of such downscaling in a group of intellectually superior female high school students. As concluded by Gerson (1986) and discussed further by Eccles (1987), women's choices about work continue to be inextricably linked with their decisions about family, and thus family role considerations limit women's investment in the occupational world. Ironically, family involvement has probably served to increase and facilitate men's career involvements because it gives them a strong rationale for achievement-related behavior.

Although the relationship of marital/familial status to women's career development has been weakening as we have witnessed tremendous increases in workforce participation among women in all marital and parental categories, the relationship of marital/parental status to career attainment, commitment, and innovation is still very strong. Theoretically, this relationship has been called the role-conflict approach (O'Connell, Betz, & Kurth, 1989) to the explanation of gender differences in work-related behavior. This approach assumes that women's work-related behavior is shaped more by family obligations than by the potential rewards associated with occupational activity.

Consistent with this approach is a vast array of data showing strong inverse relationships between being married and number of children and every measurable criterion of career involvement and achievement (see Betz & Fitzgerald, 1987, for a comprehensive review). And it is essential to note that this inverse relationship is not true among men— highly achieving men are at least as likely (if not more so) as their less highly achieving male counterparts to be married and to have one or more children. In other words, men do not have to choose, they do not have to downscale. It is, incidentally, with respect to this latter point that I disagree with authors who suggest that lack of career achievement is "OK" for women because they have different "core" values than do men (i.e., interest in people versus in achievement)—this stance seems to give too much control to something that is the product of gender-role socialization. Women, like men, deserve to have, or at least try for, "it all." Maybe most important for this goal are strategies for dealing with career-family conflict. This topic, as well as a range of issues important in counseling dual career couples, is covered in Gilbert's chapter herein.

### Mathematics: The Critical Filter for Women

The critical importance of mathematics background for entrance to many of the best career opportunities in our society—for example, engineering, scientific and medical careers, computer science, business, and the skilled trades—is now generally agreed upon (Armstrong, 1985; Chipman & Wilson, 1985; Sells, 1982; Sherman 1982), and lack of math background constitutes one of the major barriers to women's career development.

The classic study of the importance of math to career options was that of Sells (1973). In a study of freshmen at the University of California at Berkeley, Sells found that only 8% of the women, versus 57% of the men, had taken 4 years of high school math. Four years of high school math was prerequisite to entering the calculus or intermediate statistics courses required in three-fourths of the possible major field areas, and the university did not provide remedial courses to allow a student to complete the prerequisites post hoc. Thus, 92% of the freshmen women at Berkeley were prevented by lack of math background from even considering 15 of the 20 major fields at Berkeley! The five remaining "options" were predictable—such traditionally female major areas as education, the humanities, the social sciences, librarianship, and social welfare. Thus, decisions to "choose" these majors may have in many cases been by default, through failure to qualify for any major requiring math background.

Sells (1982) further elaborated the vital importance of math preparation for both career options and future earnings. Four full years of high school math are vital to surviving the standard freshman calculus course, now required for most undergraduate majors in business administration, economics, agriculture, engineering, forestry, resource management and conservation, health sciences, nutrition, food and consumer sciences, and natural, physical, and computer sciences. Only the arts, humanities, physical education, and the social sciences do not require math background. Further, Sells (1982) showed a strong and direct relationship between college calculus background and both starting salaries and employers' willingness to interview a student for a given job. Mathematics is important even for non-college-degree technical occupations; the U.S. Department of Labor's *Occupational Outlook Handbook* (U.S. Department of Labor, 1992) shows that high school math and science are a "strongly recommended" for technical and trades occupations. As so well-stated by Sells (1982), "Mastery of mathematics and science has become essential for full participation in the world of employment in an increasingly technological society" (Sells, 1982, p. 7).

Given the importance of math background to career options rather than to "choices" by default, females' tendency to avoid math coursework becomes one of the most serious barriers to their career development. Further, it is fairly clear now that it is lack of math background, rather than lack of innate ability, that is to blame for females' poorer performance on quantitative aptitude and mathematics achievement tests (e.g., Chipman & Thomas, 1985; Chipman & Wilson, 1985; Eccles & Jacobs, 1986). The critical issue is females' avoidance of math. Thus, the development of educational and counseling interventions capable of helping young women to be full participants in an increasingly technological society, may be among the most crucial strategies in attempts to broaden women's career choices. These issues are dealt with more extensively in my subsequent chapter on counseling women in the sciences.

### Cognitive Barriers

Although research on the following concepts is not conclusive, there is suggestive evidence that maladaptive cognitions related to the self may constitute barriers to women's career development. These maladaptive cognitions can be discussed in terms of the following concepts: performance or academic self-esteem, expectancies for success, and career-related self-efficacy expectations. (It should be noted that math anxiety/beliefs that girls can't do math are also maladaptive cognitions, but because of the overdetermining role of mathematics participation in either reducing or expanding career options, it has also received separate discussion in the previous section.)

*Academic and Performance Self-Esteem.* Although global self-esteem is related to stronger career orientation and greater likelihood of pursuing nontraditional careers (see Betz & Fitzgerald, 1987), even more important to women's career development is that dimension of self-concept variously called academic self-concept (Farmer, 1976), confidence in achievement situations (Lenney, 1977), intellectual self-concept

(Tinsley & Faunce, 1980), and performance self-esteem (Stake, 1979). This variable has been consistently shown to influence type and level of academic performance (e.g., Eccles et al., 1983, 1984) and occupational achievement (Gustafson & Magnusson, 1991). Thus, because females are less confident in this domain than are males of equal ability (Maccoby & Jacklin, 1974; Stake, 1979), lower levels of academic self-esteem may be a serious barrier to women's career development.

In addition to overall levels of academic self-esteem, research has utilized several related but more specific, behaviorally based concepts, including expectancies for success and self-efficacy expectations.

*Expectancies for Success.* One closely related and widely studied manifestation of women's lower academic self-esteem is their tendency to underestimate their abilities and their probable levels of future performance, a phenomenon studied in the literature as sex differences in expectancies (e.g., see Eccles et al., 1983, 1984; Meece et al., 1982). Research has shown that women tend to provide lower estimates of their abilities, performance, and expectancies for future success in many achievement situations, even when their performance is objectively better than that of males (Meece et al., 1982).

For example, if college students are asked to estimate their exam performance, most studies indicate that females estimate that they will get fewer points than males (cf. Matlin, 1987). Lower expectancies for performance have been found in females as young as preschool and elementary school age (cf. Matlin, 1987).

Additional findings suggest that females' significantly lower expectancies for success occur primarily on masculine-stereotyped tasks (Deaux, 1984), on tasks lacking clear performance feedback, and on tasks including elements of social comparison, social evaluation, or competition. Unfortunately, the conditions related to significantly lower expectancies for success among females are similar to the conditions under which career achievements must occur, that is, as involving a role pursuit that our society has traditionally defined as a masculine versus a feminine domain of activity, as usually involving some sort of social comparison or competition, and as not generally characterized by clear and unambiguous feedback. Thus, females' tendency to underestimate themselves may negatively influence their career development.

*Self-Concept in Specific Situations: Self-Efficacy Expectations.* Closely related to the concept of expectancies for success and also at the most behaviorally specific level of the heirarchy of types of self-concept is the concept of self-efficacy expectations. Developed by Bandura (1977), the notion of self-efficacy expectations refers to one's expectation or belief that one can successfully perform a given task or behavior. Bandura postulated that both behavior and behavior change are mediated primarily by expectations of personal efficacy. Efficacy expectations influence the kinds of behaviors attempted and the persistence of behavior when dissuading or disconfirming experiences are confronted. For example, self-efficacy expectations with respect to mathematics would influence approach versus avoidance behavior with respect to mathematics and the extent of persistence when a negative experience, such as failing a math test, was confronted.

Although Bandura's theory was originally used in the investigation of clinical phobias, Hackett and Betz (1981) proposed its particular utility for the understanding of women's underrepresentation in traditionally male-dominated careers. Using the concept of career-related self-efficacy expectations, Hackett and Betz contended that low career-related self-efficacy expectations mediated the effects of traditional female sex-role socialization on women's later career choices.

More specifically, Hackett and Betz suggested that female socialization provides less access to the sources of information important to the development of strong expectations of efficacy with respect to career-related behaviors; such sources of information include performance accomplishments, vicarious learning (modeling), and encouragement and support for achievement-related behaviors.

Based on their model, the research of Betz and Hackett and their colleagues (Betz & Hackett, 1981, 1983; Hackett, 1985) indicated that females report lower and weaker self-efficacy expectations with respect to their successful completion of male-dominated educational majors and careers and with respect to the study and performance of mathematics. Further, these lower expectations are related to major and occupational preferences and to the range of career options considered (Betz & Hackett, 1981; Hackett, 1985).

*Summary.*  In summary, there are a number of both environmental and socialized barriers to women's choice of a range of career fields that facilitate full utilization of women's abilities and talents. Psychologists and counselors should be aware of the potential effects of these on their women clients.

## FACILITATORS OF CAREER DEVELOPMENT

Given all the environmental and socialized barriers to women's career development, what influences allow women to surmount those barriers, to achieve to their fullest educational and occupational potentials, to have important, fulfilling careers just like men have always been able to do? Again, the environmental versus individual distinction is useful.

## Environmental Facilitators

### Family Background

The concept of socioeconomic status (SES) has been variously defined and measured; indices of SES have included the occupational or educational level of the primary breadwinner (usually the father) and family income. Although occupational level is the most commonly used index, studies vary in the indices used and, unfortunately, often fail to specify how the index of SES was obtained. In addition, the effects of intelligence on occupational attainments may be difficult to disentangle from the effects of other variables covarying with SES, for example, race and measured intelligence.

In spite of definitional variation, socioeconomic status is one of the most consistent predictors of the occupational level achieved by males; higher family SES is related to higher achieved occupational levels in sons, whereas sons of lower class backgrounds achieve lower occupational levels (Brown, 1970). As pointed out by Goodale and Hall (1976), sons are likely to "inherit" their fathers' occupational levels. In contrast, parental SES does not seem to be a consistent predictor of women's career development.

However, related variables, specifically parents' level of education and maternal employment, do predict daughters' career achievements. Research suggests that more highly educated fathers tend to have more career-oriented and innovative daughters (Russo & O'Connell, 1980), among others. Even more powerful a predictor of women's career development than father's educational level is maternal employment. Numerous studies have found that daughters of working mothers are more career oriented (versus home oriented) than are the daughters of homemakers and are more likely to pursue nontraditional occupations in comparison to daughters of homemakers (Crawford, 1978; Haber, 1980). Stephan and Corder (1985) found that girls reared in two-career families were more likely to plan to combine family and work roles than those reared in a traditional family.

Although maternal employment may influence women's career development through its provision of a model of female employment and role integration, maternal employment is also related to other variables facilitative of women's career development. Studies have suggested that the daughters of working mothers develop generally more liberal sex role ideologies (Hoffman, 1984), are less gender stereotyped (Huston,

1983), and show greater self-esteem and more positive evaluations of female competence (Hoffman, 1984) in comparison to the daughters of homemakers. All of these variables have been shown in other research to be positively related to women's career development.

Family encouragement was reported as a major facilitator by high school girls planning careers in science (McLure & Piel, 1978) and by samples of women pursuing male-dominated occupations (Haber, 1980; Houser & Garvey, 1985). Farmer (1985) found that parent support was one of the strongest predictors of young women's career aspirations and motivation. Gustafson and Magnusson (1991) reported that highly achieving girls tended to have families believing in higher education and strongly believing in their daughters' capabilities, and that these families included low as well as high SES levels.

Possibly as important as parental encouragement of daughters' achievements is a concomitant lack of pressure toward the traditional female role. Parents who exert less pressure on their daughters to date, marry, and have children have also been found to have more career-oriented daughters (Haber, 1980).

Whereas parental variables, then, appear to be importantly related to women's career development, a major limitation of this research is the assumption that both parents are present while the girl is growing up. Dramatic increases in the number of single-parent families across all racial/ethnic groups (e.g., Ferraro, 1984) suggest that research based on nuclear family assumptions will be increasingly irrelevant to an understanding of the career development of many women and men.

### Education as Facilitator

It is probably difficult to overestimate the importance of education to career development and achievement. The nature and level of obtained education are importantly related to subsequent career achievements and to adult socioeconomic status and lifestyle. For example, an undergraduate degree is now a necessary minimum requirement for the pursuit of many occupations, and graduate or professional education is the only route to careers in many professions. In general, appropriate educational preparation is a major "gate" for occupational entrance. Education creates options, while lack of education closes them; without options, the concept of "choice" itself has no real meaning. Thus, the decisions the individual makes concerning his or her education, both the level and major areas of study, will be among the most important career decisions that individual ever makes. Further, success and survival in the educational programs chosen will be critical to the successful implementation of these career decisions.

Although education received is an important variable in the study of men's career development, the nature and level of obtained education are strongly related to almost every major dependent variable used in the description of women's career development. Along with marital status and family-related priorities, education can be considered the most important variable in women's career development. One of the most striking and consistent relationships is that the more education a woman receives, the more likely she is to be working outside the home as an adult, regardless of her marital or parental status (e.g., Vetter, 1980). For example, in 1977 62% of women with bachelor's degrees and 85% of those with master's degrees were in the labor force (Vetter, 1980). The effect of higher education was particularly striking for women with degrees in science and engineering—from 63% to 84% of science BAs, from 78% to 88% of science MAs, and from 90% to 96% of science PhDs or women with professional degrees were employed. And close to half of BAs and MAs *not* in the labor force were so because they were working on advanced degrees.

In addition to its relationship to career orientation and achievements, higher education in women is also related to a greater tendency to remain single, to higher rates of marital disruption (e.g., divorce), and to lower fertility rates (Houseknecht & Spanier, 1980). And higher education in women is related to more liberal attitudes toward women's roles and to such characteristics as autonomy and the desire for direct, versus vicarious, achievement (cf. Betz & Fitzgerald, 1987). Thus, educational level is related to a number of other major variables positively related to women's career development.

The influence of educational level on career achievements and the pursuit of nontraditional occupations has been even stronger for graduates of women's colleges (Tidball, 1986). Graduates of women's colleges are twice as likely to attend medical school as are women graduates of coeducational colleges (Tidball, 1986) and are also twice as likely to have earned research doctorates (Tidball, 1986). Women's colleges have the advantage, first, of providing women with greater opportunities for academic and campus leadership than do coeducational colleges (Astin, 1977). In part this is because in the absence of the men to whom they have traditionally deferred, women must take leadership roles. But, in addition, many women are more willing to assume leadership and to behave in dominant, assertive ways when they aren't worried about offending men or reducing their femininity in men's view (Tidball, 1986). A second advantage of women's colleges is that they tend to encourage women to pursue nontraditional areas of study and therefore encourage women's pursuits of traditionally male career fields (Tidball, 1980). And even though women's colleges, like coeducational colleges, have been dominated by male faculty, there are at least a few more females in faculty and administrative positions to provide models for female students.

Given the importance of education, attention to issues of educational fairness and equality and educational enrichment for women are probably among the most crucial facilitators. Randour et al. (1982) suggested that given women's continued lack of equality in higher education, continued monitoring of the level and nature of women's involvement is essential.

Continued attention to educational equity for women is particularly important given that the 1980s began with a national administration hostile to affirmative action programs and resistant to the enforcement of antidiscrimination legislation. This resistance has continued into the 1990s. Psychologists, educators, and others committed to facilitating women's career development must ensure that research and positive change within the educational system continue to receive effort and attention.

### Individual Facilitators

Of the following individual facilitators, most if not all can be viewed as socialized, just as the internal (as opposed to environmental) barriers were. However, in the case of these facilitators, most go counter to prevailing stereotypes, to prevailing female socialization practices, and thus they might be better termed "unsocialized" or nontraditionally reinforced. In fact, the advantages of nontraditional and androgynous rearing, of a childhood allowing exploration of both traditionally male and traditionally female domains and activities, appear to be far-ranging (Lemkau, 1979). Broader views of the meaning of being female in this society are strongly related to higher achievement and stronger career orientation, possibly through their influence on the development of several significant individual facilitators of career development, as discussed later.

Many individual facilitators merely represent the inverse of the barriers discussed in the previous section; accordingly, further citations are avoided in order to conserve space. Just as marriage and children often have a downscaling effect, later marriage and/or single status and few or no children are strongly associated with career achievement. Just as math avoidance is an impediment to career options, math participation serves to preserve or create options. And just as socialized belief systems such as low self-esteem or low career self-efficacy can serve as internal barriers, higher self-esteem, career-related self-efficacy, and characteristics reflective of a transcendence of the traditional female role are important facilitators of women's career development.

An entire chapter could easily be devoted to the concepts of gender-role-related personality characteristics, so the following can be only a brief summary (for more information see Beere, 1990; Cook, 1987; Robinson Shaver, & Wrightsman, 1991). The study of gender-role-related personality characteristics began, of course, with research on the correlates of "masculinity" and "femininity." Although the terms masculinity and femininity are no longer used as much, having been replaced in the literature by terms such as "instrumentality" and "expressiveness" (Gilbert, 1985; Spence & Helmreich, 1980), much research exists that used them. The terms masculinity and femininity have been criticized because they perpetuate stereotypes and assumptions that behavior is gender based (Lott, 1985), because they imply false dichotomies that overemphasize between-gender and underemphasize within-gender differences (Lott, 1985), and because they aren't descriptive of behavior. Rather, the term *instrumentality*, referring to the capabilities of self-assertion and competence, has been suggested by Spence and Helmreich to descriptively summarize the key aspects of traditional stereotypes of masculinity. The term *expressiveness* best summarizes the central aspects of traditional femininity, that is, nurturance, interpersonal concern, and emotional expressiveness and sensitivity.

Regardless of the labels used to report the results of research in this area, this research has consistently and convincingly shown the importance of instrumentality to women's career development. More specifically, instrumentality appears to be strongly related to both the extent and the nature of women's career pursuits. Higher levels of instrumentality are related to stronger career orientation (Greenglass & Devins, 1982; Marshall & Wijting, 1980), to a greater extent of labor-force participation following the birth of the first child (Gaddy, Glass, & Arnkoff, 1983), and to greater career achievement among working women (Wong, Kettlewell, & Sproule, 1985). Orlofsky and Stake (1981) reported that masculinity was related to stronger achievement motivation and to greater performance self-esteem and self-perceived capabilities among college women. Metzler-Brennan, Lewis, and Gerrard (1985) found that masculinity both in personality and in childhood activities distinguished career-oriented from home-oriented women.

Most strongly related to instrumentality, however, is pursuit of careers in nontraditional fields for women. Among younger women, masculinity is related to stronger interests in and greater pursuit of math and science, more confidence in one's math abilities, and a greater likelihood of selecting a math-related college major (Hackett, 1985). Greater willingness to consider nontraditional college majors, or, alternatively stated, less susceptibility to the limiting influences of traditional female socialization was the major explanation of Wolfe and Betz' (1981) finding that masculine-typed women were more likely than feminine-typed women to prefer careers congruent with their measured vocational interests. Thus, the trait-factor or matching model as a basis for career decision making may be more likely to be used among women who have at least in some ways surmounted gender stereotyping.

Thus, the instrumentality associated with traditional masculinity appears to be importantly and positively related to career innovation and achievement in women. The extent to which the possession of traditionally feminine characteristics is related to career involvement is less clear. Although some studies have suggested a relationship between expressiveness (or femininity) and home orientation (Marshall & Wijting, 1980), other studies have suggested that career-oriented women score no differently on measures of femininity than do home-oriented women (Metzler-Brennan et al., 1985). Farmer (1985) reported that highly career-motivated young women tended to be androgynous, possessing relatively high levels of both instrumentality and expressiveness.

In addition to an apparent transcendence of gender-stereotypic personality characteristics is transcendence of traditional attitudes toward women's roles as an important predictor of women's career development. One of the most consistent (and, it should be noted, inherently logical) findings in the research literature concerns the greater tendency of career-oriented women to express liberal or feminist attitudes toward women's roles (e.g., Stafford, 1984; Tinsley & Faunce, 1980). More liberal gender-role attitudes are related to greater labor force participation (Atkinson & Huston, 1984; Stafford, 1984), to higher levels of educational aspiration and attainment (Lyson & Brown, 1982; Zuckerman, 1981), and to stronger career motivation and higher career aspirations (Fassinger, 1985, 1990; Komarovsky, 1982; Lyson & Brown, 1982).

Finally, other personality and attitudinal facilitators of women's career development, as reviewed previously, include high self-esteem, strong expectancies for academic success, and high expectations of self-efficacy. Overall, women's career development is facilitated by a constellation of personality and attitudinal characteristics emphasizing positive self-concepts, instrumentality and competence, androgyny, and liberated attitudes toward women's roles. The data clearly fit Almquist and Angrist's (1970) "enrichment" hypothesis, which may be summarized as explaining high achievement and role innovation in women as the result of an enriched background, above-average intellectual and personal assets, and an expanded view of what is possible for women.

In considering these conclusions, a final point should be made: that is, that the factors influencing women's career development will almost surely change as societal attitudes and norms change and as increasing numbers of women enter the work force. If girls and women, like boys and men, begin to assume that career pursuits will be an integral part of their lives, we may see changes in the nature of and influences on women's career choices. As so well stated by Osipow (1983), "so much social change is occurring in the area of sex and vocation that any theoretical proposal made now is likely to be premature, as would be any generalization about women's career development" (p. 271). Thus, the study of both barriers to and facilitators of these choices will be a continuing and challenging endeavor.

## SUMMARY AND IMPLICATIONS FOR COUNSELING

The preceding review was designed to provide a general overview of issues and concepts important in the study of women's career development. Because the focus of this volume is on the career counseling of women, I tried to emphasize herein the problematic aspects of women's career development, and both the barriers to and facilitators of that development. The concepts of barriers and facilitators have important implications for change because most of them are amenable to intervention, at either an individual or environmental (e.g., familial, organizational, or societal) level. But from the standpoint of the present volume, the most important facilitator (and the most pernicious barrier) is counseling itself. Because the chapters to follow each address a specific target group of women (e.g., minorities, gifted women, dual-career women, women in the sciences, women in management) or specific aspects of career counseling techniques (e.g., career assessment, feminist applications, and career adjustment counseling), my recommendations for career counseling are of necessity quite general and also very brief.

I recommend that career counseling for women focus on: (a) restoring their options to them and (b) convincing them that they, like men, not only can but deserve to "have it all."

In considering the restoration of options, it seems most helpful to view individual women from the framework of the null environment, as discussed previously. We as psychologists are in the best position to both be aware of the differentiating external environments from which women clients and students come and to counteract the limiting effects of these on the development and actualization of individual potential. In career counseling, a counselor should be aware that the choices of the woman client may already be seriously constrained by gender-role stereotypes and other barriers to women's career development, for example, home–career conflict and math anxiety. Counselors can accept these limitations as inevitable, as givens, or they can do their best to enrich the client's environment, to restore some of the options that societal pressures have taken away from her.

Restoring options in career counseling might involve: (a) asking a women client how her beliefs about the abilities and roles of women have influenced her choices and then counteracting restrictive beliefs; (b) encouraging her to make decisions, like continuing in math, that leave her options open until she is ready to reject them for good reasons; (c) using same-sex norms or sex-balanced vocational interest inventories in order to highlight directions in which her interests have developed in spite of sex role socialization; and (d) suggesting broadening experiences to help her explore previously unexplored areas.

For purposes of increasing interests and competencies in nontraditional areas, Hackett and Betz' (1981) application of Bandura's (1977) theory of self-efficacy expectations to women's career development implies four sources of information useful in increasing women's career-related self-efficacy expectations. Self-efficacy expectations can be strengthened by facilitating performance accomplishments, providing exposure to female role models, assisting girls and women to manage, if not conquer, anxiety with respect to nontraditional domains, and providing active support and encouragement of girls' and women's efforts to develop skills and competencies. An expanded discussion of the use of self-efficacy theory as a basis for career counseling interventions is contained in Betz (1992).

Counselors and educators can also give her support and encouragement when she confronts barriers to her goals—we may be the only cheerleader she has, but our support may be enough to enable her to continue the pursuit. Freeman (1989) noted that many women have surmounted the barriers to their career development and a null educational environment by stronger commitment to and persistence in their educational and career goals, in comparison to equally able men. Although this may be a past and current reality, it doesn't seem fair to women—each woman deserves the encouragement, support, and broadening ideas that will enable her to achieve her goals without carrying the entire burden herself.

In addition, young women need help combating stereotypic belief systems that serve to restrict the range of options—for example, "I can't do both," "I can't do math," and "Highly achieving women lose their femininity"—and combating belief systems that perpetuate the likelihood that she will feel completely responsible for home and family work even if she also pursues a career. Only as her self-esteem and the capability of independence and instrumentality in the management of her own life increase will she be able to demand equality and shared responsibility ("executive" as well as "labor") in her relationships. And only then will she be able to "have it all" without sinking under the weight of fatigue, overwork, and guilt.

Counseling interventions should focus on helping women in these ways: (a) to deal with realistic concerns, such as, "But I'll be the only woman in that profession—how will I survive?" and "So how will I manage a career and home responsibilities?"; (b) to obtain quality education and/or training and to gain needed skills in job hunting, resume writing, interviewing, assertion, and information seeking; (c) to locate support systems, role models, and mentors; and (d) to deal with discrimination, sexual harassment, tokenism, etc. when necessary. Doubly strong support for women of color is needed, because they face the dual barriers of gender and ethnic/minority status.

Finally, counselors should acknowledge their responsibility as social change agents, as stated in the Division 17 Guidelines for Counseling Women (Ad Hoc Committee on Women, 1979; Fitzgerald & Nutt, 1986). Thus, in addition to our work with women clients, we should be engaged in efforts to positively change society—our particular area of interest might be an educational system, an organization, an occupational field (e.g., women in science), or the legal or legislative system. Social change is necessary to address the numerous continuing external barriers to women and racial/ethnic minorities, at the same time as counseling psychologists and others engaged in career counseling work to restore freedom of choice and full life satisfaction to our women clients.

The preceding, then, is meant to serve as a general introduction to the issues confronted by counselors working to facilitate women's career development. The remaining chapters in this book should serve to expand upon and yet refine for specific needs and circumstances the ideas proposed in this chapter.

## REFERENCES

Ad Hoc Committee on Women, Division 17. (1979). Principles for the counseling/psychotherapy of women. *Counseling Psychologist, 8,* 21.

Almquist, E. M. (1989). The experiences of minority women in the United States. In J. Freeman (Ed.), *Women: A feminist perspective* (pp. 414-445). Palo Alto, CA: Mayfield.

Almquist, E., & A. Angrist, S. (1970). Career salience and a typicality of occupational choice among college women. *Journal of Marriage and Family, 32,* 242-249.

American Association of University Women. (1989). *Equitable treatment of boys and girls in the classroom.* Washington, DC: Author.

American Association of University Women. (1991). *Stalled agenda: Gender equity and the training of educators*. Washington, DC: Author.

Arbona, C. (1990). Career counseling research and Hispanics: A review of the literature. *Counseling Psychologist, 18,* 300–323.

Armstrong, J. M. (1985). A national assessment of participation and achievement of courses in mathematics. In S. F. Chipman, L. R. Brush, & D. M. Wilson (Eds.), *Women and mathematics* (pp. 59–94). Hillsdale, NJ: Lawrence Erlbaum Associates.

Arnold, K. D. (1987). *Values and vocations: The career aspirations of academically gifted females in the first five years after high school.* Paper presented at the Annual Meeting of the American Educational Research Association, Washington, DC.

Arnold, K. D. (1989). *The Illinois valedictorian project: The careers of academically talented men.* Paper presented at the Annual Meeting of American Educational Research Association, San Francisco.

Arnold, K. D., & Denny, T. (1984). *Academic achievement—A view from the top: The lives of high school valedictorians and salutatorians.* Paper presented at the annual meeting of American Educational Research Association, New Orleans, LA.

Arnold, K. D., & Denny, T. (1985). The lives of academic achievers: The career aspirations of male and female high school valedictorians and salutatorians (Report No. CE 041 582). *Resources in Education.* (Eric Document Reproduction Service No. ED 257 951)

Association for Women in Science (AWIS). (1984, December-January). *[Editorial]*, AWIS, p. 2.

Astin, A. W. (1977). *Four critical years.* San Francisco: Jossey Bass.

Astin, A. W. (1982). *Minorities in American higher education.* San Francisco: Jossey Bass.

Atkinson, J., & Huston, T. L. (1984). Sex role orientation and division of labor early in marriage. *Journal of Personality and Social Psychology, 46,* 330–345.

Bandura, A. (1977). Self-efficacy: Toward a unifying theory of behavioral change. *Psychological Review, 84,* 191–215.

Bart, P. (1971). Depression in middle-aged women. In V. Gornick & B. K. Moran (Eds.), *Women in sexist society* (pp. 163–186). New York: Basic Books.

Baruch, G. K., & Barnett, R. C. (1980). On the well-being of adult women. In L. A. Bond & J. C. Rosen (Eds.), *Competence and coping during adulthood* (pp. 240–257). Hanover, NH: University Press of New England.

Beale, F. (1970). Double jeopardy: To be black and female. In T. Cade (Ed.), *The black woman: An anthology* (pp. 90–100). New York: New American Library.

Beere, C. A. (1990). *Gender roles: A handbook of tests and measures.* Westport, CT: Greenwood Press.

Bernard, J. (1971). The paradox of the happy marriage. In V. Gornick & B. K. Moran (Eds.), *Women in sexist society* (pp. 145–162). New York: Mentor.

Bernard, J. (1976). Where are we now? Some thoughts on the current scene. *Psychology of Women Quarterly, 1,* 21–37.

Bernard, J. (1988). The inferiority curriculum. *Psychology of Women Quarterly, 12,* 261–268.

Betz, N. E. (1989). The null environment and women's career development. *Counseling Psychologist, 17,* 136–144.

Betz, N. E. (1992). Counseling implications of career self-efficacy theory. *Career Development Quarterly, 41,* 22–26.

Betz, N. E. (in press). The career choices of women. In F. Denmark & M. Palud (Eds.), *Handbook of the psychology of women.* New York: Greenwood Press.

Betz, N. E., & Fitzgerald, L. F. (1987). *The career psychology of women.* New York: Academic Press.

Betz, N. E., & Hackett, G. (1981). The relationship of career-related self-efficacy expectations to perceived career options in college women and men. *Journal of Counseling Psychology, 28,* 399–410.

Betz, N. E., & Hackett, G. (1983). The relationship of mathematics self-efficacy expectations to the selection of science-based college majors. *Journal of Vocational Behavior, 23,* 328–345.

Bingham, W. C., & House, E. W. (1973). Counselors view women and work: Accuracy of information. *Vocational Guidance Quarterly, 21,* 262–268.

Brooks, L., & Haring-Hidore, M. (Eds.) (1988). Career interventions with women [Special issue]. *Career Development Quarterly, 14* (4).

Brown, D., & Brooks, L. (1990). *Career counseling techniques.* Needham Heights, MA: Allyn.

Brown, D. (1970). *Students' vocational choices: A review and critique.* Boston: Houghton Mifflin.

Bureau of the Census. (1989). *Money, income, and poverty status in the United States, 1988.* Washington, DC: U.S. Government Printing Office.

Carnegie Commission on Higher Education. (1973). *Opportunities for women in higher education.* New York: McGraw-Hill.

Catalyst. (1987). *New roles for men and women: A report on an educational intervention with college students.* New York: Author.

Chapel Hill's coeds. (1987, January). [Editorial]. *Washington Post,* p. 4.

Chipman, S. F., & Thomas, V. G. (1985). Women's participation in mathematics: Outlining the problem. In S. F. Chipman, L. R. Brush, & D. M. Wilson (Eds.), *Women and mathematics: Balancing the equation* (pp. 1–24). Hillsdale, NJ: Lawrence Erlbaum Associates.

Chipman, S. F., & Wilson, D. M. (1985). Understanding mathematics course enrollment and mathematics achievement: A synthesis of the research. In S. F. Chipman, L. R. Brush, & D. M. Wilson (Eds.), *Women and mathematics: Balancing the equation* (pp. 275–328). Hillsdale, NJ: Lawrence Erlbaum Associates.

Cook, E. P. (1987). Psychological androgyny: A review of the research. *Counseling Psychologist, 15,* 471–513.

Crawford, J. D. (1978). Career development and career choice in pioneer and traditional women. *Journal of Vocational Behavior, 12,* 129–139.

Crites, J. O. (1969). *Vocational psychology.* New York: McGraw-Hill.

Dawis, R. V., & Lofquist, L. H. (1984). *A psychological theory of work adjustment.* Minneapolis: University of Minnesota Press.

Deaux, K. (1984). From individual differences to social categories. Analysis of a decade's research on gender. *American Psychologist, 39,* 105–116.

Dix, L. S. (1987). *Women: Their underrepresentation and career differentials in science and engineering.* Washington, DC: National Academy Press.

Eccles, J. (1987). Gender roles and women's achievement-related decisions. *Psychology of Women Quarterly, 11,* 135–172.

Eccles, J. E., Adler, T. F., Futterman, R., Goff, S. B., Kaczala, C. M., Meece, J. I., & Midgley, L. C. (1983). *Achievement and achievement motives* (pp. 75–145). San Francisco: W. H. Freeman.

Eccles, J., Adler, T., & Meece, J. L. (1984). Sex differences in achievement: A test of alternate theories. *Journal of Personality and Social Psychology, 46,* 26–43.

Eccles, J. S., & Jacobs, J. (1986). Social forces shape math participation. *Signs, 11,* 367–380.

Ehrhart, J. K., & Sandler, B. R. (1987). *Looking for more than a few good women in traditionally male fields.* Washington, DC: Project on the Status and Education of Women.

Erikson, E. (1950). *Childhood and society.* New York: Norton.

Espin, D. M. (1980). Perceptions of sexual discrimination among college women in Latin America and the United States. *Hispanic Journal of Behavioral Sciences, 2,* 1–19.

Farmer, H. S. (1976). What inhibits achievement and career motivation in women? *Counseling Psychologist, 6,* 12–14.

Farmer, H. S. (1985). Model of career and achievement motivation for women and men. *Journal of Counseling Psychology, 32,* 363–390.

Fassinger, R. E. (1985). A causal model of career choice in college women. *Journal of Vocational behavior, 27,* 123–153.

Fassinger, R. E. (1990). Causal models of career choice in two samples of college women. *Journal of Vocational Behavior, 36,* 225–240.

Ferraro, G. A. (1984). Bridging the wage gap: Pay equity and job evaluations. *American Psychologist, 39,* 1166–1170.

Ferree, M. M. (1976). The confused American housewife. *Psychology Today, 10,* 76–80.

Fitzgerald, L. F. (1980). Non-traditional occupations: Not for women only. *Journal of Counseling Psychology, 27,* 252–259.

Fitzgerald, L. F. (1986). Career counseling women. In Z. Leibowitz & D. Lee (Eds.), *Adult career development* (pp. 116–131). Washington, DC: National Vocational Guidance Association.

Fitzgerald, L. F., & Cherpas, C. (1985). On the reciprocal relationship between gender and occupation. *Journal of Vocational Behavior, 27,* 109–122.

Fitzgerald, L. F., & Crites, J. O. (1980). Toward a career psychology of women. *Journal of Counseling Psychology, 27,* 44–62.

Fitzgerald, L. F., & Nutt, R. (1986). The Division 17 principles concerning the counseling/psychotherapy of women: Rationale and implementation. *Counseling Psychologist, 14,* 180–216.

Fitzgerald, L., Shullman, S., Bailey, N., Richards, M., Swecker, J., Gold, Y., Ormerod, M., & Weitzman, L. (1988). The incidence and dimensions of sexual harassment in academia and the workplace. *Journal of Vocational Behavior, 32,* 152–175.

Fitzgerald, L., Weitzman, L. M., Gold, Y., & Ormerod, M. (1988). Academic harassment: Sex and denial in scholarly garb. *Psychology of Women Quarterly, 12,* 329–340.

Foster, C. D., Siegel, M. A., & Jacobs, N. R. (Eds.). (1988). *Women's changing roles.* Wylie, TX: Information Aids.

Freeman, J. (1989). How to discriminate against women without really trying. In J. Freeman (Ed.), *Women: A feminist perspective* (2nd, pp. 217–232). Palo Alto, CA: Mayfield.

Gaddy, C. D., Glass, C. R., & Arnkoff, D. B. (1983). Career development of women in dual career families. *Journal of Counseling Psychology, 30,* 388–394.

Gerson, K. (1986). *Hard choices: How women decide about work, career, and motherhood.* Berkeley: University of California Press.

Gettys, L. D., & Cann, A. (1981). Children's perceptions of occupational sex stereotypes. *Sex Roles, 7,* 301–308.

Gilbert, L. A. (1985). Measures of psychological masculinity and femininity: A comment on Gadd, Glass, and Arnkoff. *Journal of Counseling Psychology, 32,* 163–166.

Gonzales, J. T. (1988). Dilemmas of the high-achieving Chicano: The double-bind factor in male-female relationships. *Sex Roles, 18,* 367–380.

Goodale, J. G., & Hall, D. T. (1976). Inheriting a career: The influence of sex, value, and parents. *Journal of Vocational Behavior, 8,* 19–30.

Gottfredson, L. S. (1981). Circumscription and compromise: A developmental theory of occupational aspirations. *Journal of Counseling Psychology, 28,* 545–579.

Gove, W. R., & Tudor, J. F. (1973). Adult sex roles and mental illness. *American Journal of Sociology, 78,* 812–835.

Green, G. P., & Epstein, R. K. (Eds.). (1988). *Employment and earnings* (Vol. 35, 2). Washington, DC: U. S. Dept. of Labor.

Greenglass, E. R., & Devins, R. (1982). Factors related to marriage and career plans in unmarried women. *Sex Roles, 8,* 57–72.

Gustafson, S. B., & Magnusson, D. (1991). *Female life careers: A pattern approach.* Hillsdale, NJ: Lawrence Erlbaum Associates.

Haber, S. (1980). Cognitive support for the career choices of college women. *Sex Roles, 6,* 129–138.

Hackett, G. (1985). The role of mathematics self-efficacy in the choice of math-related majors of college women and men: A path analysis. *Journal of Counseling Psychology, 32,* 47–56.

Hackett, G., & Betz, N. (1981). A self-efficacy approach to the career development of women. *Journal of Vocational Behavior, 18,* 326–339.

Hall, R. M., & Sandler, B. R. (1982). *The classroom climate: A chilly one for women.* Washington, DC: PSEW, AAC.

Hall, R. M., & Sandler, B. R. (1984). *Out of the classroom: A chilly classroom climate for women?* Washington, DC: PSEW, AAC.

Harmon, L. W. (1977). *Career counseling for women.* In E. Rawlings & D. Carter (Eds.), *Psychotherapy for Women.* Springfield, IL: Charles C. Thomas.

Henry, M. D. (1985). Black reentry females: Their concerns and needs. *Journal of the National Association for Women Deans, Administrators, and Counselors, 48,* 8.

Hesse-Biber, S. (1985). Male and female students' perceptions of their academic environment and future career plans. *Human Relations, 38,* 91–105.

Hoffman, L. W. (1984). Maternal employment and the young child. In M. Perlmutter (Ed.), *Mother/child interaction and parent/child relations in child development* (pp. 101–128). Hillsdale, NJ: Lawrence Erlbaum Associates.

Houseknecht, S. K., & Spanier, G. B. (1980). Marital disruption and higher education among women in the United States. *The Sociological Quarterly, 21,* 375–389.

Houser, B. B., & Garvey, C. (1985). Factors that affect non-traditional vocational enrollment among women. *Psychology of Women Quarterly, 9,* 105–117.

Howe, L. K. (1977). *Pink collar workers.* New York: Putnum.

Howe, F. (1979). Introduction: The first decade of women's studies. *Harvard Educational Review, 49,* 413–421.

Huston, A. C. (1983). Sex typing. In E. M. Hetherington (Ed.), *Carmichael's manual of child psychology* (4th ed., pp. 116–144). New York: Wiley.

Hyde, J. S. (1985). *Half the human experience: The psychology of women* (3rd ed.). Lexington, MA: D. C. Heath.

Ilfeld, F., Jr. (1977). *Sex differences in psychiatric symptomatology.* Paper presented at the meeting of the APA, San Francisco.

Key, M. R. (1975). Male and female in children's books. In R. K. Unger & F. L. Denmark (Eds.), *Women: Dependent or independent variable?* (pp. 55–70). New York: Psychological Dimensions.

Klein, S. S., & Simonson, J. (1984). Increasing sex equity in education: Roles for psychologists. *American Psychologist, 39,* 1187–1192.

Knapp, R. R., Knapp, L., & Knapp-Lee, L. (1985). Occupational interest measurement and subsequent career decisions. *Journal of Counseling Psychology, 32,* 348–354.

Komarovsky, M. (1982). Female freshman view their future: Career salience and its correlates. *Sex Roles, 8,* 299–314.

LaFromboise, T. D. (1988). American Indian mental health policy. *American Psychologist, 43,* 388–397.

Lemkau, J. P. (1979). Personality and background characteristics of women in male-dominated occupations: A review. *Psychology of Women Quarterly, 4,* 221–240.

Lenney, E. (1977). Women's self-confidence in achievement settings. *Psychological Bulletin, 84,* 1–13.

Loo, C. M., & Rolison, G. (1986). Alienation of ethnic minority students at a predominantly white university. *Journal of Higher Education, 57*(1), 67.

Lott, B. (1985). The potential enrichment of social/personality psychology through feminist research and vice versa. *American Psychologist, 40,* 155–164.

Lyson, T. A., & Brown, S. S. (1982). Sex-role attitudes, curriculum choice, and career ambition: A comparison between women in typical and atypical college majors. *Journal of Vocational Behavior, 20,* 366–375.

Maccoby, E. E., & Jacklin, C. N. (1974). *The psychology of sex differences.* Stanford, CA: Stanford University Press.

MacKay, W. R., & Miller, C. A. (1982). Relations of SES and sex variables to the complexity of worker functions in the occupational choices of elementary school children. *Journal of Vocational Behavior, 20,* 31–37.

Marshall, S. J., & Wijting, J. P. (1980). Relationships of achievement motivation and sex role identity to college women's career orientation. *Journal of Vocational Behavior, 16,* 299–311.

Martin, J. R. (1982). Excluding women from the educational realm. *Harvard Educational Review, 52,* 133–148.

Matlin, M. W. (1992). *The psychology of women* (2nd ed.). New York: Holt, Rinehart & Winston.

Matthews, K. A., & Rodin, J. (1989). Women's changing work roles. *American Psychologist, 44,* 1389–1393.

McLure, G. T., & Piel, E. (1978). Career bound girls and science careers. *Journal of Vocational Behavior, 12,* 172–183.

Meece, J. L., Eccles, J., Kaczala, C. M., Goff, S. B., & Futterman, R. (1982). Sex differences in math achievement. *Psychological Bulletin, 91,* 324–348.

Metzler-Brennan, E., Lewis, R. J., & Gerrad, M. (1985). Childhood antecedents of adult women's masculinity, femininity, and career role choices. *Psychology of Women Quarterly, 9,* 371–382.

Moore, L. (1986). *Not as far as you think.* Lexington, MA: Lexington Books.

National Science Foundation. (1990). *Women and minorities in science and engineering.* Washington, DC: Author.

O'Connell, L., Betz, M., & Kurth, S. (1989). Plans for balancing work and family life: Do women pursing nontraditional and traditional occupations differ? *Sex Roles, 20,* 35–46.

Orlofsky, J., & Stake, J. (1981). Psychological masculinity and femininity: Relationship to striving and self-concept in the achievement and interpersonal domains. *Psychology of Women Quarterly, 6,* 218–233.

Osipow, S. H. (1983). *Theories of career development* (3rd ed.). Englewood Cliffs, NJ: Prentice-Hall.

Paludi, M. A., & Fankell-Hauser, J. (1986). An idiographic approach to the study of women's achievement strivings. *Psychology of Women Quarterly, 10,* 89–100.

Panek, P. E., Rush, M. C., & Greenwalt, J. P. (1977). Current sex stereotypes of 25 occupations. *Psychological Reports, 40,* 212–214.

Pearson, C., Shavlik, D., & Touchton, J. (Eds.). (1988). *Prospectus for educating the majority: How women are changing higher education.* Washington, DC: American Council on Education.

Perun, P. J., & DelVento-Bielby, D. (1981). Towards a model of female occupational behavior: A human development approach. *Psychology of Women Quarterly, 6,* 234–252.

Poole, M. E., & Clooney, G. H. (1985). Careers: Adolescent awareness and exploration of possibilities for self. *Journal of Vocational Behavior, 26,* 251–263.

Radloff, L. (1975). Sex differences in depression: The effects of occupation and marital status. *Sex Roles, 1,* 249–265.

Randour, M., Strasburg, G., and Lhipman-Blumen, J. (1982). Women in higher education: Trends in enrollment and degrees earned. *Harvard Educational Review, 52,* 189–202.

Richardson, M. S., & Johnson, M. (1984). Counseling women. In S. D. Brown & R. W. Lent (Eds.), *The handbook of counseling psychology* (pp. 832–877). New York: J. Wiley.

Robertson, J., & Fitzgerald, L. F. (1990). The (mis) treatment of men: Effects of client gender role and life-style on diagnosis and attribution of pathology. *Journal of Counseling Psychology, 37,* 3–9.

Robinson, J. P., Shaver, P., & Wrightsman, L. S. (1991). *Measures of personality and social psychological attitudes.* New York: Academic Press.

Rosenthal, D. A., & Chapman, D. C. (1982). The lady spaceman: Children's perceptions of sex-stereotyped occupations. *Sex Roles, 8,* 959–966.

Rosser, P. (1989). *The SAT gender gap.* Washington, DC: Center for Women Policy Studies.

Russo, N. F. & Denmark, F. L. (1984). Women, psychology and public policy: Selected issues: *American Psychologist, 39,* 1161–1165.

Russo, N. F. & O'Connell, A. (1980). Models from our past: *Psychology's foremothers. Psychology of Women.*

Sadker, M., & Sadker, D. (1985). The treatment of sex equity in teacher education. In S. S. Klein, (Ed.), *Handbook for achieving sex equity through education* (pp. 147–149). Baltimore: Johns Hopkins University Press.

Scarr, S., Phillips, D., & McCartney, K. (1989). Working mothers and their families. *American Psychologist, 44,* 1402–1409.

Scott, K. P. (1981, April). Whatever happened to Dick and Jane? Sexism in texts reexamined. *Peabody Journal of Education,* 135–140.

Sears, P. S., & Barbie, A. H. (1977). Career and life satisfaction among Terman's gifted women. In J. C. Stanley, W. George, & C. Solano (Eds.), *The gifted and creative: Fifty year perspective* (pp. 72–106). Baltimore: Johns Hopkins University Press.

Sells, L. (1973). High school mathematics as the critical filter in the job market. In *Developing opportunities for minorities in graduate education.* Proceedings of the Conference on Minority Graduate Education, University of California, Berkeley.

Sells, L. (1982). Leverage for equal opportunity through mastery of mathematics. In S. M. Humphreys (Ed.), *Women and minorities in science* (pp. 7–26). Boulder, CO: Westview Press.

Sherman, J. A. (1982). Mathematics the critical filter: A look at some residues. *Psychology of Women Quarterly, 7,* 338–342.

Shinar, E. H. (1975). Sexual stereotypes of occupations. *Journal of Vocational Behavior, 7,* 99–111.

Smith, E. J. (1982). The black female adolescent: A review of the educational, career, and psychological literature. *Psychology of Women Quarterly, 6,* 261–288.

Spence, J. T., & Helmreich, R. L. (1980). Masculine instrumentality and feminine expressiveness: Their relationships with sex role attitudes and behaviors. *Psychology of Women Quarterly, 5,* 147–153.

Spokane, A. R. (1991). *Career intervention.* Englewood Cliffs, NJ: Prentice-Hall.

Stafford, I. P. (1984). Relation of attitudes toward women's roles and occupational behavior to women's self-esteem. *Journal of Counseling Psychology, 31,* 332–338.

Stake, J. E. (1979). The ability/performance dimension of self-esteem: Implications for women's achievement behavior. *Psychology of Women Quarterly, 3,* 365–377.

Stephan, C., & Corder, J. (1985). The effects of dual career families on adolescents' sex-role attitudes, work and family plans, and choice important others. *Journal of Marriage and the Family, 47,* 921–929.

Terman, L. M., & Oden, M. H. (1959). *Genetic studies of genius: V. The gifted group at midlife.* Stanford, CA: Stanford University Press.

Tidball, M. E. (1980). Women's colleges and women achievers revisited. *Signs, 5,* 504–517.

Tidball, M. E. (1986). Baccalaureate origins of recent natural science doctorates. *Journal of Higher Education, 57(6),* 606–620.

Tinsley, D. J., & Faunce, P. S. (1980). Enabling, facilitating, and precipitating factors associated with women's career orientation. *Journal of Vocational Behavior, 17,* 183–194.

Tyler, L. E. (1978). *Individuality.* San Francisco, CA: Jossey-Bass.

U.S. Department of Labor. (1988). *Facts on U.S. working women* (Fact Sheet 88-1). Washington, D.C.: Office of the Secretary, Women's Bureau.

U.S. Department of Labor. (1989). *Labor force statistics derived from the current population survey: A databook.* Washington, DC: Author.

U.S. Department of Labor, (1992). *Occupational outlook handbook.* Washington, DC: U.S. Government Printing Office.

Vasquez, M. (1982). Confronting barriers to the participation of Mexican-American women in higher education. *Hispanic Journal of the Behavioral Sciences, 4,* 147–165.

Vetter, B. M. (1980). Working women scientists and engineers. *Science, 207,* 28–34.

Vetter, B. M. (1988). Women in engineering. *Bulletin of the American Association of Engineering Societies, 86.*

Vetter, B. M., & Babco, E. L. (1986). *Professional women and minorities: A manpower data resource service* (6th ed.). Washington, DC: Commission on Professionals in Science and Technology.

Walsh, W. B., & Osipow, S. H. (Eds.). (1986) *Advances in vocational psychology. Vol. I: The assessment of interests.* Hillsdale, NJ: Lawrence Erlbaum Associates.

Walsh, W. B., & Osipow, S. H. (Eds.). (1988). *Advances in vocational psychology. Vol. II. The assessment of career decision making.* Hillsdale, NJ: Lawrence Erlbaum Associates.

Walsh, W. B., & Osipow, S. H. (Eds.) (1990). *Advances in vocational psychology. Vol. III. Career counseling.* Hillsdale, NJ: Lawrence Erlbaum Associates.

Weishaar, M. E., Green, B. J., & Craighead, L. W. (1981). Primary influences of initial vocational choices for college women. *Journal of Vocational Behavior, 18,* 67–78.

White, M., Kruczek, T., Brown, M., & White, G. (1989). *Journal of Vocational Behavior, 34,* 289–298.

Wolfe, L., & Betz, N. (1981). Traditionality of choice and sex role identification as moderators of the congruence of occupational choice in college.

Wong, P. T. P., Kettlewell, G., & Sproule, C. F. (1985). On the importance of being masculine: Sex role, attribution, and women's career achievement. *Sex Roles, 12,* 757–768.

Yang, J. (1991). Career counseling of Chinese American women: Are they in limbo? *Career Development Quarterly, 39,* 350–359.

Zappert, L., & Stansbury, K. (1984). *In the pipeline: A comparative analysis of men and women in graduate programs in science, engineering, and medicine at Stanford University.* Stanford, CA: Stanford University Press.

Zeff, S. B. (1982). A cross-cultural study of Mexican-American, Black American, and White American women at a large urban university. *Hispanic Journal of the Behavioral Sciences, 14,* 245–261.

Zuckerman, D. M. (1981). Family background, sex-role attitudes, and the goals of technical college and university students. *Sex Roles, 7,* 1109–1126.

Zuckerman, D. M., & Sayre, D. H. (1982). Cultural sex role expectations and children's sex role concepts. *Sex Roles, 8,* 853–862.

# ❧ 2 ❧

# Career Assessment and Counseling for Women

Gail Hackett
*Arizona State University*

Susan D. Lonborg
*Central Washington University*

The reader may rightfully question the need for a chapter on assessment issues specifically for female clients. Many of the issues addressed in the now quite extensive literature on career assessment certainly apply equally to women and men. Yet there are some issues unique to women in that broader literature, for example, sex bias in testing. However, the sex bias debates are only the tip of the iceberg. The issue is not only how standardized tests and other career assessment methods may inhibit women's career choices, or may apply differently to women than to men. More fundamentally, we must consider how gender influences women's career development, and therefore how gender is addressed in the context of assessment in career counseling.

Betz (Chapter 1, this volume) examined the internal and external limitations on women's career choices that result in women occupying a disadvantaged place in the work force. Unfortunately, testing and assessment procedures have too often reinforced existing constraints and barriers (Betz, 1992). The question addressed in this chapter, then, is: How can career counselors approach assessment in their work with female clients in a way that facilitates confrontation and surmounting of limits, rather than in a manner that perpetuates the status quo? Consequently, our discussion of assessment issues must take place in the context of the broader issues of the goals, purposes, and theories guiding career counseling.

We cannot proceed, however, without the usual disclaimers about space and scope. We assume that readers of this chapter: (a) are conversant with basic psychometric concepts; (b) have a knowledge of test user guidelines regarding competent and ethical use of assessment procedures; (c) possess a working knowledge of career assessment; and (d) have at least some familiarity with the career development of women. Useful resources on testing include Anastasi's (1988) *Psychological Testing* and Walsh and Betz's (1990) *Tests and Assessment*. Likewise, the APA *Ethical Principles* (APA, 1990) and *Standards for Educational and Psychological Testing* (AERA, APA, & NCME, 1985) are germane. Several recent publications addressing assessment in counseling and career counseling are useful, particularly Watkins and Campbell's, (1990) *Testing in Counseling Practice*, and Zunker's (1990) *Using Assessment Results for Career Development*. Betz's (1992) chapter in the second edition of the *Handbook of Counseling Psychology*, addressing critical issues in career assessment, is an extremely useful companion piece to this work. Finally, although we discuss specific career tests and inventories, the reader needs to consult the appropriate technical manuals and test reviews for complete information (e.g., Hood & Johnson, 1991; Kapes & Mastie, 1988).

## ASSESSMENT WITHIN CAREER COUNSELING FOR WOMEN

When assessment takes place, it occurs within the context of the counselor's theoretical assumptions about and general approach to counseling. The goals of career counseling have expanded over the years. With the increasing acknowledgment of life-role perspectives on career development, career counseling is now viewed as a much more complex enterprise than the old notions of simple choice that have been manifested in matching models (Brown & Brooks, 1991). Perhaps a very general goal that would fit most approaches to career counseling would be that career counselors attempt to promote and facilitate satisfying and realistic decision making and career adjustment throughout the life span. Thus, goals for career counseling must necessarily encompass assisting clients with acquiring the knowledge and developing the sklls needed to make and implement career decisions, adjust to work circumstances, and negotiate work and other life roles. These overall goals are compatible with the goals of career counseling with women, but often do not lead to specific counselor behaviors that promote effective assessment and counseling with women.

### Career Counseling for Women

Fitzgerald and Crites (1980) noted some time ago that women's career development is not so much different from men's as it is more complex.

We echo this statement and extend it to career counseling: Career counseling (and assessment) with women is similar to and more complicated than career counseling (and assessment) with men. For ethical and effective career counseling with female clients, counselors must not only be good career counselors, but their counseling and assessment practices must be informed by the extensive literature on the career psychology of women and principles for counseling women (see Betz, Chapter 1, this volume; Fitzgerald & Nutt, 1986). The APA ethical principles (American Psychological Association, 1990) concerning assessment techniques and competence underscore this point, that is, the necessity of recognizing differences among people associated with sex, socioeconomic status, and ethnicity.

More fundamentally, we as career counselors need, at the very least, to adopt some variant of gender-sensitive counseling if we are to work equitably with all of our clients, but particularly with female clients. Counselors who treat female clients in a gender-blind manner often merely serve to perpetuate and/or reinforce the gender-role stereotyping that has already occurred and continues throughout clients' lives (Betz, in press; Brown & Brooks, 1991). Even when no active bias on the part of counselors is perceived, that is, when clients report being treated in a sex-fair manner by their counselors, errors of omission are still common. For example, in a recent survey former clients reported that counselors often inadvertently promoted acceptance of the status quo, failed to actively explore gender roles, and missed issues of victimization (Sesan, 1988). All of these problems reflect the failure of counselors to adequately assess important gender-related aspects of client's concerns.

We recommend Good, Gilbert, and Scher's (1990) guidelines for gender-aware therapy as a useful guide for incorporating gender in assessment and counseling. In their view, effective counseling requires: (a) regarding conceptions of gender as integral aspects of counseling and mental health (to which we would add, career development); (b) considering client concerns within their societal context (see Betz, Chapter 1, this volume); (c) actively addressing gender injustices; (d) collaborative therapeutic relationships; and (e) respect for client's freedom to choose. These assumptions are reflected throughout the rest of this chapter.

## GENDER ISSUES IN THEORY AND APPROACHES TO ASSESSMENT

The influence of gender and gender-role socialization on assessment and counseling is apparent at many levels. Although the problem of sex bias in testing comes readily to mind, there are some underlying issues, embedded in many of the fundamental assumptions of counselors, that surface at different points in counseling (L. S. Brown, 1990). Gender-aware counseling is not a theory of counseling per se, but rather an approach to conceptualizing and working with client problems applicable across theoretical perspectives. We must therefore examine the possible gender issues embedded in the broadest of our conceptual frameworks, that is, in our theoretical models of career counseling.

### Theory-Based Career Assessment

Assessment and intervention are always guided by some conceptual framework, and often by a formal theory of career counseling. Each of the major theories of career counseling contains clear implications for diagnosis/assessment, but it is rare to see any attention to gender issues in this literature. Most of the writings on theories of career counseling have followed Crites' (1974) original delineation of five theoretical perspectives: trait and factor, client-centered, psychodynamic, developmental, and behavioral, now social learning (see Walsh & Osipow, 1990). We offer a few illustrations of the potential strengths and limitations of the major theoretical models of career counseling in guiding assessment of women's career concerns.

Within the individual differences perspective (including trait factor and person–environment, or P–E, fit theories), assessment occupies a prominent place. Exploration of aptitudes, abilities, interests, personality, needs, and values is considered crucial to informed decision making. An ongoing problem in assessment within the individual differences or P–E fit approaches to career counseling is the relative absence of consideration of two very basic dimensions of individual differences, namely, gender and ethnicity (Betz, 1992). The individual differences perspective may therefore be useful in understanding the career development of men and nontraditional women, but is probably inadequate in attempts to understand the majority of women (Betz, in press).

Specific diagnostic categories used within the individual differences perspective present some dilemmas for career counselors working with female clients. One of the major foci of diagnosis within this tradition has been the concept of career choice realism (Crites, 1981). *Realistic* choices refer to those demonstrating congruence between level of ability, interests, and the requirements of the chosen occupation. When women choose careers that are clearly incongruent with their interests and measured ability levels, they are diagnosed as having made "unrealistic" career choices. Unrealistic career choices may reflect a choice that is significantly below a woman's ability levels (labeled unfulfilled), or "coerced" choices, reflecting appropriate ability levels for the job but an incongruence in interests (Crites, 1981). However, vocational choice realism is only part of the issue for most women (Fitzgerald & Weitzman, 1992). Many women are primarily responsible for childrearing, and therefore women's occupational choices, narrowly considered, may be unrealistic. Yet in the context of other life roles, plans, and priorities, these same choices might be very appropriate. That is, decontextualizing women's career issues from the rest of their lives results in assessment of only a few narrow aspects of the overall picture.

Fitzgerald and Weitzman (1992) suggested reconceptualizing career choice realism for women, and proposed two alternate concepts to explain the choice process of women seeking to negotiate both work and family role: *satisficing*, or making choices that are "good enough," and *optimization*, or actively seeking to maximize outcomes in both family roles and careers. Ideally, career counselors ought to explore optimizing options with their female clients. However, in keeping with the Good et al. (1990) principle of respect for the client's choices, satisficing options might also be explored. The question of how far the career counselor should pursue the issue of women's "settling" or satisficing is a thorny one (see Betz, Chapter 1, this volume).

Whereas P–E fit conceptions include consideration of both the person and the work environment, little attention has been devoted to possible gender differences in subjective perceptions of work environments, or to the assessment of work environments. Research indicates that gender influences observer evaluations of work performance (Betz & Fitzgerald, 1987). How then might scores on an instrument such as the Minnesota Satisfactoriness Scales (Dawis & Lofquist, 1984), based on observer ratings of employee job performance, be influenced by the gender of the rater and the employee? Could there be gender differences in the experience of the same work environment, particularly for women entering male-dominated occupations or job settings? How might such factors affect assessments of the potential for P–E fit?

Within the developmental perspective the goal of career counseling is to develop a dynamic description of the client's career through various means, including a mixture of directive and nondirective interview techniques as well as qualitative and quantitative methods (Crites, 1981; Jepson, 1990). Despite the absence of specific attention to gender, developmental career counseling does have much in common with feminist notions of the role of assessment and testing in counseling female clients. For example, Good et al. (1990) recommended a collaborative relationship between counselor and client along with respect for a client's freedom to choose, seeing these as crucial elements of gender-aware counseling. Within developmental career counseling the client is intimately involved in the assessment process, including the selection of any instruments, and assessment procedures are geared to the client's developmental level (Jepson, 1990). Moreover, developmental approaches to career counseling reflect developmental theory's concern with the various life roles of the client (Jepson, 1990). Super's (1980) life space/life span model is one of the few views of career development that actually addresses the intersection of roles that must be considered in career decision making, an extremely important consideration for most female clients (Fitzgerald & Weitzman, 1992).

Although the developmental perspective offers much in guiding assessment with female clients, it does not specifically address gender roles or internal and external barriers. Equal treatment of the life roles of males and females without consideration of how those life roles play out differentially by gender can be problematic (Betz & Fitzgerald, 1987). Can anyone truly accept that the homemaker role is considered an equally viable choice for men and women in our society? Or that a combination of parenting and worker roles is experienced similarly by men and women? For women, the worker role is usually added on to home and family roles; parenting responsibilities are rarely shared equally (Betz & Fitzgerald, 1987). Research indicates that role conflict and role overload are critical issues in the lives of many employed women (Gilbert, 1987). Thus, developmental career assessment must be expanded substantially to be considered appropriate for women.

Although social learning perspectives on career counseling account for their influence on learning experiences (Krumboltz & Nichols, 1990), gender and ethnicity are viewed as background variables, rather than as integral factors influencing ongoing learning experiences. The social learning view of vocational interests as learned preferences is one aspect of the model that is particularly advantageous in working with women. A central issue in career assessment has been the restriction of women's career interests due to limited exposure to and experience with nontraditional activities (Betz, Chapter 1, this volume). Adoption of a learning perspective on the development of interests provides theoretical guidance for understanding, assessing, and providing appropriate corrective experiences to encourage the development of nascent but undeveloped preferences.

Specific gender influences on cognitions also remain relatively unexplored within the social learning tradition. Nevertheless, the literature on the career development of women is replete with examples of gender differences in cognitions and related cognitive processes (Betz & Fitzgerald, 1987). The internal, psychological barriers to women's career development discussed by Betz (Chapter 1, this volume) reflect, to a great degree, the limiting nature of gender-circumscribed cognitions, and point to ways in which a social learning perspective on assessment might be expanded to more thoroughly address gender dynamics. Career self-efficacy theory (Hackett & Betz, 1981), while not yet adequately integrated into the social learning model of career decision making, also holds promise for career assessment and counseling of women (Hackett & Lent, 1992).

We see in the next section that the nondirective interviewing procedures that figure prominently within person-centered approaches to career counseling pose problems for the valid assessment of women's career concerns. And finally, psychodynamically based approaches have historically presented formidable obstacles to the equitable treatment of women in counseling. Because of the pervasive assumptions about innate gender differences underlying many projective and other dynamically based assessment methods, career counselors must be particularly cautious in their use and interpretation. Assessments based on Adlerian principles—for example, the assessment of early recollections, lifestyle, and autobiographies—are less likely to pose serious problems, and may, in fact, serve as vehicles for accessing possible gender role conflicts (Watkins & Savickas, 1990).

## Gender Issues in Approaches to Assessment

Gender issues arise not only within a counselor's theory or conceptual model of career counseling, but also within the approaches used to gather information across theoretical perspectives. Therefore, we now turn to considerations of gender issues that may arise in a career counselor's views of the purposes of career assessment, and in the specific approaches used to gather information.

### Purposes of Career Assessment

The primary purpose of any type of assessment within the context of counseling is to gather information to understand and address the client's concerns (Hood & Johnson, 1991). Put simply, "psychological assessment is a process of understanding and helping people cope with problems. In this process, tests are frequently used to collect meaningful information about the person and his or her environment" (Walsh & Betz, 1990, p. 12). Yet many writers attest to other uses of test and assessment information. For example, according to V. L. Campbell (1990), assessment information can: (a) serve as a source of feedback, (b) provide new perspective, (c) teach or present new ideas, and (d) serve as a stimulus for discussion.

Essentially, assessment serves to advance counseling most simply through its informational function, but information itself can serve to create new awareness and redefine goals and directions. Moreover, a number of writers have discussed assessment procedures, particularly self-guided interest inventories and qualitative assessment methods, as career interventions (Goldman, 1990; Slaney & MacKinnon-Slaney, 1990; Spokane, 1990, 1991). For example, assessment can be used to unearth conflicts or problems that may impede the progress of career counseling, can be employed to motivate clients to engage in career behaviors, and is sometimes useful in providing clients with cognitive structures for evaluating career alternatives (Spokane, 1991). Goldman (1990) argued that qualitative assessment methods provide a closer link between assessment and counseling than standardized test procedures.

Although the general purposes of assessment revolve primarily around information gathering, the specific procedures employed with individual clients depend on the nature of the problem, the issues to be addressed, and the type of information needed. Put another way, "The business of assessment—of any variety—is essentially directed toward collecting observations on some dimension of interest" (Phillips & Pazienza, 1988, p. 1). However, specification of these "dimensions of interest" within the context of career counseling is heavily influenced by the conceptual framework and approach of the counselor. That is, a career counselor's basic assumptions about the nature of the individual, along with the counselor's theoretical views about career development and career counseling, will determine what is considered important or salient given similar client concerns, and, in fact, what is attended to as relevant to assessment and counseling. Unfortunately, gender is rarely considered as a "dimension of interest" in career assessment.

## Major Approaches to Assessment

After examining one's theoretical/conceptual views and one's views of the purposes and goals of career counseling, the career counselor must also address gender issues that may arise within one's approach to assessment. We focus next on the general procedures employed by counselors to assess client concerns, that is, interviewing techniques, tests and inventories, cognitive and behavioral assessment techniques, and qualitative assessment.

*The Interview.* Assessment in career counseling begins, and may sometimes end, with the interview. Person-centered career counselors often use only this (Crites, 1981), but all counselors rely to a greater or lesser degree on the information obtained in the counseling interview (Walsh & Betz, 1990). At a minimum, the counseling interview serves as a vehicle for clarifying the presenting concern, establishing rapport, and exploring the client's frame of reference and perspectives on presenting concerns (Zunker, 1990). However, skilled career counselors can also gather much information about individual differences, career development, and the cognitions, skills, and aspirations of clients via interviewing (Brown & Brooks, 1991). More generally, the information gathered in the early stages of the counseling interview serves to inform decision making about the desirability of other types of assessment information that may be necessary, as well as treatment planning. If gender issues fail to be considered in these early stages, the counselor's developing "picture" of the client, her concerns, and her circumstances will be sorely flawed if not outright inaccurate. Integration of gender into the assessment interview is particularly important in career counseling, in that lack of attention to gender issues will cause the counselor to miss crucial information about life-role considerations, sources of stress and strain, and possible gender influences on the consideration of occupational alternatives and career directions (Betz, Chapter 1, this volume).

L. S. Brown (1990) has lamented the lack of attention to gender issues in the clinical assessment interview; her comments are as relevant to career counseling as they are to counseling for personal/interpersonal concerns. Sex per se is of far less importance than gender, which has been defined as the socially constructed attributions, assumptions, and expectations assigned to individuals on the basis of their biological sex (Unger, 1979). In addition to considering the dynamics of gender, counselors must also address the influence of gender role, gender stereotyping, and potential gender-role conflict to develop a genuine understanding of the client and her concerns (for further discussion see D. Brown & Brooks, 1991). Equally important, however, is the career counselor's awareness and consideration of the counselor's own gender issues, that is, basic values and assumptions that might be affected by societal attitudes about gender and appropriate gender-role behavior (L.S. Brown, 1986, 1990). Consequently, counselors must consider gender at various stages of the counseling interview, beginning before a counselor ever sees clients (L.S. Brown, 1990). Such considerations of gender encompass an ongoing examination of the counselor's "conscious and nonconscious biases and expectations regarding gender" (L. S. Brown, 1990, p. 14), as well as continuing efforts by counselors to educate themselves about the career psychology of women (Betz & Fitzgerald, 1987).

Within the counseling session the career counselor might actively pursue the meaning of gender in clients' lives, within their family and cultural circumstances, as well as in the broader societal context in which clients find themselves (L. S. Brown, 1990). Issues surrounding acquiescence to or deviation from internal or externally imposed gender stereotypes and expectations must also be addressed, and are of particular importance in considering clients' career options. D. Brown and Brooks (1991) provide several examples of specific lines of inquiry in career counseling reflecting attention to gender, for example, asking female clients about the meaning of achievement and career success or failure as a women, or exploring expectations about life roles and the influence of gender socialization on such expectancies. Gender-role analysis (discussed more extensively in a subsequent section) can be an effective strategy for exploring the possible costs and benefits of adherence to or noncompliance with gender-role expectations or pressures (L. S. Brown, 1986).

Although we are focusing specifically on gender issues in this chapter, we would be remiss not to discuss cultural bias. Creation of a contextually sensitive "picture" of the client and her career-related concerns includes assessment of the specifics of a client's family culture and current circumstances; this is important for the Anglo/Caucasian client, but particularly vital for women of color (L. S. Brown, 1986; Smith, 1983). Definitions of gender and appropriate gender-role behaviors differ between and within cultural groups (Betz, in press; L. S. Brown, 1986). The career counselor might explore contextual information such as:

> Age cohort, religions raised in and currently practicing, . . . family history with regard to ethnicity and participation in ethnic culture, generation from immigration (where appropriate), languages spoken in the home, . . . family roles of men and women, class background and education of parents. . . . (L. S. Brown, 1986, p. 246)

Although such an extensive exploration of background information may not be necessary for every client, at least some attention to these and related matters is, Brown (1986) argued, necessary to providing "the sociological framework for the phenomenological inquiry into what meaning gender membership gave to life experiences, [and] what was normal and useful for women and men in the world of this individual" (p. 246). Certainly, race, class, and culture influence career decision making and vocational behavior in profound and complex ways, and some consideration of the intersection between gender and ethnicity is fundamental to understanding the career concerns of women of color (Fitzgerald & Weitzman, 1992).

Finally, there is a growing recognition that cross-cultural counseling competencies encompass not only appropriate beliefs and attitudes equipping one with a sensitivity to and appreciation for other cultures and specific knowledge and information about cultural differences, but also cross-culturally appropriate skills (Sue & Sue, 1990). For example, some interviewing methods may be less appropriate than others in counseling women from varying cultural backgrounds. The competent cross-cultural counselor must be able to generate culturally sensitive verbal and nonverbal responses (Atkinson, Morten, & Sue, 1989; Sue & Sue, 1990); these interviewing skills are particularly important at the assessment stage, and crucial to gaining an adequate understanding of women of color and their career concerns.

*Tests and Inventories.* Issues of race and sex bias in standardized tests and interest inventories have been raised and debated extensively over the years, prompting revisions in the most commonly used instruments for career counseling (Betz, 1990; Lewin & Wild, 1991; Selkow, 1984). Improvements in the technical quality of tests and inventories has not, however, totally resolved the widespread concern about bias in testing. Two interrelated issues have surfaced in the literature addressing fairness in testing: the technical quality of the test, and the social policy issues about the use and impact of testing. Attention to the first issue, technical quality, has resulted in improvements in the validity of the instruments we use (e.g., interest inventories); research has demonstrated the absence of widespread, blatant bias. Technical quality reflects the question, "Is the test a good measure of what it purports to assess?" Attention to the psychometric properties of tests cannot, however, address the underlying value issues that arise from the adverse impact test results may have on certain groups in our society, for example, women and people of color. Social policy concerns reflect the question, Should a test, even if it is valid, be used? (Cole, 1981).

Career counselors must first be concerned with the technical quality of the tests and inventories they use. Cultural and sex bias in testing are manifested psychometrically in a number of ways: content bias, bias in internal structure, and selection or predictive bias (Cole, 1981; Walsh & Betz, 1990). All three reflect concerns about different aspects of the validity of an instrument. All tests are culture bound in that they have been developed within the context of the norms, values, assumptions, and experiences of a particular culture. More specifically, most of our psychological tests are developed within the context of the dominant white, middle-class culture, and thus may not be entirely suitable across different cultural groups within the United States (Walsh & Betz, 1990).

*Content bias* refers to words, examples, or the content of questions that may be more familiar to one group than another, and is a concern for women as well as for people of color. Content bias may occur at the item level or at the overall test score level. For example, items on interest inventories about auto mechanics, plumbing, or other stereotypically masculine activities are likely to be foreign to most women (Walsh & Betz, 1990). Sexist occupational titles (e.g., mailman) are another example of sex bias in interest inventory content. Gender differences in mathematics do not appear on problems requiring symbolic manipulation (e.g., computation), but do appear for story-based word problems. Research evidence suggests that differential familiarity with sex-typed word problem content accounts for these observed gender differences in math performance (Chipman, Marshall, & Scott, 1991). Cultural content bias on achievement tests may also result from differential familiarity of problem content, for example, problems requiring knowledge of farm animals that may be disadvantageous to inner-city African-American children (Walsh & Betz, 1990). Content bias may also arise from cross-cultural or gender differences in the values or perceptions of the appropriateness of different behaviors. For example, women tend to view achievement differently than men, and cultural differences in perspectives on cooperation and competition have been identified (Betz & Fitzgerald, 1987; Walsh & Betz, 1990). Experts in the field are in general agreement that offensive, biased, or stereotypical item content ought to be modified for the sake of equity and the general social welfare, as well as to reduce the possibility of inadvertent cultural or gender bias (Cole, 1981). Fortunately, most test developers have made considerable strides, particularly with vocational interest inventories, in eliminating facial bias in content (Cole, 1981).

Sex and cultural bias may also be evident in the internal structure of tests. If the scores of different groups (such as men versus women) yield different relationships, or the factor structures for the groups are different, then a test is considered to be biased (invalid). Traditional psychometric procedures such as examination of item difficulties, item-total correlations, and factor analyses are used to explore the internal structure of tests for bias (Walsh & Betz, 1990). Most career assessment instruments either have been revised to address concerns about bias in internal structure or have not shown problems on this dimension (Cole, 1981; Walsh & Betz, 1990).

*Selection bias*, however, has been of concern to career researchers and counselors. If a test score is differentially predictive across groups, selection bias is operating. A vast amount of research has been conducted exploring selection bias in intelligence, ability, and achievement tests. The consensus in the literature is that achievement and aptitude tests predict about as well for people of color as for Anglos (Anastasi, 1988; Cole, 1981; Walsh & Betz, 1990). For women, there is some evidence for selection bias in that achievement test scores (e.g., SATs, GREs) *underpredict* women's college and graduate school performance compared to men's (Betz, 1990). Career counselors must be mindful of this trend in forming their "picture" of a client's abilities.

Attempts to address bias in testing have taken several forms. All of the major interest inventories and most standardized ability, aptitude, and achievement tests have been revised to minimize content bias. Teams of expert raters are often used to identify culture-bound and sex-typed items and questions (Cole, 1981). Selection bias due to differential predictive validity has been addressed through methods such as changing the selection procedures of Universities and employers (Betz, 1990). However, as mentioned previously, improvements in the psychometric adequacy of tests do not necessarily produce fairness in the use of tests. Thus, test developers have revised not only their instruments but also their interpretive materials, and professional organizations have developed extensive guidelines to promote fairness in testing (AERA/APA/NCME *Joint Technical Standards for Educational and Psychological Testing*; APA's *Code of Fair Testing Practices in Education*). In addition to being familiar with professional ethical and technical guidelines, career counselors must consider test scores as only one piece of evidence about their client's abilities, aptitudes, or interests. Numerous factors aside from the characteristic being measured may influence test scores. Lack of motivation, lack of experience in taking standardized tests, and poor educational preparation are concerns for all test-takers, whereas for women of color there is the additional possibility of alienation due to cultural bias; all are important considerations in evaluating the accuracy of aptitude and achievement test scores (Walsh & Betz, 1990). As Walsh and Betz (1990) reminded us: "A test taker's score should not be accepted as a reflection of lack of ability with respect to the characteristic being tested without alternative explanations for the test taker's inability to perform on that test at that time" (AERA, APA, & NCME, 1985, p. 43). A case in point is the issue of sex restrictiveness in interest inventories.

As most career counselors know, in the past many of the major interest inventories employed separate forms for men and women (Hansen, 1986). All of the major interest inventories now have merged forms for use with women and men, prompted by concerns about sex bias (Borgen, 1986; Hansen, 1986). Yet women and men continue to respond differently to inventory items, resulting in gender differences in the overall patterns of occupational interests. Women tend to express interests congruent with the traditional female gender role (e.g., social, artistic, and child welfare), whereas men express more interest in traditionally masculine domains such as scientific, technical, and mechanical activities (Walsh & Betz, 1990). The end result is that the use of interest inventories with female clients may result in reinforcement of traditional feminine socialization rather than facilitate exploration of viable options (Betz, Chapter 1, this volume; Betz & Fitzgerald, 1987).

The thorny problem of sex restrictiveness in vocational interest inventories is not caused by vocational interest inventories, but uninformed use of inventories that reinforce traditional gender-role socialization can perpetuate the internal and structural pressures detrimental to women. Due to continuing occupational segregation in the work force, the percentage of women and men in different occupational fields persists, with women overrepresented in lower paying, lower status jobs across a circumscribed range of fields (Betz & Fitzgerald, 1987). Differential gender-role socialization and consequent gender differences in life experiences from early childhood influence the gender differences in interest patterns reflected in responses to interest inventories (Betz & Fitzgerald, 1987). Thus, women's interest patterns may be more indicative of experiences, or the lack thereof, than of genuine interests. The fact of gender differences in interest inventory results is generally accepted. The debate revolves around what to do about it (Walsh & Betz, 1990). Is it the career counselor's job to explore what is? Holland (1982) argued that it is unethical to tamper with gender-role socialization, and therefore concluded that interest inventories should be interpreted straightforwardly. We argue that career counselors who fail to consider the adverse impact of gender-role socialization and differential life experiences in the interpretation of interest inventories and tests are merely unwitting accomplices of the status quo.

The controversy surrounding sex restrictiveness has resulted in several approaches to the selection, use, and interpretation of vocational interest inventories. Although most of the major interest inventories use raw scores or combined-sex norms, we agree with Walsh and Betz (1990) that career counselors should use at least one of two alternatives: same-sex norms, or interest inventories with sex-balanced items. If same-sex norms are used to interpret scores, women's raw scores are compared to the patterns of scores of other women. Thus, women who have some nontraditional interests may be more readily identified. The counselor may then explore the impact of gender-role orientation, beliefs about women's roles, and lack of experience and exposure to nontraditional activities, in an effort to promote active examination and exploration of options. Alternatively, there are several interest inventories that have been developed to minimize gender differences in responses at the item level, most notably, the Vocational Interest

Inventory (VII; Lunneborg, 1981) and the Unisex version of the ACT-IV (UNIACT; Lamb & Prediger, 1981). The VII and the UNIACT include an even balance of items typical of both feminine and masculine gender role socialization so that few gender differences result at the item level. Both of the recommended approaches (use of same-sex norms or sex-balanced items) are aimed at identifying interests that female clients have developed *despite* their socialization experiences (Walsh & Betz, 1990).

*Cognitive and Behavioral Assessment.* Behavioral and cognitive assessment procedures were developed in reaction to traditional psychometric assessment, and rest on fundamentally distinct conceptual assumptions. Traditional psychometric assessment attempts to measure intrinsic traits, whereas cognitive and behavioral assessment procedures focus on discrete, situational thoughts or behaviors (Merluzzi & Boltwood, 1990). Although there are distinctions between behavioral and cognitive assessment, both focus on obtaining samples of performance (i.e., behaviors or thoughts).

The sine qua non of behavioral assessment is direct observation of performance (Merluzzi & Boltwood, 1990). In career counseling, for example, observation of live or simulated job interviewing behavior provides information not available from retrospective reports of interview performance. Behavioral assessment methods have been expanded to include behavioral interviews, self-report questionnaires, self-monitoring, and psychophysiological assessment (Merluzzi & Boltwood, 1990). The unique contribution of behavioral assessment rests in its focus on behavior per se. Behavioral self-report methods, for example, focus on tallying the frequency of behavior, along with antecedent conditions and consequences, to analyze the functional relationships of behavior and situational influences (MacDonald, 1984).

Because of the emphasis on observable behavior, behaviorists have assumed that their assessment methods are valid, unbiased, and equally applicable to women and men (MacDonald, 1984). Thus the literature on gender bias within the behavioral assessment tradition is scant, and does not compare to that which exists within the psychometric tradition. In fact, "there has been essentially no attention given to feminist issues in the behavioral assessment literature" (MacDonald, 1984, p. 60). Nevertheless, MacDonald (1984) has criticized behavioral assessment methods, recommending attention to many of the gender issues we have already discussed in this chapter. A linchpin in MacDonald's arguments is the behavioral emphasis on situational assessment. To assess women's behavior in context, the sociopolitical realities and gender-related experiences and influences on behavior must be examined, else any functional analysis will be invalid or misleading (Mac-Donald, 1984).

The research on assertion is an example of some of the problems resulting from ignoring gender in behavioral assessment. Assertiveness training became a popular intervention for women in the 1970s, based on reported gender differences in assertion, and the links among assertion, career choice, and work behavior (Jakubowski, 1977; Nevill & Schlecker, 1988). Behavioral assessment and intervention efforts focused on women's assertion deficits. Yet research indicates that: (a) reported differences between men's and women's assertive behavior reflect women's choices not to act assertively in certain situations, rather than skill deficits (Hollandsworth & Wall, 1977); (b) when women choose not to act assertively, those choices are often based on gender-related beliefs and expectancies (Solomom & Rothblum, 1985); (c) the nature of men's and women's assertiveness issues are different, for example, women are more assertive in expressing feelings (Solomon & Rothblum, 1985); and (d) social perceptions of assertion vary by gender and situation. This is, very real costs are incurred by women who act assertively, especially when that behavior is perceived as gender-role incongruent (Gervasio & Crawford, 1989; Linehan & Seifert, 1983).

Cognitive assessment is actually a hybrid, evolving out of cognitive-behavioral assessment procedures, but also influenced by other perspectives, including social cognitive theory, information processing models, and personal construct theory (Merluzzi, Glass, & Genest, 1981). The major assumption underlying cognitive assessment is that changes in cognitions result in changes in behavior and affect (Merluzzi et al., 1981). Cognitions may include self-statements and self-talk, attributions or explanatory style, imagery, beliefs, efficacy expectations, and cognitive style, depending on the theoretical perspective (Segal & Shaw, 1988). Cognitive assessment procedures include thought-listing and "think aloud" methods, prompted recall, and self-report questionnaires assessing attributions, self-efficacy, and beliefs (Merluzzi & Boltwood, 1990). In the career literature, Krumboltz's *Career Beliefs Inventory* (Krumboltz, 1991) and career self-efficacy measures (Hackett & Lent, 1987) are examples of cognitive assessment.

Gender issues have received little more attention in the cognitive assessment literature than in the behavioral literature. In practice, counselors generally adopt a combined cognitive-behavioral approach to assessment, so many of the issues mentioned in the context of behavioral assessment with women apply equally to cognitive assessment. The example of assertion is relevant; clearly, the role of gender-related beliefs and expectations, in combination with the very real social consequences for women acting assertively, underscore the need for assessing gender, cognitions, behaviors, and affect in interaction to understand the complexity of gender issues in social situations (Gervasio & Crawford, 1989). Although gender differences in irrational beliefs about assertive behavior have received some attention (Jakubowski, 1977), little attention has been devoted to the appropriateness of irrational beliefs per se as a focus of cognitive assessment for women. To extend the assertion example, women's choices to refrain from acting assertively under certain conditions may actually be quite rational, reflecting acknowledgement of unacceptable social consequences of assertion. Nor have gender issues in the assessment of career cognitions (e.g., Krumboltz, 1991; Mitchell & Krumboltz, 1990) been examined to any great extent, save for the work on career self-efficacy (Hackett & Betz, 1981; Hackett & Lent, 1992). However, there has been some work done in identifying the cognitive themes salient for women at different stages of career development (Richman, 1988); this work is a starting point for cognitive career assessment in a developmental context.

*Other Assessment Methods.* A number of alternate approaches to career assessment may be roughly termed "qualitative" (Goldman, 1990). A wide range of methods fit under the qualitative assessment rubric, and are characterized more by what they are not (i.e., standardized tests and inventories) than by what they are (Goldman, 1990). Goldman (1990) cited several examples of qualitative career assessment, including vocational card sorts, values clarification exercises, the vocational lifeline exercise, work samples, and observation. To this list we would add the various career exploration exercises described in the literature (e.g., Brown & Brooks, 1991), such as vocational autobiographies, genograms, fantasy and imagery techniques (e.g., occupational daydreams and the ideal future day exercise), and gender-role analysis (Brown & Brooks, 1991; Spokane, 1991). Qualitative career assessment techniques may be used to explore interests, values, personality, abilities, functional skills, and gender issues—indeed, every aspect of career decision making and adjustment.

The advantages of qualitative assessment in career counseling for women are several: They encourage the active participation of clients in assessment; they tend to promote a holistic and integrated view of career concerns; and they make it easier to incorporate cultural and gender issues at a very fundamental level (Goldman, 1990). Many of the qualitative career assessment techniques are in fact interventions as well (e.g., career lifeline, fantasy, and values clarification exercises), facilitating the intimate connection between career assessment and counseling that is so crucial (Goldman, 1990). Further, "in practice, a comprehensive and meaningful psychological assessment is based on information that emerges from both qualitative and quantitative methods of assessment" (Walsh, 1990, p. 262). Qualitative career assessment methods can be used alone, but may be more effective in combination with standardized assessment tools. Although the use of qualitative career assessment methods facilitates attention to gender and cultural issues, it does not guarantee their incorporation. In the section of this chapter devoted to specific techniques, we show that even the use of a "nonsexist" vocational card sort may be insufficient in promoting gender-aware career counseling.

## GENDER ISSUES IN CAREER ASSESSMENT METHODS

In this section we focus primarily on gender issues in the use and interpretation of tests, inventories, and techniques. Only the most commonly used tests and inventories are highlighted, and selected alternate methods particularly useful for career assessment with women are explored. The reader is referred to other sources for detailed technical and interpretational information (Anastasi, 1988; Kapes & Mastie, 1988; Walsh & Betz, 1990; Watkins & Campbell, 1990; Zunker, 1990).

### Assessment of Individual Differences

#### Interest Assessment

Super and Crites (1949) described four types of interests: (a) expressed interests, or what people say when asked about their likes, dislikes, or preferences; (b) manifest interests, or assessments based on observations of people's behavior across different situations; (c) tested interests, or inferences based on people's knowledge of special information about a topic; and (d) inventoried interests, or people's reports of likes, dislikes, and preferences among a list of items. Of these, the inventory method of assessing interests is probably the most widely used, and receives the most attention herein. However, Borgen (1986) reminded us that expressed interests "are at least as predictive of future career behavior as inventory results" (p. 112). We highly recommend that the reader consider interest assessment via the interview and other qualitative methods in exploring women's vocational preferences. At the very least, interpretation of interest inventory results should occur in conjunction with exploration of expressed interests.

*The Big Three Interest Inventories.* Borgen (1986) characterized the Strong Interest Inventory (SII), the Kuder inventories (e.g., the Kuder

Occupational Interest Scale, KOIS), and Holland's measures (especially the Self-Directed Search, SDS) as the "Big Three" of interest assessment. Of these, the SII and the KOIS are true interests inventories, whereas the SDS is a self-administered and -scored assessment procedure. Some gender-related issues in use and interpretation are shared by all three (and other methods as well), whereas some are instrument specific.

In considering the use of any interest inventory with female clients, at least four issues are salient: the basic assumptions underlying the development of interest inventories in general, questions about what the inventory is actually measuring (or construct validity), issues about how sex restrictiveness in vocational interests is addressed (e.g., use of single-sex or combined-sex norms, or sex-balanced items), and concern about the validity—or hit rates—of the instrument when examining the career choices of people of color.

Most of the major interest inventories rest on the assumption that responses to unfamiliar as well as familiar items are equally indicative of basic interests (Hansen, 1990). Yet we have seen that women's gender-role socialization often results in traditional patterns of interests that may reflect differential experience much more so than fundamental preferences. Although the same argument holds for men who have been traditionally socialized, the circumscription of career options is more serious for women than men. Thus, as a rule of thumb for all the interest inventories, Betz (1992) suggested that "interpretation of low scores on interest scales as indicative of a lack of interest should be deferred until alternative explanations, such as lack of background exposure to a particular area, have been considered" (p. 461).

Of the major interest inventories, the SII has the longest continuous history (Hansen, 1990). The current edition of the SII utilizes same-sex norms for the Occupational Scales in an effort to reduce sex bias (Hansen, 1984, 1990). Despite continuing debates about the most effective manner in which to address sex restrictiveness in interest inventories, the use of single-sex Occupational Scales on the SII offers some advantages. First, female clients' scores on the Occupational Scales can be compared to separate male and female criterion samples, thus allowing a female career client to examine the ways in which her scores are similar and dissimilar to both occupational reference groups. Second, women can compare their scores to those of other women. "Interpretation based on the client's own sex typically provides the most valid and reliable information and the most options for exploration of interests in areas considered non-traditional for one sex or the other" (Hansen, 1990, p. 181). Finally, comparisons between a woman's own interests and the interests of men dominating a particular field of work may be especially helpful for women considering nontraditional occupations. Knowing the extent to which their broad patterns of interests resemble the interest patterns of their potential colleagues may assist women in anticipating issues of choice implementation and occupational adjustment.

In addition to familiarizing themselves with issues of sex bias, users of the SII should also be aware of the results of available research on the appropriateness of the SII for use with people of color. Although Hansen (1990) concluded that the inventory may be used "with a variety of special populations, such as cross-ethnic or international populations, disabled clients, and culturally disadvantaged clients" (p. 179), most of the validity data on this instrument have been gathered with college student populations. Consequently, the interpretation of profiles for non-college-age women of color must be made with caution. Counselors must also consider acculturation issues when working with women of color. The client's degree of familiarity with the dominant culture helps provide a larger context in which to interpret interest inventory results.

The Kuder Occupational Interest Survey, Form DD (KOIS), differs from the SII in the construction and scoring of occupational scales. Rather than constructing scales based on differences in the patterns of responses of a general reference sample and members of an occupational criterion group, Kuder chose to examine differences in the proportions of two occupational groups endorsing responses to the occupational interest inventory items (Diamond, 1990). The subsequent use of Cleman's lambda coefficient allows for comparison of a client's scores directly to those of the occupational groups. An individual's scores are also rank-ordered separately, by gender, for occupational and college major scales.

As is the case with other major interest inventories, gender differences in patterns of scores have been found. Thus, clients should be encouraged to compare their rankings on the KOIS for same- and other-sex samples (Zytowski & Kuder, 1986). On the KOIS women tend to score lower than men on the mechanical and science Vocational Interest Estimates (VIE) scales, whereas men score lower than women on the social service and art VIE scales. Research on the predictive validity of the separate-sex scales on the KOIS has demonstrated roughly equivalent predictive validity of the two sets of norms (Zytowski & Laing, 1978).

The major advantages associated with the use of the KOIS with women include provision of same-sex and other-sex scale rankings and a broader range of occupations than most of the other major interest inventories. A limitation of the KOIS is the imbalance in the number of male-dominated versus female-dominated occupations and college majors included in the inventory. The 1985 edition of the KOIS contains only 29 out of 104 occupational scales and 17 out of 39 college major scales that have been developed with female samples (Diamond, 1990). In deciding whether or not to use the KOIS, counselors may need to consider whether the limited range of options related to female occupations and college majors will hinder a client's exploration of a variety of traditional and nontraditional occupations. The absence of some type of occupational clustering of scores (such as the Holland codes for the SII) and the lack of male and female general reference samples must also be considered. On the other hand, Zytowski and Kuder (1986) argued that Holland codes may mask subtle differences in work environments, a factor that may be problematic for women. Thus, ranked listings of occupations and college majors on the KOIS might, in fact, be useful in encouraging female clients to develop their own meanings for the results.

The Self-Directed Search (SDS; Holland, 1985a, 1987) is the major self-administered, self-scoring, self-interpreting career interest inventory (Spokane, 1990). As such, it presents some unique advantages but also idiosyncratic problems in career assessment with women. First, the absence of same-sex norms flies in the face of guidelines for eliminating sex bias in interest assessment (Betz, 1992). An equally important problem concerns the construct validity of the measure. Although two of the four sections of the Assessment Booklet ask the client to assess her interests, the remaining two sections ask for estimates of ability or competence. However, scores for all four sections are combined in order to identify the client's three-digit Holland code (Holland, 1985a). In turn, the Holland codes identified by the SDS are used in selecting occupations for further exploration. When interest assessments are combined with estimates of competence or ability, what do the combined scores actually represent? The problem is further complicated when we consider the research data that suggest that women tend to report lower self-efficacy or confidence in their abilities than men with respect to traditionally male-dominated activities and occupations (Hackett & Betz, 1992). One likely outcome of combining women's interest and ability estimates on the SDS is that female clients may find themselves with sex-stereotypical Holland codes. According to Isaacson (1985), "Because access to many of the activities and competencies have been gender-restricted in the past, the SDS must be used with extreme caution, especially with female clients" (p. 172). To circumvent possible limitations in the use of the SDS, counselors may find it most beneficial to actively work with female clients in interpreting SDS results, rather than relying on a completely self-guided process.

Despite the drawbacks, there are several benefits in using the SDS with women. The SDS has the advantage of providing immediate feedback to the client about her occupational interests, self-estimates, and Holland codes, and may engender a greater sense of involvement in the career assessment process (Spokane, 1990). The accompanying Occupations Finder now includes a vast range of occupational titles serving to expose women to a wide range of occupations (Spokane, 1990). The unscored Occupational Daydreams section of the SDS Assessment Booklet may provide a rough measure of the degree to which a female client's expressed interests are sex typed (Holland, 1985a). Similarly, an inspection of a client's responses to the sections of the Assessment Booklet requiring self-estimates of ability or competence may provide both client and counselor with specific information about the areas in which the client feels particularly competent, providing a rough screening of the client's career-related self-efficacy.

*Other Interest Inventories.*   Alternatives to the "big three" are briefly mentioned here as illustrative of other issues for career counselors to consider. The current edition of the Vocational Preference Inventory (VPI; Holland, 1985b) incorporates revisions eliminating sex-biased occupational titles. Unfortunately, no new reliability or normative data have been provided, despite changes in the item content of the inventory. Several reviewers (e.g., Drummond, 1986; Rounds, 1985) have expressed concern about the lack of evidence for the reliability and validity of this version. Reliability data provided in the 1985 manual indicate that VPI scores appear somewhat less stable for women than for men. Thus, although prima facie sex bias appears to have been reduced in the VPI, questions remain about the technical validity of the instrument.

Career counselors considering using the VPI with female clients should also consider the extent to which there is evidence for the interpretations provided in the manual. For example, the source of the validity data used in developing the empirical summary for the Masculinity/Femininity scale of the VPI is unclear. Because the clinical interpretation of this scale makes reference to preferences for traditionally male and female careers, interpretation of the M/F scale with clients should proceed cautiously.

Several interest inventories have been developed for use with noncollege populations. The Career Assessment Inventory (CAI; Johansson, 1982), patterned after the SII, was originally designed for individuals who are seeking immediate entry into an occupation, or who wish to pursue technical or business school training (McCabe, 1988). The CAI relies upon the use of combined-sex occupational scales, eliminating sex bias at the item level. Drawbacks include the lack of same-sex normative data, little supporting research, and the absence of predictive validity data (McCabe, 1985).

Two other major interest inventories, the Vocational Interest Inventory (VII; Lunneborg, 1981) and the Unisex edition of the ACT Interest Inventory (UNIACT; Lamb & Prediger, 1981), employ homogeneous interest scales. The VII is intended to produce sex-balanced suggestions of occupational alternatives, but questions about its success have arisen. Efforts to eliminate gender differences at the item level on the VII have not been entirely effective (Hansen, 1985). The VII is probably most useful in promoting career exploration and predicting college major choice, whereas disadvantages include questionable predictive validity for occupational choice and the absence of empirically keyed occupational interest scores (Krumboltz, 1988).

Finally, the UNIACT is one part of the ACT assessment program; it is used nationally and its impact is extensive (Borgen, 1986). On the whole, the UNIACT and the VII appear comparable in eliminating sex bias in item content, but the UNIACT has the edge in predictive validity (Johnson, 1985; Kifer, 1985). Decided advantages of the UNIACT are the use of Holland's classification system, and the additional keying of interests to the data/people/things orientation used to classify occupations in the *Dictionary of Occupational Titles* (DOT; U.S. Department of Labor, 1977).

*Vocational Card Sorts.* Thirty years after Tyler (1961) outlined an occupational card sort procedure, there are numerous commercially available vocational card sorts, most preserving her basic ideas. Although there are advantages to norm-based assessment methods (such as interest inventories), vocational card sorts can offer much in the assessment of the unique ways in which individual women approach the task of career decision making. Vocational card sorts can also serve as a structured method for assessing clients' gender-role beliefs, values, interests, occupational stereotypes, and self-perceptions.

As the client is asked to sort occupations into piles such as "might choose," "would not choose," and "in question," and to identify common reasons for these decisions, both the counselor and client have an opportunity to explore the kinds of perceptions and experiences that may limit or expand the client's perceptions of her career options. The opportunity for women to collaborate with counselors in the career assessment process may be particularly empowering for those women who have typically relied on the feedback and expertise of significant others in their lives. Career counselors who wish to explore gender-role stereotyping can modify card-sort procedures to include a step in which clients sort the occupations as if they were a member of the opposite sex, thus facilitating discussions of the client's perceptions of her options as a female (Slaney & MacKinnon-Slaney, 1990). Cultural influences might also be explored through modifying card sort procedures.

The main disadvantage of the vocational card-sort technique is the absence of normative and psychometric data. Two lines of argument have been pursued to address the psychometric issue: (a) data supportive of the predictive validity of expressed interests have been marshaled as evidence for the predictive validity of card sorts, and (b) card-sort techniques have been conceptualized as interventions rather than assessment methods (e.g., Goldman, 1983; Slaney & MacKinnon-Slaney, 1990). Whether an assessment tool, an intervention, or (in our view) both, card-sort procedures are clearly a useful tool for career counseling with women, offering definite advantages over alternate interest assessment methods (Slaney & MacKinnon-Slaney, 1990).

At present, several different vocational card sorts are commercially available, for example, the Non-Sexist Vocational Card Sort (NSVCS; Dewey, 1974), the Missouri Occupational Card Sort (Krieshok, Hansen, & Johnston, 1982), the Occ-U-Sort (Jones, 1979), the Missouri Occupational Preference Inventory (Moore & Gysbers, 1980), the Vocational Card Sort, part of Holland's Vocational Exploration and Insight Kit (VEIK; Holland & Associates, 1980), and Slaney's (1978) Vocational Card Sort. The reader is referred to Slaney and MacKinnon-Slaney (1990) for an in-depth review of the major vocational card sorts. We mention only a few highlights related to career assessment with women.

Dewey's NSVCS is often mentioned as a nonsexist approach to assessing women's (and men's) vocational choices. Gender-neutral terms in occupational titles are used, and the interactive process of the technique allows the counselor and client to explore issues related to gender-role stereotyping and sex bias. Unfortunately, the use of the term "nonsexist" in the label may lead some career counselors to believe that the nonsexist approach is inherent in the technique itself. To the contrary, as with any other assessment tool, gender bias may enter into the administration and interpretation of the NSVCS. For example, the occupations represented in the NSVCS are not equally distributed across the six Holland codes; in fact, the frequencies range from a low of 9 occupations in the Conventional category to a high of 21 in the social category. The fact that 28% of the occupations in the card sort are in the class (Social) in which traditionally female occupations predominate raises some concerns about the extent to which this technique will stimulate consideration of nontraditional occupational alternatives. The other card sorts available differ too in their representation of field, level, and gender-relatedness of the occupations represented, as well as in the quality of interpretational material available (see Slaney & MacKinnon-Slaney, 1990).

### Ability/Aptitude Assessment

Concerns about the assessment of women's career-related aptitudes and abilities usually reflect issues in interpretation rather than in the technical adequacy of aptitude and ability tests. Commonly used aptitude batteries such as the Differential Aptitude Tests (DAT) or the General Aptitude Test Battery (GATB) are probably about as useful for women as for men. Career counselors must, however, keep in mind that so-called aptitude tests are in reality measures of developed abilities. Abilities develop from combined experience and exposure as well as from innate aptitude. Thus, career counselors must exercise caution in interpreting women's low aptitude test scores as indicative of inherent ability deficits, particularly in traditionally masculine domains such as science, mathematics, and mechanical reasoning (Betz, 1992).

Likewise, mathematics test scores on scholastic achievement tests such as the ACTs, SATs, and GREs must be viewed holistically. Sex bias in item content does seem to be a problem on math achievement tests (Chipman et al., 1991), but other factors such as math anxiety, low math self-efficacy, and lack of experience and background in mathematics have all been identified as contributing to findings of gender differences in math achievement (Betz & Fitzgerald, 1987). In fact, many of the factors contributing to lowered math performance are open to remediation. As previously mentioned, the career counselor must consider the tendency of achievement tests scores to underpredict women's academic achievement (Betz, 1992). Finally, in the course of most career counseling, ability assessment is based primarily on client's self-reports. Yet significant gender differences in self-confidence in abilities (or self-efficacy) have been consistently found, especially with respect to gender-typed tasks, behaviors, and activities (Hackett & Betz, in press). Thus the counselor is encouraged to consider abilities and self-efficacy jointly when attempting to assess ability.

### Work Values, Needs, and Career Salience

*Values/Needs.*  In the career literature, the terms *values, needs,* and *preferences* are often defined quite differently, yet the empirical literature indicates that the various work values, needs, and worker preference inventories measure much the same thing (Betz, 1992). Essentially, the scales described in this section all tap into "the kinds of things people look for in satisfying work" (Betz, 1992, p. 464). Unlike some of the other career assessment techniques, work values scales often have direct roots in theory; both the individual differences and developmental perspectives emphasize the role of needs and values in career assessment. Problems with blatant sex bias are not of major concern with these inventories.

The Work Values Inventory (WVI; Super, 1970) is most appropriate as a career exploration tool for high school and college students, although it has been used with adult workers as well (Zunker, 1990). Scores are reported for 15 work values; norms for both sexes are available, but the norm groups have predominantly been high school students, limiting the usefulness of the WVI with adult workers. Nevertheless, the WVI, along with the MIQ (described later), are the most psychometrically sound of the work values/needs measures (Bolton, 1985). The WVI has the edge over the MIQ because of ease of administration and interpretation.

Nevill and Super (1989) have constructed a new measure, the Values Scale (VS), which has great potential for career assessment with women. Developed as part of the Work Importance Study, the VS contains 21 scales measuring both work-related and general values. The VS is particularly useful with female clients as it taps multiple ways in which values may be met, that is, through work as well as other life roles. It appears to have cross-cultural applicability and does not appear to be sex-biased; no significant gender differences have been found on any scales (Harmon, 1988). The major drawbacks of the VS are that it is still under development and considerable psychometric sophistication is required for adequate interpretation (Harmon, 1988).

The Minnesota Importance Questionnaire (MIQ; Rounds, Henly, Dawis, Lofquist, & Weiss, 1981), developed in the context of research on the theory of work adjustment, has been widely used in research. Its major advantage, aside from psychometric adequacy, is that the MIQ was designed for use with adult workers. In addition to scores for 20 worker needs, the MIQ profile also includes measures of correlation between the test-taker's needs profile and that of needs satisfied in occupational settings. It is therefore useful not only in assessment for career choice, but also in counseling for career adjustment. A disadvantage in assessing women's work-related needs is the absence of specific attention to gender issues; however, extensive norms on both male and female workers are available.

*Career/Work Salience.* People vary not only in what they look for in satisfactory work, but also in the degree to which work is important. The issue of career salience is of special importance to women (Betz & Fitzgerald, 1987) and is a neglected dimension in assessment in career counseling. Greenhaus' (1971) Career Salience Inventory has been the most visible measure of work-role salience in the research literature, but has not been widely used in career counseling. More recently, Nevill and Super (1986) introduced the Salience Inventory (SI), a measure of the "participation, commitment, and values expectations for five roles: Studying, working, community service, home and family, and leisure" (Zytowski, 1988, p. 151). As with the VS, the SI was constructed as part of the Work Importance Study, and reflects Super's theoretical statements about life roles (Super, 1980). The SI is only available in a research edition, so the limitations of the VS hold for the SI, although interpretational guidelines are provided for career counselors (Zytowski, 1988). Given the importance of issues of role salience and role conflict in women's career development, we predict increasing use of the SI and like measures.

### Personality Assessment

There are a number of objective personality instruments that have been used as an adjunct to career assessment (Zunker, 1990). Among the more commonly used is the Myers-Briggs Type Indicator (MBTI; Myers & McCaulley, 1985). Other measures of "normal" personality have also been used for career assessment, but their use in this context is arguable. Although a number of career development theories address personality factors, few inventories have been developed to specifically assess career theory-based dimensions of personality (Zunker, 1990). In career counseling with women, a drawback in the use of personality assessment is that attention to individual dynamics may be reinforced to the neglect of the environmental barriers and challenges known to complicate women's career development. Possible sex bias in personality measurement must also be considered; personality test developers have not responded to the feminist critique to the extent to which developers of vocational assessment procedures have (Lewin & Wild, 1991; Rosewater, 1985). Nonetheless, personality assessment has been employed in career counseling as a self-awareness tool, to clarify worker roles and activity preferences, and to examine sources of job dissatisfaction (Brown & Brooks, 1991).

*Myers-Briggs Type Indicator.* The MBTI was developed to measure four dimensions of Jung's theory of personality types (McCaulley, 1990). Scores obtained on the MBTI across the four Jungian dimensions or functions can be combined to form 16 types; one's type can then be used to explore personal strengths (Hood & Johnson, 1991). What makes the instrument particularly attractive to career counselors is the extensive work that has been done in delineating the 16 types and correlating these with various occupational demands (McCaulley, 1990). Thus, in career assessment and counseling, data about a client's type can be used to understand and explore preferences for work activities, promoting both self and occupational exploration (Willis & Ham, 1988).

The MBTI test manual (Myers & McCaulley, 1985) and available supporting materials offer the career counselor a great deal of information to guide the use of this inventory (Hood & Johnson, 1991). There is some research to support the linkages between types and career preferences (McCaulley, 1990), and norms are available for both men and women. Little guidance is provided for exploring gender issues in Jungian type development, a surprising trend given Jung's original theory. Still, the MBTI does not appear to suffer unduly from sex bias. If used in the context of a thorough career assessment with female clients, the instrument has decided advantages over many of the alternatives.

*Other Personality Measures.* The Sixteen Personal Factor Questionnaire (16PF) was intended as an objective test of 16 "source traits" of personality (Cattell, Eber, & Tatsuoka, 1970). The attractiveness of the instrument for career counselors is that personality patterns derived from 16PF scores can be related to important career exploration issues, for example, problem solving and preferences for career activities (Wholeben, 1988).

Counselors who are considering use of the 16PF with female career clients should attend to several cautions associated with the use of this instrument. First, the terminology employed in naming and describing the 16PF scales appears to have some inherent biases; there is ample opportunity for misinterpreting scale scores given the colloquial meaning of many of the terms used in describing the scales (e.g., emotional stability). Second, some of the bipolar scales used in the 16PF may produce sex-stereotypical interpretations. For example, emotional sensitivity, a traditionally feminine trait, and self-reliance, a traditionally masculine attribute, are presented as polar opposites, reinforcing dichotomous notions of gender roles. Third, significant gender differences have been found for the 16PF. And fourth, there is a long history of controversy about the technical adequacy of the instrument for any use (Anastasi, 1988; Butcher, 1985; Zuckerman, 1985).

An alternative to the 16PF is the California Psychological Inventory (CPI; Gough, 1957). The CPI was designed to assess everyday normal human attributes or qualities referred to as "folk concepts." Folk concepts are described as widely recognizable human attributes. Known as the "sane person's MMPI," the CPI actually contains a large number of items drawn from the MMPI, but item content is generally less objectionable (Hood & Johnson, 1991). The most recent version of the CPI appears to be applicable for use in career and occupational exploration (Wegner, 1988). Overall, the CPI compares favorably with alternative personality measures, being fairly easy to interpret and having acceptable reliability and validity (Walsh & Betz, 1990). There is also some evidence that the CPI might be fairly appropriate for cross-cultural use (Gough, 1990). On the other hand, the masculinity–femininity scale presents some interpretational problems for use with female career clients (Beere, 1990; Gough, 1990). Baucom (1980) has introduced procedures whereby the CPI's bipolar M–F scale can be transformed into two unipolar scales reflecting instrumentality and expressiveness.

## Assessment of Career Process Variables

One of the most commonly expressed goals of career counseling is vocational choice. Despite the seeming simplicity of this outcome, there has been considerable debate about definitions and measurement of career indecision (Slaney, 1988). Further, developmental perspectives require attention to the process of decision making, not just choice content. In this section we review assessment tools for measuring constructs emanating from developmental theory and focusing on career process variables. Attention to career indecision allows for differential diagnosis of decision making problems and issues, whereas career maturity measures contribute to developmental assessments of client functioning (Savickas, 1990).

### Career Decision Making

Career indecision seems to be multidimensional, but the literature remains unclear about the specific nature and number of the dimensions of indecision (Betz, 1992). Total scores on career indecision scales may thus reflect aspects of the decision-making process such as clarity and certainty as well as indecision (Betz, 1992). Distinctions have also been made between developmentally normal undecidedness (or simple indecision) and indecisive, or chronically undecided, individuals (Betz, 1992); determinations of developmental versus chronic undecidedness have important implications for intervention.

Several measures have been found to be useful in understanding the career decision status of clients and identifying sources of career indecision. The Career Decision Scale (CDS; Osipow, 1987) is widely used, psychometrically sound, and useful for working with women. The

CDS provides a measure of undecidedness and information about the sources of indecision (Osipow, 1987). When using the CDS with women, same-sex norms should be used, and information from the scale about the antecedents of indecision may need to be fully explored to check on the extent to which gender is an issue.

Holland, Daiger, and Power's (1980) My Vocational Situation (MVS) was designed to provide information about indecision and the type of vocational assistance needed. Scores for vocational identity (i.e., clarity and stability of one's career-related attributes), lack of information, and perceptions of barriers are provided. The MVS has potential as an instrument to assist in exploring the perceptions of environmental obstacles and barriers, an important issue for women. However, research support for the use of the MVS as a diagnostic tool is not yet available (Westbrook, 1988).

Finally, Swanson and Tokar (1991) developed a measure of perceptions of barriers to career development, including barriers of unique concern to women. This instrument has potential in identifying factors contributing to women's (and men's) career indecision, but is also still in the development phase. Harren's (1979) Assessment of Career Decision Making may be very helpful in understanding women's decision making styles.

### Career Maturity and Adjustment

*Career Maturity.*   Crites' (1978) Career Maturity Inventory (CMI) is a measure of the attitudes and competencies indicative of career maturity in adolescence. Although reviewers have expressed concerns about the reliability of the CMI, and construct validity is an issue for all of the measures of career maturity, the CMI is widely used (Betz, 1988). We have previously addressed concerns about how well career maturity scores predict choice realism for women. Because of the complex issues related to definitions of the construct, the career counselor must be cautious in making assumptions derived from CMI scores about women's career status. Betz's (1988) model of career maturity suggested that antecedents such as intelligence and school performance, career-related experiences, and cultural values must be considered in interpreting the meaning of the results of career maturity measures. The appropriate consequences of career maturity, in her view, are "realistic career decisions; consistency of choices over time, field, and level (outcome variables in Crites' theory of career maturity); and later, indicators of vocational success and satisfaction" (Betz, 1992, p. 467). No research has been conducted on Betz's propositions, but they are useful in interpreting CMI and other career maturity scores of female clients.

The Career Development Inventory (CDI; Super, Thompson, Lindeman, Jordaan, & Myers, 1984), like the CMI, contains both attitude and knowledge scales. Reviewers are largely in agreement that the CDI represents the type of theory-based measure rarely found in the career literature (Savickas, 1990), but the CDI shares with the CMI problems with reliability and construct validity (Betz, 1992).

*Adult Career Adjustment.* Adult workers have different concerns and issues than adolescents and young adults, yet until recently measures of adult career adjustment were unavailable. The Adult Career Concerns Inventory (ACCI; Super, Thompson, & Lindeman, 1988) measures career issues in the later stages of career development. Likewise, the Career Mastery Inventory (CMAS; Crites, 1990) assesses "mastery of six developmental tasks postulated to be important in the Establishment stage of career development" (Betz, 1992, p. 468). The ACCI has supporting research and a technical manual, whereas Crites has not yet published the CMAS manual. Widespread use of both awaits further research.

Of immediate usefulness in career assessment is R. E. Campbell and Cellini's (1981) diagnostic taxonomy of adult career problems. Their diagnostic classification includes attention to problems in career decision making, implementing career plans, and organizational/institutional performance and adaptation. Included in this taxonomy are some of the career adjustment issues widely experienced by women, for example, sexual harassment. Other common career concerns of women are included under more general problems that are not totally descriptive. For example, role conflict seems to be subsumed under "adverse off-the-job personal circumstances or stressors" (Campbell & Cellini, 1981, p. 180). When using this taxonomy with women, the career counselor may need to supplement it by additional exploration of concerns such as discrimination, role conflict, and sexual harassment.

Other measures useful in the assessment of career adjustment include measures of the work environment (Spokane, 1991), particularly the Occupational Stress Inventory (OSI; Osipow & Spokane, 1987). Occupational stress, role strain, and personal coping resources are measured on the OSI in a manner that allows for analyses of the sources of stress, and, of course, the identification of sources of occupational stress has clear treatment implications. The OSI is based on the assumption that stress in the workplace is a function of the interaction of external stressors, personal affective reactions, and lack of appropriate coping resources. As such, it offers much in work with women.

### Career-Related Cognitions

Many writers have argued for the importance of assessing career-related cognitions in exploring the process of career development (Betz,

1992). Brown and Brooks (1991) devoted considerable attention to the assessment of cognitive clarity; Spokane (1991) spoke to the need for acquiring a cognitive structure to evaluate career alternatives; Rounds and Tracey (1990) argued for an information processing approach to career assessment and counseling; Neimeyer (1988) proposed cognitive vocational schema as important; and cognitive problem-solving and decision-making abilities have long been considered crucial to career development (Brown, Brooks, & Associates, 1990). Two major types of career cognitions have received enough attention to warrant routine consideration in career assessment with women: career beliefs and career-related self-efficacy (Betz, 1992).

*Career Beliefs.* Several measures of irrational beliefs have been developed, but Krumboltz's (1991) Career Beliefs Inventory (CBI) measures specific cognitions that interfere with career decision making. The manual for the CBI contains helpful suggestions for its use in career counseling, but the inventory itself contains no items specifically addressing gender-role beliefs. Potentially quite useful in counseling women, the CBI will nonetheless need to be augmented by gender-role assessment to produce a comprehensive understanding of women's "private rules about the self" (Mitchell & Krumboltz, 1990) that may interfere with career decision making.

*Career Self-Efficacy.* Considerable evidence now exists that significant gender differences in career self-efficacy (SE), or confidence in one's career-related abilities, are related to gender differences in educational and career choice (Hackett & Betz, 1992). Career counselors are advised to routinely assess women's SE expectations hand-in-hand with abilities, especially with reference to traditionally masculine-typed activities, tasks, and occupations. Within the interview, career SE can be assessed through questions that tap the client's confidence in her ability to succeed in a domain. A number of assessment instruments are available in the research literature, but only Rooney and Osipow's (1992) occupational self-efficacy scale (OSES) was developed with a counseling use in mind. The OSES provides information about task-specific self-efficacy; thus it might be particularly helpful in identifying sources of low self-efficacy, and may be more generally useful than some of the other measures.

Research instruments have been developed to assess SE with respect to occupational choices, mathematics, academic milestones, career decision making, and home–career conflict (see Hackett & Betz, in press). Although there are a number of unresolved methodological issues in the measurement of career self-efficacy, overall the internal consistency and predictive validity data are decent for most measures (Lent & Hackett, 1987). Aside from their nascent state of development, a disadvantage of using career self-efficacy measures, and a point of confusion for many, is the need for SE to be assessed with reference to some specific set of behaviors or tasks. SE is not, conceptually, a stable personality trait. SE is more accurately defined as a cognitive appraisal of one's capabilities (Hackett & Lent, 1992). There is no one "self-efficacy measure," but rather multiple measures; the career counselor must select the measure most appropriate for a particular client's concerns. On the up side, SE assessments are easily tailored to suit the specific needs of clients and are amenable to assessment within the counseling interview. The research literature is replete with suggestions for how to integrate career SE assessment with other important career issues (Hackett & Betz, in press).

## Assessment of Gender Role Issues

It is evident by now that we recommend considering gender issues centrally in any career assessment with female clients. Yet too often counselors mistake awareness of gender differences per se for under-standing gender dynamics. In this section we review inventories and assessment techniques specifically designed to promote a greater appre-ciation for the dynamics of gender. All have the potential for serving as career interventions as well as assessment tools. Unfortunately, most of the gender-role measures have been developed for research purposes rather than for use in counseling. With this caveat, we begin our discussion with gender-role analysis because of its potential for stimu-lating a comprehensive career assessment with women.

### Gender-Role Analysis

Gender-role analysis is an extremely useful assessment tool in devel-oping an accurate understanding of a female client in her sociocultural context. We assume that the career counselor will routinely take issues of gender and culture into account in the context in career assessment. However, gender-role analysis, a structured technique for examining the meaning and influence of gender in a client's life, is a useful adjunct to standard interview procedures. Introduced as the major technique of feminist (or gender-aware) counseling and therapy (Brodsky, 1975), gender-role analysis assists the client in analyzing the potential costs and benefits of traditional and nontraditional gender role behavior—an analysis, by the way, that can be equally useful for male and female clients (Rawlings & Carter, 1977). For example, a counselor might help a woman in clarifying the potential costs and benefits that might accrue from traditionally feminine behaviors such as nurturance, dependence on others, living through and for others, and passivity. Additionally, the counselor might explore the benefits of nontraditional feminine gender-role behavior, such as psychological and economic autonomy and development of a full range of interpersonal competencies and behaviors, along with perceived costs. The gender-role analysis would thus serve to bring unconscious assumptions and limits to the forefront of consciousness, assist clients in evaluating their self-imposed gender-role constraints, and facilitate informed decision making about gender-role-related choices and behaviors. Gender-role analysis can easily be extended to the evaluation of career options. Fitzgerald (1985) offered specific illustrations of a gender-role analysis of the consequences of the homemaker role versus traditional and nontraditional career options.

### Measures of Gender role

*Attitudes Toward Women.*  Perhaps the most widely used measure of attitudes toward women and women's roles has been Spence and Helmreich's (1972) Attitudes Toward Women Scale (ATW). Consequently, the reliability and predictive validity of the various versions of the ATW are acceptable, and the research literature is quite extensive (Beere, 1990). Betz and Fitzgerald (1987) reported that "liberated" sex-role values, of the type tapped by the ATW, are facilitators of women's career development. Use of the ATW may therefore assist career counselors in identifying and exploring the specific attitudes toward women and beliefs about women's roles that may serve as barriers to informed career choice. A drawback of the ATW is that the scale "tops out," failing to discriminate among individuals who have fairly liberated attitudes. In cases where this may be an issue—for example, with feminist clients—the counselor might consider the use of an attitudes toward feminism scale (see Beere, 1990).

Another alternative to the ATW is the Feminist Identity Development Scale (FID; McNamara & Rickard, 1989). This and other FID scales are very recent developments, based conceptually on Downing and Roush's (1985) model, and describing the developmental stages women pass through in their efforts to come to terms with sexism in our culture. Women in the earliest stage of feminist identity development, that is, passive or unconscious acceptance, often need help in becoming aware of gender influences on their lives. Women in the early stages of awareness of sexism may need to express anger, while women in the later stages of feminist identity development may require other types of assistance in coming to terms with sexism in their lives (McNamara & Rickard, 1989). Although FID measures are still in the developmental stage and thus not ideally suited for counseling use, career counselors can pursue feminist identity via interviewing procedures.

*Gender-Role Orientation.* Better known than any other gender role measure is Bem's (1981a) Sex Role Inventory (BSRI). Originally developed to assess androgyny, the BSRI has been reconceptualized by Bem (1981b) as a measure of gender schema. The 60-item scale produces two scores, a "masculinity" score and a "femininity" score, each representing the degree to which individuals characterize themselves in terms of stereotypically masculine or stereotypically feminine adjectives. In the past the two scores have been combined to produce a fourfold classification: masculine or feminine sex-typed, androgynous, or undifferentiated. Current usage varies considerably, but our recommendation for career counselors is congruent with Gilbert's (1985): Masculinity and femininity scores on the BSRI and similar inventories should be viewed as indicators of only limited aspects of the masculine and feminine gender roles. Specifically, masculinity scores actually reflect *instrumental* characteristics such as independence and self-assertiveness, whereas femininity scores tap the dimension of *expressiveness* or nurturance. High instrumentality scores have been found to be predictive of achievement-related behavior and nontraditional career choices (Betz & Fitzgerald, 1987).

Bem's (1981b) work on gender schema theory incorporates current thinking and research in cognitive psychology. In this view, BSRI scores are seen as reflections of the degree to which an individual processes information in gender stereotypical ways; sex-typing is viewed as a result of gender-schematic processing. Women who score in a sex-typed manner on the BSRI would, theoretically, tend to see potential occupational choices as gender-appropriate or gender-inappropriate, rather than view occupational alternatives in the context of their unique interests, needs, and values. Gender schema theory offers the career counselor a conceptual base and accompanying techniques for determining which clients might require more active confrontation of gender-restricting beliefs and perceptions. Interestingly, career researchers have begun to explore the role of cognitive structures and vocational schema in career decision making (Neimeyer, 1988). Career counselors attempting to understand the cognitive vocational schema of their clients might benefit from attention to the interplay of gender and vocational schema.

The Personal Attributes Questionnaire (PAQ; Spence, Helmreich, & Stapp, 1974), though less widely known than the BSRI, is in many ways

the preferable measure of gender-role orientation. Although both measures assess instrumentality and expressiveness, the items on the PAQ
represent socially desirable gender-related attributes; the BSRI contains
many undesirable gender-typed attributes, especially on the "femininity" scale (e.g., gullible, childlike) (Beere, 1990).

### Role Conflict

Vocational researchers have been increasingly attentive to what career
counselors have long known—that career choice occurs in the context of
other life roles. We have already discussed career and role salience
measures as important to understanding women's career development.
But there are alternative measures constructed to assess dimensions of
role conflict untapped by the Career Salience scale and the SI. Interventions aimed at decreasing or resolving role conflict and role strain
depend on a careful assessment of the origins of the personal, interpersonal, and environmental pressures women experience in coping with
multiple roles. Farmer's (1984) Home–Career (H–C) Conflict scale, for
example, provides a measure of the extent of conflict experienced by
women who value both work and family roles but perceive these as
incompatible. High scores on this scale have been found to be predictive
of lowered career motivation (Farmer, 1984). For counseling purposes,
the H–C measure has the potential for identifying sources of psychological distress in female clients. Beere (1990) describes numerous
measures assessing job–home demands, role strain, role overload, and
role conflict. Choosing an appropriate assessment tool requires knowledge of the multiple-role literature (Betz & Fitzgerald, 1987).

## SUMMARY RECOMMENDATIONS

We briefly recap our recommendations for career assessment with
women: Counselors must be intimately familiar with the literature on
the career psychology of women and with career assessment procedures, including the technical aspects of test construction, as well as the
issues of bias in testing. Assessment in career counseling is best viewed
as an integral component of intervention rather than as a discrete
activity; thus, career counselors need to examine the conceptual underpinnings of their approach to career counseling, being aware of the
possibilities for bias. In assessment, the career counselor should routinely view female clients within a sociocultural context, adopting some
variant of gender-aware counseling—and utilizing gender-role analysis
as an integral component of the career assessment process. Career

counselors should routinely make use of qualitative alternatives to standardized testing such as vocational card sorts. Finally, we as counselors must continually examine and work on our own gender-related issues if we are to be maximally effective and ethically responsible in delivering career services to women.

## REFERENCES

American Educational Research Association, American Psychological Association, & National Council on Measurement in Education. (1985). *Joint technical standards for educational and psychological testing*. Washington, DC: Authors.

American Psychological Association. (1990). Ethical principles of psychologists. *American Psychologist, 45*, 390–395.

American Psychological Association, Joint Committee on Testing Practices. (1988). *Code of fair testing practices in education*. Washington, DC: Author.

Anastasi, A. (1988). *Psychological testing* (6th ed.). New York: Macmillan.

Atkinson, D. R., Morten, G., & Sue,. D. W. (1989). *Counseling American minorities: A cross-cultural perspective* (3rd ed.). Dubuque, IA: W. C. Brown.

Baucom, D. H. (1980). Independent CPI masculinity and femininity scales: Psychological correlates and a sex-role typology. *Journal of Personality Assessment, 44*(3), 262–271.

Beere, C. (1990). *Gender roles: A handbook of tests and measures*. Westport, CT: Greenwood Press.

Bem, S. L. (1981a). *Bem Sex-Role Inventory: Professional manual*. Palo Alto, CA: Consulting Psychologists Press.

Bem, S. L. (1981b). Gender schema theory: A cognitive account of sex-typing. *Psychological Review, 88*, 354–364.

Betz, N. E. (1988). The assessment of career development and maturity. In W. B. Walsh & S. H. Osipow (Eds.), *Career decision making* (pp. 77–136). Hillsdale, NJ: Lawrence Erlbaum Associates.

Betz, N. E. (1990). Contemporary issues in testing use. In C. E. Watkins, Jr. & V. L. Campbell (Eds.), *Testing in counseling practice* (pp. 419–450). Hillsdale, NJ: Lawrence Erlbaum Associates.

Betz, N. E. (1992). Career assessment: A review of critical issues. In S. D. Brown & R. W. Lent (Eds.), *Handbook of counseling psychology* (2nd ed., pp. 453–484). New York: Wiley.

Betz, N. E. (in press). Women's career development. In M. Paludi & F. Denmark (Eds.), *Handbook of the psychology of women*. Westport, CT: Greenwood Press.

Betz, N. E., & Fitzgerald, L. F. (1987). *The career psychology of women*. San Diego, CA: Academic Press.

Bolton, B. (1985). Work values inventory. In D. J. Keyser & R. C. Sweetland (Eds.), *Test critiques* (Vol. II, pp. 835–843). Kansas City, MO: Test Corporation of America.

Borgen, F. H. (1986). New approaches to the assessment of interests. In W. B. Walsh & S. H. Osipow (Eds.), *The assessment of interests* (pp. 83–126). Hillsdale, NJ: Lawrence Erlbaum Associates.

Brodsky, A. M. (1975, March). *Is there a feminist therapy?* Paper presented at the annual meeting of the Southeastern Psychological Association, Atlanta.

Brown, D., & Brooks, L. (1991). *Career counseling techniques*. Boston: Allyn & Bacon.

Brown, D., Brooks, L., & Associates. (1990). *Career choice and development: Applying contemporary theories to practice* (2nd ed.). San Francisco: Jossey-Bass.

Brown, L. S. (1986). Gender-role analysis: A neglected component of psychological assessment. *Psychotherapy, 23,* 243–248.

Brown, L. S. (1990). Taking gender into account in the clinical assessment interview. *Professional Psychology, 21,* 12–17.

Butcher, J. N. (1985). Review of the Sixteen Personality Factor Questionnaire. In J. V. Mitchell, Jr. (Ed.), *The ninth Mental Measurements yearbook* (Vol. II, pp. 1391–1392). Lincoln, NE: Buros Institute of Mental Measurements.

Campbell, R. E., & Cellini, J. V. (1981). A diagnostic taxonomy of adult career development problems. *Journal of Vocational behavior, 19,* 175–190.

Campbell, V. L. (1990). A model for using tests in counseling. In C. E. Watkins, Jr. & V. L. Campbell (Eds.), *Testing in counseling practice* (pp. 1–7). Hillsdale, NJ: Lawrence Erlbaum Associates.

Cattell, R. B., Eber, H. W., & Tatsuoka, M. M. (1970). *Handbook for the Sixteen Personality Factor Questionnaire (16PF).* Champaign, IL: IPAT.

Chipman, S. F., Marshall, S. P., & Scott, P. A. (1991). Content effects on word problem performance: A possible source of test bias? *American Educational Research Journal, 28,* 897–915.

Cole, N. S. (1981). Bias in testing. *American Psychologist, 36,* 1067–1077.

Crites, J. O. (1974). Career counseling: A reviewed major approaches. *Counseling Psychologist, 4*(3), 3–23.

Crites, J. O. (1978). *Theory and research handbook for the Career Maturity Inventory.* Monterey, CA: CTB, McGraw-Hill.

Crites, J. O. (1981). *Career counseling.* New York:McGraw-Hill.

Crites, J. O. (1990). *Career mastery inventory.* Boulder, CO: Crites Career Consultants, Inc.

Dawis, R., & Lofquist, L. (1984). *A psychological theory of work adjustment.* Minneapolis: University of Minnesota Press.

Dewey, C. R. (1974). Exploring interests: A non-sexist method. *Personnel and Guidance Journal, 52,* 311–315.

Diamond, E. E. (1990). The Kuder Occupational Interest Survey. In C. E. Watkins, Jr. & V. L. Campbell (Eds.), *Testing in counseling practice* (pp. 211–239). Hillsdale, NJ: Lawrence Erlbaum Associates.

Downing, N. E., & Roush, K. L. (1985). From passive acceptance to active commitment: A model of feminist identity development for women. *Counseling Psychologist, 13,* 695–709.

Drummond, R. J. (1986). Vocational Preference Inventory. In D. J. Keyser & R. C. Sweetland (Eds.), *Test critiques* (Vol. V, pp. 545–548). Kansas City, MO: Test Corporation of America.

Farmer, H. S. (1984). Development of a measure of home-career conflict related to career motivation in college women. *Sex Roles, 10,* 663–675.

Fitzgerald, L. F. (1985). Career counseling women. In Z. Leibowitz & D. Lea (Eds.), *Adult career development* (pp. 116–131). Alexandria, VA: AACD.

Fitzgerald, L. F., & Crites, J. O. (1980). Toward a career psychology of women: What do we know? What do we need to know? *Journal of Counseling Psychology, 27,* 44–62.

Fitzgerald, L. F., & Nutt, R. (1986). The Division 17 principles concerning the counseling/psychotherapy of women: Rationale and implementation. *Counseling Psychologist, 14,* 180–216.

Gervasio, A. H., & Crawford, M. (1989). Social evaluations of assertiveness. *Psychology of Women Quarterly, 13,* 1–25.

Gilbert, L. A. (1985). Measures of psychological masculinity and femininity: A comment on Gaddy, Glass, and Arnkoff. *Journal of Counseling Psychology, 32,* 163–166.

Gilbert, L. A. (Ed.). (1987). Dual career families in perspective. *Counseling Psychologist, 15,* 3–145.

Goldman, L. (1983). The Vocational Card Sort technique: A different view, *Measurement and Evaluation in Guidance, 16,* 107–109.

Goldman, L. (1990). Qualitative assessment. *Counseling Psychologist, 18,* 205–213.

Good, G. E., Gilbert, L. A., & Scher, M. (1990). Gender aware therapy: A synthesis of feminist therapy and knowledge about gender. *Journal of Counseling and Development, 68,* 376–380.

Gough, H. G. (1957). *Manual for the California Psychological Inventory.* Palo Alto, CA: Consulting Psychologists Press.

Gough, H. G. (1990). The California Psychological Inventory. In C. E. Watkins, Jr. & V. L. Campbell (Eds.), *Testing in counseling practice* (pp. 37–62). Hillsdale, NJ: Lawrence Erlbaum Associates.

Greenhaus, J. H. (1971). An investigation of the role of career salience in vocational behavior. *Journal of Vocational Behavior, 1,* 209–216.

Hackett, G., & Betz, N. E. (1981). A self-efficacy approach to the career development of women. *Journal of Vocational Behavior, 18,* 326–336.

Hackett, G., & Betz, N. E. (1992). Self-efficacy perceptions and the career-related choices of college students. In D. H. Schunk & J. L. Meece (Eds.), *Student perceptions in the classroom: Causes and consequences* (pp. 229–246). Hillsdale, NJ: Lawrence Erlbaum Associates.

Hackett, G., & Betz, N. E. (in press). Career choice and development. In J. E. Maddux (Ed.), *Self-efficacy, adaptation, and adjustment: Theory, research, and application.* New York: Plenum.

Hackett, G., & Lent, R. W. (1992). Theoretical advances and current inquiry in career psychology. In S. D. Brown & R. W. Lent (Eds.), *Handbook of counseling psychology* (2nd ed., pp. 419–451). New York: Wiley.

Hansen, J. C. (1976). Exploring new directions for Strong–Campbell Interest Inventory occupational scale construction. *Journal of Vocational Behavior, 9,* 147–160.

Hansen, J. C. (1984). *User's guide for the SVIB-SCII.* Stanford, CA: Stanford University Press.

Hansen, J. C. (1985). Review of the Vocational Interest Inventory. In J. V. Mitchell (Ed.), *The ninth mental measurements yearbook* (Vol. II, pp. 1677–1678). Lincoln: Buros Institute of Mental Measurements.

Hansen, J. C. (1986). Strong Vocational interest blank/Strong-Campbell interest inventory. In W. B. Walsh & S. H. Osipow (Eds.), *The assessment of interests* (pp. 1–30). Hillsdale, NJ: Lawrence Erlbaum Associates.

Hansen, J. C. (1990). Interpretation of the Strong Interest Inventory. In C. E. Watkins, Jr. & V. L. Campbell (Eds.), *Testing in counseling practice* (pp. 177–209). Hillsdale, NJ: Lawrence Erlbaum Associates.

Harmon, L. W. (1988). Review of the Values Scale. In J. T. Kapes & M. M. Mastie (Eds.), *A counselor's guide to career assessment instruments* (2nd ed., pp. 156–158). Alexandria, VA: National Career Development Association.

Harren, V. A. (1979). A model of career decision making for college students. *Journal of Vocational Behavior, 14,* 119–133.

Holland, J. L. (1982). The SDS helps both females and males: A comment. *Vocational Guidance Quarterly, 30,* 195–197.

Holland, J. L. (1985a). *The Self-Directed Search: Professional manual.* Odessa, FL: Psychological Assessment Resources.

Holland, J. L. (1985b). *Manual for the Vocational Preferance Inventory.* Odessa, FL: Psychological Assessment Resources.

Holland, J. L. (1987). *Manual supplement for the Self-Directed Search.* Odessa, FL: Psychological Assessment Resources.

Holland, J. L., & Associates. (1980). *Counselor's guide to the Vocational Exploration and Insight Kit (VEIK).* Palo Alto, CA: Consulting Psychologists Press.

Holland, J. L., Daiger, D. C., & Power, P. G. (1980). *My Vocational Situation*. Palo Alto, CA: Consulting Psychologists Press.

Hollandsworth, H. G., & Wall, K. E. (1977). Sex differences in assertive nehavior: An empirical investigation. *Journal of Counseling Psychology, 24*, 217–227.

Hood, A. B., & Johnson, R. W. (1991). *Assessment in counseling: A guide to the use of psychological assessment procedures*. Alexandria, VA: AACD.

Isaacson, L. E. (1985). *Basics of career counseling*. Newton, MA: Allyn & Bacon.

Jakubowski, P. A. (1977). Self-assertion training procedures for women. In E. I. Rawlings & D. K. Carter (Eds.), *Psychotherapy for women: Treatment toward equality* (pp. 168–190). Springfield, IL: C. C. Thomas.

Jepson, D. (1990). Developmental career counseling. In W. B. Walsh & S. H. Osipow (Eds.), *Career counseling* (pp. 117–158). Hillsdale, NJ: Lawrence Erlbaum Associates.

Johansson, C. B. (1982). *Manual for the Career Assessment Inventory* (2nd ed.). Minneapolis: National Computer Systems.

Johnson, R. W. (1985). Review of the Vocational Interest Inventory. In J. V. Mitchell (Ed.), *The ninth Mental Measurements yearbook* (Vol. II, pp. 1678–1679). Lincoln: Buros Institute of Mental Measurements.

Jones, L. K. (1979). Occ-U-Sort: Development and evaluation of an occupational card sort system. *Vocational Guidance Quarterly, 28*, 56–62.

Kapes, J. T., & Mastie, M. M. (Eds.). (1988). *A counselor's guide to career assessment instruments* (2nd ed.). Alexandria, VA: National Career Development Association.

Kifer, E. (1985). Review of the ACT assessment program. In J. V. Mitchell (Ed.), *The ninth Mental Measurements yearbook* (Vol. I, pp. 31–36). Lincoln: Buros Institute of Mental Measurements.

Krieshok, T. S., Hansen, R. N., & Johnston, J. A. (1982). *Missouri Occupational Card Sort manual (college form)*. Available from the Career Planning and Placement Center, 100 Noyes Hall, University of Missouri-Columbia, Columbia, MO.

Krumboltz, J. D. (1988). Review of the Vocational Interest Inventory. In J. T. Kapes & M. M. Mastie (Eds.), *A counselor's guide to career assessment instruments* (2nd ed., pp. 137–142). Alexandria, VA: National Career Development Association.

Krumboltz, J. D. (1991). *Manual for the Career Beliefs Inventory*. Palo Alto, CA: Consulting Psychologists Press.

Krumboltz, J. D., & Nichols, C. W. (1990). Integrating the social learning theory of career decision making. In W. B. Walsh & S. H. Osipow (Eds.), *Career counseling: Contemporary topics in vocational psychology* (pp. 159–192). Hillsdale, NJ: Lawrence Erlbaum Associates.

Lamb, R. R., & Prediger, D. J. (1981). *Technical report for the unisex edition of the ACT Interest Inventory (UNIACT)*. Iowa City, IA: American College Testing Program.

Lent, R. W., & Hackett, G. (1987). Career self-efficacy: Empirical status and future directions [Monograph]. *Journal of Vocational Behavior, 30*, 347–382.

Lewin, M., & Wild, C. L. (1991). The impact of the feminist critique on tests, assessment, and methodology. *Psychology of Women Quarterly, 15*, 581–596.

Linehan, M. M., & Seifert, R. F. (1983). Sex and contextual differences in the appropriateness of assertive behavior. *Psychology of Women Quarterly, 8*, 79–88.

Lunneborg, P. W. (1981). *The Vocational Interest Inventory manual*. Los Angeles: Western Psychological Services.

MacDonald, M. L. (1984). Behavioral assessment of women clients. In E. A. Blechman (Ed.), *Behavior modification with women* (pp. 60–93). New York: Guilford.

McCabe, S. P. (1985). Career Assessment Inventory. In D. J. Keyser & R. C. Sweetland (Eds.), *Test critiques* (Vol. II, pp. 128–137). Kansas City, MO: Test Corporation of America.

McCabe, S. P. (1988). Career assessment inventory—The enhanced version. In J. T. Kapes & M. M. Mastie (Eds.), *A counselor's guide to career assessment instruments* (2nd ed., pp. 76–80). Alexandria, VA: National Career Development Association.

McCaulley, M. H. (1990). The Myers-Briggs Type Indicator in counseling. In C. E. Watkins, Jr. & V. L. Campbell (Eds.), *Testing in counseling practice* (pp. 91–134). Hillsdale, NJ.: Lawrence Erlbaum Associates.

McNamara, K., & Rickard, K. M. (1989). Feminist identity development: Implications of feminist therapy with women. *Journal of Counseling and Development, 68*, 184–189.

Merluzzi, T. V., & Boltwood, M. D. (1990). Cognitive and behavioral assessment. In C. E. Watkins, Jr. & V. L. Campbell (Eds.), *Testing in counseling practice* (pp. 135–176). Hillsdale, NJ: Lawrence Erlbaum Associates.

Merluzzi, T. V., Glass, C. R., & Genest, M. (Eds.). (1981). *Cognitive assessment*. New York: Guilford.

Mitchell. L. K., & Krumboltz, J. D. (1990). Social learning approach to career decision making: Krumboltz's theory. In D. Brown, L. Brooks, & Associates (Eds.), *Career choice and development* (pp. 145–196). San Francisco: Jossey-Bass.

Moore, E. J., & Gysbers, N. L. (1980). *Missouri Occupational Preference Inventory*. Columbia, MO: Human Systems Consultants, Inc.

Myers, I. B., & McCaulley, M. H. (1985). *Manual: A guide to the development and use of the Myers-Briggs Type Indicator*. Palo Alto, CA: Consulting Psychologists Press.

Neimeyer, G. J. (1988). Cognitive integration and differentiation in vocational behavior. *Counseling Psychologist, 16*, 440–475.

Nevill, D. D., & Schlecker, D. I. (1988). The relation of self-efficacy and assertiveness to willingness to engage in traditional/nontraditional career activities. *Psychology of Women Quarterly, 12*, 91–98.

Nevill, D. D., and Super, D. E. (1986). *Manual for the Salience inventory: Theory, application, and research*. Palo Alto, CA: Consulting Psychologists Press.

Nevill, D. D., & Super, D. E. (1989). *Manual for the Values Scale* (2nd ed.). Palo Alto, CA: Consulting Psychologists Press.

Osipow, S. H. (1987). *Career Decision Scale: Manual*. Odessa, FL: Psychological Assessment Resources.

Osipow, S. H., & Spokane, A. R. (1987). *Manual for the Occupational Stress Inventory*. Odessa, FL: Psychological Assessment Resources.

Phillips, S. D., & Pazienza, N. J. (1988). History and theory of the assesment of career development and decision making. In W. B. Walsh & S. H. Osipow (Eds.), *Career decision making* (pp. 1–31). Hillsdale, NJ: Lawrence Erlbaum Associates.

Rawlings, E. I., & Carter, D. K. (1977). *Psychotherapy for women*. Springfield, IL: Charles C. Thomas.

Richman, D. R. (1988). Cognitive career counseling for women. *Journal of Rational Emotive and Cognitive Behavior Therapy, 6*, 50–65.

Rooney, R. A., & Osipow, S. H. (1992). Task-specific occupational self-efficacy scale. *Journal of Vocational Behavior, 40*, 14–32.

Rosewater, L. B. (1985). Feminist interpretation of traditional testing. In L. B. Rosewater & L. E. Walker (Eds.), *Handbook of feminist therapy* (pp. 266–273). New York: Springer.

Rounds, J. B. (1985). Vocational Preference Inventory. In J. V. Mitchell, Jr. (Ed.), *The ninth Mental Measurements yearbook* (Vol. II, pp. 1683–1684). Lincoln, NE: Buros Institute of Mental Measurements.

Rounds, J. B., Henly, G. A., Dawis, R. V., Lofquist, L. H., & Weiss, D. J. (1981). *Manual for the Minnesota Importance Questionnaire*. Minneapolis: Vocational Psychology Research, University of Minnesota.

Rounds, J. B., & Tracey, T. J. (1990). From trait-and-factor to person-environment fit counseling: Theory and process. In W. B. Walsh & S. H. Osipow (Eds.), *Career counseling: Contemporary topics in vocational psychology* (pp. 1–44). Hillsdale, NJ: Lawrence Erlbaum Associates.

Savickas, M. L. (1990). The use of career choice process scales in counseling practice. In C.

E. Watkins, Jr. & V. L. Campbell (Eds.), *Testing in counseling practice* (pp. 373–418). Hillsdale, NJ: Lawrence Erlbaum Associates.

Segal, Z. V.,& Shaw, B. F. (1988). Cognitive assessment: Issues and methods. In K. S. Dobson (Ed.), *Handbook of cognitive-behavioral therapies* (pp. 39–81). New York: Guilford.

Selkow, P. (1984). *Assessing sex bias in testing*. Westport, CT: Greenwood.

Sesan, R. (1988). Sex bias and sex-role stereotyping in psychotherapy with women: Survey results. *Psychotherapy, 25,* 107–116.

Slaney, R. B. (1978). Expressed and inventoried vocational interests: A comparison of instruments. *Journal of Counseling Psychology, 25,* 520–529.

Slaney, R. B. (1988). The assessment of career decision making. In W. B. Walsh & S. H. Osipow (Eds.), *Career decision making* (pp. 33–76). Hillsdale, NJ: Lawrence Erlbaum Associates.

Slaney, R. B., & MacKinnon-Slaney, F. (1990). The use of vocational card sorts in career counseling. In C. E. Watkins, Jr. & V. L. Campbell (Eds.), *Testing in counseling practice* (pp. 317–371). Hillsdale, NJ: Lawrence Erlbaum Associates.

Smith, E. J. (1983). Issues in racial minorities' career behavior. In W. B. Walsh & S. H. Osipaw (Eds.), *Handbook of vocational psychology: Foundations* (Vol. 1, pp. 161–222).

Solomon, L. J., & Rothblum, E. D. (1985). Social skills problems experienced by women. In L. L'Abate & M. M. Milan (Eds.), *Handbook of social skills training and research* (pp. 303–325). New York: Wiley.

Spence, J. T., & Helmreich, R. L. (1972). The Attitudes Toward Women Scale: An objective instrument to measure attitudes toward the rights and roles of women in contemporary society. *JSAS Catalog of Selected Documents in Psychology, 2,* 66 (Ms. No. 153).

Spence, J. T., Helmreich, R. L., & Stapp, J.(1974). The Personal Attributes Questionnaire: A measure of sex role streotypes and masculinity–femininity. *JSAS Catalog of Selected Documents in Psychology, 4,* 43 (Ms. No. 617).

Spokane, A. R. (1990). Self-guided interest inventories and career interventions. In C. E. Watkins, Jr. & V. L. Campbell (Eds.), *Testing in counseling practice* (pp. 285–316). Hillsdale, NJ: Lawrence Erlbaum Associates.

Spokane, A. R. (1991). *Career intervention*. Englewood Cliffs, NJ: Prentice-Hall.

Sue, D. W., & Sue, D. (1990). *Counseling the culturally different: Theory and practice* (2nd ed.). New York: Wiley.

Super, D. E. (1970). *Work Values Inventory manual*. Chicago: Riverside Publishing Company.

Super, D. E. (1980). A life span, life-space approach to career development. *Journal of Vocational Behavior, 16,* 282–298.

Super, D. E., & Crites, J. O. (1949). *Appraising vocational fitness*. New York: Harper & Row.

Super, D. E., Thompson, A. S., & Lindeman, R. H. (1988). *Adult Career Concerns Inventory: Manual for research and exploratory use in counseling*. Palo Alto, CA: Consulting Psychologists Press.

Super, D. E., Thompson, A. S., Lindeman, R. H., Jordan, J. P., & Myers, R. A. (1984). *Technical manual for the Career Development Inventory*. Palo Alto, CA: Consulting Psychologists Press.

Swanson, J. L., & Tokar, D. M. (1991). College student's perceptions of barriers to career development. *Journal of Vocational Behavior, 38,* 92–106.

Tyler, L. E. (1961). Research explorations in the realm of choice. *Journal of Counseling Psychology, 8,* 195–201.

Unger, R. K. (1979). Toward a redefinition of sex and gender. *American Psychologist, 34,* 1085–1094.

U.S. Department of Labor, Employment and Training Administration. (1977). *Dictionary of occupational titles* (4th ed.). Washington, DC: U.S. Government Printing Office.

Walsh, W. B. (1990). Putting assessment in context. *Counseling Psychologist, 18,* 262–265.

Walsh, W. B., & Betz, N. E. (1990). *Tests and assessment* (2nd ed.). Englewood Cliffs, NJ: Prentice-Hall.

Walsh, W. B., & Osipow, S. H. (Eds.). (1990). *Career counseling.* Hillsdale, NJ: Lawrence Erlbaum Associates.

Watkins, C. E., & Campbell, V. L. (Ed.). (1990). *Testing in counseling practice.* Hillsdale, NJ: Lawrence Erlbaum Associates.

Watkins, C. E., & Savickas, M. L. (1990). Psychodynamic career counseling. In W. B. Walsh & S. H. Osipow (Eds.), *Career counseling* (pp. 79–116). Hillsdale, NJ: Lawrence Erlbaum Associates.

Wegner, K. W. (1988). Review of the California Personality Inventory, 1987 revised edition. In D. J. Keyser & R. C. Sweetland (Eds.), *Test critiques* (Vol. VII, pp. 66–75). Kansas City, MO: Test Corporation of America.

Westbrook, B. W. (1988). My Vocational Situation. In J. T. Kapes & M. M. Mastie (Eds.), *A counselor's guide to career assessment instruments* (2nd ed., pp. 187–190). Alexandria, VA: National Career Development Association.

Wholeben, B. E. (1988). Sixteen PF Career Development Profile. In J. T. Kapes & M. M. Mastie (Eds.), *A counselor's guide to career assessment instruments* (2nd ed., pp. 238–242). Alexandria, VA: National Career Development Association.

Willis, C. G., & Ham, T. L. (1988). The Myers-Briggs Type Indicator. In J. T. Kapes & M. M. Mastie (Eds.), *A counselor's guide to career assessment instruments* (2nd ed., pp. 230–233). Alexandria, VA: National Career Development Association.

Zuckerman, M. (1985). Review of the 16 Personality Factor Questionnaire. In J. V. Mitchell, Jr. (Ed.). *The ninth Mental Measurements yearbook* (Vol. II, pp. 1392–1394). Lincoln, NE: Buros Institute of Mental Measurements.

Zunker, V. G. (1990). *Using assessment results in for career development* (3rd ed.). Pacific Grove, CA: Brooks/Cole.

Zytowski, D. G. (1988). Review of the Salience Inventory. In J. T. Kapes & M. M. Mastie (Eds.), *A counselor's guide to career assessment instruments* (2nd ed., pp. 151–154). Alexandria, VA: National Career Development Association.

Zytowski, D. G., & Kuder, F. (1986). Advances in the Kuder Occupational Interest Survey. In W. B. Walsh & S. H. Osipow (Eds.), *Advances in vocational psychology, Vol I: The assessment of interests* (pp. 31–54). Hillsdale, NJ: Lawrence Erlbaum Associates.

Zytowski, D. G., & Laing, L. (1978). Validity of other-gender-normed scales on the KOIS. *Journal of Counseling Psychology, 25,* 205–209.

# ❧ 3 ❧

# Feminism and Career Counseling

Linda Brooks
*University of North Carolina*

Linda Forrest
*Michigan State University*

This chapter explicates the influence of feminism on the research and practice of career counseling. The chapter begins with a brief description of the major tenets of feminism articulated during the last three decades. Next, research critiques developed by feminist researchers within the larger scientific community are outlined, as well as the recommendations for improving research that emanate from these critiques. We then review the last decade of research on vocational behavior and career counseling to evaluate whether and to what extent these feminist recommendations have been incorporated into the research practices of psychologists studying vocational behavior and career counseling.

After completion of the research critique, we turn to the practice of career counseling. We provide an overview of the feminist critiques of mental health practices and the tenets of feminist therapy that developed from these critiques. These feminist therapy tenets are used as criteria to evaluate the literature on career counseling practice.

Finally, we use the tenets of feminist therapy to make specific recommendations about the practice of career counseling with women. In our conclusion, we summarize the current state of the art of feminist influences on the research and practice of career counseling, and make recommendations for future action by career counseling researchers and practitioners.

## TENETS OF FEMINISM

The major tenets of feminism build from the belief in social, political, and economic equality between women and men and freedom for

everyone to develop their potential unhampered by "artifically dichotomous sex roles" (Sturdivant, 1980, p. 6). Feminism is "both an ideology
and a movement for sociopolitical change based on a critical analysis of
male privilege and women's subordination" (Offen, 1988, p. 151).
Consequently, feminists believe it is important to challenge sexist
attitudes, beliefs, and practices based on a double standard for men's
and women's behavior that exists within our social order. Feminists
strive to analyze and eliminate understandings that devalue women,
view women as deficient, or place women in secondary roles to men.
Feminism is pro-woman, but not necessarily anti-man; "indeed in time
past, some of the most important advocates of women's causes have
been men" (Offen, 1988, p. 181). Feminists oppose "women's subordination to men in the family and society along with men's claims to
define what is best for women without consulting them" (Offen, 1988, p.
151), and encourage egalitarian, nonhierarchical relationships between
people, including husband and wife, parent and child, worker and boss.

"The core of feminism is simply the insistence that personal autonomy
is essential for every woman" and "that women should have both the
freedom and responsibility to direct all important aspects of their lives:
emotional, intellectual, economic, and sexual" (Sturdivant, 1980, p. 6).
Feminists reject biological determinism (i.e., because women differ
biologically from men, they should serve different social functions and
roles than men) and assert the importance of sociocultural conditions in
determining what behaviors are allowed and rewarded for women and
men. Sociocultural conditions have prevented women from functioning
and contributing according to their potential, because they have relegated and enforced secondary roles for women. "The movement seeks
an end to the myth that men are superior to women and an end to those
practices and institutions of the society that are perpetuating that myth"
(Sturdivant, 1980, p. 44). "Feminism has been, and remains today, a
political challenge to male authority and hierarchy in the most profound
sense" (Offen, 1988, p. 182). Thus, feminists see political, economic, and
social action as necessary to accomplish the structural changes in
society. These basic feminist tenets are the springboard from which
feminist critiques of research and practice have been launched.

## FEMINIST CRITIQUES OF PSYCHOLOGICAL RESEARCH

Feminist critiques of psychological research are based on and originated
from the feminist values and assumptions covered in the previous
section. Initially, feminist critiques of research focused on the problems
associated with studying men and generalizing to women. Soon it was

apparent that just "adding" women was not sufficient to solve the problems of androcentric bias (Harding, 1987), because all aspects of research process were affected by sexist attitudes (Grady, 1981; McHugh, Koeske, & Frieze, 1986; Wallston, 1981). Thus, the critique moved to examining each step of the research process for bias, from the generation of questions (Wallston, 1981) to the interpretation of results. Suggestions for removing sexist bias were also viewed as insufficient. These concerns caused some feminist researchers to look for alternative methodologies outside the traditions of the logical positivists and their scientific methods.

Initially, all feminist critiques were assumed to originate from similar value systems and commitments. However, since the mid- 1980s there has been a growing understanding that there is not one feminist challenge of research design and methodology, but many (Harding, 1987a; Lykes & Stewart, 1986; Maracek, 1989). By the 1990s, the major elements of the various different feminist critiques of research had been identified (Harding, 1987b; Hawkesworth, 1989; McHugh et al., 1986). Yet, according to Lykes and Stewart (1986), feminist critiques of research have had limited influence outside journals committed to the psychology of women. Walsh (1989) agreed that many of the feminist suggestions for improving research have not yet been integrated into research practice, even within the psychology of women literature.

Still, feminist critiques remain alive and well, and examples of improving and stretching our research methods to address questions of importance to women appear with more regularity. A recent edition of the *Psychology of Women Quarterly* was devoted to the theory and methods of feminists psychology that raised questions about the relationship among epistemology, metatheory, and methods, including how we know what we know, the production and justification of knowledge, the social and historical position of the knower, and the relationship between knowledge and power. The increasing differentiation within feminist critiques creates a fertile ground for further debates about research methodology. Marecek (1989) stated that

> Thus far, feminist psychology has been predominantly oriented toward producing facts; we are ready now to theorize those facts. The turn to metatheory and epistemology allows us to see how the discipline of psychology disciplines us: how it structures the categories we think in, regulates the knowledge we produce, and restrains our imagination. (p. 375)

In this section, we (a) review major elements of feminist critiques of research, (b) summarize recommendations for the conduct of research that arise from feminist critiques of research, and (c) examine current research on vocational behavior and career development to determine if feminist recommendations are being incorporated.

## MAJOR ELEMENTS OF FEMINIST CRITIQUES
## OF RESEARCH

### The Inclusion and Confusion About Sex

Early feminist critiques raised two concerns. First, psychologists often left out information about the sex of research participants, suggesting a lack of interest in variance between or within the sexes. Second, feminists were concerned about the large numbers of studies in which only men were studied, yet conclusions were being drawn as if they were applicable to women (Grady, 1981; Lott, 1985). Feminist critiques addressed this problem, encouraging researchers to study both sexes, to select male and female subjects similarly (Peplau & Conrad, 1989), and once selected to provide both sexes the same treatment.

Feminists also proposed clarifying the terminology used to study sex and sex differences. McHugh et al. (1986) listed possible different meanings for the term *sex* and urged researchers to define terms with precision. More specifically, Unger (1979) recommended using the word *sex* to describe biological aspects of being male or female, and using the word *gender* to describe aspects of sex "for which biological causality has not been established" (Unger, 1990, p. 108) and "that are culturally regarded as appropriate to males or to females" (Unger, 1979, p. 1086). Creating this distinction between sex and gender reduces the likelihood that researchers will assume implicit parallels between biological (i.e., physical attributes like penis, vagina, uterus) and psychological sex. Later research confirmed that in certain instances gender, not biological sex, was the significant contributor to the variance in observed behavior.

Another thoughtful criticism developed around how the variable "sex" was conceptualized in the research design. Most research focused on sex as a subject variable (i.e., a subject is female or male), thus attempting to determine and explain how women and men differ on various behaviors, traits, and capabilities (Deaux, 1984; Parlee, 1981). However, over time feminists also recognized the significance of sex as a stimulus variable. In this approach, providing information about the sex of an individual allows research respondents to exhibit their expectations about an individual's behavior based on the respondent's beliefs and attitudes about the social category of gender. Feminists recommended the inclusion of sex not only as a subject, but also as a stimulus variable in research designs (Deaux, 1984; Eagly, 1978; Grady, 1981; Lott, 1985; Maccoby, 1988, 1990; Unger, 1990; Wallston, 1981).

Feminists were also concerned about researchers who (a) included gender as a variable without theoretical or conceptual agruments for doing so (Grady, 1981; McHugh et al., 1986; Wallston, 1981), and (b) drew conclusions about significant gender differences without exploring multiple plausible explanations for such differences. In the first instance, simple descriptions of the differences found would have been in order, yet authors generated explanatory differences without grounding these explanations in the larger theoretical and empirical literature, creating a literature "replete with inconsequential, accidental and incidental findings of 'sex differences' " (Grady, 1981, p. 632). Grady suggested that sex is a surface explanation that needs further exploration, because sex is a medium for complex psychological processes. In the second instance, authors who purported a single explanation for differences often produced an explanation grounded in biology (McHugh et al., 1986) that was inherently biased against women. Models that explain gender differences by viewing women as deficient (e.g., the literature on moral development or achievement motivation) or deviant (e.g., the literature of sex differences in mental illness) often revert to internal, stable traits or biological differences without identifying the mechanisms and processes involved. These researchers ignored other equally plausible explanations for the data (sociocultural explanations that recognize women's experiences in the larger world around them) that would have been more positively disposed to women.

## Bias as a Consequence of Focus on the Individual

Feminists (Kahn & Yoder, 1989; Lott, 1985; Unger, 1981, 1990) voiced concern about how often gender is treated as a simple, stable, internal individual variable rather than a complex, multifaceted, social variable that varies depending upon social and environmental circumstances. Many researchers have built their studies on the assumption that gender was a stable, internal trait (perhaps because of the implicit assumption about differences having biological origins). This assumption creates blind spots, perhaps explaining why researchers do not include social context variables in their research designs. This focus on the individual limits both the type of research designed and the possible explanatory models developed to organize our thinking about observed similarities and differences between the sexes.

Accordingly, feminists have pointed to empirical evidence that documents social context as a major explanation for the type and degree of gender differences observed (Deaux, 1984; Eagly, 1978, 1983; Frodi,

Macauley, & Thome, 1977; Zanna & Pack, 1975). For example, Carli (1990) found that the way people speak depends more on the gender of the person with whom they are speaking than on their own style and that certain styles of speaking are more influential than others, depending on the gender of the person to whom they are speaking (i.e., the social context). Thus, a women using certain patterns of speech (speaking hesitantly rather than assertively) may not be acting from some internal trait, but may be accurately reading her environment (the man she is with prefers and responds to this style) and actively choosing to have influence on another. This study points to the importance of including measures of social context.

This line of research also suggests that power and influence are critical factors in determining under what circumstances gender similarities and differences are observed. Several authors (Henley, 1977; Snodgrass, 1985) provided empirical evidence to support the conclusion that when gender differences are found, what is actually being measured is not differences in gender but differences in access to power and influence.

Because "gender by situation interactions are more the rule than exception" (Lott, 1985, p. 185) and account for more variance than either situation or person variables (Wallston, 1981), feminists call for researchers to attend to the person/situation interactions that create a much fuller, more accurate explanation of gender differences. Research designs limited by their focus on internal traits of the individual have not been able to explore the multifaceted nature and complex social processes of gender that are now well documented by authors who used more sophisticated methods to study gender (Deaux, 1984; Eagly, 1978, 1983; Maccoby, 1988, 1990).

As Wallston (1981) articulated, one serious consequence of not attending to situational variables in understanding gender is the misattribution of causality to individuals. This leads researchers to make recommendations that focus on changing individuals rather than organizations or social contexts. Misattribution of causality resulting in efforts to change individuals (e.g., assertiveness training) may have limited impact, because the societal expectations and rewards remain the same. Research designs that include social context variables may prove more fruitful because they allow researchers to consider social and organizational change recommendations as well.

## Challenging the Hierarchical Relationship Between Scientist and Citizens

Feminists have challenged hierarchical relationships that are embedded in the conduct of science, and are concerned about the impersonal approach and lack of attention paid to research participants throughout the research process (Wallston, 1981; Walsh, 1989; Unger, 1983). The inequality between researcher and research participants may create responses by the research participants that represent their behavior when in passive, subordinate positions. Researchers who enter studies with predetermined hypotheses may "remain outsiders who fail to elicit critical insider information or to recognize the potential harm of their approach" (McHugh et al., 1986, p. 880).

Feminists' commitment to nonhierarchical, democratic relationships provides the philosophical underpinnings for research participants to be more involved in all aspects of the research process (e.g., the generation of important questions, the selection of representative samples, the decisions about which variables to study, their reactions to the accuracy and relevance of the operationalization and measurement of variables, data analysis, and interpretation). When researchers locate themselves in the same sphere as the research participants (Harding, 1987b), rather than jeopardizing objectivity, they create opportunities for research participants to provide feedback that improves research designs and findings. Eliciting participants' viewpoints "may be one way to 'get behind' the inequality and the limited self presentation potentially inherent in all researcher-participant interactions" (McHugh et al., 1986, p. 880). Several authors (McHugh et al., 1986; Walsh, 1989) recommended that initial results be shared with the participants and their input sought to gain a more accurate understanding of their responses. Such interactions might uncover biases the researcher holds, methodological limitations, and problems with researchers' interpretations. Lott (1985) suggested that more involvement with research participants throughout the research process might create better understanding of the effects of the research protocol on the participants. Given the influence of social context on the type and degree of gender differences observed in various research studies, the demand characteristics of the research protocol when studying gender seem particularly relevant and important to assess (Unger, 1981).

## Challenging the Assumptions of Objectivity

A major focus of the feminist critiques has been to challenge some of the basic assumptions of objectivity deeply embedded in the scientific method and the logical positivist traditions. Feminists reject the claim that well-conducted research using the scientific method can "effectively safeguard against the intrusion of values and bias into the production of knowledge" (Marecek, 1989, p. 369).

Because the values, attitudes, and social position of the researcher can have a systematic effect on all stages of the research process (McHugh et al., 1986; Wallston, 1981), several feminist authors have called for providing more information about who the researcher is in scientific write-ups. The current practices of most psychological journals do not require personal data about the researcher. Furthermore, within the logical positivist traditions, the overemphasis on objectivity discourages authors from acknowledging personal positions or tendencies and hides the fact that researchers are often examining "data with an eye to the construction of a convincing case" (McHugh et al., 1986, p. 882).

Evidence exists that personal identity, including one's social history, political commitments, and professional activities, affects one's world-views and beliefs about human nature (Ricketts, 1989), suggesting that personal information about the researcher may be critical and central to evaluating the quality of any research (Harding, 1987b). Harding (1987b) suggested that reporting this subjective information about the re-searcher would increase the ultimate objectivity of the research and decrease the objectivism that hides this personal information from public scrutiny. Whereas most psychologists see the knowledge pro-duced by traditional scientific method based on a commitment to objectivity as the most accurate and bias-free knowledge, feminist are more likely to see objectivity and the scientific method as one position among many for creating knowledge with its own unique strengths and limitations.

## Challenging Psychology's Lack of Commitment to Social Change

Feminist researchers have criticized mainstream psychology for its inadvertent support of the current social order that places women at great risk (Kahn & Yoder, 1989). Psychology's heavy reliance on individualistic approaches that minimize the effects of social, cultural, and environmental influences on shaping behavior and see solutions at the individual level causes psychology as a discipline to play a major role in maintaining the status quo in society (Kahn & Yoder, 1989). In contrast, the scholarship of feminist psychology developed in the midst of the women's movement, where political agendas, commitment to social change, and close links to public policy issues were acknowl-edged. Feminists admit freely the difficulty they have in separating scientific concerns from political concerns (Grady, 1981). They argue that this separation between research and social change is, in fact, an unhealthy one. Wittig (1985) argued "that scholarship informs political action and that the political stance of the researcher affects aspects of the research endeavor" (p. 804). Many feminists (Tangri & Strasburg, 1979;

Wallston, 1981) criticize mainstream psychology for its lack of attention to critical social policy issues, especially those affecting the lives of women and children (e.g., childcare, occupational and consequently economic discrimination against women, sexual and domestic abuse, abortion).

Several authors (Millman & Kanter, 1975; Wallston, 1981) have recommended that psychologists consider the potential policy ramifications of their research throughout the research process. Wallston (1981) suggested that researchers consider potential outcomes from their research while they are developing their research questions and design, thus, formulating productive questions and generating data for input into the social policy discussions. Millman and Kanter (1975) recommended alternating between social reform activities and reflecting on the process of social reform through research production, thus generating more useful data for social policy decisions. Unger (1983) suggested adding a criterion for making publishing decisions (i.e., measuring "the degree to which studies are helpful to the target population," p. 28).

## Methodological Bias

According to Harding (1987a), feminists differ from other researchers in the theories they use, the ways they apply theory to specific problems, and their general beliefs about how knowledge is construed, yet feminists use the techniques and methods available to all researchers. Although Harding did not consider methods to be a defining feature of feminist research, feminists have criticized psychology for respecting only one epistemological position, that of the logical positivists. This position relies heavily on tight experimental control (Parlee, 1981), often strips away the context in which behavior occurs (Fine, 1985), assumes linear relationships among variables, restricts the type of psychological questions considered (Wallston, 1981) and the type of behaviors that can be studied due to operationalization and measurement constraints, and limits the acceptable methods for analyzing data. Feminists have also questioned the limitations created by the tight cause-and-effect reasoning that requires discrete variables isolated from each other, removed from their situational and historical context (Unger, 1983), and available for independent manipulation. This cause-and-effect reasoning also assumes linear relationships between variables (Parlee, 1981). These limitations are especially apparent when so many psychologically important questions require understanding complex, perhaps nonlinear, relationships among variables that may be impossible to isolate from each other and manipulate independently. Questioning the actual usefulness of this compartmentalization, control, and manipulation of variables, many feminist writers have wondered if a more open attitude toward other epistemological positions and consequently other methodological traditions might not provide greater clarity and understanding of human behavior. Other feminists have documented the lack of methodological diversity within the field of psychology, including the subdiscipline of the psychology of women (Lykes & Stewart, 1986; Walsh, 1989). In their evaluation of the degree of inclusion of feminist recommendations on published research, Lykes and Stewart noted that it was in methodology that they observed the greatest reluctance to change. They concluded that methodology can be viewed as the major gatekeeper in psychology for addressing questions important to women.

In addition to questions raised about methodological diversity, feminists have written extensively about the various ways that sex bias is embedded in specific aspects of methodology.

*Sampling Bias.* As mentioned in an earlier section, male single-sex research designs were common, yet conclusions from these studies were generalized to all humans. With the addition of women as research subjects, another problem presented itself. Several authors (Grady, 1981; Maccoby & Jacklin, 1974; Marecek, 1989; McHugh et al., 1986; Unger, 1990) noted that studies reporting gender differences were evaluated as more interesting and important, and consequently were more likely to be published, than studies where no differences were found. The consequence of these publishing practices within psychology is that similarities are obscured and differences are emphasized.

Because sex of the subject cannot be manipulated and randomized, Parlee (1981) revealed another problem arising from sample selection that creates biased results and conclusions, that is the selection of appropriate comparison groups. She used as an example the selection of a control group of women for an ongoing study on aging originally involving men only. The men were "intelligent, highly educated, professionally active and successful, and by a number of psychological and physical criteria they seem to be aging very well" (p. 639). The social scientists wanted to select a sample of women who were matched on these social variables, whereas the biomedical researchers wanted to select the female siblings of the men already in the study. Each of the researchers' choices represented their understanding of the important comparisons to be made. In the case of the social scientists they wanted the two groups carefully matched on social dimensions, whereas the biomedical scientists believed heredity and physiological similarities were more important for understanding differences and similarities in aging between men and women. Parlee highlighted the underlying assumptions and theoretical frameworks apparent to her in the selection of the comparison group. She commented that when selection of control groups is discussed solely as a methodological issue, the researcher can ignore or deny the influence of the researcher's personal histories, values, and assumptive frameworks on decisions. In addition, the researcher may miss the influence of the sampling decision on the results, thus drawing incomplete or inaccurate interpretations about the data.

Finally, numerous feminist writers have raised the concern about the lack of sampling diversity (i.e., the overuse of college students from introductory psychology courses) in psychological research (Grady, 1981; Lott, 1985; Peplau & Conrad, 1989; Unger, 1990). In calling for expanded diversity in sampling decisions, feminists suggest selecting samples from the people who are most affected by the topic under study and working to include individuals from all income situations, diverse ethnic and racial backgrounds (Peplau & Conrad, 1989), all ages, all types of sexual orientation (Peplau & Conrad, 1989), and physical abilities.

*Bias in Topic Selection.* Historically, topics of importance in women's lives have received little attention in the psychological literature (Denmark, cited in Grady, 1981). Until the last two decades certain topics (e.g., the psychological processes required to balance work and family life, or the effect of household responsibilities on career advancement) were not addressed within psychology, and certain questions (e.g., questions about the psychological consequences of sexual abuse, incest, or sexual harassment) had never been asked (Grady, 1981), because there were not sufficient researchers interested in and committed to women and the lives women lead. In addition, some questions were asked (e.g., the effect of mother's employment on children), but stereotyped attitudes about women and their appropriate place in society guided the research design (e.g., the psychological effects of marriage and children on women's mental health and career development were not asked) and the interpretation of the results.

The conditions of women's lives viewed positively and centrally from the perspective of women creates a whole new set of questions for researchers (Lerman, 1986; Lott, 1985; Wallston, 1981). For example, the psychological consequences on women of male dominance in male–female relationships is unlikely to be asked by researchers who do not see male dominance in these relationships (Millman & Kanter, 1975). Questions such as "What are the consequences of men's lack of involvement in childcare and household responsibilities on women's career development?" are of great interest to many women, but may not be burning questions for men (Harding, 1987a).

Feminist-standpoint theorists (Hartsock, 1987) argue that women's position in the societal hierarchy allows them to see certain relationships among variables that cannot be seen by those in power. They suggest that once a woman acknowledges the power hierarchy embedded in society, she will ask different questions about social relations. The Division 35 (Psychology of Women) Taskforce on Guidelines for Nonsexist Research in Psychology (as reported in McHugh et al., 1986) noted that feminist researchers provide a vital function by presenting an alternative perspective of the "outsider," thus generating new theoretical conceptualizations about human behavior and new research agendas.

*Bias in the Operationalization of Variables.*  Bias can also exist in how researchers select variables and tasks to study, operationalize the variables, and determine the methods of measuring the variables. For example, in her review of a decade's research on gender, Deaux (1984) observed that differences between men and women were highly influenced by the task selected to study a behavior (i.e., the sex linkage of the task in studies of helping behavior, reward allocations, and conformity influenced the direction and size of sex difference found). She concluded that "some tasks may not be neutral arenas for a test of possible sex differences, but rather influential sources of those differences" (p. 107).

Another example comes from McKenna and Kessler (1977), who evaluated over 500 studies on aggression and interpersonal attraction and found that when females were subjects, the independent variable manipulation was less likely to involve active treatment or arousal (paper and pencil measures instead of overt acts of aggression) and the dependent variable was less likely to involve active behavior (rating feelings of aggression instead of acts of aggression) than when males were the subjects. They concluded that the pattern of results indicate that "the relationship between sex of subject, the variables studied, and how the variables are measured and manipulated is not random, but reflects sex-role stereotyping" (McKenna & Kessler, 1977 p. 125).

Bias can also appear when researchers select the coding responses available. For example, Bart (1971) reported on a study that coded women's responses to sexual intercourse with the following categories: passive, responsive, resistant, aggressive, deviant and other. She reflected that an "active" response to sexual intercourse for women would either fall into the aggressive, deviant, or other category and would not be recognized by the researchers. Bart asked whether the category of "active" would have been left out if men's responses to sexual intercourse were being coded.

Another source of bias can be in the labels or terms used to describe variables. For example, Tavris (1991) provided examples of conclusions from previously published research that exhibited bias, because the terms selected assumed men to be the standard. For each example, the conclusion from previous research is provided first, followed by Tavris' restatement:

1. "Women have lower self-esteem than men do" (Sanford & Donovan, 1984) or "Men are more conceited than women."
2. "Women do not value their efforts as much as men do, even when they are doing the same work (Major, 1987) or "Men overvalue the work they do" or "Men are not as realistic and modest as women in assessing their abilities."
3. "Women are more likely than men to say they are 'hurt' than to admit they are 'angry' " (Biagggio, 1988) or "Men are more likely than women to accuse and attack others when they are unhappy, instead of stating that they feel hurt."
4. "Women have more difficulty than men in developing a 'separate sense of self' " (Aries & Olver, 1985) or "Men have more difficulty than women in forming and maintaining attachments" (Tavris, 1991, pp. 94–95).

McHugh et al. (1986) argued that terminology conveys cultural attitudes about the preferred behavior for men and women. They recommended terminology that reflects tolerance for differences rather than terminology that suggests preferred or privileged standard of behavior.

***Bias Based on Limited Sources of Data.*** Feminists have criticized the standards of psychological research for its dependence on a narrow range of ways that are acceptable for measuring variables. Many psychological studies rely heavily on paper and pencil standardized measures that were developed on men and are now used for both men and women. Excessive confidence in standardized measures with good reliability and validity often provides researcher with protection that does not encourage checking closely for potential sex bias in the instrument.

Millman and Kanter (1975) criticized mainstream research designs for their lack of attention to subjective experiences of women. Wallston (1981) recommended using more data generated from the personal experiences of women. She argued that these subjective data were rich, full, and complex measures of the "real" lives of women. Lykes and Stewart (1986) recommended developing more strategies for using "experience near" data. And others have recommended more interactive strategies for collecting data.

*Sex of Experimenter Bias.* Unger (1981) described traditional psychology's attitude about the relationship between the experimenter and subjects as a variable that needs to be controlled. Feminists are more likely to see the social interactions between the researcher and participants in the study as a critical, integral component of context that might be influencing the phenomenon under study. Thus, attention to controlling interactions between the researcher and participants to remove the effect is less important than observing interactions to better understand the complex social processes that affect individual behavior.

There are numerous examples of sex of experimenter effects on results. Bickman (1974) found that men and women were more likely to volunteer for opposite sex experimenters. Sex of the evaluator also interacts with the public and private nature of the task participants are asked to perform (Eagly, 1978)—that is as the degree of public scrutiny increases, so does stereotypic sex-related behavior. Eagly and Carli (1981) also found disturbing evidence of research results interacting with the sex of the experimenter. Researchers were more likely to report behaviors that were socially desirable for members of their own sex (e.g., males reported evidence of female conformity and male independence, whereas females reported greater female superiority in nonverbal decoding). The combination of all of these studies suggests that the sex of the experimenter is interacting with other aspects of methodology and affecting results. Also, given the clear indication from the research on social context showing the influence of context on the type and degree of gender differences observed, feminists call for special attention to sex of experimenter effects on results.

## FEMINIST RESEARCH RECOMMENDATIONS: ARE THEY OBSERVABLE IN THE VOCATIONAL RESEARCH LITERATURE?

Are the recommendations for improving research that emanate from feminist critiques observable in the research on vocational behavior and career development? We reviewed two major journals (the *Journal of Vocational Behavior* and the career development section of the *Journal of Counseling Psychology*). We selected 1980 as a starting point, because the process of conducting research can take several years prior to publication and we wanted to provide sufficient time for feminist critiques of research to have influenced the research process. Thus, we anticipated that some of the early critiques from the 1970s might be observable in the research published in the early 1980s.

We reviewed the majority of the articles in each volume to determine trends. We provide our general impression of whether and to what degree a specific feminist recommendation has been incorporated into the research on vocational behavior and career counseling. We also describe exemplary studies that included one or more of the recommendations originating from feminist research critiques.

We reviewed more carefully each article that had in its title either "women" or "gender" because we assumed that these authors were more likely to have read the feminist writings than authors not focusing on women or gender. Prior work by Lykes and Stewart (1986) found that researchers publishing in psychology of women journals were more likely to include examples of feminist principles in their research methods, design, and writeup than were researchers publishing in other psychological journals.

Although we do not consider our review to be either systematic or comprehensive, we believe our general impressions reflect the reality of research published in the last decade. However, we also encourage others to investigate the degree to which feminist principles of research are observable.

## The Inclusion and Confusion About Sex

We observed several studies in which the researcher provided no information about the sex of the research participants, and numerous studies where the author identified the number of men and women research participants but never mentioned sex again, including not analyzing the results to see if men and women responded similarly or differently to the variables under study. There were just as many studies that provided information about the number of women and men research participants, and analyzed the data for sex or gender differences, yet did not provide theoretical arguments for doing so or ground their analyses in the literature on gender. When these authors noted gender differences, they often built superficial explanations for their results without understanding how their results fit into a larger contextual understanding of gender. Solomon, Bishop, and Bresser (1986) noted this problem commenting that "the literature on . . . gender differences in career development is characterized by conceptual complexity and a lack of integration of research studies, each of which examines a different single facet of the problem" (p. 28).

Several authors acknowledged the importance of attending to similarities between the sexes (Fitzgerald & Rounds, 1989; Hackett, Lent, & Greenhaus, 1991; Scozzaro & Subich, 1990). For example, Hackett et al. (1991) stated that "perhaps the most widespread conclusion at this time is that women and men are more similar than different in most work-related variables" (p. 20). Or Fitzgerald and Rounds (1989) concluded that "although . . . gender differences in vocational behavior do exist, the similarities between women and men are more numerous and probably more significant than differences" (p. 108). Scozzaro and Subich (1990) reported both differences and similarities between women and men in job outcome perceptions.

There were numerous examples of authors misusing the terms "sex" and "gender". Some authors used these terms interchangeably. Other authors used sex when the more appropriate term would have been gender, because the author was referring to social and cultural roles, not biological sex. Several authors were careful to avoid terms like masculinity and femininity when measuring behaviors that could be highly influenced by social conditioning and sex-role stereotyping (see Douce & Hansen, 1990).

There were many examples of authors paying attention to the difference between biological sex and sex role socialization, though there were still some problems with careful attention to terminology. For example, Gaddy, Glass, and Arnkoff (1983) looked beyond biological sex by using a measure of psychological androgyny to assess women's social roles and the effect of these roles on women's career involvement. Though Gianakos and Subich (1986) did not define their terms carefully, they did recognize the importance of separating the sex of the subject from the subject's sex-role orientation. Their results showed the importance of making this distinction, because they found no sex of subject differences (though they labeled this variable "gender"), but sex-role orientation differences on vocational undecidedness.

We found only one study in which the authors understood the importance of using sex as a stimulus variable or understanding that research participants respond to gender as a social category (Kinicki & Griffeth, 1985). Several studies would have definitely been improved if the authors had understood the importance of assessing the effects of sex as a stimulus variable (e.g., Beehr, King, & King, 1990, examined the relationship among social support, occupational stress, and talking to supervisors without examining the sex of the supervisor effect).

In summary, our review suggests that authors need to be more careful in identifying the sex of the research participants, and need to build a case for why the results should either be analyzed or not for differences between men and women. Authors also need to define the terms they use to describe sex, gender, and sex or gender role with more care. We also recommend that authors read the literature that clarifies these issues and makes definitional recommendations for the consistent use of these terms. Finally, when explaining similarities and differences between the sexes, authors need to ground their explanations in the empirical and theoretical literature on gender differences.

## Bias as a Consequence of Focus on the Individual

Our review suggests that most authors continue to study vocational behavior from the perspective of the individual, with little attention to measuring social context variables. For example, Chusmir and Koberg (1986) studied gender differences in creativity of managers by measuring participant's self-report of job satisfaction, job involvement, and so on. They did not consider context variables in designing their study; thus they may have missed major explanations for gender differences in the creativity of managers.

We found only two studies that measured the influence of context variables on women's career aspirations and choice (Hackett, Esposito, & O'Halloran, 1989; Matsui, Ikeda, & Ohnishi, 1989) However, in both cases situational variables were measured by relying on the individual's self-report. Thus, even when authors did attend to concepts of social context, they used the individual as the source of information. Several authors mentioned the importance of contextual variables (e.g., role models, the availability of childcare, type and quality of supervision, pay inequities, communication problems within organizations), yet they did not include in their methods mechanisms for measuring these social context variables (Abush & Burkhead, 1984). We found no authors that included measures of power and influence in their study design. However, in their annual review of vocational literature, Greenhaus and Parasuraman (1986) noted under the subsection Power and Influence the importance of contextual variables like sex-segregated networks and situational factors such as management style and resource scarcity as examples of variables to consider in determining gender differences in power and influence.

An excellent example of understanding the importance of social context is provided by Harmon's (1989) study of longitudinal changes in women's career aspirations. Because the historical context in which women grow up may have powerful effects on women's career aspirations, Harmon compared two samples of women, one of women who were approximately 18 years old in 1968 and the other of women who were 18 in 1983. She was able to tease apart developmental effects from historical effects and determine that there were sociocultural influences on women's career aspirations that have changed over time.

For the vast majority of authors, context variables do not seem to receive the attention they deserve, nor are authors conscientious about identifying creative ways to measure context variables.

## Challenging the Hierarchical Relationship

We reviewed the literature for examples of integrating research participants as collaborators in a nonhierarchical relationship throughout the process of creating, conducting, and evaluating studies. We found several examples where researchers involved research participants in eliciting constructs, either through structured formats on questionnaires (Leso & Neimeyer, 1991; Randall, Fedor, & Longnecker, 1990; Swanson & Tokar, 1991), or through open-ended questions during interviews (Chusid & Cochran, 1989; Gaddy et al., 1983). For example, Leso and Neimeyer (1991) examined the influence of providing researcher-determined constructs or having the participant generate their own constructs and concluded that the active process of construct elicitation by participants functions as an exploratory stimulus or intervention that enhances participants' levels of differentiation. Similarly, Randall et al. (1990) concluded that "employees may not share researchers' views of how commitment should be expressed" (p. 219).

We discovered one example of researchers checking their results and interpretations for accuracy and face validity with research participants (Chusid & Cochran, 1989). Finally, we reviewed one article that used the results generated by research participants to assist these same individuals by conducting a workshop on coping strategies and problem solving (Heppner, Cook, Strozier, & Heppner, 1991). The feedback provided to the participants in this study highlights one of the feminist recommendations, being committed to using results to benefit the research participants.

These examples suggest that a few researchers are seeing the benefits of creating opportunities for research participants to be more involved in the generation of constructs and categories. However, none of these examples suggest that we are seriously challenging our understanding of the researcher's relationship to participants, nor are we developing new ways to include research participants in other aspects of the research process. The large majority of studies still utilize research participants solely as sources of data, and inadvertently participate in a hierarchical relationship with research participants.

## Challenging the Assumption of Objectivity

In our review we did not find any examples of researchers providing information about their personal values and beliefs, or background information about their social position in society. Nowhere were we able to find a researcher who openly provided this information so the reader could evaluate the influence of these factors on the research design and methodology as well as the results and interpretation.

## Challenging Psychology's Lack of Commitment to Social Change

The large number of studies on women's career choice and development suggests that the researchers have been aware of the social circumstances of women's lives. However, we did not find a publication in which the authors acknowledged that they were studying a particular question because they wanted to provide data for public policy debate or to affect social change. Some authors did mention issues of social change when discussing potential implications of their findings. In general, though, we did not observe any examples of authors readily admitting that their research was intimately tied to social change agendas or current public policy debates.

## Methodological Bias

In our review we observed a methodological narrowness. In their annual review, Greenhaus and Parasuraman (1986) commented on the disproportionate use of quantitative rather than qualitative approaches and techniques. Many of the recommendations that were made by these authors mirror the feminist recommendations for improving research.

*Sampling Bias.* There were a few studies that did not mention the sex of the research participants, and other studies where a small percentage of the participants was women, yet the author discussed the results as if they applied to women (see Kinicki, 1989). We found one study in which women were the predominant research participants, yet the results and discussion made no mention of being careful in generalizing the results to men (Blau, 1989). However, the more common practice when studying women only was that authors identified their reasons for doing so and then confined their discussion to women.

Sampling diversity was clearly observable in both journals. In their annual review, Greenhaus and Parasuraman (1986) noted the increase in use of diverse population. We found examples of studies using disadvantaged youth, Mexican-Americans, the unemployed, retirees, immigrants, managers, husbands and wives in dual career families, and men in female-dominated occupations. There were several studies of women only samples that also showed commitment to diversity. Russell and Rush (1987) commented that "ignoring the differences among women has implied that women have homogeneous concerns" (p. 293).

*Bias in Topic Selection.* The 1980s began with a publication by Fitzgerald and Crites (1980) that summarized the current state of affairs in understanding women's career development. This often-cited article sparked researchers' interest in new aspects of women's career development and laid the theoretical groundwork for many of the research studies that followed during the 1980s.

Many of the annual reviews of the career literature published in the *Journal of Vocational Behavior* during the 1980s mentioned the large increase in the number of articles on women's career development or gender influences on vocational behavior (Borgen, Layton, Veenhuizen, & Johnson, 1985; Greenhaus & Parasuraman, 1986; Slaney & Russell, 1987; Tinsley & Heesacker, 1984). For example, in analyzing 1983 publications by topic, Tinsley and Heesacker (1984) reported 79 articles published on the "vocational behavior of women," more than twice as many as any other topic. Slaney and Russell (1987) agreed that the concern about women's vocational behavior "can be seen as leading to some of the most interesting, energetic, and sophisticated research and thought in the entire domain" (p. 118). Clearly, women's vocational behavior and career development received increased attention from researchers during the 1980s.

Common topical themes for studies published during the early 1980s were: (a) sex differences on vocational interest inventories, (b) studying the "special" features of women's career development (e.g., career and homemaker conflicts), (c) studying the influence of sex-role orientation on career aspirations and choice, and (d) studying differences among women (e.g., traditional vs. nontraditional careers). By the mid-1980s, we observed more studies on (a) dual-career couples and family and work roles, (b) the effects of role models on women's career development, (c) interest in the gendered nature of occupational settings, and (d) studies on the special needs and concerns of reentry women. We observed a trend in topic selection moving from understanding women's career development as an internal process (e.g., the woman's sex-role orientation) to understanding women's career development within the social contexts of relationships (e.g., studies on work and family roles for both members of the dual-career couple), historical cohorts (e.g., the interplay of developmental stage and age cohort on career aspirations or choice), or work environments (e.g., sexual harassment, sex discrimination, mentoring).

*Bias in Operationalization and Measurement of Variables.* We found several examples of authors not understanding that vocational tasks may be sex-linked and consequently that task selection may affect results. For example, Pond and Hay (1989) studied the impact of job task preview on the recipient's self-efficacy. The authors did not assess whether these tasks might be viewed as more associated with women or men. However, Hackett, Betz, O'Halloran, and Romac (1990) were careful to acknowledge the potential influence of gender-linked tasks on results, and hypothesized that task success or failure would interact with gender, which in turn results in differential self-evaluation of performance for women and men on gender-linked tasks.

In their investigation of how family relations influence the career decision-making and commitment process in college students, Blustein, Walbridge, Friedlander, and Palladino (1991) included measures of attachment as well as separation to parents. Their addition of attachment measures was an improvement on previous studies that had focused on psychological separation and ignored the influence of attachment on the development of identity, a concept clearly indicated as important in women's development by the theoretical work published by the women at the Stone Center (Jordan, Kaplan, Miller, Striver, & Surrey, 1991) and the qualitative studies of Gilligan (1982).

We observed another example of authors not attending to sex effects when operationalizing their variables. In their analogue design, Cleveland, Festa, and Montgomery (1988) had participants respond to an imaginary job applicant, yet used only males as job applicants in their vignettes. They did not discuss the consequences of this methodological decision on their results.

*Bias Based on Limited Sources of Data.* Like Greenhaus and Parasuraman (1986), we are concerned about the overreliance on paper and pencil measures as a means for measuring variables. In many cases, authors relied on standardized instruments to measure only internal psychological processes, completely ignoring social and situational effects on individuals. We are also concerned about the tendency to rely solely on the individual, rather than requesting information from others in the individual's environment. This becomes more critical as our questions become more sophisticated about the importance of context on behavior and how behaviors within one individual change based on the changing social contexts.

*Sex of Experimenter Bias.* We were unable to find an example of a study that understood the potential confounding effects of the sex of the experimenter on the data the research participants were generating about their experiences.

In summary, our review suggests that most authors are not well informed about the feminist recommendations for improving the conduct of research. Authors were not careful to ground their explanations of gender differences in the larger literature on gender, nor did they attend to context variables in their research designs. Most studies continue to use research participants solely as data sources. The greatest improvements during the last two decades have occurred in the increased attention to topics of importance to women.

## THE FEMINIST CRITIQUES OF TRADITIONAL THERAPY

Feminist critiques of society and its institutions led inevitably to critiques of mental health practice. The criticisms focused on Freudian theory and practice, particularly the distinction between clitoral ("immature") and vaginal ("mature") orgasms; the insistence that anatomy is destiny; the idea that penis envy is inevitable in all women; the view of women as inherently passive, narcissistic, and masochistic; and the belief that the source of women's problems resides within the woman.

Feminists argued that anatomy is not destiny (e.g., biological functions such as the capacity for child bearing do not inherently limit roles for women), women's envy of men is not of their penises but rather their power and status, and the passivity and narcissism observed by Freud were not due to biological tendencies but rather to socially prescribed behavior. Further, feminists asserted that the aloofness of the analyst and the hierarchical nature of the relationship in which the analyst is the expert created, rather than resolved, problems (e.g., dependency and low self-esteem), and served to invalidate women's reports of their experiences.

Critiques of Freudian theory and practice expanded quickly to psychotherapy as a profession (Sturdivant, 1980). According to Sturdivant, criticisms came first from women consumers charging sex bias in practice. Mental health professionals soon joined women clients in faulting psychotherapy for perpetuating sexist beliefs and attitudes. Chesler's intensive analysis of sexism in mental health practice in *Women and Madness* (1972) was a major impetus to other mental health professionals to examine sexism in practice. She likened therapy to marriage and asserted that both were the tools of oppression—that is, they are both based on unequal relationships, isolate women from one another, emphasize individual rather than collective solutions to women's distress, and are based on women's helplessness and dependency on a strong male authority figure.

Feminist critiques of traditional therapy have continued over the last two decades. Feminists critiques are summarized next under four major headings (Nassi & Abramowitz, 1978): ideology, structure, criteria, and content.

*Ideology.* Feminists charged that traditional psychotherapy is a form of social control rather than one of social change. Theories of practice focus on intrapsychic or internal explanations of women's problems rather than the external, sociocultural factors that are prejudical, discriminatory, and demeaning of women. Such views about the etiology of women's problems lead to goals of therapy that are focused on women adjusting to society. Thus, the solutions offered in traditional therapy are individual and personal, directed at changing the "sick" woman, rather than collective, social action approaches aimed at changing a "sick" society.

*Structure.* The structure of traditional therapy is inherently unequal and hierarchical. The therapist, usually a male, is thus in a position of authority over a woman patient. The therapist as expert determines the goals and direction of therapy, and thus replicates the patriarchical structure of society where male is dominant and female is subordinate.

*Criteria.* Traditional therapists' attitudes and beliefs reflect a sexist double standard of mental health. In the widely cited study by Broverman, Broverman, Clarkson, Rosenkrantz, and Vogel (1970), therapists described mentally healthy adults and males as independent, aggressive, rational, and so forth, whereas healthy females were described as more submissive, less independent, more emotional, and disliking math and science. This double standard of mental health places women in a double bind: To aspire to be healthy as an adult, she needs to be "masculine" and thus run the risk of losing societal support and having her femininity questioned. If she chooses to be healthy as a woman, then she is adopting less socially desirable traits and is relegated to second-class status (Broverman et al., 1970).

*Content.* Finally, traditional therapy was criticized by feminists for its "sins of omission." More specifically, traditional therapists either underestimate, undermine, or ignore women's problems with marriage, career conflicts, job discrimination, the division of labor in the family, abortion, rape, incest, domestic violence, sexual harassment, and so forth.

## COMMON TENETS OF FEMINIST THERAPIES

Given this critique of traditional psychotherapy, the call went out for a new form of therapy—one that would focus on the pathology of the culture rather than that of women, help women overcome and resist restrictive role expectations rather than help them adjust to narrow societal expectations, offer an egalitarian rather than a hierarchical client–therapist relationship—in short, a therapy based on feminist values.

In the early 1970s, the development of feminist therapy came from women working at the grassroots level who were not professionally trained and who identified primarily with the radical feminist philosophy. These women complained that traditional therapies replicated the patriarchal structure of American society (because most therapists were men and most clients were women). They lambasted the professional elite who had neglected women's issues such as rape, violence against women, sexual abuse, womens' economic dependence on men, and so forth. They were instrumental in establishing consciousness-raising groups as well as peer counseling services for women outside of the mental health establishment (e.g., rape crisis centers and hotlines, shelters for battered women). They borrowed many ideas from the radical and growth-oriented, humanistic therapies (Greenspan, 1983; Kaschak, 1981). Early on, feminism itself was declared a form of therapy (e.g., Mander & Rush, 1974). The leaderless consciousness-raising group, where women met in small groups and recognized that societal problems had been misidentified as women's personal problems, was also declared a form of therapy (Brodsky, 1973).

In a review of the first decade of feminist therapy, Kaschak (1981) predicted a future synthesis in the form of a cohesive and conceptually sophisticated school of thought. Yet, after approximately 20 years, feminist therapy is still considered primarily a philosophical-value orientation to therapy rather than a stand-alone theory or school of therapy. Since feminist therapy principles have been applied to a variety of groups (e.g., ethnic minorities, men, incest survivors, borderlines) and integrated into a variety of existing theories (e.g., cognitive-behavioral, Gestalt, Adlerian), some believe that there are not one but many feminist therapies (Douglas & Walker, 1988).

At this time, consensus has not been reached regarding the principles or tenets of feminist therapy. One factor that has undoubtedly contributed to this lack of consensus is the existence of different philosophical stances about feminism in general, and feminist therapy in particular. The most common positions are the radical, the liberal, and the socialist, although these stances are seldom made explicit in writings about feminist therapy. These groups differ primarily in their views about the source of women's oppression and thus the solutions proposed for achieving equality for women. For example, the radical feminists believe that women's oppression is due to patriarchy (i.e., male dominance and control), whereas the liberal feminists locate the source of women's oppression in sexist ideas, laws, habits, and so forth that are a part of society. Socialists/Marxists, on the other hand, locate the cause of women's oppression in the existing economic system and political processes, namely, capitalism that entails competition, control, self-interest, hierarchical forms, and valuing of wealth and power.

Despite the lack of consensus, four general principles are commonly agreed on across different types of feminists (Sturdivant, 1980). These principles speak to four important aspects of the therapeutic endeavor:

1. Diagnosis and problem conceptualization (what are the causes of psychological distress).
2. The focus of therapeutic interventions.
3. The therapist–client relationship.
4. The outcomes or goal of therapy.

Each of these principles is next discussed in some detail.

## Sociocultural Conditions as Primary Source of Women's Problems

Central to feminist therapy is the belief that social structures have molded and limited women's experiences and opportunities. As stated by Ballou and Gabalac (1985), "Feminist therapy holds that external social, economic, political, cultural, class, race, and interpersonal conditions felt in women's lives through sex discrimination, sex role behavior and attitudes, and internalized in family, relationships, and self image, are the causes of pathology" (pp. 65–66). Thus, the common problems of women such as depression and low self-esteem are not due to intrapsychic conflicts; rather, women have developed these problems because sex-role prescriptions encourage them. Problems of low-esteem and feelings of powerlessness, for example, stem from American society's denigration and oppression of women. Variables associated with women's sex roles, such as the nonexpression of negative feelings, an orientation toward satisfying a male partner to the neglect of oneself, passivity, learned helplessness, exaggerated femininity, and "other directedness" play a primary role in mental illness (Brodsky & Hare-Mustin, 1980). In this sense, women's symptoms are adaptive solutions to societal expectations or oppressions rather than individual psychopathology (Porter, 1985). To counteract the intrapsychic determinism viewpoint of traditional therapy, feminist therapists place priority on environmental interpretations of women's problems.

## The Personal is Political

This tenet is a natural extension of the first and lies at the heart of consciousness-raising. The reasoning of this tenet goes something like the following:

1. All women in American society are oppressed.
2. Therefore, all women in American society share common problems.
3. For women to develop an understanding of their problems, political awareness is essential. "Clients must learn how social structures have molded and limited them, the extent to which they have been denigrated and how they have developed prejudices against themselves and other women" (Faunce, 1985).
4. The solutions to women's problems are political; therefore, women must work together to forge common solutions (Sturdivant, 1980).
5. Problems and politics are intertwined.

Given the above, the feminist political analysis of society is the sine qua non of feminist therapy (Kaschak, 1981). Thus, a primary focus of feminist therapies becomes helping "clients look outward as well as inward and differentiate clearly what belongs to the society and is being imposed and what is internal." The client is helped to "differentiate between what she has been taught and has accepted as socially appropriate and what may actually be appropriate for her . . . This process enhances the individual's sense of her personal power" (Lerman, 1976, pp. 379–380), as well as self-esteem, and teaches that the woman herself is not crazy. Anger is an inevitable outcome, and therefore "an essential part of feminist therapy" (Lerman, 1976, p. 381).

"The importance of helping women clients to differentiate between external, relatively uncontrollable sociocultural conditions (such as prejudice in the job market) and internal feelings and reactions to these conditions (which are changeable) is emphasized in all the more comprehensive papers on feminist therapy" (Sturdivant, 1980, p. 79).

However, this analysis of the environmental causes of psychopathology does not preclude or replace, the individual's responsibility. "Both levels of analysis and change are essential" (Kaschak, 1981, p. 397).

Because realization of the common problems of women, and thus political analysis, occurs more easily in groups, some feminist therapists work primarily with groups rather than individuals. In this setting women overcome their prejudices against themselves as well as other women and develop less reliance on approval of men. The sense of community that is necessary to effect individual and social change is also facilitated (Sturdivant, 1980). A woman's power as an individual is "inextricably bound to the collective power of women as a group" (Greenspan, 1983, p. 142).

## The Relationship is Egalitarian

To avoid coercion and abuse of power, and therefore fostering of client dependency, the feminist counselor establishes a relationship based on equal worth. The nature of the relationship is to be collaborative rather than hierarchical.

Early feminist therapy writings advocating an egalitaran relationship between client and therapist were understandably criticized for being unrealistic because the very nature of the therapeutic enterprise demands therapist expertise, power, and authority. As Brown (1985) stated, "To deny differences in power between ourselves and our clients on the grounds of shared womanhood is as naive a belief as the notion that there exists a value-free therapist" (p. 300).

Feminist therapists thus found themselves in the dilemma of believing, on the one hand, that it was desirable to equalize the relationship, yet knowing on the other hand that if they denied their expertise they would be ignoring reality and could discredit themselves in the eyes of the client. As a result, the "relationship is egalitarian" principle has been modified and clarified to mean "equal worth" although not equal therapeutic competence. "While feminist therapists recognize the necessity for the therapist to have greater therapeutic competence, they insist that therapist and client are absolutely equal in personal worth" (Sturdivant, 1980, pp. 81–82). Thus, rather than denying or ignoring their power or the authority that therapists derive from technical expertise, feminist therapists diminish the kinds of power that set up unnecessary hierarchies, interpersonal dominance, or exploitation. Feminist therapists must be keenly aware of the sources of their power, the ways power can be abused, and make efforts to diminish power differences that are harmful or exploitive and reinforce passivity and dependency (Gannon, 1982).

In their analysis of the power dimension, feminists therapists have pointed out several therapeutic procedures that unnecessarily maintain and/or exacerbate the power differential: (a) the therapist reveals no personal information to the client, thus suggesting that he/she is free from personal problems; (b) the therapist assumes the role of expert on the client; (c) the therapist tries to substantiate hypotheses about the client by directing the dialogue; and (d) the therapist uses psychological jargon or obscure clinical terms (Gannon, 1982).

To minimize power differences between therapist and client, feminists and therapists use power-sharing strategies such as assuming "that the client is the 'expert' on her own feelings and experiences" (Sturdivant, 1980, p. 81), encouraging clients to take advantage of adjuncts to individual therapy, such as bibliotherapy and women's support groups, urging clients to take a consumer approach to selecting a therapist, and engaging in therapist self-disclosure. Although therapist self-disclosure has been warned against on grounds that therapeutic distance is necessary for the development of the transference relationship (Greenspan, 1986), feminist therapists counter that self-disclosure does not include inappropriate emotional unloading leading to therapist–client role reversal, but rather is a judicious acknowledgment that the therapist has also experienced oppression, discrimination, and difficulties that are similar to those of the client. Whereas early feminist therapists also advocated fee negotiation to minimize power differences, this practice clashes with the feminist principle of valuing women and women's work (Brown, 1985).

## Essentials for Women's Mental Health

This tenet points to the goals of feminist therapy and is in direct opposition to what is perceived to be the goal of traditional therapy — that is, individual adjustment to social conditions. Instead, feminist therapy rejects social conformity in favor of personal self-definition and self-determination. A basic belief is that both psychological and economic independence is essential for all women (Cammaert & Larsen, 1988). "The belief in the sociocultural roots of women's emotional distress commits us to a feminist growth/developmental model of therapy within which both personal and social change are significant therapeutic goals, and political action an integral part of therapy" (Faunce, 1985, p. 2). "Thus, the purpose of feminist therapy might best be described as being to bring women closer to a state of individually defined optimal functioning" (Sturdivant, 1980, pp. 162–163).

This feminist growth model of mental health "politicalizes personal problems" (rather than "personalizing social problems") (Rawlings &

Carter, 1977, pp. 23–24) by placing more emphasis on environmental causes of distress and viewing symptoms as healthy attempts to adapt to a restricted society. Problem resolution comes through behavioral, attitudinal, and affective change based on an awareness of the ways that society has constricted or limited individual options. This requires that clients cease cooperating in their own oppression—the "external sources of oppression and the internal sources of collusion with that oppression—including internalized sex roles, devaluation of their own and other women's abilities, and so forth" (Sturdivant, 1980, p. 139).

One issue that has been raised is whether the goals include urging clients to become feminists who are active in social change. Lerman's (1976) response to the former is "Yes" if being a feminist means being aware of oppression and gaining a self-definition within it. The answer is "No" if feminist means espousing *specific* tenets of feminism.

## FEMINIST PERSPECTIVES: EVALUATION OF THE CAREER COUNSELING PRACTICE LITERATURE

A predominant theme in the feminist literature is that women are oppressed and restricted in their life roles. Although various examples of restricted roles are identified, a central one is that women occupy a narrow range of work and achievement roles. Historically, career counselors have been vitally concerned with helping individuals identify compatible and satisfying work environments. Thus, it would be surprising if the feminist agenda of achieving equality for women in the labor force had not infiltrated the literature on career counseling with women.

To address the question of the influence of feminist ideas on career counseling with women, we reviewed the literature from 1969 to the present. We focused our attention on two professional journals expected to contain the major articles on career counseling practice with women: the *Journal of Counseling and Development* (formerly the *Personnel and Guidance Journal*) and the *Career Development Quarterly* (formerly the *Vocational Guidance Quarterly*.) In addition, we consulted major books concerned with women's career development issues (e.g., Hansen & Rapoza, 1978) and special issues of *The Counseling Psychologist* on counseling women (Birk & Tanney, 1976; Harmon & Fitzgerald, 1973; Hill et al., 1979). We make no claim that our review is comprehensive; we do believe, however, that it is representative of the literature. We are uncertain about the extent to which this review captures typical career counseling practice with women because, unfortunately, many counselors do not write about their practice and to our knowledge no survey has been completed about feminism and career counseling practice. Finally, we make no claim about the absolute or ultimate truth of our analysis; others might come to different conclusions.

What follows is our analysis of the extent to which the four feminist therapy principles (e.g., the personal is political) have been incorporated into suggestions for career counseling with women.

## Sociocultural Conditions as Primary Source of Women's Problems

The career counseling literature on women over the past two decades has identified a multitude of problems that women experience in their career choice and development. For the most part, every article either implicitly or explictly referred to one source of these problems as being sex-role prescriptions, for example, that women are more likely to pursue occupations that are compatible with sex role stereotypes, or that society's ideas about appropriate roles for women have limited their "dreaming," etc. Cook (1985), for example, presented a model for linking work and sex roles and urged counselors to "recognize the power of sex roles in shaping behaviors," which she deemed an "integral part of the career and life-planning process" (p. 218).

One of the most common themes in the literature has been that women's expected roles as marriage partner and mother have been the most limiting. For example, Betz and Fitzgerald (1987), in a major review of the career literature on women, stated that "the premise of our book [is] that the interface of home and work is the most salient characteristic of women's vocational behavior" (p. 89). Despite recognition of the influence of sex-role stereotypes and cultural prescriptions for women to be wives and mothers, many authors still conceptualized internal barriers as the primary source of women's career development problems. For example, despite the multitude of needs of reentry women identified by Manis and Mochizuki (1972), no mention was made of the social etiology of these problems. Moreover, many authors suggested that the primary focus of counseling would be to help women overcome these "internal" barriers and/or teach them coping skills (e.g., assertiveness skills, job search skills). DiSabatino (1976) went so far as to suggest that even if the external barriers were removed (e.g., men were more willing to promote women), the internal factors, which are more detrimental, would remain. Brandenburg (1974) suggested that reentry women should be helped to explore the extent to which they prevented their own success by, for example, projecting resistance on others.

Nevertheless, a few authors identified the social/political conditions as being the primary source of womens' career development concerns.

Gardner (1971) hinted at this principle when she noted that it may not be the client but rather the system that needed adjusting. Brizzi (1986) gave more explicit attention to this idea in her description of the circular process involved in socialization. "Early perceived limitations imposed by the environment are incorporated into the self-concept, which in turn restricts subsequent interactions with the environment, thereby reducing the information available for further development of the self-concept" (p. 229).

Hansen stands out, however, with her consistent message that the socialization process should be targeted (Hansen, 1972, 1978; Sundal-Hansen, 1984, 1985). To cite but one representative sample of her ideas, Hansen criticized traditional career counseling for its failure to consider the effects of socialization and stereotyping on both sexes and the reality that many "unconscious" decisions have been made by individuals before counseling for decision making begins. She urged "greater emphasis . . . on the influence of environmental factors on career development and not only intrapsychic factors" (Sundal-Hansen, 1985, p. 209).

**The Personal is Political**

We found no instances of specific references to the feminist principle that the personal is political. Gardner (1971) came the closest when she stated: "Personal problems are really not personal, but class problems" (p. 711). Despite this lack of explicitness, it was clear to us that this principal has infiltrated the career counseling literature in the forms of urging counselors (a) to be activists and change agents, (b) to offer alternatives to individual counseling in the form of consciousness-raising groups and support groups, and (c) to use interventions that explored the effects of sex bias or sex role stereotypes on the client.

One of the earliest advocates of a more activist position for career counselors was Vetter (1973). "It seems time for counseling psychology to pick up the challenge . . . to become involved in social action" (p. 64). Hansen (1972) also asserted that confining our efforts to the individual as a vehicle of change would be insufficient. Rather, she recommended a multipronged, proactive effort that would among other things involve public school curricular adjustments and intense work with teachers and parents. BORN FREE, a collaborative consultation project created by Hansen and her colleagues, was designed to achieve that goal (Hansen & Keierleker, 1978). Similarly, Schlossberg (1972) challenged counselors to be activists, to do programming as well as counseling, and to work for system change. "The counselor's . . . task is to help change the context in which women live, so that as dreams expand, so will the possibility of their implementation" (p. 138). Like Schlossberg, Oliver (1975) urged counselors to engage in action that would help women, for example, establishing child care facilities, and helping placement offices combat discrimination in interviewing and hiring.

With regard to the use of groups as an alternative or adjunct to individual counseling, most if not all of the articles on reentry women, for example, recommended group counseling or support groups (e.g., Brandenburg, 1974; Gray, 1980). Groups were viewed as desirable from a number of standpoints—to establish commonality of problems, to learn coping strategies, to obtain support and increase confidence, and to forge common solutions to problems. (Brandenburg, 1974; Gray, 1980; Kahn, 1983; Katz & Knapp, 1974). Gardner (1971) urged the use of consciousness-raising groups as a way for women to recognize their oppression.

### The Egalitarian Relationship

We found only one explicit suggestion that the client–counselor relationship should be characterized as collaborative and cooperative. In a chapter on gender and career counseling, D. Brown and Brooks (1991) identified specific strategies that career counselors could use to set the stage for this collaboration (e.g., "Make it clear to the client that he or she can reject or accept suggestions growing out of data or those made by counselor," p. 188).

### Essentials for Women's Mental Health

As was pointed out earlier, this principle of feminist therapy is concerned with the appropriate goals for counseling. Feminist therapists reject the goal of "adjusting to society." Career counselors have also apparently rejected adjustment as a goal. Women's rights and responsibilities are to develop "their own individual potential, not to subordinate that development to men's and society's needs" (Gardner, 1971, p. 706). Hansen (Sundal-Hansen, 1984) asserted that "Freeing women and men from rigid sex-role constraints perpetuated by stereotypes and socialization and implemented in societal institutions, structures, and policies would seem to be a valid goal for career guidance and counseling" (p. 228).

The feminist therapy literature urges that a goal for women is financial autonomy and independence. Sundal-Hansen (1985) agreed that the goals of career counseling should include "increased preparation for economic independence for women" (p. 235). Similarly, Harmon (1978) stated, "It is important that every woman, adolescent or middle-aged, be sure that she can independently meet her needs for food and security" (p. 449).

Finally, several authors suggested that interventions should be focused on helping women overcome the limiting effects of sex-role stereotypes. Schlossberg (1972), for example, suggested that counselors must help clients free themselves to dream—"free to act in ways appropriate to their interests and their values—not their sex" (p. 139). Sundal-Hansen (1984) urged counselors to help clients become aware of career socialization and the ways that the sex-role system had limited them. Betz and Fitzgerald (1987) advocated that counselors confront the socialization process, "pointing out both the advantages and disadvantages of 'bucking the system'. In doing so, counselors can change, rather than tinker with the system" (p. 87). Hawley (1978) agreed but was somewhat pessimistic about whether counselors could overturn internalized stereotypes. "The insidious thing about psychological barriers is they are often so subtle and located at such an unconscious level that they are not recognized as barriers at all but are seen as evidence of 'the way things are' " (p. 342).

Despite the assertion that counselors should help women overcome the influence of sex roles on their career choice and development, few specific techniques have been offered in the literature. In an early influential article, Dewey (1974) offered an innovation in the form of a nonsexist card sort. One of the aims of this technique is to notice clients' expressed sex-role biases in the selection of preferred options and then to explore these with the client. Two later writings suggested a way to adapt the feminist therapy sex-role analysis technique to career counseling (Brown & Brooks, 1991; Fitzgerald, 1986).

One of the most frequent ideas mentioned for encouraging women to consider a wider variety of career and lifestyle options was to expose them to role models—those who were successful in their careers as well as those who demonstrated successful management of integrating work and home roles (e.g., Eyde, 1970; Farmer, 1971; Kahnweiler & Kahnweiler, 1980; Plotsky & Goad, 1974; Rudnick & Wallach, 1980; Sandmeyer, 1980).

In summary, our review of the literature suggests an uneven incorporation of feminist therapy tenets into career counseling with women. Although references to all but one of the tenets (i.e., nonhierarchical client–counselor relationship) were found, they were seldom if ever mentioned as arising from feminist origins. Further, the ideas were unevenly scattered throughout the literature. What follows is our attempt to present an integrated model of feminist career counseling.

## AN APPLICATION OF FEMINIST TENETS TO
## CAREER COUNSELING

In this section, we discuss ways of incorporating the principles of feminist counseling into career counseling. We do not intend a thorough presentation of career counseling practice; rather, we outline the basic parameters of feminist career counseling. We remind the reader that feminist therapy is a philosophy of treatment rather than a comprehensive theory of therapy. "Philosophy of treatment is an implicit value system defined by personal and cultural beliefs about the innate nature of human beings, about the causes of psychological distress and interpretation of its symptoms, about the desired relationship between people .. . ., and about the goals of the helping endeavor" (Sturdivant, 1980, p. 35). The value system in this case is, of course, feminism. What follows is a discussion of each of the four common feminist tenets as it applies to career counseling.

### Sociocultural Conditions as Primary Source
### of Women's Problems

This feminist therapy tenet speaks to the issue of how problems are conceptualized. As Lerman (1985) and others have noted, "how a problem is defined determines how and where one looks for a solution" (p. 9). Incorporation of this tenet into the career counseling process means that the feminist career counselor approaches the assessment and diagnosis process with the attitude that social structures and societal prescriptions have molded and limited women's career development experiences and opportunities. Thus, in addition to the usual appraisal process of identifying the client's aptitudes, interests, work values, needs, personality characteristics, educational background, and so forth, the counselor also assesses the ways in which gender-role issues have affected the client and created barriers to her career development.

One approach to this additional assessment task is what L. S. Brown (1986, 1990) has termed gender-role analysis. One goal of gender-role assessment is to gain some understanding of how the individual interprets her gender-role socialization experience and the degree to which gender-role concerns play a part in the client's strengths and deficits. Another goal is to assess whether under- or overconformity to society's sex-role expectations might be creating barriers to the client reaching her goals. Finally, the very nature of the counselor's inquiry stimulates the client to engage in a political analysis of women's roles via examining her own experience. Whereas L. S. Brown's writings are focused on psychotherapy, D. Brown and Brooks (1991) adapted her guidelines to the career counseling situation. The following suggestions for conducting a gender-role analysis with a career client are guided primarily by the writings of L. S. Brown (1986, 1990) and D. Brown and Brooks (1991).

### Preassessment Strategies

1. Counselors familiarize themselves with research and scholarship on the relationship between gender and career development, including the interaction between gender and demographic variables, such as race and class; critical incidents that affect the career development of women, such as models, mentors, encouragement/discouragement; and discriminatory practices that might occur in the educational system and workplace.

2. "Counselors with strongly traditional sex-role attitudes probably should not attempt to do career counseling with women" (Fitzgerald, 1986, p. 130). Accordingly, counselors examine their own conscious and nonconscious biases and expectations about women and career development, including feelings and attitudes about compliance and defiance to gender roles. A counselor "must take on a particular mind-set in order to facilitate the process of gender role analysis. This perspective is one in which the assessor continually calls into question her or his taken-for-granted notions about what is usual and 'normal' in regard to gendered phenomenon" and in American White society (L. S. Brown, 1990, p. 13). Deviance from the culture's prescribed gender roles (e.g., a woman interested in skilled trades) may be a sign of "pathology" or of ego strength. Compliance that interferes with reaching achievement goals may be ignored by counselors who have not examined their nonconscious beliefs.

*The Assessment Process.* One of the central tasks of gender-role assessment is to determine how the client has experienced gender-role socialization. Collier (1982) asserted the wisdom of assuming that each client will in some respects be "unrealistic about and ignorant of the realities of working women's lives" (p. 158) and may not recognize limitations that have been internalized.

In gender-role analysis, the counselor first assumes a sociological perspective and gathers contextual data on, for example, the culture of the client's family of origin, family roles for men and women, and the client's perception of societal gender-role prescriptions for her age cohort. Second, the counselor assumes a phenomenological framework and inquires how the client transformed and gave meaning to her own life within her sociological culture. What, for example, does it mean to her to be a female in her family of origin, in her current environment, and in relationship to changing gender roles over the lifespan? What lessons were learned about gender roles, for example, what "commandments" were given by the client's mother and father about how to be a girl? (Sargent, 1977). What experiences has she had with individuals who deviated from or complied with gender-role norms, including herself, and what were the rewards and penalities for such behavior? What meaning does the client attach to gender as it relates to career? What does it mean to be a success or failure in one's career for a man? For a woman?

From this inquiry, the counselor develops hypotheses about the gendered aspects of the client's career development. At least three types of clients are common as to how gender role conceptions may be limiting their career options (Fodor & Rothblum, 1984). The *overly stereotyped* client may respond to career problems with passivity and dependency. Such learned helplessness may manifest itself in a variety of ways, such as an inability to act on her own career goals as distinguished from the goals of important others, hopelessness regarding changing her present work situation, etc. Overly stereotyped clients may also express interest only in "female" typed occupations, despite obvious talents and interests in nontraditional areas. The client who is *attempting to conform more to stereotypes* may degrade herself for not fitting in and/or not meeting the occupational "ideal" with regard to age, physical attractiveness, weight, etc. The client who is *attempting to conform less to stereotypes* may wish to overcome her original gender-role programming and engage in nontraditional behaviors (e.g., assertiveness, negotiation) and pursue nontraditional career options (e.g., architecture, chief executive officer of a major corporation) with a greater sense of security and confidence. Hypotheses about the client are generally shared with the client for verification or refutation. However, counselors need to monitor their hypotheses for their own biased conclusions. For example, D. Brown and Brooks (1991) provided the following case as an example of a career counselor's failure to detect the personal biases underlying his hypotheses about the causes of the client's problems.

> R., a married full-time graduate student with a part-time job, entered career counseling with a concern about whether she was in the right field. Among her concerns was whether she should continue to pursue a field that demanded a high level of professional commitment. Both her husband and her husband's parents wanted her to quit graduate school so that she could more adequately attend to matters at home, especially keeping the house in better order. She expressed much distress about the situation because she wanted to continue her education, but she was upset that she could not handle her duties at home more effectively. The

counselor decided that R would be unable to attend to her career concerns without first resolving her distress with her husband and his parents. Thus, he proceeded to help her develop time-management skills so that she could more effectively perform "her" household chores. In this case, the counselor failed to explore R's feelings about the gender role demands of the husband and thus reinforced the client's self-degradation. (p. 191)

Depending on the preferences of the counselor, gender-role assessment could be conducted entirely during an interview or included as part of a structured homework assignment. Several exercises that have been used in groups could be used with individuals. Sargent (1977) used a fantasy exercise that helped clients examine the conflict within themselves about gender roles. The client imagines a man and a woman who each have ideas about what occupations she should pursue. For each, the client completes sentences that begin "Be _____ " and "Don't be _____ ." The client imagines the man and woman having an argument and identifies the content of the argument in terms of agreement and disagreement.

Another exercise aimed at increasing awareness of gender-role expectations and limitations also uses the sentence completion technique. Clients answer the question, "Since I am a woman, I am required to be _____ ; I am allowed to be _____ ; I am forbidden to be _____ ." A second question begins with "If I were a man" and is followed by the same stimuli.

In summary, a key task of gender-role analysis is to identify ways in which social structures and gender-role prescriptions have affected the client. The conclusions drawn from the assessment then guide the goals and process of counseling. Gender-role issues are more salient with some clients than others, but it is difficult to imagine any situation where they are totally irrelevant. "All women have in some way been negatively affected by political, economic, and social forces" (Devoe, 1990, p. 33).

## The Personal is Political

The principle that the personal is political is a natural extension of the first feminist therapy tenet, which asserts that a primary cause of women's problems lies in social structures and prescriptions. A focus of the counseling interventions, then, is to help clients develop a political awareness of the ways the social structure has molded and limited them, for example, restricted perceptions of occupational options, focus on nurturing roles to the neglect of achieving roles, etc. Through gaining an awareness of the ways in which the environment has affected women's career choice and development, clients reduce self-blame for conditions over which they had no control. For example, a client comes to view the stress she experiences at her nontraditional job as due to a social environment that is distressing, rather than to her oversensitivity or pathology (Greenspan, 1983).

Identifying what belongs to society and is imposed may be a natural by-product of the gender-role assessment process described here. However, because all-women's groups can often facilitate this process, feminist career counselors often provide services in a group setting. Groups provide the opportunity for women to congregate in a supportive atmosphere to examine their experiences as women, to find the commonalities of their career development experiences that are due to the political and economic conditions (Adams & Durham, 1977), and, in some cases, to gain encouragement and support for social and political action

## The Egalitarian Relationship

As noted previously, this principle advocates a client–counselor relationship characterized by equal worth. Toward that end, the counselor does not deny therapeutic competence nor the greater power that such expertise affords her; rather, she works to avoid abuse of power and uses power sharing strategies. For example, the counselor views the client as competent and as the expert on her own feelings, thoughts, and needs. The counselor helps the client validate her own experience rather than undercut her through the use of authoritarian position (e.g., the heavy use of interpretations or assuming only the counselors' interpretations are accurate). The feminist career counselor realizes that judicious sharing of her own reactions to sex-role conflict can be validating and supporting for the client (Fitzgerald, 1986).

To implement this principle, feminist career counselors work toward (a) establishing the relationship as collaborative and facilitative rather than hierarchical, (b) informing the client about the procedures and goals of counseling and the philosophy of the counselor, (c) urging the client to give feedback to the counselor, and (d) encouraging the client to shop for a counselor. Counselors may make these points explicit either through a written contract or a verbal exchange with the client.

Achieving a collaborative and facilitative relationship often requires ongoing dialogue with career counseling clients, since many come to counseling with the expectation that the counselor will take the major responsibility for the course of counseling. Nevertheless, setting the stage for a nonhierarchical relationship occurs during the first session. In general, the counselor emphasizes that the client is expected to be an active participant in counseling, that the counselor will use her expertise in helping the client but that the client is the best expert on herself, and that the task is to work together to help the client reach her goals. Words such as cooperative, mutual, or collaborative can be used to convey the expected type of relationship. Power-sharing strategies, as discussed previously, should also be uppermost in counselor's mind.

Although counselors may refrain from asserting their feminist values, at a minimum, they can indicate their beliefs about the variables that are important to consider in making effective career decisions, including the influence of gender-role expectations. For example the counselor could state:

> CO: My belief is that our career choices are influenced by many factors. One of my tasks is to help you discover those factors that are influencing you—those that are encouraging and facilitating and those that are discouraging and inhibiting. The goal is to help you make fully informed choices. Some of the factors that I believe influence all of us are: the desires of important others, such as parents, family members, friends, the success and failure experiences we have had. I also hold the belief that American society gives us strong messages about what is appropriate and "good" for our sex. These messages often have a stronger influence on us than we realize. I think it is very important that we explore rather carefully how those messages have influenced you.

Finally, during this first session, the counselor makes it clear that the clients have a choice about who they select for a counselor, and whether they "shop around" for a counselor who feels more compatible, or pursue an alternative helping system, such as support groups, group counseling, self-help materials, etc. Indeed, providing all of the information suggested in the preceding paragraphs is intended, in part, to enable the client to make an informed choice (Hare-Mustin, Marecek, Kaplan, & Liss-Levenson, 1979).

In summary, the counselor emphasizes the collaborative nature of the counseling, makes it clear that the client should provide feedback to the counselor about any dissatisfactions with counseling, informs the client about her philosophy and values about career counseling and gender roles, and encourages the client to be an informed consumer of counseling.

## Essentials for Women's Mental Health

This fourth feminist therapy tenet speaks to the goals of counseling. The overall goal of feminist counseling is the empowerment of the client toward self-determination. Thus, counselors help clients gain the skills, knowledge, and attitudes necessary to take control over her own life (i.e., personal power) and to begin to influence others (i.e., interpersonal power) (Smith & Siegel, 1985). Further, feminist career counselors believe that "women should have the means or the skills to be financially independent" (Rawlings & Carter, 1977, p. 60); that is, they are economically as well as psychologically autonomous. As Fitzgerald (1986) stated, "it is not in anyone's best interest to be totally economically dependent on the good will and good health of another person" (p. 129). Thus, she believes that counselors must engage woman clients in "damage control," and at a minimum ensure that they develop some salable skills. In most instances, reaching these goals will necessarily entail helping clients analyze how gender-role expectations and myths have limited their choices, plans, and satisfaction; determine strategies for overcoming and coping with internal and external barriers; and develop new information, skills, attitudes, and behaviors regarding alternative roles and career options.

Reaching these goals often requires special techniques and strategies. As Collier (1982) and Fitzgerald (1986) have asserted, the career development needs of women are different from and more complex than those of men. Along these lines, various strategies have been suggested for facilitating the career choice and development of women, many of which have been mentioned in previous sections (e.g., use of groups, exposure to role models, gender-role analysis, nonsexist card sorts, interventions into the curriculum and other social structures, life-planning). One unique strategy that has emerged from feminist therapy is sex-role analysis. This technique is similar to the more general gender-role assessment discussed earlier in that the goal is to identify the client's expectations regarding gender roles. As used in career counseling, it is a specific activity directed at eliciting the client's views about costs and benefits of pursuing traditional versus nontraditional careers (for specific examples see D. Brown & Brooks, 1991; Fitzgerald, 1986). Another technique that can be used to challenge clients to develop new ideas about their options is the *nonsexist occupational card sort* (Dewey, 1974). Brooks (1988) and D. Brown and Brooks (1991) described this technique in more detail than we have space for and the interested reader can consult these references. In general, however, the technique involves giving clients a stack of cards, each of which contains the name of an occupation. The cards should contain equal numbers of traditionally male occupations and traditionally female occupations. Clients sort the cards into three stacks: Would consider, Not sure, and Would not consider. The counselor then sorts the cards from the Would consider and Would not consider into stereotypically male and stereotypically female and asks the client to discuss the positive and negative features of each. In addition to stimulating clients to consider new options, this discussion can help both the counselor and the client determine the extent to which perceptions about the gender appropriateness of occupations are creating barriers.

Another technique to expand the client's ideas about career options is Sargent's (1977) *discarded dream* exercise. Clients are asked to write down dreams that have been encouraged by important others and dreams that have been discouraged. They then select one or two dreams, play them out, identify the encouragement they would need to follow through on them, and devise strategies for getting the support they need.

Finally, because it seems clear that most women will need to plan for and integrate multiple roles, life-career planning strategies can encourage women to engage in long-term planning and thereby exert some control over their future (for suggestions for life-planning techniques see D. Brown & Brooks, 1991; Collier, 1982).

## SUMMARY AND CRITIQUE

We have presented our view on the influence of feminism and the women's movement on the research and practice of career counseling. In this process, we identified the common tenents of feminism, reviewed the feminist critiques of research and practice, and analyzed representative literature on career counseling and research on vocational behavior for the extent to which feminist thinking has been an influence. We have also indicated how feminists critiques might be more fully incorporated into research and practice of career counseling.

We have presented our conclusions throughout the chapter, so only a brief review of our thinking is presented here. In general, it seems quite clear that feminist thinking has influenced our research on and practice with women's career issues, but in limited, circumscribed ways. The influence has been felt more in the career counseling than research literature, however.

In the research area, the only notable influence has been in the area of bias on topic selection. As the annual reviews of the career literature in the *Journal of Vocational Behavior* document, research on women's vocational behavior is clearly one of the most popular topics in the field. Moreover, we see evidence of studying diverse populations of women and a small beginning in research that incorporates new theory about women (e.g., the study of attachment as well as separation). For the most part, however, we did not find that feminist critiques of research have had a major impact. For example, we found numerous examples of the failure to distinguish between and use accurately the terms sex and gender, only one study that recognized the importance of sex as a stimulus variable, few examples of considering the social context versus focusing on the individual, no studies that explored the effects of power and influence, and so on.

The picture is somewhat brighter in the career counseling literature. We noticed several writers urging counselors to be social activists, although we found no explicit reference to the feminist therapy principle that the personal is political. We also found much recognition, albeit more implicit than explicit, that counselors need to include an awareness that women's career development takes place in a social context. On the other hand, we found only one book chapter that urged a collaborative, nonhierarchical client–therapist relationship, and no examples of an explication of a well-developed feminist philosophy of treatment. Finally, we found very, very few acknowledgments that suggestions for career counseling with women had their origin in feminist thinking.

This more implicit rather than explicit incorporation of feminist critiques, especially in the practice literature, leads us to wonder if researchers and writers are skittish about identifying with the feminist perspective. Alternatively, perhaps feminist ideas have infiltrated our thinking at a more subliminal level, or perhaps many of the critiques made by feminists are also made by others who have critiqued, for example, psychology's excessive focus on the individual, lack of methodological diversity, predominant use of the epistemology of the positivists, and so on.

One question that we suspect some readers will raise is: Why should we incorporate feminist thinking into our research and practice? Is it not simply a value system or a bias of another sort? We would argue that stripped of the label "feminist," many of the same points have been made by those who do not espouse a feminist philosophy (e.g., methodological diversity, overreliance on college sophomores for research participants), and these are important and valid suggestions for increasing our understanding of vocational behavior. To take just one example, who can deny on simply intuitive grounds that women's vocational behavior is a product of the interaction between individual and social contextual variables? And yet, our research and our practice are heavily biased toward understanding the individual apart from the social context. Psychology's focus on the individual too frequently leads to "blame the victim" attributions, whereas sociology's focus leads too easily to "blame society" explanations. Perhaps the balance can begin to be achieved if we started thinking more like social psychologists, a discipline that is commonly defined as "the study of how the thoughts, feelings, and actions of individuals are influenced by the actual, imagined, or implied presence of others" (Lott, 1991, p. 506).

We hope this chapter will stimulate readers to carefully review their practice and their research in light of feminist critiques.

## REFERENCES

Abush, R., & Burkhead, E. J. (1984). Job stress in midlife working women: Relationships among personality type, job characteristics, and job tension. *Journal of Counseling Psychology, 31,* 36–44.

Adams, H. H., & Durham, L. (1977). A dialectical base for an activist approach to counseling. In E. I. Rawlings & D. K. Carter (Eds.), *Psychotherapy for women* (pp. 411–428). Springfield, IL: Charles C. Thomas.

Aries, E., & Olver, R. (1985). Sex differences in the development of a separate sense of self during infancy: Directions for future research. *Psychology of Women Quarterly, 9,* 515–532.

Ballou, M., & Gabalac, N. W. (1985). *A feminist position on mental health.* Springfield, IL: Charles C. Thomas.

Bart, P. (1971). Sexism and social science: From the gilded cage to the iron cage, or, the perils of Pauline. *Journal of Marriage and the Family, 33,* 734–735.

Beehr, T. A., King, L. A., & King, D. W. (1990). Social support and occupational stress: Talking to supervisors. *Journal of Vocational Behavior, 36,* 61–81.

Betz, N. E., & Fitzgerald, L. F. (1987). *The career psychology of women.* Orlando, FL: Academic Press.

Biaggio, M. (1988, August). *Sex differences in anger: Are they real?* Paper presented at the annual convention of the American Association for the Advancement of Science, Atlanta, GA.

Bickman, L. (1974). Sex and helping behavior. *Journal of Social Psychology, 93,* 43–53.

Birk, J. M., & Tanney, M. F. (1976). Counseling women II. *Counseling Psychologist, 6,* 2–63.

Blau, G. (1989). Testing the generalizability of a career commitment measure and its impact on employee turnover. *Journal of Vocational Behavior, 35,* 88–104.

Blustein, D. L., Walbridge, M. M., Friedlander, M. L., & Palladino, D. E. (1991). Contributions of psychological separation and parental attachment to the career development process. *Journal of Counseling Psychology, 38* 39–50.

Borgen, F. H., Layton, W. L., Veenhuizen, D. L., & Johnson, D. J. (1985). Vocational behavior and career development, 1984: A review. *Journal of Vocational Behavior, 27,* 218–270.

Brandenburg, J. B. (1974). The needs of women returning to school. *Personnel and Guidance Journal, 53,* 11–18.

Brizzi, J. S. (1986). The socialization of women's vocational realism. *Vocational Guidance Journal, 34,* 225–232.

Brodsky, A. M. (1973). The consciousness-raising group as a model for therapy with women. *Psychotherapy: Theory, Research, and Practice, 10,* 24–29.

Brodsky, A. M., & Hare-Mustin, R. (Eds.). (1980). *Women and psychotherapy.* New York: Guilford Press.

Brooks, L. (1976). Supermoms shift gears: Re-entry women. *Counseling Psychologist, 6,* 33–37.

Brooks, L. (1988). Encouraging women motivation for non-traditional career and lifestyle options: A model for assessment and intervention. *Journal of Career Development, 14,* 223–241.

Broverman, I. K., Broverman, D. M., Clarkson, F. E., Rosenkrantz, P. S., & Vogel, S. R. (1970). Sex-role stereotypes and clinical judgments of mental health. *Journal of Consulting and Clinical Psychology, 34,* 1–7.

Brown, D., & Brooks, L. (1991). *Career counseling techniques.* Boston: Allyn & Bacon.

Brown, L. S. (1985). Ethics and business practice in feminist practice. In L. B. Rosewater & E. A. Walker (Eds.), *Handbook of feminist therapy* (pp. 297–304). New York: Springer.

Brown, L. S. (1986). Gender role analysis: A neglected component of psychological assessment. *Psychotherapy: Theory, Research, Practice, Training, 23,* 243–248.

Brown, L. S. (1990). Taking account of gender in the clinical assessment interview. *Professional Psychology: Research and Practice, 21,* 12–17.

Cammaert, L. P., & Larsen, C. C. (1988). Feminist framework of psychotherapy. In M. A. D. Douglas & L. E. A. Walker (Eds.), *Feminist psychotherapies: Integration of therapeutic and feminist systems* (pp. 3–11). Norwood, NJ: Ablex.

Carli, L. L. (1990). Gender, language, and influence. *Journal of Personality and Social Psychology, 59,* 941–951.

Chesler, P. (1972). *Women and madness.* Garden City, NY: Doubleday.

Chusid, H., & Cochran, L. (1989). Meaning of career change from the perspective of family roles and dramas. *Journal of Counseling Psychology, 36,* 34–41.

Chusmir, L. H., & Koberg, C. S. (1986). Creativity differences among managers. *Journal of Vocational Behavior, 29,* 249–253.

Cleveland, J. N., Festa, R. M., & Montgomery, L. (1988). Applicant pool composition and job perceptions: Impact on decisions regarding an older applicant. *Journal of Vocational Behavior, 32,* 112–126.

Collier, H. V. (1982). *Counseling women: A guide for therapists.* New York: Free Press.

Cook, E. P. (1985). Sex roles and work roles: A balancing process. *Vocational Guidance Quarterly, 33,* 213–220.

Deaux, K. (1984). From individual differences to social categories: Analysis of a decade's research on gender. *American Psychologist, 39,* 105–116.

Devoe, D. (1990). Feminist and nonsexist counseling: Implications for the male counselor. *Journal of Counseling and Development, 69,* 33–36.

Dewey, C. R. (1974). Exploring interests: A non-sexist method. *Personnel and Guidance Journal, 52,* 311–315.

DiSabatino, M. (1976). Psychological factors inhibiting women's occupational aspirations and vocational choices: Implications for counseling. *Vocational Guidance Quarterly, 25,* 43–49.

Douce, L. A., & Hansen, J. C. (1990). Willingness to take risks and college women's career choice. *Journal of Vocational Behavior, 36,* 258–273.

Douglas, M. A. D., & Walker, L. E. A. (Eds.). (1988). *Feminist psychotherapies: Integration of therapeutic and feminist systems.* Norwood, NJ: Ablex.

Eagly, A. H. (1978). Sex differences in influenceability. *Psychological Bulletin, 85,* 86–116.

Eagly, A. H. (1983). Gender and social influence: A social psychological analysis. *American Psychologist, 38,* 971–981.

Eagly, A., & Carli, L. (1981). Sex of researchers and sex-types communications as determinants of sex differences in influenceability. A meta-analysis of social influence studies. *Psychological Bulletin, 90,* 1–20.

Eyde, L. D. (1970). Eliminating barriers to the career development of women. *Personnel and Guidance Journal, 49,* 25–28.

Farmer, H. S. (1971). Helping women to resolve the home-career conflict. *Personnel and Guidance Journal, 49,* 795–801.

Faunce, P. S. (1985). Teaching feminist therapies: Integrating feminist therapy, pedagogy, and scholarship. In L. B. Rosewater & L. E. A. Walker (Eds.), *Handbook of feminist therapy* (pp. 309–320). New York: Springer.

Fine, M. (1985). Reflections on a feminist psychology of women: Paradoxes and prospects. *Psychology of Women Quarterly, 9,* 167–183.

Fitzgerald, L. (1986). Career counseling women: Principles, procedures, and problems. In Z. Leibowitz & D. Lea (Eds.), *Adult career development* (pp. 116–131). Alexandria, VA: American Association for Counseling and Development.

Fitzgerald, L. F., & Crites, J. O. (1980). Toward a career psychology of women: What do we know? What do we need to know? *Journal of Counseling Psychology, 27,* 44–62.

Fitzgerald, L. & Rounds, J. (1989). Vocational behavior, 1988: A critical analysis. *Journal of Vocational Behavior, 35,* 105–163.

Fodor, I., & Rothblum, E. D. (1984). Strategies for dealing with sex-role stereotypes. In C. M. Brody (Ed.), *Women therapists working with women* (pp. 86–95). New York: Springer.

Frodi, A., Macauley, J., & Thome, P. R. (1977). Are women always less aggressive than men? A review of the experimental literature. *Psychological Bulletin, 84,* 634–660.

Gaddy, C. D., Glass, C. R., & Arnkoff, D. B. (1983). Career involvement of women in dual-career families: The influence of sex role identity. *Journal of Counseling Psychology, 30,* 388–394.

Gannon, L. (1982). The role of power in psychotherapy. *Women and Therapy, 1,* 3–11.

Gardner, J. (1971). Sexist counseling must stop. *Personnel and Guidance Journal, 49,* 705–714.

Gianakos, I., & Subich, L. M. (1986). The relationship of gender and sex-role orientation to vocational undecidedness. *Journal of Vocational Behavior, 29,* 42–50.

Gilligan, C. (1982). *In a different voice: Psychological theory and women's development.* Cambridge, MA: Harvard University Press.

Grady, K. E. (1981). Sex bias in research design. *Psychology of Women Quarterly, 5,* 628–636.

Gray, J. D. (1980). Counseling women who want both a profession and a family. *Personnel and Guidance Journal, 59,* 43–46.

Greenhaus, J. H., & Parasuraman, S. (1986). Vocational and organizational behavior, 1985: A review. *Journal of Vocational Behavior, 29,* 115–176.

Greenspan, M. (1983). *A new approach to women and therapy.* New York: McGraw-Hill.

Greenspan, M. (1986). Should therapists be personal? Self-disclosure and therapeutic distance in feminist therapy. *Women and Therapy, 5,* 5–17.

Hackett, G., Betz, N., O'Halloran, S., & Romac, D. (1990). Effects of verbal and mathematics task performance on task and career self-efficacy and interest. *Journal of Counseling Psychology, 37,* 169–177.

Hackett, G., Esposito, D., & O'Halloran, M. S. (1989). The relationship of role model influences to the career salience and educational and career plans of college women. *Journal of Vocational Behavior, 35,* 164–180.

Hackett, G., Lent, R. W., & Greenhaus, J. H. (1991). Advances in vocational theory and research: A 20-year retrospective. *Journal of Vocational Behavior, 38,* 3–38.

Hansen, L. S. (1972). We are furious (female) but we can shape our own development. *Personnel and Guidance Journal, 51,* 87–96.

Hansen, L. S. (1978). Promoting female growth through a career development curriculum. In L. S. Hansen & R. S. Rapoza (Eds.), *Career development and counseling of women* (pp. 425–442). Springfield, IL: Charles C. Thomas.

Hansen, L. S., & Keierleker, D. L. (1978). BORN FREE: A collaborative consultation model for career development and sex-role stereotyping. *Personnel and Guidance Journal, 56,* 395–399.

Hansen, L. S., & Rapoza, R. S. (Eds.). (1978). *Career development and counseling women.* Springfield, IL: Charles C. Thomas.

Harding, S. (1987a). Introduction: Is there a feminist method. In S. Harding (Ed.), *Feminism and methodology* (pp. 1–14). Bloomington: Indiana University Press.

Harding, S. (1987b). Conclusion: Epistemological questions. In S. Harding (Ed.), *Feminism and methodology* (pp. 181–190). Bloomington: Indiana University Press.

Hare-Mustin, R. T., Marecek, J., Kaplan, A. G., & Liss-Levenson, N. (1979). Rights of clients, responsibilities of therapists. *American Psychologist, 34,* 3–16.

Harmon, L. (1978). Career counseling for women. In L. S. Hansen & R. S. Rapoza (Eds.), *Career development and counseling of women* (pp. 443–453). Springfield, IL: Charles C. Thomas.

Harmon, L. W. (1989). Longitudinal changes in women's career aspirations: Developmental or historical? *Journal of Vocational Behavior, 35,* 46–63.

Harmon, L., & Fitzgerald, L. (1973). Counseling women I. *Counseling Psychologist, 4.*

Hartsock, N. C. (1987). The feminist standpoint: Developing the ground for a specifically feminist historical materialism. In S. Harding, (Ed.), *Feminism and methodology* (pp. 157–180). Bloomington: Indiana University Press.

Hawkesworth, M. (1989). Knowers, knowing, known: Feminist theory and claims of truth. *Signs, 14,* 533–557.

Hawley, P. (1978). Empirically based counseling practices for women. In L. S. Hansen & R. S. Rapoza (Eds.), *Career development and counseling of women* (pp. 338–353). Springfield, IL: Charles C. Thomas.

Henley, N. (1977). *Body politics.* Englewood Cliffs, NJ: Prentice-Hall.

Heppner, P. P., Cook, S. W., Strozier, A. L., & Heppner, M. J. (1991). An investigation of coping styles and gender differences with farmers in career transition. *Journal of Counseling Psychology, 38,* 167–174.

Hill, C. E., Birk, J. M., Blimline, C. A., Leonard, M. M., Hoffman, M. A., & Tanney, M. F. (1979). Counseling women III. *Counseling Psychologist, 8,* 2–63.

Jordan, J. V., Kaplan, A. G., Miller, J. B., Striver, I. P., & Surrey, J. L. (1991). *Women's growth in connection: Writings from the Stone Center,* New York: Guilford Press.

Kahn, A. S., & Yoder, J. D. (1989). The psychology of women and conservatism: Rediscovering social change. *Psychology of Women Quarterly, 13,* 417–432.

Kahn, S. E. (1983). Development and operation of the women's employment counseling unit. *Vocational Guidance Quarterly, 32,* 125–129.

Kahnweiler, J. B., & Kahnweiler, W. M. (1980). A dual-career family workshop for college undergraduates. *Vocational Guidance Quarterly, 28,* 225–230.

Kaschak, E. (1981). Feminist psychotherapy: The first decade. In S. Cox (Ed.), *Female psychology.* New York: St. Martin's Press.

Katz, J. K., & Knapp, N. H. (1974). Housewife, mother, other: Needs and helpers. *Personnel and Guidance Journal, 53,* 105–109.

Kinicki, A. J. (1989). Predicting occupational role choices after involuntary job loss. *Journal of Vocational Behavior, 35,* 204–218.

Kinicki, A. J., & Griffeth, R. W. (1985). The impact of sex-role stereotypes on performance ratings and causal attributions of performance. *Journal of Vocational Behavior, 27,* 155–170.

Lerman, H. (1976). What happens in feminist therapy. In S. Cox (Ed.), *Female psychology: The emerging self* (pp. 378–384). Chicago: Science Research Associates.

Lerman, H. (1985). Some barriers to the development of a feminist theory of personality. In L. B. Rosewater & L. E. A. Walker (Eds.), *Handbook of feminist therapy* (pp. 5–12). New York: Springer.

Lerman, H. (1986). From Freud to feminist personality theory: Getting here from there. *Psychology of Women Quarterly, 10,* 1–18.

Leso, J. F., & Neimeyer, G. J. (1991). Role of gender and construct type in vocational complexity and choice of academic major. *Journal of Counseling Psychology, 38,* 182–188.

Lott, B. (1985). The potential enrichment of social/personality psychology through feminist research and vice versa. *American Psychologist, 40,* 155–164.

Lott, B. (1991). Social psychology: Humanist roots and feminist future. *Psychology of Women Quarterly, 15,* 505–519.

Lykes, M., & Stewart, A. (1986). Evaluating the feminist challenge to research in personality and social psychology: 1963–1983. *Psychology of Women Quarterly, 10,* 393–412.

Maccoby, E. E. (1988). Gender as a social category. *Developmental Psychology, 26,* 755–765.

Maccoby, E. E.(1990). Gender and relationships: A developmental account. *American Psychologist, 45,* 513–520.

Maccoby, E. E., & Jacklin, C. N. (1974). *Psychology of sex differences,* Stanford, CA: Stanford University Press.

Major, B. (1987). Gender, justice, and the psychology of entitlement. In P. Shaver & C. Hendrick (Eds.), *Sex and gender* (pp. 213–225). New Haven, CT: Yale University Press.

Mander, A. V., & Rush, A. K. (1974). *Feminism as therapy.* New York: Random House.

Manis, L. G., & Mochizuki, J. (1972). Search for fulfillment: A program for adult women. *Personnel and Guidance Journal, 50,* 594–599.

Marecek, J. (1989). Introduction. *Psychology of Women Quarterly, 13,* 367–377.

Matsui, T., Ikeda, H., & Ohnishi, R. (1989). Relations of sex-typed socializations to career self-efficacy expectations of college students. *Journal of Vocational Behavior, 35,* 1–16.

McHugh, M., Koeske, R., & Frieze, I. (1986). Issues to consider in conducting nonsexist psychology research. *American Psychologist, 41,* 879–890.

McKenna, W., & Kessler, S. J. (1977). Experimental design as a source of sex bias in social psychology. *Sex Roles, 3,* 117–128.

Millman, M., & Kantor, R. M. (1975). *Another voice: Feminist perspectives on social life and social science.* New York: Anchor Books.

Nassi, A. J., & Abramowitz, S. I. (1978). Raising consciousness about women's groups: Process and outcome research. *Psychology of Women's Quarterly, 3,* 139–156.

Offen, K. (1988). Defining feminism: A comparative historical approach. *Signs: Journal of Women in Culture & Society, 14,* 119–157.

Oliver, L. W. (1975). Counseling implications of recent research on women. *Personnel and Guidance Journal, 53,* 430–437.

Parlee, M. B. (1981). Appropriate control groups in feminist research. *Psychology of Women Quarterly, 5,* 637–644.

Peplau, L. A., & Conrad, E. (1989). Beyond nonsexist research: The perils of feminist methods in psychology. *Psychology of Women Quarterly, 13,* 379–400.

Plotsky, F. A., & Goad, R. (1974). Encouraging women through a career conference. *Personnel and Guidance Journal, 52,* 486–488.

Pond, S. B., & Hay, M. S. (1989). The impact of task preview information as a function of recipient self-efficacy. *Journal of Vocational Behavior, 35,* 17–29.

Porter, N. (1985). New perspectives on therapy supervision. In L. B. Rosewater & L. E. A. Walker (Eds.), *Handbook of feminist therapy* (pp. 332–343). New York: Springer.

Randall, D. M., Fedor, D. B., & Longenecker, C. O. (1990). The behavioral expression of organizational commitment. *Journal of Vocational Behavior, 36,* 210–224.

Rawlings, E. I., & Carter, D. K. (Eds.). (1977). *Psychotherapy for women.* Springfield, IL: Charles C. Thomas.

Ricketts, M. (1989). Epistemological values of feminists in psychology. *Psychology of Women Quarterly, 13,* 401–415.

Rudnick, D. T., & Wallach, E. J. (1980). Women in technology: A program to increase career awareness. *Personnel and Guidance Journal, 58,* 445–448.

Russell, J., & Rush, M. (1987). Age-related variations in women's views of management careers. *Journal of Vocational Behavior, 30,* 280–294.

Sandmeyer, L. E. (1980). "Choices and changes": A workshop for women. *Vocational Guidance Quarterly, 28,* 352–359.

Sanford, L., & Donovan, M. (1984). *Women and self-esteem*. New York: Doubleday.

Sargent, A. G. (1977). *Beyond sex roles*. St. Paul, MN: West.

Schlossberg, N. K. (1972). A framework for counseling women. *Personnel and Guidance Journal, 51*, 137–143.

Scozzaro, P. & Subich, L. (1990). Gender and occupational sex-type differences in job outcome factor perceptions. *Journal of Vocational Behavior, 36*, 109–120.

Slaney, R., & Russell, J. (1987). Perspectives on vocational behavior, 1986: A review. *Journal of Vocational Behavior, 30*, 111–173.

Smith, A. J., & Siegel, R. F. (1985). Feminist therapy: Redefining power for the powerless. In L. B. Rosewater & L. E. A. Walker (Eds.), *Handbook of feminist therapy* (pp. 13–21). New York: Springer.

Snodgrass, S. E. (1985). Women's intuition: The effect of subordinate role on interpersonal sensitivity. *Journal of Personality and Social Psychology, 49*, 146–155.

Solomon, E. E., Bishop, R. C., & Bresser, R. K. (1986). Organization moderators of gender differences in career development: A facet classification. *Journal of Vocational Behavior, 29*, 27–41.

Sturdivant, S. (1980). *Therapy with women: A feminist philosophy of treatment*. New York: Springer.

Sundal-Hansen, L. S. (1984). Interrelationships of gender and career. In N. C. Gysbers & Associates, *Designing careers* (pp. 216–247). San Francisco: Jossey-Bass.

Sundal-Hansen, L. S. (1985). Work-family linkages: Neglected factors in career guidance across cultures. *Vocational Guidance Quarterly, 33*, 202–212.

Swanson, J. L., & Tokar, D. M. (1991). College students' perceptions of barriers to career development. *Journal of Vocational Behavior, 38*, 92–106.

Tangri, S. S., & Strasburg, G. L. (1979). Can research on women be more effective in shaping policy? *Psychology of Women Quarterly, 3*, 321–343.

Tavris, C. (1991). The mismeasure of woman: Paradoxes and perspectives in the study of gender. In J. D. Goodchilds (Ed.), *Psychological perspectives on human diversity in America* (pp. 91–137). Washington, DC: American Psychological Association.

Tinsley, H. E. A., & Heesacker, M. (1984). Vocational behavior and career development, 1983: A review. *Journal of Vocational Behavior, 25*, 139–190.

Unger, R. K. (1979). Toward a redefinition of sex and gender. *American Psychologist, 34*, 1085–1094.

Unger, R. K. (1981). Sex as a social reality: Field and laboratory research. *Psychology of Women Quarterly, 5*, 645–653.

Unger, R. K. (1983). Through the looking glass: No wonderland yet! (The reciprocal relationship between methodology and models of reality). *Psychology of Women Quarterly, 8*, 9–32.

Unger, R. K. (1990). Imperfect reflections or reality: Psychology constructs gender. In R. T. Hare-Mustin & J. Marecek (Eds.), *Making a difference: Psychology and the construction of gender* (pp. 102–149). New Haven, CT: Yale University Press.

Vetter, L. (1973). Career counseling for women. *Counseling Psychologist, 4*, 54–66.

Wallston, B. S. (1981). What are the questions in psychology of women? A feminist approach to research. *Psychology of Women Quarterly 5*, 597–617.

Walsh, R. (1989). Do research reports in mainstream feminist psychology journals reflect feminist values? *Psychology of Women Quarterly, 13*, 445–458.

Wittig, M. A. (1985). Metatheoretical dilemmas in the psychology of gender. *American Psychologist, 40*, 800–811.

Zanna, M. P., & Pack, S. J. (1975). On the self-fulfilling nature of apparent sex differences in behavior. *Journal of Experimental Social Psychology, 11*, 583–591.

# ❧ 4 ❧

# Gender and Dual-Career Families: Implications and Applications for the Career Counseling of Women

Lucia Albino Gilbert
Marybeth Hallett
*University of Texas, Austin*

Natalie S. Eldridge
*Boston University Counseling Center*

## DUAL-CAREER FAMILIES IN PERSPECTIVE

In 1969, the Rapoports, working in England, first used the term *dual-career family* to describe what they considered to be an unusual and revolutionary type of dual-wage heterosexual family that emerged as the result of complex social changes. Revolutionary from their perspective was the dual-career families' apparent inconsistency with traditional notions of gender. In these families, the woman and man both pursued a lifelong career, relatively uninterrupted, and also established and developed a family life that often included children.

Interestingly, discussions of dual-wage heterosexual families often overlook the uniqueness of the dual-career family and how, in theory, it challenges traditional notions of gender (cf. Gilbert & Rachlin, 1987). Employment of women in low-paying jobs is neither new nor radical and thus does not necessarily challenge traditional assumptions about work and the family. In contrast, women and men as equal partners provides a dramatically different view of work and family, one that assumes certain changes in women's and men's self-concepts as well as in societal norms and structures.

Three assumptions appear particularly important to dual-career family functioning and hence to career counseling in this area. The first of these is a presumed equality between the partners economically, which in turn implies for heterosexual couples an economic equality between women and men. The second is a presumed compatibility of

135

occupational and family systems. The third pertains to the partners themselves. It is presumed that spouses' self-concepts as women and men allow for the establishment of a relationship characterized by role-sharing and mutuality and by an interdependency free of the constraints of gender. Particularly crucial to the relationships between women and men is the assumption that neither spouse would expect women to accommodate to men's assumed superiority nor for men to have authority over women.

Theory and reality, however, often differ in great measure, and such is the case for dual-career families. This chapter first describes what appears to be the case with regard to these three assumptions and then uses emerging gender perspectives to further elucidate and explain processes that may keep theory from becoming reality. Factors influencing women's choices about occupations and family life are then considered from this broader gender perspective, followed by discussions of choices, dilemmas, and sources of support characteristic of dual-career families. Because the issues in career counseling with regard to dual-career relationships differ in many respects for lesbian and heterosexual women, separate sections of the chapter are at times devoted to each.

Often overlooked, in fact, is that not all dual-career families are heterosexual and that the integrating and sharing of occupational and family roles, which is emerging for women in heterosexual dual-career relations, is normative among lesbian women. Indeed, much of the interest and excitement about the dual-career-family patterns center around changes in the power relations between contemporary women and men, changes that are crucial to viewing it as an emerging family form. The situation is obviously different for dual-career relationships in which neither the power dynamics implicit in heterosexual relationships nor the norms and roles of marriage as an institution operate. By identifying as lesbians, women generally accept a lifelong responsibility to support themselves and their children. Both this economic reality and their being socialized to value egalitarian relations with other women engender role-sharing relationships in lesbian couples.

## THE TWO-CAREER FAMILY IN ACTUALITY

Today, only 10% of American families fit the traditional model of a two-parent family with children, a wage-earning husband, and a homemaker wife. Even among two-parent heterosexual families, the proportion where the husband is the only wage-earner has dropped to 20%; for minority families it is even lower (Spain, 1988). For married women with children under 6 years old, 56.1% are in the labor force, and of these 69.4% are employed full time. For married women with children under the age of 18, these percentages increase to 65% employed and 72.9% employed full time. The average working wife with full-time employment contributes approximately 40% of the family's annual income (U.S. Bureau of Labor Statistics, 1989).

The comparable statistics for lesbian couples are not readily available, although current statistics likely include women whose partners are women. Lesbian working women are clearly a hidden population; their presence in the workforce typically goes unrecognized by employers, co-workers, and those who observe and conduct research on women in the workplace. Unlike a person's race or sex, an individual's sexual orientation cannot be determined on the basis of physical cues. The pervading heterosexual bias (Morin, 1977) that is a part of our socialization usually leads to assumptions that everyone is heterosexual unless there is clear evidence to the contrary. Indeed, because our society discriminates heavily against those who are not heterosexual, gays and lesbians often collude with this heterosexual bias in order to avoid the consequences of being identified as deviant. In one study of working lesbians in committed relationships, 65% of the sample indicated that they had not disclosed their lesbianism to their employers, whereas 37% indicated that no one in their work environment knew they were lesbian (Eldridge & Gilbert, 1990). A significant proportion of these women had children.

Clearly, not only is the number of dual-earner families increasing, but also the number of families having partners who both consider themselves in careers. Women today have more opportunities for career placement and advancement than ever before in our history, and many heterosexual women want and push for the "revolutionary" two-career family with men envisioned by the Rapoports (Ferree, 1990; Guelzow, Bird, & Koball, 1991). Research indicates that approximately one third of heterosexual and most lesbian dual-career families do establish what they and objective others would consider an egalitarian relationship (Eldridge & Gilbert, 1990; Gilbert, 1985, 1993). Moreover, there is much evidence of men's increased involvement in home roles and parenting, overall, and of the personal benefits for men who do so (e.g., Barnett & Baruch, 1987; Pleck, 1985, 1987). However, these women and men manage to do so despite the fact that two of the three assumptions described earlier are not entirely the case.

The first of these assumptions was economic equality between women and men in general and hence between heterosexual spouses. The reality is that, in addition to still earning significantly less than men, women are greatly underrepresented in nearly all professional areas, and experience significant attrition in male-dominated professions (Rix, 1987; U.S. Bureau of Labor Statistics, 1989). Moreover, the occupational distribution of women within the labor force has changed only slightly over time: Women and men are still typically found in different occupations (Scott, 1982; Spain, 1988). Lesbians, like women in general, earn less than men on average, but the impact for them is reflected not in differences in partners' incomes but in lower joint earnings as a couple (Schneider, 1986).

The second assumption concerns the compatability of occupational and family systems. As discussed later, there is still considerable resistance to altering the structure of professional work and providing policies based on the assumption that both women and men, not just women, involve themselves in family work. Paternity leaves apparently pose unique difficulties for organizations because granting them would sanction men as caregivers and alter firmly held views that families accommodate to the structure of men's work (Fowlkes, 1980, 1987).

The next section explains how these realities, which dramatically impact on the lives of individuals in dual-career families, derive from complex gender processes. Many women today want to establish egalitarian relationships with men in the workplace and in their personal relationships. Yet society continues to question whether two individuals, both of whom are career-oriented, can successfully achieve a loving and enduring relationship with each other and with their children and also progress in their chosen fields. This is especially true with regard to relationships between women and men because historically women were expected to accommodate to men's achievement needs regardless of their own talents and abilities. A poignant cartoon by Cline (1988) cuts to the essence of this reality in its depiction of a professional-looking couple contemplating the purchase of a book. The wife in the cartoon says to the husband, "It's by a woman who still thinks marriage is possible."

This is not the first time women have questioned whether relationships with men were possible given the societal structure and its explicit and implicit policies. Lucy Stone and Henry Blackwell, early American feminists, at the time of their wedding in 1855 publicly announced their intent to live their private lives outside the institutional constraints of the time. They said:

> While we acknowledge our mutual affection by publicly assuming the relationship of husband and wife . . . we deem it a duty to declare that this act on our part implies no sanction of, nor promise of voluntary obedience to such of the present laws of marriage as refuse to recognize

the wife as an independent, rational being, while they confer upon the husband an injurious and unnatural superiority. (Flexner, 1959, p.64)

Husbands in the United States no longer have custody of the wife's person, yet the issues of male dominance and superiority and female obedience and dependency identified in the Stone-Blackwell statement persist today—some 100 years later—and profoundly influence women's self-concept and choices. Hare-Mustin (1991), a keen observer of gender processes, concluded that "Women live under the kind of patriarchy that is represented, not by outright oppression, but by the unacknowledged preeminence of men's desires and the subordination of their own" (p. 56).

## A GENDER PERSPECTIVE

The previous section makes clear how the personal lives of individuals are always played out within the constraints of societal norms, values, and institutions. Particularly important to the purposes and goals of this chapter is understanding how many of the constraints implicit in the two-career family form are inextricably tied to gender processes.

In this chapter the term *sex* refers to whether a person is biologically male or female, and to characteristics determined by that biology. For example, the female sex has the capacity to bear children, and the male sex has the capacity to fertilize eggs. The term *gender*, in contrast, acknowledges the broader meaning typically associated with being born biologically female or male. Gender refers to the psychological, social, and cultural features and characteristics that have become strongly associated with the biological categories of female and male (Deaux, 1985). For example, women and men in our society are as likely to become parents (i.e., biologically, conception requires a female and a male), but disproportionately more women than men are involved in the day-to-day care of children (i.e., culturally, women rear children). From a gender perspective, women typically rear children, not because men are less nurturing than women by nature, but because societal expectations associated with sex prescribe that women more than men should engage in nurturing activities. From a gender perspective, then, many of the traits and behaviors traditionally assumed to be determined by biological sex have become "constructed by the social reality" of individual women and men (Hare-Mustin & Marecek, 1990). The ways in which gender meanings and practices come to be accepted in modern society is a focus of feminist postmodern theory and discourse analysis (Hare-Mustin, 1991).

Broadening the meaning of behaviors typically associated with biological sex shifts the locus of assumptions about the causes of behavior (cf. Deaux & Major, 1987; Sherif, 1982; Unger, 1990). Rather than focusing on intrapsychic and individual variables presumably tied to biological sex, perspectives now shift to viewing individuals' behavior as emerging from a web of interactions between their biological being and their social environment. For example, early studies on women's stress in combining multiple roles primarily looked at intrapsychic variables such as guilt, self-esteem, and occupational aspirations. More recent studies reconceptualize the personal experience of role conflict within the context of family and employment variables and demonstrate that both individual well-being and relationship satisfaction are related to such contextual variables as partners' participation in family work, childcare availability and quality, and employer policies (Aldous, 1990; Crosby, 1987; Gilbert, 1988; Thompson & Walker, 1989).

## Gender and Its Relation to Societal Institutions and Policies

We now conceptualize gender as extending beyond individual women and men and their socialization to the social structures and principles of organizations (Sherif, 1982). For example, women and men are still found in different occupations and we worry about the feminization of psychology (Ostertag & McNamara, 1991). Overall, men have a wider base of power and easier access to valuable resources, and women continue to earn significantly less than men (U.S. Bureau of Labor Statistics, 1989). Positions of power and leadership in business organizations and academic institutions are still predominantly held by men, and the structures of career participation have not changed appreciably (Fowlkes, 1987). Current employment benefits and policies enable women more than men to ask for and receive the accommodations necessary for combining work and family responsibilities (e.g., maternity leaves, flexible schedules). However, the availability of such accommodations for the nonbiological or legally unrecognized parent in a lesbian family is as yet untested.

Studies that conceptualize gender as structure, although still quite rare, are appearing with increased frequency in the dual-career literature. Pleck (1990), for example, reported on how employer policies regarding paternity leave influence men's participation in parenting. Hyde and Clark (1989) are in the early stages of a longitudinal study of the relationship between maternity leave options and family members' well-being. Thus, rather than viewing multiple role occupancy as a problem for marriages, these researchers are focusing on structures (i.e., employer attitudes and policies) that prohibit/inhibit the beneficial integration of multiple roles for both partners, particularly when they are parents. As we mention later, employers are increasingly recognizing the corporate benefit of changes in their organizational structures. A large number of companies already provide "family friendly benefits," and many more have plans underway (Moskowitz & Townsend, 1991).

## Gender and Its Relation to Interpersonal Processes

Recent theorists also emphasized how gender is a process engaged in by women and men (Deaux, 1984; Sherif, 1982; Unger, 1990). That is, as individuals we internalize societally based constructions of women and men and are encouraged and rewarded for playing them out in our interpersonal interactions—particularly in those kinds of interactions where gender is salient. Deaux (1984), in her review of a decade of work on gender, concluded that views of gender as a static category must give way to, or at least be accompanied by, theories that treat sex-related phenomena as a process—"a process that is influenced by individual choices, molded by situational pressures, and ultimately understandable only in the context of social interaction" (p. 115).

A study by Holland and Eisenhart (1991) provides a particularly relevant illustration of this process in an older group of students, college-aged women and men. They reported that female students at two Southern universities scaled down their ambitions over their 4 years in co-ed colleges so that most ended up with desired heterosexual relationships but only a marginal career and inferior preparation as a wage earner. Thus, women and men may consciously or unconsciously act on beliefs or assumptions of male entitlement and prerogative and women's accommodations to men's rights. Doing so is likely related to indices of personal and occupational well-being as well as to the degree of role-sharing achieved by heterosexual partners.

Parallel dynamics occur in work settings. That is, interpersonal processes based on assumed or unconsciously held views of gender-related characteristics, such as male superiority, may maintain interpersonal dynamics that keep men in dominant positions they may not even want. A series of studies with college students indicated that under certain situational constraints women, even those who are high in dispositional dominance, might accept the legitimacy of men's assumed power or status and then act in accordance with this assumption (Davis & Gilbert, 1989). More specifically, these authors found that high dominant women paired with low dominant men became leaders 71% of the time. However, high dominant women paired with high dominant men assumed the leadership role only 31% of the time. Thus, men's expectancies may be a more important determinant of interaction sequences in mixed-sex dyads than are women's, and women in mixed-sex dyads may inadvertently confirm men's behavioral expectancies more than men confirm women's (e.g., Davis & Gilbert, 1989).

Conscious and unconscious assumptions about how women and men should behave also may help understand the well-documented gender differences in the patterning of both verbal and nonverbal communication and in topics of discourse (Aries, 1987). Tannen (1990) argued that women and men fail to understand one another because men see themselves in an hierarchical social order in which they are either one-up or one-down. In the world as they construe it, conversations are negotiations in which people either try to achieve the upper hand or protect themselves from others' attempts to have the upper hand and put them down. She argued that women, in contrast, perceive themselves as part of a network of connections. In the world as they know it, conversations are negotiations for closeness in which people try to "seek and give confirmation and support, and to reach consensus" (p. 25).

Men's difficulty in establishing close working relations with women may relate to men's self-view that they should control and dominate interactions with women (McGill, 1985; Pleck, 1981). Withholding themselves from relations with women not only provides men with the illusion of an independent stance but also reinforces their dominant position. But, as Pleck (1981) also points out, by engaging in these kinds of interactions, men give women the ability to make them feel like men since maintaining their dominant position depends on women seeing men as superior to them. Interpersonally, then, women and men likely engage in behaviors prompted by gender-related beliefs and constraints more often than they realize.

In summary, gender processes such as those we have described can influence women's relationships with men in the workplace and in their personal lives both directly and indirectly. Views of men as superior to women and entitled, sexually and otherwise, continue to influence employers' policies and practices as well as women's and men's self-views and expectations. Realities such as the underrepresentation of women in most professional areas and the inequities in men's and women's salaries clearly are associated with societal views of, and sanctions for, male dominance. In the earlier words of Stone and Blackwell, they confer on the man "an injurious and unnatural superiority."

Gender-related dynamics of this kind, although prevalent in the workplace (cf. Morrison, White, Velnor, & the Center for Creative Leadership, 1987), are also particularly pertinent to relations between partners in dual-career families. We next address how these realities pertain to the career counseling of women who are planning or have already involved themselves in dual-career relationships. Many of the factors we discuss are intuitively related to gender as process (e.g., participation in family work, decision making about locating and relocating) and gender as structure (e.g., implicit and explicit policies for promotions, family benefits).

## FACTORS INFLUENCING WOMEN'S CHOICES

Nearly all women planning careers assume they will be in long-term romantic relationships (Tittle, 1981). These women not only need to understand factors that can help or hinder their achieving the kind of dual-career relationship they envision, but they also need to be prepared for dealing with the likely obstacles and day-to-day realities. Thus, those individuals who counsel women must address variables that interact with women's career development and, more specifically for our purposes, be aware of how these factors may have powerful crossover effects in dual-career relationships.

Broadly speaking, there are numerous variables that influence women's advancement in careers and their ability to integrate occupational and family roles. Many of these factors are mutually influencing and overlapping and occur in a social milieu that has the capacity to be both supportive and detrimental to women who are pursuing professional careers and are in committed personal relationships, often with children. It is important to note that although we divide these variables into internal sociopsychological factors and external structural factors, the division is in some ways artificial. It is rare when discussing women's career development that a factor can be discretely identified as one or the other. Much of our internal sociopsychological world is influenced by and acted out in our external structural environments—and vice versa. Nevertheless, the division is useful to examining these factors in a systematic manner. Also, where applicable, the influence of gender processes is noted.

### Internal Sociopsychological Factors

Two of the most pervasive internal psychological factors that continue to influence the career development of women with regard to dual-career families center around the concept of gender. These are the assumptions of *female dependency and nurturance* and of *male superiority and privilege* already discussed in the previous section. Related to these is a third factor we view as important, *self-efficacy* (Bandura, 1977).

There is a long history of women having little authority and depending on others for their sense of self. There is also a long history of assumed male superiority and entitlement. One consequence of these realities is women's overvaluing the importance of relationships and looking to relationships as a way to feel important or worthwhile (Heilbrun, 1988; Lerner, 1983; Westkott, 1986). Today many women are still socialized to believe that being partnered or married is a first priority in life and that achieving financial independence and career recognition are secondary to their roles as caregivers and partners. In heterosexual relationships this is further complicated by the status historically associated with being loved by a man and the promise of being taken care of financially and otherwise. That women's lives are given meaning through their attachment to men, and that men take care of women in return, remains a powerful metaphor in women's lives. Being without a man supposedly means that a woman is undesirable and unlovable, a belief that can bring about feelings of shame and inadequacy, despite a woman's career accomplishments.

The relationship between female dependency, male entitlement, and women's career development is multilayered and is played out in different ways for heterosexual and lesbian women. Heterosexual women often feel they have to choose between a career and marriage or accommodate to a husband. If the male partner is unwilling to engage in an egalitarian relationship, a woman may view the choice as one between equality and marriage. Indeed, the literature indicates that many women find themselves doing more than their share and resenting it, and at the same time feeling reluctant to challenge male dominance and privilege because of the fear of losing the relationship or of feeling less competent and assured than the male partner (Gilbert, 1988). In order to maintain the dual-career family, these women may underfunction professionally or subordinate their career desires to their partner's plans and aspirations (Lerner, 1983).

Rarely does a man wonder about the consequences of being too competent. In contrast, this is often a concern for young women thinking ahead to relationships, particularly heterosexual relationships. It is not unusual for women to struggle with the negative reactions they receive for being too competent. Being competent and professionally ambitious is still inconsistent with traditional views of what makes a woman desirable and worthwhile. The notion of women making their own choices, separate from the needs of others, is inconsistent with societal views and women's self-views of women. The role conflict experienced by women in dual-career relationships, discussed later in the chapter, can be heightened by internalized views that women are primarily nurturers and that being ambitious is tantamount to greed and selfishness.

Stone and Blackwell described so well how, in our patriarchal society, both sexes are socialized to believe that men are more valuable than women and are entitled to many rights and privileges that are attendant to that fact. Men learn to see themselves as special and superior and they learn to expect women to serve them. They are conditioned to assume that their needs and desires come before the needs and desires of women. Clearly, these beliefs do not bode well for successful, equitable relationships between women and men, for women's career development, or for the development of family-friendly policies for both sexes. Feelings of entitlement may surface regarding how to perform domestic or parenting roles, whose career is primary, or who should make the larger salary. Male entitlement issues will be a struggle for men and women as they try to develop careers in a society that remains considerably sexist and form relationships that have little historical precedence.

The *career self-efficacy* of women has obvious connections with the assumptions of female dependency and male entitlement just discussed. Several earlier chapters addressed in detail the general importance of this concept and its applicability to career counseling for women.

Gender differences with regard to career-related self-efficacy have been found in many studies (e.g., Betz & Hackett, 1981, 1983; Hackett, 1985; Hackett, Betz, O'Halloran, & Romac, 1990; Swindell, 1988). Research supports the hypothesis that women have less strong and less generalized career-related self-efficacy beliefs and that this affects both how women envision their professional life and how persistent they are in attempting to achieve what they envision. A case in point is a recent nationwide poll conducted by the Association of American University Women (Horowitz, 1991). The study was designed to assess self-esteem, educational experiences, interest in math and science, and career aspirations of girls and boys, ages 9 to 15. Key findings were the gender differences in self-esteem and the indication that girls emerge from adolescence with a much poorer self-image, more constrained views of the future and their place in society, and much less confidence in their abilities in comparison to their male peers.

Bandura (1977) defined self-efficacy as the belief in one's ability to successfully perform a given task. He proposed that all behavior is mediated by this cognitive mechanism and that given the appropriate skills and adequate incentives, self-efficacy expectations determine much of what an individual does. Later researchers successfully applied his theory to more global tasks (e.g., Betz & Hackett, 1981; Lent, Brown,

& Larkin, 1984; Nevill & Schlecker, 1988). Self-efficacy expectations are related to whether effort is initiated, how much effort is put forth, and how long that effort will be continued in the face of obstacles or aversive experiences.

Although no studies to date have specifically tied self-efficacy theory to the experiences of women in dual-career families, the findings from studies in related areas indicate its potential usefulness for career counseling. For example, the literature indicates that self-efficacy expectations may determine persistence in the face of obstacles. Women contemplating and entering dual-career relationships typically encounter a number of internal and external barriers, many of which are identified in this section of the chapter. Assessing the strength and level of a client's self-efficacy about managing career and family in general, as well as in particular areas, could prove useful to the career counseling process for women. A first step might be for women to ask themselves, "How confident am I that I can successfully manage the dilemmas that will arise in this situation?" Important additional steps would include working with them to identify what factors influence their self-efficacy expectations and whether these are tied to the gender processes described in the chapter.

## External Structural Factors

Any discussion of the factors that influence women's career development has to include the persistent societal beliefs and attitudes about women and work and the kinds of subtle and overt discrimination employed women may experience. It is essential to understand that women develop a sense of their "possible selves" with regard to work and family in the context of society's views about women and the structural constraints put on women's work (Gilbert & Dancer, 1991; Markus & Nurius, 1986). Exposure to these beliefs and limitations begins at birth. Both women and men internalize stereotypic notions about women's and men's achievement and relationships, views that are played out as individuals come together in dual-career partnerships.

*Beliefs.* The belief still persists that women cannot successfully combine domestic and waged labor. It is true that without the support of their partners and significant changes in the way that work is structured, combining work and family can be extremely difficult. Childcare and household responsibilities may prevent women from engaging in activities that will aid them in career advancement (e.g., social functions, overtime, continuing education, leisure). Many people still believe that the involvement of women in waged labor is harmful to the family system. It is important to address these beliefs when counseling women for dual-career relationships, as these women themselves may have internalized this point of view and unconsciously be acting on it.

Other persistent myths in our society include the view that achievement is not "feminine"; that the work women do and the interests that they have are not valuable; and that all women should aspire to the same goal—to be a wife and mother. These messages are "broadcast" loud and clear in the media, in the schools, and in women's homes. Even today women who do not want to define their lives by heterosexual relationships or childrearing are viewed as suspect and as contributing to the decline of the American family. In the past, many women reconciled their achievement desires and these conflicting messages by choosing "feminine" occupations, by not attempting to advance in their careers, or by adopting stereotypic roles in the work place (e.g., nurturer, sex object). Women and men who see their careers as integrating work and family in a new way may find that they too have internalized such extant attitudes to some degree. Recognizing and altering their belief systems to accommodate a desired dual-career relationship would be an important component of career counseling.

*Forms of Discrimination.* Discrimination is certainly not a new phenomenon. Women and other minorities have been the victims of discrimination for decades, if not centuries. Even today with the existence of federal laws that prohibit sexual discrimination, women are still largely segregated into low-income, low-status positions, not promoted at near the rate that men are, and paid only a percentage of what men in comparable positions are paid. Discrimination against women exists both in the workplace and in educational settings. In the work setting, this discrimination can include unfair practices in terms of selection, promotion, or compensation. Theoretically, two types of discrimination have been identified. The first type is called *taste discrimination.* Employers who discriminate on the basis of taste are unfair or sexist in their practices simply because they prefer not to associate with or work with women. This could be for reasons that are misogynistic, or simply misguided, or this could occur for economic reasons. By keeping women out of the work force—especially out of male-dominated occupations—men do not have to compete with women and therefore their jobs are not threatened. Preventing women from entering the labor force also prevents men from having to "take up the slack" in domestic labor.

The second type of discrimination that has been identified is called *statistical discrimination.* The assumption behind this type of discrimination is that the capitalist labor market requires that employers get a good return on their investment in employees. Employers are considered benign, fair, and rational, and they make employment decisions based on *probabilities*. According to proponents of this type of discrimination, it is probable that men will be a better return on their investment. In other words, it is probable that men will work more continuously, more effectively, and be more committed to their work because of their primary "breadwinner" role. These employers are supposedly just looking out for their investment. They assume that because women in this culture are primarily responsible for the home and family, they will likely be tardy or absent, leave their jobs, or be generally unreliable and unmotivated because of their domestic obligations. After all, there are only so many hours in a day and a person only has so much energy. Research has shown, however, that these negative job variables (absenteeism, tardiness, etc.) are inversely related to occupational status. In other words, the higher the occupational status of the position, the lower the employee turnover, absenteeism, tardiness, and so on. Women are more likely to be in low-status jobs that are conducive to job instability, but this is because of job segregation. Men in low-status jobs are as likely to exhibit job instability as women are.

Discrimination is also seen in the workplace in terms of *differential evaluations* and *rewards based on gender*. For example, several studies have demonstrated that there are differential rates of return on education for men and women (England, Chassie, & McCormack, 1982; Sewell, Hauser, & Wolf, 1980). Women and men may put the same amount of time, energy, and money into their education, and do equally as well, but on average male students will benefit from that education much more than female students. Many of these studies involve women who have worked full time continuously throughout their adult life, and still are unable to receive the same types and amounts of status and salary as their male counterparts. Today, a male high school graduate on average still earns more than a woman with a 4-year college degree. In higher education overt discrimination can be seen in admission practices, faculty attitudes towards female students, and financial aid awards (e.g., athletic scholarships, GI Bill, ROTC, and prestigious fellowships such as the Rhodes scholarship, which was until recently only given to men) (Betz & Fitzgerald, 1987). A recent government report indicated that in the federal government "basically the old boys' network is still very much in effect" (Miller, 1991). The male director of the Equal Employment Opportunity Commission (EEOC), in commenting on the report, said he was embarrassed by his agency's failure to enforce equal opportunity laws within the federal government! Clearly it is difficult for a woman to advance in her career pursuits if she encounters these types of overt discrimination.

Another phenomenon that can seriously impede the careers of women is *sexual harassment*. Gilbert (1984) stated that "the quickest way to de-skill a woman is through eroticism." Sexual harassment is seen in occupational settings in many forms. It takes the form of innuendo, overt sexual comments, or even sexual coercion. This type of debasement and domination can have extremely harmful effects on women both personally and professionally. Sexual harassment devalues a woman's abilities and ambitions and defines women as essentially sexual. Treating a woman in a seductive, suggestive, or sexually aggressive manner creates a dynamic of eroticized power that is difficult to deal with. The laws are supposedly supportive of women in this situation, but often proof of sexual harassment is difficult to come by. It usually boils down to his word against hers. Like discrimination, this is a phenomenon with which men are not necessarily personally familiar. Struggles with sexual harassment likely affect the dual-career relationship. In heterosexual couples, male partners may become educated about sexual harassment and become a source of support for their spouse. In addition, a supportive spouse may make it easier for women to leave their work environment. However, in lesbian couples, where both partners may have to deal with harassment as well as homophobia, it may be harder for partners to confront the harassment dynamics and harder for them to leave the work environment because of economics.

A related external factor is the *lack of role models and mentors for professional women* (Douvan, 1976). The relationship between good mentoring and successful career advancement is well documented (Kram, 1988). Mentoring helps provide the kinds of knowledge, contacts, and self-visions necessary for developing and extending one's career options. The importance of role models has also been shown to be crucial for career development. Particularly crucial for women are models for ways to successfully combine careers and family responsibilities (Gilbert & Evans, 1985). Historically, women looked to men as role models and mentors because there were few women in careers. However, these relationships were often limited in their effectiveness because of processes related to gender, such as the potential of heterosexual relationships becoming sexualized or male mentors not being able to address the unique issues that women in the professions face (Gilbert & Rossman, 1992).

The final kind of discrimination to be considered is one less talked about—*homophobia and heterosexism*. Homophobia is the irrational fear, intolerance, and, in its most severe form, hatred of people who are gay or lesbian (Pharr, 1988). This type of prejudice leads to persistent beliefs in negative stereotypes toward gays and lesbians, and supports discriminating actions against these groups in areas such as jobs, housing, and child custody. Lesbians and gays, socialized in the same values, often internalize these negative stereotypes and develop some degree of self-hatred or low self-esteem, a form of internalized homophobia (Margolies, Becker, & Jackson-Brewer, 1987).

When homophobia is combined with cultural and institutional power, the result is heterosexism: a belief in the inherent superiority of heterosexuality and its right to dominance. This is analogous to sexist and racist attitudes, combined with the cultural and institutional power to enforce these attitudes, resulting in sexism and racism. As an external, structural factor, then, heterosexism can have a powerful influence on a woman's choice to envision, enter, or stay in a dual-career relationship with another woman. Being "out" on the job can have devastating repercussions to the woman's career advancement or even to her rights to remain employed. Choosing to "be discreet" can have great personal costs in terms of feeling isolated, compartmentalized, and unaffirmed. Heterosexism in the workplace could be viewed as supporting the necessity of a dual-career family model for lesbians. Few employers extend benefits to an "unmarried" partner or to biological children of that partner, practices that make the more traditional one-earner family model less possible for same-sex female partners.

The anger, discontentment, despair, and stress that all of these discriminatory practices can produce affect how a woman manages her career and her relationship as part of a dual-career couple. Moreover, many women and men come to understand and truly recognize the existence and extent of discrimination as they watch their own partners experience it. This can, in turn, affect how they manage their own career and family responsibilities. Learning to recognize forms of discrimination and becoming informed about what to do should a woman or her partner become a target represent crucial components of effective career counseling.

## CHOICES, DILEMMAS, AND SOURCES OF SUPPORT CHARACTERISTIC OF DUAL-CAREER FAMILIES

Certain realities come with dual-career family relational patterns. Partners need to be prepared for the kinds of choices they may need to make and the possible dilemmas they may face. The dilemmas typically center around the gender processes already described and the constraints of an occupational world that assumes families accommodate to the demands of occupational work (Brown, 1987). Several aspects of normal family life can become troublesome or difficult to dual-career family functioning. Personal, relational, and contextual factors influence couples' choices and decisions in all these areas.

Before addressing these, it is important to note certain similarities between lesbian and heterosexual dual-career families. First of all, correlates of relationship satisfaction found in studies of lesbian relationships are quite similar to those of women in dual-career heterosexual relationships (cf. Eldridge & Gilbert, 1990; Schneider, 1986). These include higher levels of dyadic attachment and shared decision making, intimacy in the relationship, especially emotional intimacy, equality of power, equality of involvement in the relationship, and a similarity of attitudes and backgrounds. Higher valuing of personal autonomy and higher levels of role conflict are typically associated with lower relationship satisfaction.

Dissimilarities for lesbian and heterosexual women are less in individual differences between these two groups of women than in the differences between the two types of partnerships. In the case of power, for instance, women place a higher value on equality of power in their relationships than do men, although men also express a value in equality. In a study of college students (Peplau, 1979), both women (95%) and men (87%) indicated that dating partners should have equal say in their relationships. However, only 49% of the women and 42% of the men reported equal power in their current relationships. When power was unequal, it was usually the male that had greater power. In a study comparing lesbian, gay male, heterosexual cohabiting, and married couples, the amount of money a person earned established the relative power in the couple relationship in every group except the lesbian couples (Blumstein & Schwartz, 1983). The authors attributed this finding to gender socialization, suggesting that it is the presence of male socialization in relationships that leads to the equating of money and power. In taking on "the good provider role," men are socialized to feel entitled to exercise control if they have proved their worth by being financially successful (Bernard, 1981). This example of power dynamics in relationships illustrates both the similarity of heterosexual and lesbian women, and the distinct contextual difference in the relationships these women experience. This distinct contextual difference is important in understanding the issues involved in the four areas described next. For example, combining work and family within the relationship is much less of a problem for lesbian couples than for heterosexual couples, whereas the heterosexist bias in employers' policies typically makes combining work and family harder for lesbian families than for heterosexual families.

## Combining Work and Family

Numerous studies describe the variability among heterosexual dual-career couples on this dimension of family functioning and how such variability relates to the personal, interpersonal, and contextual factors summarized in Table 4.1 (cf. Crosby, 1987; Gilbert, 1987, 1988, 1993). Approximately one third of heterosexual families studied fall into the category labeled "conventional dual-career family," approximately one third into the category "role-sharing dual-career family," and the remaining one third into the category "participant." In the conventional dual-career families, both partners are involved in careers but the responsibility for family work is retained by the women. Typically both partners agree to the premise that work within the home is women's work, and men help out as long as doing so does not interfere with their career pursuits. Far more professionally ambitious than their spouses, the men in these families typically command much higher salaries and see the choice of whether to combine a career with family life as belonging to women.

In contrast, role-sharing dual-career heterosexual families fit the description initially envisioned by the Rapoports in 1969. Both partners are actively involved in family life and in career pursuits. This variant of the dual-career family is the most egalitarian and best represents the pattern many couples strive for. In participant dual-career families, parenting is typically shared by spouses, but female partners do much more of the household work.

Not surprisingly, differences among the variations of the dual-career heterosexual families involve gender-related variables associated with

TABLE 4.1
Factors That Influence How Couples Combine Occupational and Family Roles

*Personal Factors*
    Personality (e.g., how important is a partner's need to dominate, be emotionally intimate, be number one in her or his field)
    Attitudes and values (e.g., partner's beliefs about rearing a child, gender and power, being "out")
    Interests, abilities, stages in careers (e.g., partner's commitment to occupational work, family relations; partner's work satisfaction and career plans, is one partner peaking career-wise and the other thinking about retirement)

*Relationship Factors*
    Equity and power (how are decisions made; what seems fair; how do partners come to agreements about household work, parenting, money)
    Partner support (e.g., can partner's count on each other for support in all areas)
    Shared values and expectations (e.g., do partners share life goals)

*Environmental/Societal Factors*
    The work situation (e.g., are work hours flexible, any sex discrimination, homophobia)
    Employer's views (e.g., kinds of family policy provided, general attitude about employees who involve themselves in family life)
    Childcare availability and quality
    Support systems (family, friends, colleagues, community)

individual partners and with places of employment. For instance, husbands in conventional dual-career families are reported to differ from husbands in role-sharing dual-career families on such indices as dominance, needs for closeness and inclusion, and the differential between spouses' salaries (Gilbert, 1985). Men in role-sharing marriages typically report lower dominance needs, higher needs for closeness and inclusion, and more comparable spouse salaries. They also feel emotionally closer to spouses and to their children.

## Occupational Placement, Advancement, and Mobility

Finding a position of choice or moving from a current position may very well be the most difficult issue for members of dual-career families. Couples often wish to give equal weight to the interests of both partners. In reality, locations or relocations among heterosexual couples often are based on the husbands' opportunities. Companies, however, report increasing employee resistance to relocating because of the reluctance of one partner to relocate if it puts the other partner at a disadvantage. Many companies provide assistance to the accompanying spouse, but even this assistance is often not sufficient to convince couples that relocating is advantageous overall to their family life. Locating or relocating is further complicated for partners in lesbian couples who may be reluctant to mention their dual-career situation to employers.

## Whether to Parent and Handling Childcare

Deciding whether, when, and how to have a child involves a somewhat different set of questions, issues, and realities for lesbian partners than for heterosexual partners. Whereas heterosexual couples face societal expectations that they will have a child, lesbians generally are stigmatized for becoming parents (Slater & Mencher, 1991). Moreover, the "how" of having children, which typically goes unquestioned by heterosexual partners, is very complex for lesbian partners and requires resources as well as sources of support outside of the relationship. Once the decision to parent is made and the method of impregnating or adopting established, heterosexual and lesbian couples face additional questions of how childcare will be handled. As already mentioned, parenting in our society is still equated with mothering. Current employment benefits and policies, although increasingly recognizing men as parents, still make it easier for female partners who are legal or biological mothers to ask for and receive accommodations associated with parenting.

Identifying quality day care is an early and important task. Many books and services are available to assist parents in locating care most consistent with partners' values and needs. Most parents prefer group care for children older than 3 years, but they show no clear preference for individual or small-group care for children under 3 years.

Despite early fears about the negative effects of maternal employment, the results of many studies indicate that children are not at added risk if they receive child- or day care instead of parental care for some portion of the day, and that in some ways children may benefit from it (Hoffman, 1989; Scarr, Phillips, & McCartney, 1990). Both girls and boys, for example, develop less stereotypic gender role attitudes and girls more self-confidence and independence of spirit.

Normal role conflict of varying degrees occurs when partners meet the responsibilities and demands of parenting and occupational pursuits. Generally, role conflict and day-to-day stress associated with parenting and both partners continuing in careers are lowest under the following conditions (Gilbert, 1988; Guelzow et al., 1991):

Employers of both partners have benefit policies that are family responsive.

Both partners actively participate in parenting.

Partners feel comfortable sharing the parenting with childcare personnel.

Partners are satisfied with the childcare they are using.

Partners are happy in their occupational work.

## Resources for Support

Partners in dual-career families need support in a number of areas and from a number of different sources. Various coping responses and resources mediate the impact of stresses on individual partners and on the relationship. The resources helpful to dual-career families are conceptually similar to those listed in Table 4.1. There are personal, relational, and societal sources of support.

*Personal Resources.* These include partners' personal characteristics such as personality attributes, financial resources, abilities to deal with life's stresses, beliefs about love and work, coping strategies typically employed in dealing with role strain, and so forth. Particularly important to effectively managing a dual-career family is commitment to this lifestyle, the capacity to be flexible, compromising, and realistic, and the use of cognitive restructuring coping strategies (e.g., overlooking the difficulties of the dual-career lifestyle and focusing on the good things; seeing your family as lucky to be doing what each partner wants and managing as well as you are).

*Family Resources.* Jessie Bernard (1974) noted some time ago that spousal or partner support and sensitivity play a key role in heterosexual dual-career families. The importance of husbands' sensitivity has been noted repeatedly in studies of heterosexual couples (e.g., Gilbert, 1985; Thompson & Walker, 1989; Vannoy-Hiller & Philliber, 1989). The most essential family resource in heterosexual families is partner support, followed by support from parents and friends. Lesbian couples tend to derive less support from family and to rely more on friendship networks than do married heterosexual couples. Also, heterosexual bias and homophobia may prevent including colleagues from the workplace among friendship networks.

Inextricably tied to the ability to be sensitive and give support is how the need for support is conceptualized by each partner and the meaning each attributes to providing support. Present views, implicitly derived from views of gender as difference, assume that the person with "needs" is lacking in some way and remains unchanged despite interactions with others, and that a female partner is more needy than a male partner (i.e., the stereotypic view that women are basically dependent and stay that way and that men are rarely dependent, regardless of the behaviors they may engage in). From this perspective, individuals meet one anothers' needs but the process of meeting another person's needs leaves both individuals basically unchanged. Partners add up what is given to them and match this total against some internal standard or norm, such as equity, that represents what each is entitled to or should be satisfied with. An illustrative example would be a wife who relocates for a husband's position, assumes the next move is for her career, and feels resentful and underbenefited when he balks at doing so when she wants to relocate some years later.

Partners in dual-career relationships must reframe social support as an interpersonal process involving both giving and receiving and mutual empowerment and strength, a reframing likely not necessary in lesbian couples because of the absence of gender. Stereotypically, dependency was assumed to be a personal variable, characteristic of women, not a dynamic interpersonal variable characteristic of an ongoing relationship. By reconceptualizing the relation between gender and dependency, heterosexual partners can move beyond viewing dependency as a characteristic on which wives and husbands differ to viewing dependency as an interpersonal process that serves as a vehicle for the development of mutuality between partners. Similarly, lesbian partners can move beyond viewing dependency as a negative characteristic associated with being female to viewing dependency as a healthy part of their relationship with another woman (Brown, 1989; Rothblum, 1989). To be able to rely on others and have them able to rely on you is enhancing and empowering to partners and to the relationship.

*Societal Resources.* The long-term acceptance of dual-career families requires support from society at large (Walker, Rozee-Koker, & Wallston, 1987). More effective coping and greater satisfaction among partners with children invariably are associated with flexibility of work schedules, family-supportive employers and benefit policies consistent with this supportive attitude, and suitable childcare (Gilbert, 1988, 1993; Guezlow et al., 1991).

Areas currently receiving attention from companies fall into three categories: dependent care, including infants, adolescents, and the elderly; conditions of work such as greater flexibility in the organization, hours, and location of work; and corporate mission or the validation of family issues as an organizational concern. Of the Fortune 500 companies, 86% will have introduced new work/family programs by January 1991. The reasons are to improve recruitment and retention, increase morale, reduce stress, and keep up with the competition (Aldous, 1990; Moskowitz & Townsend, 1991). State and national policies have not been as responsive, however (Kammerman, 1988).

## PLANNING AHEAD

In the past heterosexual women typically did not plan for their futures, assuming instead that their decisions would be preempted by their husbands or that they would not have to work (Angrist, 1974; Kriger, 1972; Osipow, 1975). Career planning was comparable to contingency training pending marriage plans. Over the last few decades, this situation has changed dramatically. Most women today work, and many work in professional fields. To ensure that women and men are both able to engage in home and family life and pursue career aspirations, planning ahead is imperative.

We summarize in Table 4.2 factors identified in our research as important to young women's decisions to plan for and enter heterosexual dual-career relationships (Gilbert & Dancer, 1991; Gilbert, Dancer, Rossman, & Thorn, 1991). As can be seen from the table, these factors range from parents' choices about occupational work and involvement in household work and parenting to knowledge about the realities of dual-career family life, such as those just discussed. Some of these may apply to lesbian dual-career relationships as well. For example, women who enter into relationships with other women are also influenced by how their own parents integrated work and family responsibilities, but the influence is likely different because of the absence of heterosexual dynamics associated with gender roles. Moreover, because they grow up knowing that a man will not provide for them, women in lesbian relationships also likely have less conflict about how to integrate occupational and family roles.

**TABLE 4.2**
**Areas to Consider in Planning Ahead for a Dual-Career Relationship**

*Parents' Attitudes and Lifestyle*
   (e.g., was mother employed, was father involved in household work, what visions
   does each parent hold for their daughter?)
*Woman's Self-Views Regarding Work and Family*
   (e.g., does she hold the view that although both partners may be employed the
   woman holds primary responsibility for the home and children or does she see both
   partners actively integrating occupational and family roles; how important is
   continuing in her own career, being in a role-sharing marriage?)
*Essential Spouse Characteristics*
   (e.g., how important is a partner who shares in household work, who views women
   as equal with men, who is successful in a career? who centers life around yours?)
*Anticipating Possible Future Difficulties*
   (e.g., trying to locate two good positions, getting both partners to share household
   work, feeling competitive with one's partner career-wise, deciding on having a child)

Daughters observe and directly experience the way that their parents
combine work and family roles. Parents' decisions not only model a
family pattern but also help shape a daughter's self-concept and what she
sees as possible for herself. Was a woman's mother able to pursue full-
time employment or did her responsibilities limit her to part-time work?
Was she able to use her college degree or go on to college? Was her
employment considered a "job" or a "career"? Was a woman's father an
active participant in day-to-day parenting? Day-to-day household work?
How satisfied did each parent seem with the choices they made? Did they
communicate certain hopes and aspirations to their daughter and/or
provide experiences that broadened or narrowed her life views? Research
indicates that the lifestyle parents pursue has an effect on what daughters—and sons—see as possibilities for themselves (Hoffman, 1989). Our
research, for example, indicates that daughters who perceived their parents as role-sharing are more likely to plan for role-sharing marriages than
daughters reared in more traditional family environments.

Planning ahead also includes consideration of desirable partner characteristics. Gilbert (1985) found that heterosexual partners who achieved
role-sharing marriages discussed during courtship what their expectations were for themselves and their future partner in areas such as career
pursuits, caring for children, and managing household work. Those
who did not were more likely to find themselves in traditional patterns
that they had neither wanted nor anticipated. Areas of dual-career
family life that need to be discussed with potential partners include the
importance of having a partner who is financially independent, successful in a career, and so on; attitudes about women and men,
particularly whether men are viewed as entitled and superior; and the
importance of having a child and assumptions about childrearing as
reflected, say, in the willingness to alter their own work schedules for

parenting responsibilities. Clearly a man who believes that women should not work outside the home or someone who is likely to devalue the work of her or his partner would not be a good candidate for a role-sharing, dual-career relationship. Most women planning for dual-career relationships, regardless of their sexual preference or orientation, want partners who can be supportive of their career, can enter into an emotionally intimate relationship, and are willing to share in the tasks of maintaining a home and family.

Planning ahead extends to anticipating the difficulties of this emerging lifestyle. Earlier sections of the chapter outlined the gender processes that inhibit dual-career family functioning and specific internal and external factors influencing women's choices. Anticipating the realities of a dual-career lifestyle makes it easier to cope with situations and difficulties when they occur. Certain situations almost always occur—integrating work and family, locating and relocating, deciding on whether and when to have a child and on how to handle childcare. It is not always easy to make the decisions associated with dual-career relationship patterns, but planning ahead can establish goals and values that lay the foundation for the kind of relationship desired by both partners.

All couples are different and need to find solutions that fit their values, personalities, passions, and needs. Couples need to consider how much each person would like to work (e.g., 20, 30, 40, or 50 hours a week). Will they have children, and if so, during what part of their children's lives will each work? Will childcare services be employed? How will the domestic responsibilities be managed? How will finances be negotiated? And how will work responsibilities be prioritized? Many careers require activities such as continuing education or travel that affect the other person in the relationship. Obviously, questions about location and relocation will arise. These issues are crucial to the fabric of career counseling. Planning ahead in these ways can prevent or lessen many of the struggles and concerns that generally arise.

## THE COUNSELOR

Counselors act as the carriers and enforcers of values in their work with clients. They can reinforce the gender stereotypes, patriarchal values, and heterosexist beliefs that limit all women, or they can provide an affirmative and empowering haven in which women can reach their potential. Professionals working with women who contemplate or are involved in dual-career relationships also must recognize the resistances within themselves to relationships based on the premises of male–female equality and the integration of occupational and family systems as normative. Very few practitioners have themselves experienced the kind of relationships many women today are wanting help in achieving—relationship interdependency free of the constraints of gender—a new kind of interpersonal relationship, which gives both partners the freedom to involve themselves in the human endeavors of love and work and which allows new forms of intimacy and interdependency to develop between partners and between both parents and their children.

There is another reason counselors must recognize and work through their own resistances to dual-career families. It is the counselor's responsibility to validate and normalize the myriad of emotions and thoughts that may emerge for women planning for and living in dual-career relationships. Their emotions, fears, and experiences need to be understood within the reality of the two-career family today. When a women comes in furious with her boss, her well-meaning partner, or a childcare worker, the last thing she wants to hear is, "quit." Her fury must be understood and worked through within the context of her reality and desires, not the counselor's. We have made suggestions throughout the chapter for ways to integrate this material into the ongoing process of career counseling. As our example helps illustrate, crucial to this integration is recognizing that the social context of women's lives must be brought into their career counseling.

Taking on new images of themselves as women is usually associated with a good deal of emotion. Many issues must be identified and worked through. Feelings of confusion, rage, helplessness, despair, fear, and grief are not uncommon in women struggling to work out location or relocation decisions, the dilemmas created by unsupportive work environments, the difficulties in working out role-sharing with partners, and so forth. Often career advancement will necessitate actions that force women to make choices that are unpopular with their partners or support network. This may require facing up to internalized beliefs about self-worth and entitlement. By the same token, a woman's partner may be facing decisions that feel threatening to her or the relationship. It is at this time that she may most want to explore feelings of dependency or insecurity. Alternatively, she may feel resentful about having to alter her own career path to accommodate what appears to be legitimate demands of her partner. Learning how to negotiate joint decisions is difficult, especially in relationships that take place in what remains a very much gendered society.

## SUMMARY

Recent changes in women's roles and self-perceptions have had and continue to have enormous impact in areas that range from career decisions and personal relations to societal assumptions about power and privilege. Young women now have more freedom to shape themselves than young women anywhere or at any time in history. That freedom at times is a lonely and difficult burden, particularly when tradition dampens spirits and limits opportunities. In counseling women for dual-career families the real and imagined difficulties must be addressed and their courage and self-conviction strengthened, not undermined.

Especially crucial to the counseling process with these women is an understanding of traditional and emergent views of gender and gender roles that directly pertain to the dual-career family patterns. Gender extends beyond the individual and operates in the structures of society as well as in the dynamics of work and family relationships. Gender-related internal factors such as assumptions of female dependency and nurturance and male superiority and privilege, and external factors such as homophobia, sexual discrimination, and sexual harassment influence the explicit and implicit choices made by women who enter into dual-career relationships.

Gender processes are crucial to women's career development irrespective of an individual woman's sexual orientation. Yet these perspectives necessarily differ for lesbian and heterosexual women in dual-career families because of the structural differences associated with the gender of their respective partners. For example, the construct of male and female gender roles with its accompanying expectations, which is critical to understanding the issues for counseling women entering heterosexual marriages, does not apply in a parallel way to relationships between members of the same sex (Morin, 1977). The meaning of role-sharing or establishing an egalitarian relationship differs dramatically when we move from a relationship centered around gender differences to one centered around gender sameness.

Dual-career family patterns based not only on egalitarian role relations with a partner but also on the compatability of occupational and family systems are still emerging in our society. Those doing career counseling for women wanting careers and family life are engaging in an exciting and complex process that, done well, can enhance the lives of the women (and men) they counsel as well as their own lives as individuals and as members of a changing society.

## REFERENCES

Aldous, J. (1990). The impact of workplace family policies. *Journal of Family Issues, 11*(4), whole issue.

Angrist, S. S. (1974). The study of sex roles. In C. Perucci & D. Targ (Eds.), *Marriage and the family: A critical analysis and proposal for change* (pp. 182–188). New York: McKay.

Aries, E. (1987). Gender and communication. In P. Shaver & C. Hendrick (Eds.), *Review of personality and social psychology* (pp. 149–176). Newbury Park, CA: Sage.

Bandura, A. (1977). Self-efficacy: Toward a unifying theory of behavioral change. *Psychological Review, 84*(2), 191–215.

Barnett, R. C., & Baruch, G. K. (1987). Social roles, gender, and psychological distress. In R. C. Barnett, L. Biener, & G. K. Baruch (Eds.), *Gender and stress* (pp. 122–143). New York: Free Press.

Bernard, J. (1974). *The future of motherhood*. New York: Dial Press.

Bernard, J. (1981). The good provider role: Its rise and fall. *American Psychologist, 36*, 1–12.

Betz, N. E., & Fitzgerald, L. F. (1987). *The career psychology of women*. Orlando, FL: Academic Press.

Betz, N. E., & Hackett, G. (1981). The relationship of career-related self-efficacy expectations to perceived career options in college women and men. *Journal of Counseling Psychology, 28*(28), 399–410.

Betz, N. E., & Hackett, G. (1983). The relationship of mathematics self-efficacy expectations to the selection of science-based college majors. *Journal of Vocational Behavior, 23*, 329–345.

Blumstein, P., & Schwartz, P. (1983). *American couples*. New York: William Morrow.

Brown, C. A. (1987). The new patriarchy. In C. Bose, R. Feldberg & N. Sokoloff (Eds.), *Hidden aspects of women's work* (pp. 137–160). New York: Praeger.

Brown, L. S. (1989). New voices, new visions: Toward a lesbian/gay paradigm for psychology. *Psychology of Women Quarterly, 13*, 445–458.

Cline, R. (1988, October 24). Cartoon. *The New Yorker*, p. 67.

Crosby, F. J. (Ed.) (1987). *Spouse, parent, worker: On gender and multiple roles*. New Haven, CT: Yale University Press

Davis, B. M., & Gilbert, L. A. (1989). Effect of dispositional and situational influences on women's dominance expression in mixed-sex dyads. *Journal of Personality and Social Psychology, 57*, 294–300.

Deaux, K. (1984). From individual differences to social categories: Analysis of a decade's research on gender. *American Psychologist, 39*, 105–116.

Deaux, K. (1985). Sex and gender. In L. Porter & M. Rosenzweig (Eds.), *Annual review of psychology 1985* (Vol. 36, pp. 49–81). Palo Alto, CA: Annual Reviews.

Deaux, K., & Major, B. (1987). Putting gender into context: An interactive model of gender-related behavior. *Psychological Review, 94*, 369–389.

Douvan, E. (1976). The role of models in women's professional development. *Psychology of Women Quarterly, 1*, 5–20.

Eldridge, N. S., & Gilbert, L. A. (1990). Correlates of relationship satisfaction in lesbian couples. *Psychology of Women Quarterly, 14*, 43–62.

England, P., Chassie, M., & McCormack, L. (1982). Skill demands and earning in female and male occupations. *Sociology and Social Research, 66*(2), 147–168.

Ferree, M. M. (1990). Beyond separate spheres: Feminism and family research. *Journal of Marriage and the Family, 52*, 866–884.

Flexner, E. (1959). *Century of struggle: The women's rights movement in the United States*. Cambridge, MA: Harvard University Press.

Fowlkes, M. R. (1980). *Behind every successful man: Wives of medicine and academe*. New York: Columbia University Press.

Fowlkes, M. R. (1987). The myth of merit and male professional careers: The roles of wives. In N. Gerstel & H. E. Gross (Eds.), *Families and work* (pp. 347–360). Philadelphia: Temple University Press.

Gilbert, L. A. (1984). Female development and achievement. In A. Rickel, M. Gerrard & I. Iscoe (Eds.), *Social and psychological problems of women* (pp. 5–18). Washington, DC: Hemisphere.

Gilbert, L. A. (1985). *Men in dual-career families: Current realities and future prospects.* Hillsdale, NJ: Lawrence Erlbaum Associates.

Gilbert, L. A. (Ed.) (1987). Dual-career families in perspective. *The Counseling Psychologist, 15*(1), whole issue.

Gilbert, L. A. (1988). *Sharing it all: The rewards and struggles of two-career families.* New York: Plenum.

Gilbert, L. A. (1993). *Two careers/One family.* Newbury Park, CA: Sage.

Gilbert, L. A., & Dancer, L. S. (1991). Dual-earner families in the United States and adolescent development. In S. Lewis, H. Hootsmans, & D. Izraeli, *Crossnational perspectives on dual-earner families* (pp. 151–171). Beverly Hills, CA: Sage.

Gilbert, L. A., Dancer, L. S., Rossman, K. M., & Thorn, B. L. (1991). Assessing perceptions of occupational-family integration. *Sex Roles, 24,* 107–119.

Gilbert, L. A., & Evans, S. (1985). Dimensions of same-gender student-faculty role-model relationships. *Sex Roles, 12,* 111–123.

Gilbert, L. A., & Rachlin, V. (1987). Mental health and psychological functioning of dual-career families. *Counseling Psychologist, 15,* 7–49.

Gilbert, L. A., & Rossman, K. M. (1992). Gender and the mentoring process. *Professional Psychology: Research and Practice, 23,* 233–238.

Guelzow, M. G., Bird, G. W., & Koball, E. H. (1991). An exploratory path analysis of the stress process for dual-career men and women. *Journal of Marriage and the Family, 53,* 151–164.

Hackett, G. (1985). Role of mathematics self-efficacy in the choice of math-related majors of college women and men: A path analysis. *Journal of Counseling Psychology, 32*(1). 47–56.

Hackett, G., Betz, N. E., O'Halloran, M. S., & Romac, D. S. (1990). Effects of verbal and mathematics task performance on task and career self-efficacy and interest. *Journal of Counseling Psychology, 37*(2), 169–177.

Hare-Mustin, R. T. (1991). Sex, lies, and headaches: The problem is power. *Journal of Feminist Family Therapy, 3*(1/2), 39–61.

Hare-Mustin, R. T., & Marecek, J. (1990). *Making a difference: Psychology and the construction of gender.* New Haven, CT: Yale University Press.

Heilbrun, C. G. (1988). *Writing a woman's life.* New York: Ballantine Books.

Hoffman, L. W. (1989). Effects of maternal employment in the two-parent family. *American Psychologist, 44,* 283–292.

Holland, D. C., & Eisenhart, M. A. (1991). *Educated in romance: Women, achievement, and college culture.* Chicago: University of Chicago Press.

Horowitz, E. L. (1991). Shortchanging girls, shortchanging America. *AAUW Outlook,* April/May, whole issue.

Hyde, J. S., and Clark, R. (1989, August). *Maternity leave: The mother's perspective.* Paper presented at the meetings of the American Psychological Association, Boston.

Kamerman, S. B. (1988). Maternity and parenting benefits: An international overview. In E. F. Zigler & M. Frank (Eds.), *The parental leave crisis: Toward a national policy* (pp. 235–244). New Haven, CT: Yale University Press.

Kram, K. E. (1988). *Mentoring at work: Developmental relationships in organizational life.* New York: University Press of America.

Kriger, S. F. (1972). Achievement and perceived parental childrearing attitudes of career women and homemakers. *Journal of Vocational Behavior, 2,* 419–432.

Lent, R. W., Brown, S. D., & Larkin, K. C. (1984). Relation of self-efficacy expectations to academic achievement and persistence. *Journal of Counseling Psychology, 31*(3), 356–362.

Lerner, H. E. (1983). Female dependency in context: Some theoretical and technical considerations. *American Journal of Orthopsychiatry, 53,* 697–705.

Margolies, L., Becker, M., & Jackson-Brewer, K. (1987). Internalized homphobia: Identifying and treating the oppressor within. In Boston Lesbian Psychologies Collective (Eds.), *Lesbian psychologies: Explorations and challenges* (pp. 229–241). Urbana: University of Illinois Press.

Markus, H., & Nurius, P. (1986). Possible selves. *American Psychologist, 41*, 954–969.

McGill, M. E. (1985). *The McGill report on male intimacy.* New York: Holt, Rinehart & Winston.

Miller, R. (1991, August 24). Government not model employer. *Austin American-Statesman,* p. C2.

Morin, S. F. (1977). Heterosexual bias in psychological research on lesbianism and male homosexuality. *American Psychologist, 32*, 629–637.

Morrison, A. M., White, R. P., Velsor, E. V., & the Center for Creative Leadership. (1987). *Breaking the glass ceiling: Can women reach the top of America's largest corporations?* New York: Addison-Wesley.

Moskowitz, M., & Townsend, C. (1991, October). The 85 best companies for working mothers. *Working Mother,* pp. 29–70.

Nevill, D. D., & Schlecker, D. I. (1988). The relation of self-efficacy and assertiveness to willingness to engage in traditional/non-traditional career activities. *Psychology of Women Quarterly, 12*, 91–98.

Osipow, S. H. (Ed.). (1975). *Emerging women: Career analysis and outlooks.* Columbus, OH: Merrill.

Ostertag, P. A., & McNamara, J. R. (1991). "Feminization of psychology." The changing sex ratio and its implications for the profession. *Psychology of Women Quarterly, 15*, 349–369.

Peplau, L. A. (1979). Power in dating relationships. In J. Freeman (Ed.), *Women: A feminist perspective* (2nd ed., pp. 106–121). Palo Alto, CA: Mayfield.

Pharr, S. (1988). *Homophobia: A weapon of sexism.* Little Rock, AR: Chardon.

Pleck, J. H. (1981). A men's movement analysis. In R. A. Lewis (Ed.), *Men in difficult times: Masculinity today and tomorrow* (pp. 234–244). New York: Prentice-Hall.

Pleck, J. H. (1985). *Working wives/working husbands.* Beverly Hills, CA: Sage.

Pleck, J. H. (1987). American fathering in historical perspective. In M. S. Kimmel (Ed.), *Changing men: New directions in research on men and masculinity* (pp. 83–97). Beverly Hills: Sage.

Pleck, J. H. (1990, August). *Family-supportive employer policies and men's participation.* Paper presented at the Annual Meeting of the American Psychological Association, Boston.

Rapoport, R., & Rapoport, R. N. (1969). The dual-career family. *Human Relations, 22*, 3–30.

Rix, S. E. (Ed.). (1987). *The American woman 1987–1988: A report in depth.* New York: Norton.

Rothblum, E. D. (1989). Introduction: Lesbianism as a model of a positive lifestyle for women. *Women in Therapy, 8*, 1–12.

Scarr, S., Phillips, D., & McCartney, K. (1990). Facts, fantasies, and the future of child care in the United States. *Psychological Science, 1*, 26–35.

Schneider, M. S. (1986). The relationships of cohabiting lesbian and heterosexual couples: A comparison. *Psychology of Women Quarterly, 10*, 234–239.

Scott, J. W. (1982). The mechanization of women's work. *Scientific American, 247*, 167–185.

Sewell, W. H., Hauser, R. M., & Wolf, W. C. (1980). Sex, schooling, and occupational status. *American Journal of Sociology, 86*(3), 551–583.

Sherif, C. W. (1982). Needed concepts in the study of gender identity. *Psychology of Women Quarterly, 6*, 375–398.

Slater, S., & Mencher, J. (1991). The lesbian family lifecycle: A contextual approach. *American Journal of Orthopsychiatry, 6*, 372–382.

Spain, D. (1988, November). *Women's demographic past, present, and future.* Paper presented at the Radcliffe Conference on Women in the 21st Century, Cambridge, MA.

Swindell, C. J. (1988). *Math self-efficacy, self role self-concept, and women's consideration of math-related occupations.* Unpublished doctoral dissertation, University of Texas at Austin.

Tannen, D. (1990). *You just don't understand: Women and men in conversations.* New York: William Morrow.

Thompson, L., & Walker, A. J. (1989). Women and men in marriage, work, and parenthood. *Journal of Marriage and the Family, 51,* 845–872.

Tittle, C. K. (1981). *Careers and family: Sex roles and adolescent life plans.* Beverly Hills, CA: Sage.

Unger, R. K. (1990). Imperfect reflections of reality. In R. T. Hare-Mustin & J. Marecek (Eds.), *Making a difference: Psychology and the construction of gender* (pp. 102–149). New Haven, CT: Yale University Press.

U.S. Bureau of Labor Statistics (1989). *Labor force statistics derived from the current population survey: A databook,* Washington, DC: Author.

Vannoy-Hiller, D., & Philliber, W. W. (1989). *Equal partners: Successful women in marriage.* Newbury Park, CA: Sage.

Walker, L. S., Rozee-Koker, P., & Wallston, B. S. (1987). Social policy and the dual-career family: Bringing the social context into counseling. *Counseling Psychologist, 15,* 97–121.

Westkott, M. (1986). *The feminist legacy of Karen Horney.* New Haven, CT: Yale University Press.

# ❧ 5 ❧

# Career Counseling With Ethnic Minority Women

Rosie P. Bingham
*Memphis State University*

Connie M. Ward
*Georgia State University*

Ethnic minority women can see the top rung of the career ladder, but invisible barriers prevent them from grasping it. A "glass ceiling" for the careers of women and minorities in the United States was acknowledged by the Bush presidential administration. Perhaps it is time for psychology and counseling to determine if career counseling can make a difference.

This chapter specifically looks at issues relevant to providing career counseling services to African-American, Asian-American, Arab-American, Latinas (American), and Native American women. There is a great deal of diversity between and within these groups. It is not our intention to provide historical, anthropological, or ethnographical information relevant to each ethnic group or subgroup, but rather to provide concepts the career counselor might use to better gather information about the client and how she views her opportunities in the world of work.

It is now widely accepted that there is a need for a multicultural emphasis in the fields of psychology and counseling. The need has been argued and documented eloquently by Sue (1981) and Pedersen, Draguns, Lonner, and Trimble (1989).

The integration of career counseling and multicultural counseling is in its infancy. Recent articles dealing with ethnic minorities or internationals are still investigating and identifying differences between one group and Whites or developing strategies aimed at providing career counseling to one ethnic, racial, or cultural group. Although the latter both provide theoretical and practical information, they may also deter counselors from learning multicultural counseling. These latter strategies may, unwittingly, set up the expectations for the career counselor to need to have knowledge/experience at the "cultural anthropologist" level. The former still sets up the majority White group as the standard by which other groups are judged. The prospective counselor may decide there is too much to learn and too many experiences to gain in order to be competent. Practicing career counselors may refrain from counseling clients who are racially, ethnically, or culturally different from themselves because they do not feel competent.

The push for integration of career counseling and multicultural counseling may come into conflict with the "one size fits all" and the "test them and tell them" mentality, which enjoys a certain amount of comfort in the career counseling profession. Many times the emphasis is on the manipulation of techniques and resources and not on the development of the individual.

Women requesting career counseling will increasingly present a diversity of perspectives about work, career options, and the integration of family and career, as well as different perspectives about breadth of career opportunities, perception of sexism and racism, and feelings of self-efficacy and empowerment. We contend these diverse perspectives are shaped by race, ethnicity, culture, and gender and should not be overlooked. Rather, they suggest the need for the integration of multicultural counseling and career counseling.

## ASSUMPTIONS

We make several assumptions about the type of career counseling experience for which the information in this chapter would be appropriate. These assumptions are based on our collective experiences providing career counseling to women of color. The assumptions are as follows:

1. The career counselor is familiar with theories of career development, adult development, and theories of counseling. This is a most basic assumption.

2. The career counselor is open to developing sensitivity to and understanding of how a client's world view is shaped by culture, ethnicity, race, and gender.

3. The career counselor is open to acquiring the sensitivity to and understanding of how career counseling orientation, values, and beliefs are shaped by the counselor's own culture, ethnicity, race, and gender.

4. The career counseling length is at least two to six sessions. The emphasis in this chapter is not on use of assessment tools or resources. The emphasis is on developing an interview style or ease that allows the

counselor to gain access to information about the client and helps the client to see the variety of factors, conscious or unconscious, that impact on her career decision. A framework of two to six sessions will allow this type of relationship to develop.

5. The career counselor recognizes and acknowledges the social, political, and economic realities of this nation at a given time in history. This assumption asks the career counselor not to work with the client in a vacuum, but to acknowledge the realities of the world of work the client is hoping to enter. Many times being forthright with an acknowledgment allows the client to voice her own fears or beliefs, which may be powerful inhibitors or motivators, thus giving the counselor more information about how the client views her opportunities in the world of work.

6. The career counselor is open to being challenged in ways that go beyond learning the technology of assessment instruments and familiarity with career resources. We do believe career counselors should have a good understanding of why they are assigning a client a particular assessment. We believe the counselor needs to have a good understanding of the client and her particular career questions to make these determinations. This assessment relies on being a skilled and culturally sensitive career counselor. The challenge is to not hide behind the technology of tests and instruments. We encourage career counselors to ask themselves how their client's race, ethnicity, culture, or gender might impact her test-taking intent, expectations, and the results of the assessment.

7. The career counselor, understanding that a career decision will impact all parts of the life of a client, sees career counseling as an educational process.

8. All the knowledge presented in this chapter may not be used directly in a particular session with a client, but may serve to provide a mindset/framework from which to view diverse career clients.

9. The career counselor is open to being challenged to look differently at the tasks of career counseling. This chapter is devoted to helping those counselors who are open to that challenge to expand the tasks involved in providing career counseling to women of color.

10. All clients will be treated with respect, dignity, and humanity because ultimately it is the client who has the answers to her questions. The counselor has the expert skills to facilitate her finding the answers.

## REVIEW OF LITERATURE

### Career Counseling With Ethnic Minority Female

By the year 2000, it is predicted that racial ethnic minorities will make up one third of the workforce. African-American participation in the workforce will increase by 29%, whereas Hispanic participation will increase by 72%. Given the White birth rate, it is generally accepted that their participation will increase by only 15% as the 21st century dawns. It is clear that the world will be more technological and service-oriented, thus requiring a more educated populace. Ethnic minority women have generally occupied the bottom of the employment ladder. What will happen to these women, given the anticipated economic and demographic changes? How can career counselors help ethnic racial minority women succeed in a world where even the 1992 U.S. Department of Labor admitted that there is a glass ceiling for women and minorities?

Smith (1980) maintained that the research on minority women still remained almost nonexistent. If vocational counseling was born from the changing demographics and economic needs of this century, then clearly career counseling will need to change in response to changing needs of the coming century. Further, if women and minorities will make up the significant increases in the workplace, then career counselors need methods and means for understanding and facilitating the career counseling needs of racial ethnic minority women.

The literature reveals at least five areas that probably affect the career development of racial ethnic minority women: (a) information about the world of work, (b) familial involvement and approval, (c) community influence, role models, and language, (d) impact of socialization, and (e) impact of sexism and racism. Certainly these categories cannot be neatly divided, and they overlap and perhaps are not even separable.

Manese, Sedlacek, and Leong (1988), in a study of the career needs of international students, reported their first priority was to obtain work experience, followed by a need to learn how to prepare for a career, and to talk to a career counselor. Many writers (Evansoki & Wu Tse, 1989; Martin, 1991) purported that ethnic minorities often have limited information about the world of work because they have limited exposure to role models who work in a variety of occupations.

Martin (1991) described the plight of Native Americans, particularly those that live on or near an Indian reservation. He reported unemployment rates of 33%–43%, which is more than five times the national average. So not only is there scarcity in variety of careers, there is also scarcity in the number of people working. Bowman (Bowman & Tinsley, 1991) reported other data that suggest that racial ethnic minorities lack information about the world of work. In a study assessing the concept of vocational realism, she found that lower socioeconomic status (SES) African-American college students were very unrealistic about the amount of money they would earn in various careers after they obtained a college degree. She suggested that the students needed more exposure to live role models rather than media representations.

Evansoki and Wu Tse (1989) supported the need for live role models in their description of a successful career development program for Chinese and Korean youths. They further asserted that it is critically important for role models to be bilingual, and some of the literature must also be written in the native language. Inherent in the discussion is a need for community involvement, a notion supported by Morgan, Guy, Lee, and Cellini (1986), who maintained that community, family, and home may be more central to the decision-making process for Native Americans than jobs and careers.

The role of the family in general counseling with racial ethnic minorities has been documented by numerous authors (Akbar, 1981; Comas-Diaz & Jacobson, 1987; Smith, 1983). There is a growing body of literature that further suggests that the family is equally important in career counseling (Evansoki & Wu Tse, 1989; Wehrly, 1988). Denga (1988) asserted that the family is a key factor in decision making in Nigerian individuals. The family then stresses the occupation's social prestige and influence in community affairs, family occupational stereotypes, religious convictions, and values, social mores, and folkways. Denga (1988) further stated that there is definite sex typing within the families—for example, women are discouraged from entering fields that are seen as competitive with men. For women, family is emphasized over career.

The literature, additionally, indicates that socialization does influence the career path of women. McCormick (1990) maintained that people are greatly influenced by their perception of appropriate careers for men and women. In spite of the movement toward greater vocational access, women still are perceived more often in traditional female jobs. In the self-efficacy literature, Hackett and Betz (1981) maintained that women believe that they can achieve most easily in traditional female careers and tasks. They are less secure in more male occupations. Stickel and Bonett (1991) supported the data provided by Hackett and Betz and expanded it by demonstrating that women also have greater self-efficacy regarding their ability to combine career and family. Gilligan's (1982) work may provide some clues about why women have greater self-efficacy in traditionally feminine tasks and careers. She maintained that women have a different "voice" than men. Whereas men are raised to think independently and aggressively, women are raised to be dependent and relational. It is important to help women learn that there are strengths and weaknesses in both "voices."

For racial ethnic minority women, socialization may be even more complex because added to the gender issues are the racial ethnic issues. Gainor and Forrest (1991) asserted that there are at least four self-referents that impact on the self-concept and career development process for African-American women: psychophysiological self-referent, Afro self-referent, Euro self-referent, and the myself self-referent. Each referent has unique components. For example, the psychophysiological refers to the woman's need for relationship and attachments. The Afro self-referent encompasses the social political realities that the woman believes she must deal with as a result of being a particular race. The Euro referent includes the individualistic focus as well as the messages the Anglo race has about the African-Americans. (Gainor and Forrest believed many of these messages are negative.) The myself referent is to all that is the unique personal history of the woman. Gainor and Forrest (1991) believed that the referent that is most pronounced in a woman will influence her career.

Further, the self-referents may also influence or be influenced by the woman's perception of sexism and racism. Each may affect her decision about which career to enter and how to implement the career once the choice has been made. Evans and Herr (1991) maintained that African-American women have enough anxiety about the barriers presented by sexism and racism that they avoid those careers in which the two are seen as significant barriers.

## Impact of World Views

As researchers and theoreticians included racial ethnic minorities in their work on counseling with the various groups, differences began to emerge. Sue (1981), Nobles (1976), Pedersen (1976), and others indicated that all individuals have ways of perceiving the world or world views that will influence their behavior. Various racial/ethnic groups often have world views that are peculiar to each specific group. For example, Nobles (1976) described a European world view and an African world view. In the European world view the focus is on the individual, survival of the fittest, conquering nature, etc. The African world view on the other hand has features that include a group focus, survival of the tribe or group, and being in tune with nature. Sue (1981) described world views using the concept of internal and external locus of control and internal and external locus of responsibility. He maintained that many ethnic minorities in the United States may believe that they have little external control over much of what happens in their lives. Pedersen (1976) described world views for various ethnic groups, including Native Americans, Hispanics, Asians, African-Americans, and others. Curiously, throughout many of the world views the role of the family is central. In others, as in the Nobles theory of an African world view, the community or group is also key. These notions seem consistent with the previous discussions of the centrality in Native American cultures of the family and the community rather than jobs and careers.

The concept of world views has not been generally applied to the field of career counseling. Yet if these theories are valid it seems reasonable to assume that they would have some importance for career counselors. For example, if a career counselor with a European world view is working with a client with an African world view, the sessions could quickly become less than useful. The counselor would probably believe that the individual should make her decision independent of the family and/or cultural group, whereas the client may believe that she must involve those individuals in the process. The counselor could easily view the client as having separation/individuation problems. The client might view the counselor as selfish and self-centered or possibly as just not understanding. The same kind of problem could exist if the client's family holds one world view and yet, because of exposure to an educational setting or another country, the client has begun to modify her family-of-origin world view. It then becomes crucial for the career counselor to be familiar with world views in order to facilitate the career counseling process.

Janet Helms (1990) held that even if a counselor does understand the concept of world views, more is needed in order to be an effective counselor with ethnic minority clients. Helms (1990) believed that there is a minority identity development process through which each ethnic minority individual goes perhaps continuously. Like the notions of world views, the theory of minority identity development has not been generally applied to the field of career counseling, yet it seems reasonable to believe that one's stage of development would influence the choice and implementation of a career decision. Janet Helms based much of her work on racial identity development on the Negro to Black conversion model proposed by W. E. Cross (1971).

Cross (1971) maintained that part of a Black individual's identity is shaped by her experience in the social milieu of the White majority society. He proposed a four-stage model in which a Black individual will move from a self definition based on a White frame of reference to one that is more internally determined.

First is the preencounter stage, in which the Black individual is very pro-White and anti-Black. The individual wants to be seen as just a human being without a focus on her race. In fact, the person is likely to deny her race or at least devalue it.

Next is the encounter stage. Here the individual comes face to face with racism, discrimination, or prejudice that makes it impossible to deny that her race is a factor. Perhaps she cannot get the job she wants and the only explanation is that she is Black. Or perhaps the "glass ceiling" becomes more visible and it is clear that the thing holding it in place is others' concern about her race. She now is likely to begin to question her white frame of reference. Parham (1989) maintained that there are two phases to this stage: a realization and a decision. First the individual realizes that the preencounter frame of reference is not appropriate. She then makes a decision to adopt a black identity.

The third stage is one of immersion and emersion. The individual now becomes very pro-Black and anti-White. At this stage an individual will likely adopt a Black or Afro-centric lifestyle and prefer interactions with only other Blacks. They have all the outer accoutrements of being Black, yet internally they remain insecure about their Black identity.

The final stage in the Negro to Black conversion model is internalization. Here the individual becomes internally secure with being Black and generally adopts a more pluralistic view of the world, so that while she remains pro-Black she is also pro other ethnic groups. Attitudes toward Whites are less hostile and more realistic, according to Cross (1971).

Atkinson, Morten, and Sue (1983) proposed a similar model, which they call the minority identity development model. They believed that all oppressed people go through a five-stage identity development process that is directly impacted by relationships with the majority group. In their five stages the minority individual goes from a state of depreciating herself and her group while appreciating the majority group, through stages of ever-increasing appreciation of her own group, until she finds a balance of appreciation for herself and all other groups.

Each of these models has research support for their conceptions. However, that support has most often been applied in the area of general counseling. We are proposing that the models have relevance for career counselors. However, career counseling is nearly always minimally a dyadic process. The foregoing identity models focus on the racial identity development of people who are often depicted as the client and most certainly they are the racial ethnic minority persons, yet many times the counselor is a majority-group person, usually White. Theorists have begun to raise questions about White identity development and its impact on the counseling process. Certainly the questions also apply in the career counseling arena.

Sabnani, Ponterotto, and Borodovsky (1991) have summarized the three major White racial-identity models as proposed by Helms (1984), Hardiman (1982), and Ponterotto (1988a). Like the minority identity development models, the stages are not necessarily linear and, in fact, Parham (1989) and Sabnani et al. (1991) suggested that individuals may "loop" back through stages at various points in their lives. The White racial-identity models can most easily be summarized in five stages. In Stage 1, White individuals have no sense of awareness of themselves as racial beings. In fact, Katz (1985) maintained that White individuals often do not recognize that there is a White culture. Stage 2 seems to emerge as a result of interactions with other racial ethnic groups or exposure to knowledge about other cultural groups. At this stage, White individuals will often experience a conflict about wanting to maintain a White status quo and wanting to adopt a more nonracial, humanistic acceptance of other groups. According to Sabnani et al. (1991), these individuals will sometimes experience guilt and depression or anger as a result of the conflict. Stage 3 continues to be conflictual because Whites are forced to break down previous knowledge held about racial ethnic minorities. At this point in order to alleviate some of the guilt experienced in Stage 2 some Whites will become very prominority and perhaps begin to reject internalized racist beliefs or even begin to reject Whiteness in general. Stage 4 represents the other extreme reaction to Stage 2. Here, perhaps as a result of the anger experienced in Stage 2 or perhaps because of rejection by a minority, the White individual retreats into White culture. The individual will perhaps now experience feelings of hostility and/or fear of racial ethnic minority groups members. Stage 5 represents a similar internalization stage as that found in minority identity development models. A White identity is clearly formed and the individual becomes more self and group accepting as well as more pluralist. Sabnani et al. (1991) maintained that the last stage is "marked by a culturally transcendent worldview" (p. 82).

It seems true that if these theories of racial identity development are valid then the career counseling process will be directly influenced by the stage of development of the parties in the counseling relationship. Clearly, there are then numerous variables that can shape the counseling process of career counseling with ethnic minority women. It can seem an overwhelming task, yet if a counselor is to be effective, it is time to give consideration to the cultural influences that are in the process, whether the client acknowledges them or not.

## STEPS TO CAREER COUNSELING WITH ETHNIC MINORITY FEMALE

The actual steps for counseling are really quite simple and probably do not deviate from those in any other counseling relationship. We have identified four steps or phases that require some focus on the counselor, focus on the client, client and counselor agreement on a contract, and implementation and follow-up, or (a) counselor preparation, (b) exploration and assessment of client variables, (c) negotiation and working consensus, and (d) intervention and follow-up. Each step will require the counselor to apply thinking, knowledge, and/or skills that embrace concepts of multicultural counseling.

## Counselor Preparation

We assume that counselors will have received basic skills training in various counselor education or psychological academic programs. To enhance that training we recommend that counselors become familiar with the minimum cross-cultural counseling competencies described by Sue et al. (1982). Cheatham (1990) pointed out that awareness and acceptance of the client's culture should precede the counselor assisting the client with developmental tasks. He believes that counselors need to be knowledgeable of their client's history, future, and culture for their models of intervention to serve African-Americans well. He challenged counselors to question whether their client's choices are obligated or freely exercised and whether these choices have career, social, economic, or societal values.

Counselor preparation involves the counselors, looking at their own cultural, social, political, and economic experiences. The counselors should look for cues to the development of their own world view that shapes their beliefs, values, experiences, and perceptions about the world. If career counselors take the time to identify and gain an understanding of what shapes their own world view, they may be better able to emphasize with the different factors that shape their client's world view. Some questions a career counselor might ask him or herself in the area of counselor preparation are: What cultural messages did I receive as a child about work? How does my social background shape my values about careers? Who has access to certain careers and what careers are socially acceptable? How does my SES impact my ability to emphasize with clients with different SES backgrounds? How do my political views influence my ability to help my career client?

Discussed next are some of the ways that we believe counselors can improve their level of preparation to provide career counseling for ethnic minority women.

*Cultural Sensitivity.*   Cultural sensitivity is gained by being open to the experiences of others. These experiences may seem very different or strange to the career counselor, but exposure to these varied experiences may broaden the career counselor's perspective. Exposure may also provide career counselors with additional frameworks by which to view the clients. Cultural sensitivity is a form of empathy. Being able to understand the problem from the client's perspective means acknowledging, identifying and respecting the client's own cultural experiences.

Guthrie (1976), Nobles (1976), and Warwick (1980) have noted the inappropriateness of using one's own group experience to interpret the experiences of another group. Cheatham (1990) thought the essential message for the helping professions is that the helper may be so culture-bound that the helping interventions come not from the client's cultural perspective and personal motives but exclusively from the counselor's. The notion of culture-boundness is extremely important to the career counseling process where there is a danger of the counselor perfecting a technology and using it on all career clients regardless of their cultural, ethnic, racial, or gender needs.

For example, if an African-American, Asian-American, Native American, or Latin American client is having difficulty making a career decision, it may be inappropriate to merely administer a Strong Interest Inventory, provide an interpretation, and then assume the counseling task is complete. A sensitive counselor needs to explore the client's world view for possible beliefs that make the decision difficult for the client.

*Familiarity with a Body of Cross-Cultural Knowledge.* It is virtually impossible to learn and retain cultural knowledge about all different cultural groups. Therefore, it is important to know how to acquire cultural knowledge. One way is to learn about a racial ethnic group different from one's own group. For example, if Hispanics are a major ethnic group in the geographical area, it is reasonable to study them. It is helpful to know some of the group's history, the local sociopolitical issues facing the group, general family dynamics, and attitudes toward seeking help. The client's career decision will be influenced by each of these factors. Next, it is important to interact with the group in order to increase intuitive and affective understanding of the group. When counselors are discussing sensitive issues in the decision-making process, such understanding will facilitate the counselor's ability to understand some of the nonverbal features of the session. The authors believe that if one becomes sensitive and knowledgeable about one body of cultural information, it becomes easier to apply the learning procedures to other ethnic racial minority groups.

*Sociopolitical Strengths of Ethnic Groups.* Judith Katz (1985) maintained that the field of counseling psychology is built on sociopolitical percepts. She believed that in order to be effective multicultural counselors it is important for counselors to understand the social and political nature of counseling. It is equally important to understand the social and political aspects of the clients with whom the counselor works. Otherwise the counselor can fall victim to judging and evaluating clients from a set of beliefs that disavows the logic and strength of the client and her racial ethnic group. Katz (1985) wrote that the field of counseling psychology is built on principles derived from White culture, such as a Protestant work ethic, focus on the individual, action orientation, status and power, etc. A counselor with such an orientation might overlook the social and political strength in having a group focus and a more egalitarian view of power. A client could be inadvertently viewed as weak and unable to make an individual decision. It is important to have a general understanding of the relative strengths that clients bring to the career counseling sessions.

Just as the counselor must have some sense of the strengths that clients bring as a result of being part of a cultural group, it is important to not fall prey to stereotyping clients. The theme from the environmental movement applies here: "Think globally; act locally." In other words, while remembering an ethnic group's social/political strengths, it is important to counsel from the strengths of the individual (Copeland, 1977). When working with an Asian client, then, it might be a strength to involve the family in the career decision, whereas with some African-Americans it might be wise to involve the client's spiritual leader. Those counselors wishing further information might look at the Brown-Collins and Sussewell (1986) comprehensive view of African-American self-concept formation, which incorporates personal, social, historical, or political aspects of African-American women's lives.

*Receptivity to Client as Cultural Teacher.* It is rare that a counselor will gather and maintain enough experience or knowledge about all ethnic groups to be constantly ready with knowledge and sensitivity for every ethnic minority who comes for counseling. The idea that the counselor should know all before involving self in multicultural counseling is many times a barrier to acknowledging its legitimacy. One of the most important tools of multicultural counseling is the counselor's ability to step away from an "all-knowing" role to one where the counselor is receptive to learning from the client as the cultural informant/teacher. Such receptivity will need to be balanced with the rush for answers that sometimes accompanies career clients. Arrendondo (1985) suggested that in order for counseling professionals to be effective they must examine their own biases and assumptions and be willing to ask for assistance if they do not know how to proceed. She believed asking for help gives the therapist an opportunity to learn from others and prevents the unintentional oppression of the client.

*Counselor's World View.* We have previously mentioned the importance of understanding the concept of world views. In order to be an effective career counselor it is first crucial that the counselor understand his or her own world view. It has been generally espoused that the counselor is the expert in the relationship, and much of the focus has been on the necessity of the counselor understanding the client's worldview (Sue, 1981; Pedersen, 1976; Nobles, 1976). However, it is likely to be very difficult for counselors, if they have not come to understand that they are operating from a set of beliefs about life that impact their ability to understand what the client is saying. Ibrahim (1985), in describing her use of Kluckhorn's (1951) work, maintained that individuals may use the same words, yet misunderstand each other because of the difference in the "structure of their reasoning."

It is conceivable that a client with an African world view might solicit the services of a career counselor with a European world view. The client could be having an extremely difficult time deciding between becoming a teacher and pursuing a dream to be an entrepreneur. In a typical counseling session, the client might be given a Strong Interest Inventory, opportunities to use the career library, and perhaps even shadowing experiences with teachers and entrepreneurs. Yet no decision is reached. The counselor, operating from a European world view, may have interpreted the problem as a simple individual decision-making process. In fact, the client may have been interpreting her interest in business ownership as selfish, with too little regard for her ethnic group. Unless the counselor understands that she has a world view that is different from that of her client, this potential error or others like it loom large. The counselor must therefore ask questions like: What is my world view? How is it shaped? What are my parameters of tolerance for others' world views? Can I even accept the possibility of other world views?

*Counselor's Racial Identity Development.* Parham (1989), Helms (1984), Cross (1971), Sabnani et al. (1991), and many others have indicated that racial identity development will impact the process and outcome of counseling. A counselor's racial identity development may or may not have direct bearing on a client's career decision. However, assuming the theories are accurate, the stage of the counselor's racial identity development can significantly influence the quality of the counseling relationship. For example, if the counselor is White and is in Stage 4 (Ponterotto, 1988a), he or she may experience hostile feelings toward minority clients. The counselor could begin to believe that none of the clients are able to think for themselves. If the counselor is unfamiliar with theories of racial identity development and world views, then the problems will likely be attributed to the client rather than understood in context of the counselor's own development. It thus becomes clearer that it is important for counselors to understand their own racial identity development and that of their client's. Each stage will have implications for how the counselor processes the information received from clients. Even if the counselor is in a prominority stance, the results for the career client could be negative because the counselor may overcompensate for feelings of guilt and fail to appropriately confront the client.

It is equally important for minority counselors to be aware of their racial identity development because similar kinds of results can occur. For example, if an African-American counselor in Stage 1, preencounter, is working with a minority client in the immersion–emersion stage, the relationship is likely to be conflictual with the client believing that the counselor could not possibly understand her or that it is she, the client, who should be helping the counselor. On the other hand, the counselor may see the client as hostile, unrealistic, and perhaps inappropriate. The career issues can easily be lost in the relationship issues.

*Counselor's Comfort with Engaging Ethnic Women Clients.*   Some of the work in career counseling involves helping the client to acknowledge the messages, stereotypes, and ideas she has about the world of work. Assumptions, misunderstanding, fantasies, and much false information about careers and their requirements are readily available from "well-meaning others." The career counselor may need to engage the ethnic minority client in a process to check the validity of her information. A culturally skilled career counselor will know enough about himself or herself to explore the places in the career counseling session where the counselor's discomfort may get in the way of helping the client to explore her feelings and define and meet her own needs.

Comas-Diaz (1989) wrote about the need for therapists to explore their ethnocultural identity and look for real or potential overlap with that of their client's. Her premise was that the unresolved ethnocultural issues of the therapist may be reflected back to the clients in the form of feelings. Although Comas-Diaz wrote directly about a therapeutic relationship, we believe that some of the same countertransferential feelings can present themselves in the career counseling sessions with ethnic minority women. This could become crucial when the career counselor has to engage the client in a way that helps the career client to challenge some of her assumptions about the career exploration process and careers in general.

Yang (1991) suggested using a multifaceted approach for engaging Chinese American women. She believed the career counselor should play many roles, including mentor, advisor, educator, and advocate. She encouraged the counselor to remain flexible to adapt to the client's needs.

She believed that in light of some inherent family–work–cultural conflicts, the career counselor should be active in teaching the Chinese-American women role classification and renegotiation skills, as well as skills to help these women define and meet their own needs. We think Yang's (1991) ideas are also appropriate for other ethnic minority women.

Given these various techniques, a counselor may become uncomfortable with actively engaging the ethnic minority client. Again the career counselor would want to have explored his or her own sensitivity and comfort level with engaging ethnic minority women at the level of activity Yang suggested.

## Exploration and Assessment

After appropriate counselor preparation it is time for the exploration of the client's perception of the career issue and the client's receptivity and openness to assessment of these issues. During this phase the career counselor and the client will work to clarify the career issues. Part of the clarifying process involves the assessment of how the career questions are impacted by issues such as culture, ethnicity, race, or gender. The career counselor can take a cue from the client by the amount of information provided in these areas. The counselor must keep in mind that factors such as counselor's culture, race, ethnicity, or gender may hinder or encourage the disclosure of this information. Other factors, such as familiarity with the counseling process, client comfort, counselor openness, or the type counseling relationship developed, may impact the amount of information provided.

*Identification of Career Issues.* A skilled career counselor develops a relationship with the client and helps her to probe more deeply to determine the components of her career questions. Because coming for career counseling may be the ethnic minority woman's first encounter with counseling, the career counselor will need to balance helping the client to determine her own questions with the pressure from the client for answers. Some researchers (Leong, 1985; Vontress, 1971) have indicated that ethnic minorities like counselors who are active and directive. A counselor might therefore be tempted to provide answers before either the client or the counselor understands the question. Many times the career question is complicated by financial, family, and/or academic problems/concerns. These issues and their impact on the career questions will need to be explored. The culturally skilled career counselor will work with the client to empower her to determine her career questions and develop the confidence and competence to answer these questions.

*Presence or Absence of Racial or Cultural Information.* The career counselor needs to be sensitive to whether the client presents racial or cultural information in relation to her career question. This information can be presented verbally when the ethnic minority woman talks about her career decision in the context of her ethnic, racial, or cultural identity.

Pyant and Yanico's (1991) review suggested that positive mental health for African-American women is associated with positive racial identification. The racial or cultural information could take the form of expressed limitations or obstacles. In this case, the career counselor needs to assess whether there are negative feelings associated with the client's feeling about her culture, ethnicity, or race or whether the limitations or obstacles are legitimate.

Yang (1991) maintained that Chinese-American women represent a silent subgroup whose cultural values and specific career needs remain unexpressed and even mysterious. It may be that these women's career issues could remain hidden if the career counselor is not culturally sensitive. The counselor must be able to sort through the cultural information in order to clarify the career needs.

*Client's Racial or Ethnic Identification.* It is all too easy to assume that all ethnic, racial minority clients want to be identified with their cultural groups. Some do; others do not. The counselor must assess the client's preferences. A client may look like one racial or ethnic group yet identifies as another. Given the theories on racial identity development, it is apparent that the client's identification can have a significant impact on the career counseling process. It is useful for the counselor to assess the client's ethnocultural identification. A fairly straightforward way of doing that was described by Lillian Comas-Diaz and Frederick Jacobsen (1987). The authors presented a five-step model for completing an ethnocultural assessment. First it is important to obtain a history of the ethnic and cultural heritage of the client. Critical to this step is an inclusion of the ethnocultural heritage of the client's parents. Second, the counselor needs to assess what led the client's family to move to a different cultural setting or different country. Third, assess the family's ethnocultural identification since arriving in the new culture. Fourth, the counselor needs to know how the client views her ethnocultural identity in the current culture separate from that of the family's. And finally, the counselor needs to assess his or her own ethnocultural background in order to discover similarities with that of the client. Such information can be critical to the career counselor who wants to understand something of the pressures facing the client whose family has career expectations that directly derive from the circumstances of the family's move from the culture of origin to a new culture. For example, if an ethnic minority family moved from an agrarian impoverished culture to a large urban area with the expectation that now the children would go to college and become middle-class professionals, and the child, your client, does not want the same thing, then the effect on the career counseling process can be significant. The problems can be further complicated if the client does not even claim the same ethnocultural identification as that of the family. Clients can also experience a significant impact on their career decisions when it is the family that wants to deny the original ethnocultural identification. It is incumbent upon the counselor to have some sensitivity to these ethnic and racial identification potentialities and their possible effect on the career counseling process.

*Support of Family of Origin.* Family support can mean the difference in a client selecting one occupation over another, furthering one's education, working outside or inside the home, the role of children in an ethnic minority woman's life, etc. The family can even have views that will influence the woman's comfort with seeking help. In some ethnic minority families, going for counseling is seen as weakness and sometimes as a breach of the family trust. A client could become so hesitant about seeking help as a result of such values that the counselor could view her as resistive to change. All the work of the career counselor can be sabotaged if the counselor fails to assess the client's family support. If the family is supportive of the client's wishes, then the counseling process will be considerably smoother. If, however, there is little or no familial support, then the counselor may need to help the client sort through all of the implications. In fact, it may not even be clear to the client that family support is an area of concern. A few well-worded straightforward questions may bring the issue to the surface. Questions could be as simple as, how does your family feel about your career? What do your parents want you to do/be?

*Familial Obligations.* There is an entire body of literature on the various roles and responsibilities of women. This is merely a reminder that the ethnic minority woman may have some special family obligations that cause her even more problems. For example, it is often cited in the literature that African-American families are extended. For some women that means having responsibilities for other peoples' children, distant aunts and uncles, and sometimes friends. The African-American woman may not be aware of the extent to which such obligations are dictating her career choices. Other racial ethnic minority women will have some of the same experiences. Again, it is necessary for the career counselor to assess this area and help the women resolve any surrounding issues.

*High School Experiences.* The authors have found that an ethnic minority woman's experiences with school will shape her self-concept and impact her feelings of self-efficacy. If she has had positive academic experiences and support from teachers and counselor, then she may believe there is a wide range of opportunities available to her in the world of work. If the woman has had negative experiences with school, these may transfer to her beliefs about career opportunities available to her and her ability to be successful in life.

The perceptions of the breadth or narrowness of options available to the client is influenced by the exposure to career information, role models, educational information, and so forth gained while in high school. Further exposure depends on the sensitivity of the high school administration and the energy put into sharing information with all students. Many times ethnic minority students get locked out of the information or opportunity loop for such exposure.

At other times, ethnic minority women meet with overt hostility when they strive for opportunities, which are perceived by some to be outside some teachers', counselors', and administrators' traditional expectations for them. Such individuals sometimes unwittingly place limitations on ethnic minority women based on their biases or stereotypes.

Encouragement in high school can motivate a student to tackle college even though the student may be the first of family to do so. Many times ethnic minority female clients will present a lack of confidence that has its roots in negative high school experiences. The client may have internalized the messages of limitations and may present them as her own self-assessment. It would be important to explore these messages, to seek their origins and help the woman modify her self-assessment.

*Level of Self-Esteem.* The career counselor needs to look for information regarding the ethnic minority woman's perceptions about her competence, her level of confidence in her abilities, and her feelings of self- sufficiency, because each of these will influence her level of self-esteem. The career counselor should look for verbalizations from the ethnic minority female client that reflect positive or negative perceptions of her ability to make things happen for herself. The counselor should reinforce the positive perceptions and try to find the source of the negative perceptions.

Evans and Herr (1991) maintained that African-American women may have perfected a coping system of avoiding potentially successful working environments. They believed these women may lower or alter their career goals to avoid the dual effects of racism and sexism in the workplace. The women may inadvertently avoid the more successful work environments that could positively affect their self-esteem.

Gainor and Forest (1991), in their discussion of Brown-Collins and Sussewell's (1986) models of African-American women's self-concept, made several conclusions for the models' implications for career decisions and career counseling. They concluded that:

> If we agree that self concept is important in career decisions, and if we further agree that one's historical, social, and personal experiences influence self concept, then we must agree that the unique components of the African-American women's self concept need to be considered when counseling her about her career decisions. The multiple self-referent model provides a framework for examining not only the personal experiences of Black women, but also their historical experiences in the country, the influences of the Black community and White American culture as well as the interactive effects of racism and sexism. Career counselors would be remiss in their responsibilities if they did not consider these aspects of African-American women's lives. (p. 271)

Pyant and Yanico (1991) found that racial identity attitudes are related to the psychological health of African-American woman. They found that women who endorsed pro-White/anti-Black attitudes (preencounter attitudes) reported more psychological and physical distress and lower self-esteem. The career counselor may therefore need to address self-esteem issues before proceeding to the career issues. Minimally the counselor must be aware that the level of self-esteem may be intruding upon the ethnic woman's career decision-making process.

## Negotiations and Working Consensus

After the counselor has properly assessed many of the ethnocultural issues that might affect the career counseling process, it is then time to begin to negotiate with the client and obtain consensus around the expected goals and outcomes of counseling.

*Goals for Career Counseling.* Perhaps the first item of business is agreement on definition of the terms to be used in the counseling experience. If a client is seeking career counseling help, the counselor needs to determine the extent to which she wants help and the type of help desired. For example, what does the client mean when she says she is trying to decide on a career? Does she mean she wants a job to supplement her family income? Does she mean she wants a career that has a defined path with perhaps opportunities for growth and possible promotion? Does she mean she wants a professional career like that of a medical doctor or lawyer? It is easy to assume that clients and counselors mean the same thing when they are using the same words. However, as Ibrahim (1985) reminded us, sometimes the reasoning structure is different and sometimes words just have different meanings for different cultural groups.

Such a defining process will help the client and counselor determine what the goals of the counseling process will be. Interestingly enough, Stabb and Cogdal (1990) discovered that often it is easier for an ethnic minority to come for career counseling when the real need is for personal counseling. At other times the client is actually experiencing academic trouble and seeks a career decision to solve an academic difficulty. As long as the counselor is culturally skilled, then traditional goal-setting techniques can be modified and used to help ethnic minority women establish career goals. It is just incumbent upon the counselor to remember that sometimes the roles for women in various ethnic groups are highly specified and family bound. It is probably not important or even possible to remember for which groups this applies. It is just important to remember to assess it appropriately with the client.

*Perception of Roles of Women.* Martin (1991) asserted that the individual's knowledge of the world of work depends on the breadth and depth of past work experiences and the degree of exposure to people working in a wide range of occupations. He looked at the lack of work models for Native American youth, and it would make sense that the number of working role models would be even more limited for Native American women.

Bowman and Tinsley (1991) looked at the development of vocational realism as it relates to gender and age in their study of Black college students. Their findings did not support the hypothesis that vocationally realistic Black male students would be younger than vocationally realistic Black female students. This study's findings differed from the observation of Ginzberg, Ginzberg, Axelrod, and Herma (1951) that women make final vocational decisions later than men. Bowman and Tinsley's (1991) finding indicated similar levels of career decision making progress for Black males and females. The women in the study did not seem to place their career decisions on hold or experience greater uncertainty than the men.

Granrose and Cunningham (1988) looked at the intention to work after finishing college and starting a family for Black and White college students. Their review found that both Black and White women tended to underestimate the probability that they will be working mothers. But

Black women were more likely to expect they would be working after college. The authors' intentions were to find out what factors caused the Black women to intend to work so that they might identify ways of helping all young women be more realistic about the future.

Further, they pointed out that young women make choices very early in their lives that open or close career options for them. These choices, such as pursuing higher education, majoring in a specific field, marrying early or later, or even the choice of an entry level job, will have a major impact on the type of job or childcare options available to the woman when she must decide whether to work or not work after childbirth.

Finally, the authors found the Black women in their sample to be more likely than the White women to favor earning a personal income, advancing their careers, and running a smooth, well-disciplined family. These women were more likely to indicate that they expected to gain what they value by working. The Black women were more likely than the White women to have mothers that worked and approved of their working, and these women had a more positive attitude toward working after childbirth. Although these two groups had similar family and personal incomes, the Black women expected to achieve this family income through continuous work. This study clearly demonstrated that these two ethnic groups hold different perceptions about the women's work role within the family.

Yang (1991) looked at the career concerns of first- and second-generation Chinese-American women. She saw these women experiencing "triple jeopardy" because of (a) traditional Confucian patriarchal thought not endorsing equality between males and females, (b) problems resulting from the social ramifications of sexual and racial differences, and (c) stress and strain resulting from the loss of extended family support systems and inadequate coping mechanisms necessary to reduce the conflicts inherent in living in two cultures. It was her contention that Chinese-American females are not raised to seek equality with men. The traditional value of taking care of the family and the home is still prized for women. She stated that there are few role models for balancing career and family needs for these women. She maintained that these women are unlikely to find role models within their own cultural group, and social differences may preclude them from identifying with cross-race or cross-gender models. Yang (1991) stated that women who devote their minds, skills, and hearts to their family may feel isolated and out of step with the time.

The Chinese-American woman may approach career counseling with some apprehension, because she may wonder if the career counselor will push her to want a career outside of the home or may not be sensitive to her particular concerns about working outside the home when so many American women are in the work force. The career counselor needs to be open to different perceptions and comfort levels with the role of women and work.

Arbona (1989) used data from the 1980 Census to look at the distribution of jobs among the sexes as well as between Whites, Blacks, and Hispanics. He found Black women to be overrepresented in the social and lower level conventional jobs and underrepresented in investigative and enterprising work. He found Hispanic women to be overrepresented in low-level realistic work and in moderate-level social and conventional jobs. They were underrepresented in investigative and enterprising work. Because role models are important to the development of career and world of work knowledge, many Black and Hispanic females are being exposed to a very narrow range of career options. It is our contention that this exposure will impact on the client's perceptions of the roles of women.

We encourage the career counselors to let the ethnic minority women tell them how they want work to be a part of their lives. Information about the work experiences of mothers or other adult female relatives will give the counselor some idea of the role models she has been exposed to. If the client mentions careers she is open to, the counselor might inquire how she decided to include these occupations on the list. Again her answers might reflect influences from family, friends, and others. A "career fantasy" exercise might help the woman to expand her perception of the options available to women. Small group exercises and informational interviews may broaden the client's exposure. The counselor should then be open to the possible culturally based career conflicts such exposure might elicit.

*Level of Aspirations.*    African-Americans perceive more obstacles to occupational goals than do Whites, despite similar levels of aspirations (Hawks & Muta, 1991). Because clients make career decisions based on perceived opportunities, Hawks and Muta (1991) maintained that counselors must acknowledge the reality of racism and help the clients increase their ability to master the situation by providing cognitive and behavioral coping skills.

Arbona and Nory (1991) found very few differences in the career aspirations and expectations among Black, Mexican, American, and White high school seniors and beginning college students. They believed that previously perceived ethnic barriers and stereotypes in the world of work may be less dominant in college freshman. Arbona and Nory (1991) found gender more highly associated with career choice than ethnicity, and gender was more highly associated with career expectations than aspirations. They suggested "that counselors may encounter many college women who aspire to nontraditional careers but who do not expect to be able to pursue such careers" (p. 238). Becoming very sensitive and alert to sex-role stereotypes will allow career counselors to be able to help these women identify and overcome the barriers they may perceive in pursuing their career aspirations.

Arbona (1989) suggested that clients receiving career counseling need to be aware of the direct relationship between interest in a type of work and the educational level at which work is available. The career client may need help in making that connection.

Subich (1989) proposed that career counselors and career clients concentrate on barriers such as low self-efficacy or self-limiting expectations. She encouraged individual practitioners to focus on helping clients overcome those internal constraints they have acquired through socialization processes.

Subich (1989) recommended concentrating on the "elimination of self defeating behaviors or too low expectations." Success in this area could help the career clients compete successfully in an aggressive market. She further suggested career development professionals help to identify the career-related deficits of women and minority persons and then develop interventions to replace them with more adaptive skills and attitudes. With more adaptive skills the woman is likely to experience more success and therefore an increase in her level of aspiration.

*Self-Efficacy/Locus of Control.* Rothberg, Brown, and Ware (1987) suggested that "counselors should attend to their client's perceptions of their ability to perform in a given occupation or class of occupations, in addition to their career interest and aptitudes" (p. 109). They recommended that clients only consider careers for which they have high expectations of self-efficacy. They proposed that career counselors raise or change specific career self-efficacy expectations to increase the client's willingness to choose from a wider range of careers.

*Review or Renegotiate Career Goals.* The exploration and assessment process can lead the client to change her original goals. An effective process may help her to determine that there are other personal issues that need to be resolved, or she may make a firm decision about the path down which she wants to proceed. The counselor must remain open and perhaps help the client to remain open to the possibility of renegotiating her career goals.

*Education About the Career Exploration Process.* Career counseling can proceed smoothly if the expectations about the process are agreed on by both the career counselor and the client. The career counselor will want to ask questions about the client's expectations. That will give the career counselor some idea about the client's expectations of herself in this process. Because career counseling is often the first exposure the client will have to counseling, the client may not know her responsibility or the counselor's responsibility in the counseling relationship.

The career counselor can be instrumental in helping the client to know what information is needed to make a good career decision. The career counselor can help the ethnic minority woman identify her interests, skills, values, needs, career aspirations, and career expectations. The client may readily give the counselor some of this information, but the career counselor may need to gently prod the client with questions related to the missing information. Having the client provide input can also help to bolster the client's feelings of competency and self-efficacy. It also helps the client to realize how much information she has available to enhance the career exploration process.

Once the ethnic minority woman understands the expectations in a variety of different areas, the career counseling process can proceed. The client will know that the career counselor can be a source of information, an interpreter of assessment tools, and a liaison to career information resources, but that the final career decision is up to the client. The career counselor's job is to help empower the client to make a good career decision.

In order for the career counselor to better facilitate the ethnic minority woman's career decision, the career counselor must resist the temptation to patronize the client or to set the expectations too low or to push the client into a career based on the counselor's own expectations due to race or gender. The career counselor must take care to guide the client into a better understanding of herself.

### Intervention and Follow-Up

Interventions with ethnic minority women may or may not be different from those used with majority group women. But certainly the decision-making process of the counselor regarding the interventions will be different, because the culturally skilled counselor will have given consideration to many ethnocultural issues.

We have stated throughout this chapter that career counselors need to be effective multicultural counselors. We believe that for an intervention to go smoothly the counselor must first resolve as soon as possible any cultural issues and then help the client resolve her career issues.

*Resolution of Cultural Issues.* Gainor and Forrest (1991) asserted that counselors need to be knowledgable about African-American women self-referents and possible selves because they provide a foundation for assessment and intervention. They believed career counselors need to be cognizant of the complexity of this integration process for African-American women.

Smith (1980) stated that ethnic minority women have to come to terms with the issues of race and sex and what they mean for their career development in American society. The career counselor should help the client to identify issues related to racism and sexism and how these issues relate to the client's tolerance of risk, academic achievement, motivational level, and endurance. Helping the client to express feelings related to racism and sexism can force the client away from operating under the effect of these dual discriminations.

The career counselor can then help the client to reframe some of her perceptions, expectations, and experiences. The counselor may help the client to accept her challenges as well as her competencies. The counselor may help the client to separate the facts from the myths. The counselor can help her integrate her economic, political, historical, and social realities with her career expectations and career aspirations and skills.

*Demographic Shifts.* Hawks and Muta (1991) contended that demographic shifts suggest that minorities who are educationally and occupationally prepared will face fewer racial barriers in the future labor market. They pointed to the demographic trends outlined in Workforce 2000 as a "window of opportunity" for ethnic minorities and career counselors. They believed that "unlike their predecessors," counselors today have a body of knowledge that underlines the impact of race, gender, and class on the behavior of both students and counselors. This body of knowledge can help the career counselor determine how to better serve the ethnic minority female client so that the client will prepare herself educationally and experientially to take advantage of this "window of opportunity."

Hawks and Muta (1991) challenged counselors to integrate the information about the demographic shift and the need for multicultural understanding of clients and then (a) recommit to career development and counseling, (b) ensure equal access to their career counseling services, and (c) change the context of their interventions. Among other things, they indicated that career counseling is something most students say they want, and minority students who have access to career counseling are more likely to be placed in academic versus nonacademic or vocational tracks.

*Self-Esteem Enhancement.* Ethnic minority women have self-esteem issues that will influence their career decision. In fact, Bowman and Tinsley (1991) maintained that African-American women close off many career fields because they believe that racism and sexism will pose considerable barriers to them. If sexism and racism have adversely impacted a racial ethnic minority woman she may find herself with scripts that say "You can't do that." It may be necessary for the career counselor to design exercises to enhance her self-esteem. Evansoki and Wu Tse (1989) developed a program for Chinese and Korean youths that included role models of the same ethnicity as the youths. It helped to raise the youths' belief in the possibility that if the role models could do that job or enter that career then perhaps they could, too. Included in this type of exercise could be a shadowing experience. Women could spend time on the job with other women of their same ethnicity. Sometimes the power of the word of someone who has potentially faced the same struggles will be more credible and reassuring than words from someone who is perceived as vastly different.

Sometimes the vestiges of sexism and racism may have been so great that a woman believes she is good at nothing. Arrendondo (1985) cautioned the counselor "about the tendency to overlook a woman's strengths and life management skills because she speaks with an accent or is an immigrant. The Latina client must be supported for her accomplishments and her decision to seek self care." The career counselor may therefore want to help the woman design a program of incremental successes. The exercise would be designed to ensure success. A strategy may be the one suggested by Elaine Copeland (1977). Here the counselor would begin the counseling relationship with emphasis on whatever the woman currently does well. The client is then helped to discover the devices she uses for that success. Those skills are transfered into other areas, thereby expanding her repertoire of possibilities. Such an exercise can begin to free the client to think more expansively about what she can do.

It may be necessary for the counselor to include the family in the decision-making process in order to help the client in the enhancement of her self-esteem. The counselor may need to help the family reframe its thinking about the role of women in the family and in the culture.

Other exercises might include having the client design a program that uses some of the requisite career skills in a safe environment. For an African-American woman that might mean writing a play that can be produced in her church. Mainly self-esteem exercises need to be culturally relevant and appropriate.

*Career Exercises/Assessment.* When the career counseling process has reached the stage where a counselor may want to administer a formal career instrument like an interest inventory, the career counselor is encouraged to proceed cautiously. Most of the typical instruments were designed with European Americans in mind. Cheatham (1990) maintained that they were not designed to reflect the African-American experience; nor do they account for the effects of discrimination, the cultural meaning of work, or the differential availability of career information. Martin (1991) contended that unaccounted-for ethnocultural influences cause most instruments to be inaccurate for minority groups. If the counselor chooses to use the instruments, then it is prudent to explore the literature for relevant directions and implications regarding the instruments' effectiveness with racial ethnic minority groups. For example, some of the research on Holland's Self Directed Search and Vocational Preference Inventory indicates that African-American women, regardless of high point code, tend to have a social designation as one of the high point codes (Bingham & Walsh, 1978; Ward & Walsh, 1981). The results from Holland's instruments may influence counselors to over emphasize social occupations for African-American females. In fact the instrument may be reflecting the client's world view rather than a definite career interest.

Language barriers may further complicate instrumental effectiveness with some groups. The career counselor may need to design exercises that will assess minority women's interest in a more discrete, less standardized fashion. It will probably be necessary to collaborate with other individuals who will have culturally relevant information in order to produce useful protocols. The client may be an excellent resource. Members of her group may also prove to be valuable assets. It may be effective for the counselor to help the client design a structured interview for use with an individual who is working in the client's field of interest.

Certainly the counselor will want to be aware of the sociopolitical realities facing the client. At this point, the counselor may want to broach these issues with the client if the client has not initiated the discussion. The counselor must be careful to communicate concern, care, and confidence in the client's ability, lest the client think the counselor is suggesting that because of her ethnicity she can not enter a particular career. If the counselor has developed some of the cultural competencies discussed in this chapter, and delineated by Sue et al. (1982), then due caution will be exercised with all assessment instruments.

## IMPLICATIONS FOR TRAINING AND PRACTICE

It would be easy to read this chapter and become overwhelmed with the amount of work it appears one needs to do in order to become a culturally competent career counselor. Certainly if one tried to become a competent counselor in any arena by reading a chapter in a book it would be an impossible task. Becoming a culturally skilled career counselor must begin early in one's academic training program. Academic programs must begin including ethnocultural courses at the beginning of the programs and proceed through more advanced levels as students move through the curriculum. Because the society is changing so dramatically in its ethnic and racial composition, it is essential that at least one practicum be spent working with ethnic groups different from that of the student. That of course has implications for supervision in the field. The question can be asked, who will supervise those students in the field? After all, at this point, the field of psychology has a very limited history of multicultural training. It will probably be necessary for practitioners and academicians to receive training from multicultural experts from throughout the country. It may be necessary for professionals to arrange some group self-study programs, using racial ethnic minority professionals from other disciplines to serve as guides and resource persons.

Predoctoral internships require special consideration because often they are the last formal opportunity for graduate students to receive intensive supervised training before becoming licensed professionals. Individuals who are looking for internships might list multicultural counseling training as one of their requirements for accepting a position. It would perhaps cause training programs to become more assertive about multicultural counseling training on site. On the internship sites, the program coordinators may need to ensure that interns will participate in at least a minimal ethnocultural experience. Many institutions and organizations around the country have already initiated such programs in the form of seminars and applied experiences (Parker, Bingham, & Fukuyama 1985).

Inherent in this discussion is an implied assumption that there is a body of knowledge that describes what needs to be in a training program. Actually, the information is fairly well fragmented. However, numerous authors have called for the establishment of model training programs and curricula (Sabnani et al., 1991; Sue et al., 1982). Others have called for the inclusion of multicultural counseling experiences in all American Psychological Association accredited programs (Division 17, Committee on Women, 1992). Even with all of these efforts there is still a need for courses and programs that combine multicultural with career counseling in a fairly easily accessible format if we are to succeed in breaking the barriers that face ethnic racial minority women.

## REFERENCES

Akbar, N. (1981). Mental disorder among African Americans. *Black Books Bulletin, 7*, 18–25.
American Psychological Association, division 17, Committee on Women, Accreditation

Task Force, "Guidelines for Meeting Accreditation Criteria for Programs and Internships." (1992, September). Washington, DC: Author.

Arbona, C. (1989). Hispanic employment and the Holland Typology of Work. *Career Development Quarterly, 37,* 257–268.

Arbona, C., & Novy, D. (1991). Career aspirations and expectations of Black, Mexican, American, and White students. *Career Development Quarterly, 39,* 231–239.

Arrendondo, P. (1985). Cross cultural counselor education and training. In P. Pederson (Ed.), *Handbook of cross-cultural counseling and therapy* (pp. 281–289). Westport, CT: Greenwood Press.

Atkinson, D. R., Morten, G., & Sue, D. W. (1983). *Counseling American minorities: A cross cultural perspective* (2nd ed.). Dubuque, IA: William C. Brown.

Bingham, R. P., & Walsh, W. B. (1978). Concurrent validity of Holland's theory for college degreed black women. *Journal of Vocational Behavior, 13,* 242–250.

Bowman, S., & Tinsley, H. (1991). The development of vocational realism in Black American college students. *Career Development Quarterly, 39,* 240–249.

Brown-Collins, A. R., & Sussewell, D. R. (1986). The Afro-American woman's emerging selves. *Journal of Black Psychology, 13,* 1–11.

Cheatham, H. (1990). Africentricity and career development of African Americans. *Career Development Quarterly, 38,* 334–346.

Comas-Diaz, L. (1989). *Cross-cultural psychotherapy: The therapist/patient dyad.* Proceedings, Psychotherapy of Diversity: Cross cultural treatment Issues, Boston.

Comas-Diaz, L. & Jacobsen, F. M. (1987). Ethnocultural identification in psychotherapy. *Psychiatry, 50,* 232–241.

Copeland, E. (1977). Counseling Black women with negative self-concepts. *Personal and Guidance Journal, 55*(7), 397–400.

Cross, W. E. (1971). The Negro-to-Black conversion experience: Toward a psychology of Black liberation. *Black World, 20,* 13–27.

Denga, D. I. (1988). Influence of traditional factors on career choice among Nigerian secondary school youth. *Journal of multicultural Counseling and Development, 16,* 1, 3–15.

Evans, K., & Herr, E. (1991). The influence of racism and sexism in the career development of African American women. *Journal of Multicultural Counseling and Development, 19,* 130–135.

Evansoki, P. D., & Wu Tse, F. (1989). Career awareness program for Chinese and Korean American parents. *Journal of Counseling and Development, 67,* 8, 472–474.

Gainor, K., & Forrest, L. (1991). African American women's self concept: Implications for career decisions and career counseling. *Career Development Quarterly, 39,* 261–272.

Gilligan, C. (1982). *In a different voice: Psychological theory and women's development.* Cambridge, MA: Harvard University Press.

Ginzberg, E., Ginzberg, S. W., Axelrod, A., & Herma, J. (1951). *Occupational choice: An approach to a general theory.* New York: Columbia University Press.

Granrose, C., & Cunningham, E. (1988). Post partum work intentions among Black and White college women. *Career Development Quarterly, 37,* 149–164.

Guthrie, R. V. (1976). *Even the rat was White: A historical view of psychology.* New York: Harper & Row.

Hackett, N. E., & Betz, N. (1981). A self-efficacy approach to the career development of women. *Journal of Vocational Behavior, 18,* 326–339.

Hardiman, R. (1982). *White identity development: A process oriented model for describing the racial consciousness of White Americans.* Dissertations Abstracts International, 43, 104A. (University Microfilm No. 82–10330)

Hawks, B. K., & Muta, D. (1991). Guidelines for career interventions: Facilitating the career development of minorities: Doing it differently this time. *Career Development Quarterly, 39,* 251–260.

Helms, J. E. (1984). Toward a theoretical explanation of the effects of race on counseling: A Black/White interactional model. *Counseling Psychologist, 12*(4), 153–165.

Helms, J. E. (Ed.). (1990). *Black and White racial identity: Theory, research, and practice.* Westport, CT: Greenwood Press.

Ibrahim, F. A. (1985). Effective cross-cultural counseling and pyschotherapy: A framework. *Counseling Psychologist, 13*, 625–638.

Katz, J. H. (1985). The sociopolitical nature of counseling. *Counseling Psychologist, 13*(4), 615–624.

Kluckhorn, C. (1951). Values and value-orientation in the theory of action. In T. Parsons & E. Shils (Eds.), *Toward a general theory of action* (pp. 388–433). Cambridge, MA: Harvard University Press.

Kluckhorn, C. (1962). The concept of culture. In R. Kluckhorn (Ed.), *Culture and behavior* (pp. 19–73). New York: Free Press.

Leong, F. (1985). Career development of Asian American. *Journal of College Student Personnel*, 539–546.

Manese, J., Sedlacek, W. E., Leong, F. T. (1988). Needs and Perceptions of Female and Male International Undergraduate Students. *Journal of Multicultural Counseling and Development, 16*, 24–29.

Martin, W. (1991). Career development and American Indians living on reservations: Cross-cultural factors to consider. *Career Development Quarterly, 39*, 273–283.

McCormick, T. E. (1990). Counselor-teacher interface: Promoting nonsexist education and career development. *Journal of Multicutural Counseling and Development, 18*, 2–10.

Morgan, C. O., Guy, E., Lee, B., & Cellini, H. R. (1986) Rehabilitation services for American Indians: The Navajo experience. *Journal of Rehabilitation, 52*(2), 25–31.

Nobles, W. W. (1976). Extended self: Rethinking the Negro self-concept. *Journal of Black Psychology, 2*, 15–24.

Parham, T. (1989). Cycles of psychological nigrescence. *Counseling Psychologist, 17*, 187–226.

Parker, W. M., Bingham, R. P., & Fukuyama, M. (1985). Improving cross-cultural effectiveness of counselor trainee. *Counselor Education and Supervision, 24*, 349–352.

Pedersen, P., Draguns, J., Lonner, W., & Trimbles, J. (1989). *Counseling across cultures.* Honolulu: University of Hawaii Press.

Pedersen, P. B. (1976). The field of intercultural counseling. In P. Pedersen, W. J. Lonner, & J. G. Draguns (Eds.), *Counseling across cultures* (pp. 17–41). Honolulu: University of Hawaii Press.

Ponterotto, J. G. (1988a). Racial consciousness development among White counselor trainees: A stage model. *Journal of Multicultural Counseling and Development, 16*, 146–156.

Ponterotto, J. G. (1988b). Racial/ethnic minority research in the *Journal of Counseling Psychologist*: A content analysis and methodological critique. *Journal of Counseling Psychologist, 35*(4), 410–418.

Pyant, C., & Yanico, B. (1991). Relationship of racial identity and gender-role attitudes to Black women's psychological well-being. *Journal of Counseling Psychology, 38*, 315–322.

Rothberg, H., Brown, D., & Ware, W. (1987). Career self-efficacy expectations and perceived range of career options in community college students. *Journal of Counseling Psychology, 34*, 164–180.

Sabnani, H. B., Ponterotto, J. G., and Borodovsky, L. G. (1991). White racial identity development and cross-cultural counselor training: A stage model. *Counseling Psychologist, 19*, 76–102.

Smith, E. J. (1980). Issues in racial minorities' career behavior. In W. B. Walsh & S. H. Osipow (Eds.), *Handbook of vocational psychology: Vol. 1. Foundations* (pp. 161–222). Hillsdale, NJ: Lawrence Erlbaum Associates.

Stabb, S., & Cogdal, P. (1990, April). *Needs assessment and the perception of help in a multicultural college population.* ACPA Convention Presentation, St. Louis, MO.

Stickel, S. A., & Bonett, R. M. (1991). Gender difference in career self-efficacy: Combining a career with home and family. *Journal of College Student Development, 32,* 4, 297–301.

Subich, L. (1989). A challenge to grow: A reaction to Hoyt's article. *Career Development Quarterly, 37,* 213–217.

Sue, D. W. (1981). *Counseling the culturally different. Theory and practice.* New York: Wiley.

Sue, D. W. (1990). *Counseling the culturally different. Theory and practice.* (2nd ed.). New York: Wiley.

Sue, D. W., Bernier, J. E., Durran, A., Feinberg, L., Pedersen, P., Smith, E., & Vasquez-Nuttal, E. (1982). Position paper. Cross-cultural counseling competencies. *Counseling Psychologist, 10,* 45–52.

Vontress, C. E. (1971). Racial difference: Impediments to rapport. *Journal of Counseling Psychology, 18,* 7–13.

Ward, C. M., & Walsh, W. B. (1981). Concurrent validity of Holland's theory for non college degreed Black women. *Journal of Vocational Behavior, 18,* 356–361.

Warwick, D. P. (1980). The politics and ethnics of cross-cultural research. In H. C. Triandis & W. W. Lambert (Eds.), *Handbook of cross cultural psychology perspectives* (pp. 319–371). Boston: Allyn & Baron.

Wehrly, B. (1988). Influence of traditional factors on career choice among Nigerian secondary school youth. *Journal of Multicultural Counseling and Development, 16,* 1, 3–5.

Yang, J. (1991). Career counseling of Chinese American women: Are they in Linko? *Career Development, 39,* 350–359.

# ❧ 6 ❧

# Career Counseling for Gifted Women

Barbara Kerr
Susan E. Maresh
*Arizona State University*

## THE STUDY OF GIFTED GIRLS AND WOMEN

The study of gifted women is fairly recent. Historically, the education and guidance of bright girls have been a low priority. Gifted women have appeared throughout history; however, the nature of their education and the means by which they discovered their vocations remain a mystery (Schwartz, 1980).

The first psychological study of gifted girls and women was Terman's longitudinal study of gifted children. This study, which began in 1921, followed the lives of 1,528 gifted children from childhood throughout adulthood (Terman, 1925; Terman & Oden, 1935, 1947). The subjects of the Terman Study and their children continue to be studied today.

Several findings emerged from Terman's study of gifted boys and girls that shed light on gender differences among the gifted as well as on the individual development of gifted girls and women. For example, Terman found that gifted girls are much more like gifted boys in their interests and activities then they are like average girls (Terman, 1925). In addition, Terman found that gifted girls were superior to average girls in their physical health and their psychological adjustment. These findings have important implications for the vocational development of gifted girls and women, as seen later in this chapter.

Leta Hollingworth, herself a gifted woman, studied brilliant girls attending the Speyer School in New York City (Hollingworth, 1926, 1942). Hollingworth also showed how the common practice of labeling as intellectual geniuses only those who had attained eminence led to mistaken figures on the incidence of genius among women. She showed definitively how women's societal roles precluded the manifestation of superior abilities; for example, Hollingworth observed that home-making is a field in which eminence is impossible.

In general, giftedness and its implications were eclipsed by other educational issues in the 1940s and early 1950s. Only with the launching of Sputnik and a new emphasis on educational reform was there renewed interest in the study of gifted students. The Wisconsin Guidance Laboratory for Superior Students was founded in 1957 at the University of Wisconsin to study the career development of gifted students (Sanborn, 1974). This laboratory, which held workshops and provided counseling to gifted students from 1957 through 1984, created an enormous body of research on gifted girls and gifted boys in the adolescent years. Frederickson and Rothney (1972) found that gifted girls, like gifted boys, were likely to be struggling throughout adolescence with issues of multipotentiality, the expectations of others, and discrepancies between emotional maturity and the necessity of making long-range decisions. The Wisconsin Guidance Laboratory for Superior Students provided ample evidence of the existence of multipotentiality. Multipotentiality is the capacity for selecting and developing a wide number of career options because of multiple intellectual abilities and interests. Multipotentiality often leads to career indecision and insta-bility of major and career choice.

The early 1970s marked the first time in which gifted girls were studied in their own right. Lynn Fox's pioneering study of gifted girls participating in the Johns Hopkins Study for Mathematically Precocious Youth set the tone for most of the study of gifted girls in the 1970s and early 1980s (Fox, 1976a; Fox, Benbow, & Perkins, 1983; Fox & Cohn, 1980). Fox, rather than focusing simply on sex differences in mathemat-ical ability, instead focused on the reasons that may account for the lower participation of gifted girls in enrichment opportunities and advanced mathematics course taking. The studies of Fox and her colleagues included investigations of career interests, values, attitudes toward math, and self-concept (Fox & Cohn, 1980). In addition, Fox created and evaluated programs to encourage gifted girls in their career interests in math and science (Fox, 1976b, 1981; Fox, Benbow, & Perkins, 1983).

In a similar fashion, Hollinger and Fleming carried out many studies of the construct social self-esteem and its relationship to gifted girls' career interests and aspirations (Hollinger, 1983, 1985; Hollinger & Fleming, 1985, 1988).

Kerr's (1985) *Smart Girls, Gifted Women* recounted the results of a 10-year follow-up study of gifted women who had graduated from a special program for gifted children. In addition, the book reviewed the literature of gifted girls' career development and career interventions for this group. Finally, suggestions for career interventions based on the career development of eminent women and successful career development interventions were given. A 20-year follow-up study (Kerr, 1991a) of the same cohort was recently concluded.

The clinical studies of Silverman (1986) and the theoretical work of Noble (1990) and Reis (1991) have clarified issues in the education and guidance of gifted girls throughout the last decade. The new interest in gifted girls and women culminated in an international symposium on the theme, "Girls, Women, and Giftedness," a book of the proceedings (Ellis & Willinsky, 1990), and several special issues of journals of gifted education (Kline & Kerr, 1991a, 1991b).

## DEFINITIONS OF GIFTEDNESS

There is a great deal of controversy today about the definition of intelligence. Throughout most of the 20th century the concept of general intelligence that emerged from the testing movement and from the work of Lewis Terman dominated conceptualization of intellectual ability. General intellectual ability often has been defined as general mental strength or abstract thinking ability. General intelligence is usually measured by IQ tests such as the Stanford-Binet (Terman & Merrill, 1960) or the Wechsler Intelligence Scale for Children (Wechsler, 1974). The majority of children who participate in programs for the gifted today are still admitted mainly on the basis of IQ.

A new theory of intelligence that is gaining recognition in gifted education is Gardner's theory of multiple intelligences (Gardner, 1983). According to this theory, an intelligence is an ability or set of abilities that permit an individual to solve problems or fashion products that are of consequence in a particular cultural setting. Gardner believes that there is not one but many intelligences. The evidence for this theory is drawn from neuropsychological studies of normal, gifted, and brain-damaged individuals, cross-cultural accounts of cognition, and psychometric studies. The intelligences that have been suggested by Gardner and his colleagues include linguistic, logical-mathematical, spatial-visual, musical, and bodily kinesthetic, as well as two "personal" intelligences, interpersonal and intrapersonal. This theory, so far, has no implications for gender; however, measures based on this theory hold promise for identifying a broader range of talents than more traditional intelligence tests have done.

In this chapter, giftedness of girls and women is examined in terms of both general intellectual ability and specific extraordinary talents.

A generous amount of research exists on the career development needs of academically talented young people, and there is even a small literature pertaining to the career development of academically talented women. Because the theory of multiple intelligences is so young, there have been no applications of this theory to career development. However, it makes sense to examine specific intellectual talents and the development of those talents in women. Therefore, the second section of this chapter examines career development issues in the lives of women with specific extraordinary talents in the areas of verbal, mathematical, spatial-visual, musical, and kinesthetic performance. The area of personal giftedness, which may encompass the literature of leadership, teaching, and helping, was deemed too broad and as yet ambiguous for examination in this chapter.

## CAREER DEVELOPMENT OF WOMEN WITH GENERAL INTELLECTUAL GIFTEDNESS

### Gifted Girls

Intellectually gifted girls, like gifted boys, are usually taller, stronger, and healthier than their average peers (Terman & Oden, 1935). They usually have better psychological adjustment then their average peers (Janos & Robinson, 1985; Robinson & Janos, 1986). In fact, by almost any measure gifted girls are extraordinarily well adjusted. On personality measures, gifted girls appear to be less likely to show traits associated with depression and anxiety. Gifted girls are less likely than average girls or boys to be referred for behavior disorders (Kerr, 1991b). In the area of self-concept, there are some studies that seem to show that gifted girls may have a lower opinion of themselves than gifted boys (Kerr, Colangelo, & Gaeth, 1988). Although gifted girls tend to have a high academic self-concept, they may have lower social self-concept as a result of being labeled gifted. In fact, many gifted girls feel that giftedness is a social handicap. And although girls have a higher academic self-concept, they may have less confidence in their academic abilities than their actual achievements would warrant. Gifted girls may be less conforming to social norms then girls in general. For instance, Karnes and Wherry (1983) found that gifted girls were more casual in their behavior than average girls and tended to be careless. Other studies have found gifted girls to be independent, curious, and assertive. One area in which gifted girls seem to stand out is in their possession of greater social knowledge, that is, the ability to feel empathy and to make accurate social judgments (Terman & Oden, 1935).

Therefore, throughout girlhood, intellectually gifted girls are likely to be well adjusted; implications of this fact for career development are several. First of all, good psychological adjustment may mean that most gifted girls will be perceived by teachers and counselors as needing very little guidance. Second, the excellent psychological adjustment of gifted girls may sometimes work to their detriment when they adjust to social norms rather than choosing high aspirations or nontraditional career goals. On the other hand, it may be possible that for gifted girls, good psychological adjustment would serve to prepare them to encounter the barriers and challenges that bright women are likely to face in pursuit of their career goals.

Gifted girls' interests are more like those of gifted boys then they are like average girls (Hollingworth, 1926; Kerr, 1985; Terman & Oden, 1935). What this means is that gifted girls are likely to be interested in the kind of play activities that emphasize exploration, problem solving, adventure, and active outdoor play. Like boys, they may be interested in competitive sports and aggressive physical activities. Because play interests in childhood sometimes provide a clue to later adult interests, the implications for bright girls' career development are clear. The nontraditional play interests of gifted girls could be guided into career goals that emphasize problem solving, exploring, adventure, and leadership.

The career aspirations of gifted girls, like their play interests, are similar to those of gifted boys. Gifted girls, unlike average girls, are likely to have high aspirations and sometimes vivid, dramatic career fantasies (Kerr, 1985).

Gifted girls may show the early signs of multipotentiality in their tendency to have many varied interests and abilities (Sanborn, 1974). Gifted girls may excel in most of their school subjects throughout their education. They may also claim an interest in four or five different career goals well into adolescence, as well as changing their interests and career goals frequently according to their current fascinations and passions. It may be hard to detect, in the gifted girl's constantly changing stream of multiple interests, a thread of consistent career possibilities.

## Adolescence of Gifted Girls

Adolescence is a difficult time for most gifted girls. During this time it is likely that the gifted girls' habits of achievement and strong interests in high level career goals come into conflict with societal expectations of women (Silverman, 1990). Adolescent girls are often faced with the choice of developing intellectually or socially. Developing intellectually may mean taking advanced math and science courses in which there are few girls; attending summer institutes at universities where there are few friends or acquaintances from one's own home school; and taking advantage of special tutoring and lessons that may take place during the time that most adolescents are engaged in social activities with one another. The gifted girl who chooses to emphasize social development may find herself minimizing the importance of good grades and academic achievement.

As recently as the mid-1980s, patterns of declining career aspirations were easy to detect in gifted girls. However, it is less likely now that bright girls will show an interest in low-level or very traditionally feminine occupations (Dolny, 1985). Instead, bright girls may choose lofty-sounding career goals with little understanding of those goals and the means to reach them (Kerr, 1989).

It is during the adolescence of the gifted girl that the role of the math/science filter comes into play. The math/science filter (Sells, 1980; Tobin & Fox, 1976), is the process by which gifted young women often sabotage their own career goals by refusing to take the necessary math and science courses that will prepare them for the careers to which they aspire. Math anxiety and low academic self-concept may account for much of the attrition in math/science courses among gifted girls. Although there is much less evidence of math anxiety among gifted girls than in previous decades (Weiner & Robinson, 1986), many gifted girls still profess to be afraid of taking math courses. Some gifted girls, despite high grades in mathematics and science-related courses, continue to believe that they have little proficiency in that area.

Whatever the reason for declining interest in math/science courses during adolescence, the fact remains that gifted girls often give up advanced course taking in these areas as soon as the opportunity is presented. Unfortunately, teachers and counselors sometimes collaborate with gifted girls in the process (Eccles, 1984). Many guidance counselors advise gifted girls away from those courses that they perceive as having a negative impact on the girls' grade-point average. The result is that many adolescent women are ill prepared for the achievement test that will determine the higher education institutions to which they will go.

They also enter college with much less preparation for the courses that are necessary to their academic majors. Most college majors that lead to high-status and high-salary occupations allowing autonomy and the potential for growth require math and science. Therefore, a single decision made by an adolescent gifted girl to discontinue her studies in math and science may have far-reaching consequences on her career options.

It is also during adolescence that gifted girls may begin to have decreasing self-esteem. A recent study commissioned by the American Association for University Women showed a precipitous decline in girls' self-esteem compared to boys during adolescence (Greenberg Lake Analysis Group & AAUW, 1991). Self-esteem may be a very important determinant of career aspirations. As a component of self-efficacy, self-esteem seems to predict the degree to which girls and young women will consider careers in nontraditional fields in areas of high aspiration (Betz & Hackett, 1981).

In adolescence and young adulthood, the impact of the peer group is probably one of the most important factors to consider in predicting a women's career aspirations. The pressure on gifted girls to channel their considerable intellectual ability into social achievement instead of intellectual achievement is great (Kerr, 1985).

Despite their tendency to take less rigorous academic courses, gifted girls continue to receive high grades in high school and to have moderately high college and career aspirations. Nearly as many gifted girls as gifted boys expect to have college major in prelaw and premedicine and to pursue careers as lawyers and doctors (Kerr & Colangelo, 1988). Expectations of gifted girls for participation in majors in engineering and the physical sciences remain very low, however. Most gifted adolescent women now have career plans that include both career and family. The majority of gifted students plan on a professional career, marriage, and children, according to a study by Dolny (1985). In this study, however, more gifted females than males felt that work and family was a combination that could be accomplished without major conflict.

An interesting sidelight on the issue of gifted adolescent females' attitudes toward careers and relationships is given by a study by Bakken, Hershey, and Miller (1990). In this study, gifted adolescent females were assessed with regard to their opinions about gender equality in educational, professional, and intellectual pursuits. They were also assessed with regard to their beliefs concerning gender equality, dating, marital relationships, and the area of social etiquette. Seventy-five percent of this sample strongly agreed that women should expect equality in professional and educational areas, but only 34% of the young women strongly agreed that there was gender inequality in dating relationships and etiquette. In fact, there was wide variability in terms of attitudes toward dating and marriage. It may be that gifted adolescent females do not see a connection between inequality in relationships and inequality in the workplace.

## Gifted Young Women in College

Gifted young women enter college, then, with a puzzling constellation of characteristics. Their career goals are higher than those of average women and, except for physical sciences and engineering, as high as those of gifted men. Their educational aspirations are correspondingly high. Nevertheless, their self-esteem by the time they enter college may be lower than that of gifted men. Gifted women may enter college with somewhat naive attitudes toward relationships with men.

There is increasing evidence that the typical American college campus is not an environment that is conducive to maintaining the high aspirations of most gifted women or remediating the low self-esteem and fears of those gifted women who are already handicapped by negative attitudes toward their own career development. Sandler's (1983) study of the status of women on college campuses concluded that college campuses provide a "chilly climate" for women. The evidence from this particular survey suggested that male students receive more attention in the classroom, greater leadership opportunities, and in general a more supportive environment for the achievement of their goals than do women students.

Holland and Eisenhart (1990) provided a devastating portrait of women in college in their book, *Educated in Romance*. This book described the long-term ethnographic study that was performed by the authors at two large universities, one a historically Black institution and one a predominantly White institution. Women at these universities were followed from their early months in college throughout the period in which they attempted to establish themselves after graduation. Two-thirds of the women studied abandoned their career plans or subordinated them to those of their husbands. The authors concluded that the primary barrier to the women's successful achievement of their goals was what they termed the "culture of romance" on college campuses. The culture of romance is essentially a system of intense peer pressure that focuses women's interests almost entirely on their attractiveness to men rather than on achievement in college.

There is strikingly little written about the gifted women in college (Phelps, 1991). Terman and Oden's (1947) gifted women in college tended to achieve well but to aspire to fewer high-status and high-salary careers than their male gifted peers. Far fewer females than males in this study chose to continue to graduate or professional school. The gifted females in Kerr's (1985) follow-up study also apparently lost ground during college, sometimes to the point of dropping out. The majority of women in this study gave up career goals while they were in college.

A long-term study of male and female valedictorians and salutatorians is being conducted by Arnold and Denny (1985). In this study, the women's self-estimated reports of their own intelligence declined between high school and their sophomore year of college, whereas the men's did not. In this study, the women also shifted their career goals toward less demanding careers, apparently because of concerns regarding work and future family responsibilities.

**Adulthood of Gifted Women**

Gifted women's achievement and aspirations decline throughout adulthood (Card, Steele, & Abeles, 1979; Reis, 1991). Despite the extraordinary changes in the role of women in our society, gifted women continue to fail to realize their full potential.

Half of Terman's gifted women were homemakers at midlife (Terman & Oden, 1947). Of those women who were employed, 30% were working in secretarial and clerical positions. Forty years later a group of gifted women selected according to the same criteria as Terman's women had precisely the same proportions of women in homemaking and traditional careers at age 30, despite the vastly increased opportunities for women in the 1980s (Kerr, 1984). The 20-year follow-up of this group found increased education, but little change in career status among the women (Kerr, 1991a). White (1984) also found that the achievement levels of gifted females who had attended a New York City school for the gifted were much lower then those of their male counterparts.

Kaufmann's (1981) sample of gifted women, the U.S. Presidential Scholars for 1964–1968, were a group of highly gifted girls that Kaufmann followed up in 1979 and 1981. Although these very academically talented women were found in about the same proportions as males in professional and academic positions, the discrepancies in the salaries of the males and females were extraordinary: Males were earning about twice the salary of their female counterparts in the same professions.

Kaufmann's more recent data analysis seemed to show that gifted women have a great many unsolved questions about their own abilities. Noble (1989) found that women disclaimed the label of giftedness but were quite ready to label their children or their partners in this way. Half of the gifted women in this study claimed that self-doubt was the major reason for changing their career aspirations and was the primary obstacle in inhibiting the development of their potential.

Three studies shed some light on the multiple roles that gifted adult women play. These studies have examined the impact of family and career combinations upon gifted women's satisfaction and realization of potential. Rodenstein and Glickhauf-Hughes (1979) showed convincingly that gifted women could successfully integrate career and family responsibility. Thirty-year-old gifted women who had all been identified as intellectually superior as children were grouped into three categories—career only, family only, and integraters. It was found that integraters were as satisfied with their careers as the career-only women and as satisfied with their families as those women who were homemakers. These gifted women integraters were apparently able to feel competent and satisfied while playing both roles, although many remarked on the fatigue that can be produced by such a lifestyle.

Sears and Barbee's (1977) study of Terman's gifted women at age 62 also gives insight into the impact of early decisions about role combinations. Sears and Barbee also grouped gifted women according to their lifestyle. They found that the single women who had been career-oriented enjoyed the greater degree of life satisfaction compared to married women with income-producing work or those who had been homemakers only. A more recent study by Kerr (1991a), which was a 20-year follow-up study of female graduates of a gifted program, found that although some gifted women were capable of transforming their lives at midlife, overcoming earlier barriers or missed educational opportunities, a large number of gifted women who had decided not to pursue careers were now beset by financial problems and overwhelming family responsibilities.

## Conclusions About the Career Development
## of Gifted Women

A few conclusions can be drawn from a review of the literature of gifted females from girlhood to adulthood. First, it is clear that the high aspirations and career fantasies of gifted girls are not predictive of their actual attainments. Second, the decisions that bright women make in early adolescence have long-term consequences for their adult achievement and eventual life satisfaction. Thus, a 15-year-old girl who chooses not to continue with trigonometry and advanced algebra sabotages her own dream to be a physician.

Third, excellent academic performance in high school and college may not be associated with academic self-confidence, high social self-esteem, or high career aspirations. Fourth, the college and young adult years seem to be a critical period for gifted women, in which college environment can have a permanent impact on the realization of these women's potential. The college freshman who allows her academic performance to decline as she becomes caught up in the culture of romance loses the options of graduate or professional school. The young gifted career woman who cannot find adequate child care and who receives little support for her own career goals may eventually see her male colleagues surpass her in promotions and salary, while she stops out to fulfill her family responsibilities.

Finally, it appears that developmental metaphor, with its implications of blossoming and unfolding, may not be appropriate to describe the vocational behavior of gifted girls and women. What happens to gifted girls and women hardly seems to be career "development," but rather a sort of gently downward spiral as gifted young women adjust their interests, aspirations, and achievements to fit their own perceived limitations in the absence of guidance and support.

## CAREER DEVELOPMENT OF WOMEN WITH SPECIFIC EXTRAORDINARY TALENTS

### Types of Talents and Career Development Issues

A small literature is beginning to develop on the needs of young people with specific extraordinary talent. Led by the pioneering work of Stanley and his colleagues at Johns Hopkins University, a great deal of interest formed around the needs of mathematically precocious students (Benbow & Stanley, 1984). It became clear that mathematically gifted students had many needs that were similar to those of academically gifted students in general, as well as some unique needs. Interest in students with other specific talents has also slowly been growing. Specific talents that have been examined by researchers are verbal giftedness or writing ability, mathematical giftedness, spatial-visual giftedness, musical giftedness, and athletic giftedness.

### Verbal Giftedness

The area of verbal ability, or linguistic intelligence, is the one domain in which females have tended to excel. In fact, Colangelo and Kerr (1990) found that there were twice as many female as male perfect scorers on the English subtest of the ACT. Writing and other verbal careers such as teaching have had a longer history of female participation then most other careers. Verbal giftedness does not seem to bear the same stigma for girls as mathematical giftedness. However, as in most other fields, eminence is largely reserved for males.

According to Gardner (1983), linguistic giftedness is one of the later developing abilities because it relies on life experience for its full flowering. Although many people who have high achievement in verbal careers were verbally precocious and were precocious readers, the converse is not necessarily true: all precocious readers and speakers do not become verbally gifted adults. Girls are more likely to speak, to read, and to write earlier than boys. It may be that verbal giftedness in the young girl is often simply ascribed to the developmental edge that girls have over boys in this area (Silverman, 1986). Verbally gifted girls may be more likely to suffer emotional and social difficulties than girls in other talent areas (Brody & Benbow, 1986). Appropriate career guidance may be difficult to obtain for verbally gifted girls. The careers that seem obvious for those with extraordinary linguistic abilities—that is, writing, teaching of English, and careers associated with foreign languages—are those that are frequently discouraged. This is possibly because of the difficulty of finding jobs in those fields during the 1980s. In fact, only a very small percentage of those students with perfect scores in English were planning on pursuing careers in English in Colangelo and Kerr's (1990) study. Creative writing is a notoriously difficult profession in which to attain eminence. Therefore, a great many gifted females may be discouraged quite early from fully developing their greatest gift.

A study of successful creative writers by Barron (1972) showed that the five items most characteristic of the group of creative writers were intellectual capacity; high valuing of intellectual and cognitive matters; high value on independence and autonomy; verbal fluency; and aesthetic reactivity. Scores on the California Psychological Inventory for writers show that writers are superior to the general population in social presence, self-acceptance, capacity for social status, psychological mindedness, and achievement through independence. They are significantly lower in achievement via conformance. They tend to have low scores on socialization, on self-control, on sense of well-being, and on desire to make a good impression. They are distinctly more introverted than extroverted. To the degree that these characteristics are dissimilar to the characteristics that are reinforced in females, there will be difficulty for young gifted women to attain creative eminence. Independence and nonconformity of writers may be necessary to their work; however, these are characteristics that are seldom rewarded in bright girls. In fact, Bachtold and Werner (1973) found that women writers tend to be loners, preferring to work alone on their writing.

Verbally gifted young women are likely to be found in many other careers besides writing. Education at all levels, languages and translation, performance in radio, television, cinema, and theater, and all areas of business may attract verbally talented females. Because verbally precocious young women tend to score very high on the artistic scale of vocational interest tests (Fox, 1982), most careers that involve creativity, expressiveness, spontaneity, and originality would be attractive and congruent with needs of verbally gifted young women. Many of the careers in which linguistic abilities are primary have been those careers that have been the most open to women. Even as gifted young women are attracted in greater numbers to science and mathematically oriented careers, the careers requiring great verbal ability will probably continue to be the most attractive to gifted girls. Unfortunately, many verbally gifted girls are not aware of the value of their gift.

Therefore, verbally gifted girls may need help identifying their verbal talent and understanding the link between abilities and careers. They may need encouragement to believe that their talents are rare enough that they will probably be rewarded in the job market. Given the extreme independence, nonconformity, and desire for aloneness of verbally gifted females, guidance might prove extremely difficult. These women may be very unlikely to seek help with career development. Nevertheless, verbally gifted girls and young women may benefit from realistic, encouraging career guidance.

## Mathematical Giftedness

Mathematically gifted girls and women have been the subject of study by a number of researchers at Johns Hopkins University Study for mathematically precocious youth (Fox, 1976a, 1976b). Mathematically gifted girls do differ from their less gifted counterparts in their interests, needs, and aspirations. They also differ from male mathematically gifted peers. Compared to average girls, these girls tend to have talented mothers who do not work outside the home; in fact, many of them have mothers with PhDs. There is a predominance of Asian girls among mathematically gifted girls; even among female mathematicians of the 1960s, the influence of other ethnicities besides majority culture was very evident (Helson, 1983). Clearly, mathematical interests are not reinforced in mainstream American culture among females. Mathematically gifted girls tend to score higher than average girls on the Holland Investigative and Conventional Scales on vocational interest tests.

In fact, the combination of investigative and conventional interests in mathematically gifted girls aspiring to nontraditional mathematics jobs was of concern to Hollinger (1986), who wrote that the conformity that is associated with conventional career interests may work against the creativity that is required for higher level mathematics occupations. She wrote:

Since the non-traditional science career aspirants score significantly lower than non-traditional math career aspirants on the conventional dimension it would appear as though while both math and science are perceived as requiring investigative attributes, the investigative attributes of math career aspirants may be tempered by or superseded by conventional attributes. While such conventional attributes may serve the bookkeeper quite well, investigative attributes are essential to the higher level careers in mathematics. (p. 143)

Hollinger was also concerned that the nontraditional math career aspirants in her study may have been a high-risk group in terms of a tendency to abandon their math aspirations. Because of their high conventional scores they would tend to be more conforming then was necessary for those who wish to pursue nontraditional, stereotypically masculine careers. If these girls were to persist they would need extraordinary support for their choices.

Helson's (1983) study focused upon a comparison of creative women mathematicians with their less creative counterparts in mathematics. In general, the creative women mathematicians were more productive than other women mathematicians, having earlier PhDs and more papers, fellowships, and grants. They apparently were more independent and they preferred to do things their own way. Creative women mathematicians described themselves as inventive and ingenious and were less interested in salary, promotion, and teaching. They had more unusual leisure pursuits, and, according to Piirto (1991), creative women mathematicians simplify their lives by doing a few things that they care greatly about.

Creative female mathematicians were not similar to creative male mathematicians on the California Psychological Inventory (CPI). Males were significantly higher on social ascendancy and intellectual efficiency. In general, personality assessment of creative male mathematicians and creative female mathematicians shows creative male mathematicians to be more ambitious, more focused on their own achievements, and more confident and adventurous. Creative women are more inner focused then creative male mathematicians.

Subotnik (1988) investigated variables that characterized students who had won the 1983 Westinghouse Science Talent Search Contest. These young people were among some of the most extraordinarily talented young scientists in the United States. Females and male subjects did differ in a number of important areas. The female talent search participants reported more concern with the social impact of scientific research. There was less variability in their self-image as a scientist. They also tended to attribute their success to hard work and dedication rather than to intelligence or creativity, as did the male subjects. As in Fox's study of mathematically gifted girls, this study showed once again the importance of social concerns to bright young women in math and science. Many more mathematically gifted females than males wish to have careers in mathematics and science in order to improve the human condition or promote some social good. However, curiosity is still the major reason that both male and female winners pursued science, rather than bettering the human condition or prestige.

It is significant that the greatest part of the research on mathematically gifted females has focused on sex differences in mathematical ability (Eccles, 1984). Despite the fact that gender differences in mathematics ability appear to be diminishing rapidly with time and despite the fact that biological gender differences appear to account for only a very small proportion of the variance in scores between boys and girls (Hyde, 1981), a disproportionate amount of discussion has taken place in the literature and in the popular media concerning gender differences in mathematical ability. It is true that among gifted young people the differences favoring males are the strongest (Benbow & Stanley, 1983). However, it has often been automatically assumed that these differences are biological in nature, whereas the biological link that has been made is extremely tenuous. Benbow and Stanley based the biological hypothesis almost entirely on their findings of increased lefthandedness and allergy problems among mathematically gifted youth, two characteristics that are genetically linked to males. On this small finding a great deal of discussion has emerged, a discussion that has had a great impact on gifted girls and their attitude toward their own abilities. Jacobs and Eccles (1985) found that media reports of sex differences in mathematics had an impact on parental attitude toward girls' mathematical ability, with mothers seeing their girls' abilities lower than they had before the report and fathers seeing girls' abilities as somewhat higher than they had before media reports of gender differences in mathematics. Gifted girls continue to have less confidence in their mathematical abilities than gifted boys and to see less relevance of mathematics to their own lives. The extreme emphasis in literature on gender differences in mathematics is unlikely to contribute to the encouragement of girls in career development in mathematics-related professions. Mathematically gifted girls need guidance that corrects stereotypes about mathematical ability and gender. In addition, they need continued encouragement to persist in mathematics course taking. Finally, women teachers and role models may be very important to these gifted girls' development (Fox, Benbow, & Perkins, 1983).

## Musical Giftedness

Although music is a field in which many women singers and musicians have excelled, there are still very few women among the ranks of leading composers and conductors of orchestras (Piirto, 1991). Therefore, there seems to be a great difference in the acceptance and success of women in musical performance versus musical leadership and creation. Trollinger (1983) studied creative women musicians during childhood, adolescent, and college years. She found that creative women musicians throughout the lifespan were solitary people, preferring their creative activities to all other pursuits. Parents were nurturing, and fathers were particularly encouraging of creative and musical activities. Surprisingly, gifted female musicians did not have high participation in school musical activities. Like successful female visual artists and writers, successful female composers have been found to be more dominant and more self-sufficient than their less successful female peers. For the most part, however, successful women composers have personality profiles very similar to successful male composers (Shuler-Dyson, 1985). Female performers may not resemble female composers in personality. In considering the career development of musically gifted women, therefore, it is important to recognize that there may be differences in the needs of performers and those whose aspirations include conducting and composition.

Musical giftedness is one of the earliest developing talents. Gardner (1983) claimed that many child prodigies are musical prodigies, because musical talent does not necessarily depend on life experience and maturity. Many parents notice a strong early interest in music in bright girls and arrange for their instruction. In fact, private instruction at an early age seems to be critical to the development of musical talent (Bloom, 1985). Girls whose talent is neither identified nor nurtured at an early age may never manifest their talent.

Few schools provide special programs for musically gifted students. Although most high schools have a band or orchestra, the development of musical talent is left up to parents until adolescence. As has been pointed out, female gifted musicians may not seek out these opportunities. Musically gifted children are often not included in gifted programs. The traditional means of nurturing musical talent include private lessons, practice, auditions, and performance. In the last two decades, Suzuki methods of teaching music have combined guidance with education (Gardner, 1983). How education and guidance for the musically gifted girl must differ from that of the musically gifted boy has not been investigated by researchers in the area of talent development. It is likely, however, that musically gifted girls need training and guidance that will develop their identities as musicians as well as developing the specific musical talent (Bloom, 1985).

## Spatial-Visual Giftedness Intelligence

*Definition of Spatial Intelligence.*   Education for gifted and talented students has overvalued verbal and mathematical abilities in academic programs with students whose talents are academically and intellectually advanced. For more than 50 years there has been a neglect of the arts due to this emphasis. Historically, the study of children with superior abilities in the visual arts is now at a place comparable to the study of gifted children with superior intellectual abilities in the 1920s. It has been an article of faith for years among students of intelligence that there is an ability to solve problems efficiently apart from straight logical or linguistic ability. A number of individuals have strongly argued for the existence and independence of spatial ability. Gardner (1983) proposes that spatial intelligence comprises a variety of loosely held capacities. It is the ability to recognize instances of the same visual element; the ability to transform or to recognize the transformation of one element into another; the ability to conjure up mental imagery and then to transform that imagery; and the capacity to produce a visual likeness of spatial information. He believes these operations are independent of one another and could develop or break down separately. Conceptually, they tend to function as a family, and the use of each operation might provide reinforcement for the use of these others.

*Historical Overview of Research and Assessment.*   In the view of many, spatial intelligence is another intelligence that should be considered equal in importance to linguistic intelligence. There were a number of research studies from the early 1900s through the 1940s that focused on behaviors of students with superior abilities in the visual arts and characteristics of their artwork (Ayer, 1916; Hollingworth, 1923; Manuel, 1919; Meier, 1939). At the Cleveland Museum of Art in 1933 under the direction of Munro one of the most important studies of students' artistic ability was begun (Munro, 1956). Over a number of years 1,300 students were in involved in performing a series of standardized tasks. On the basis of these standardized tasks the children were grouped into special and average classes. The Seven Drawing Test was used to differentiate the two groups by including drawing from memory, copying, and drawing from imagination. Later development of aesthetic response tasks over specified periods of time made it possible for more factors to be researched. Later reports from the Cleveland studies used additional characteristics with which it attempted to differentiate between average and special groups of students. This pioneering work established various sets of criteria to describe the differences between average and superior students, such as aesthetic judgment and drawing ability.

It has been suggested that a portfolio of artwork be kept for individual students and that outside experts should be used to evaluate the contents and identify students with superior art abilities.

*Identification of Talented Students.* Talented students in the visual arts were distinguished by the content, depth, proportion, originality of expression, uses of media, and visual expression in their artwork and by their ability to respond to works of art. Important characteristics that could be used to identify students with potential for high achievement included the role of interest, desire, persistence, and self-motivation to do artwork. Additional research in the 1960s attempted to describe the factors that distinguished gifted from average children (Hildreth, 1966; Lowenfeld & Brittain, 1964; Yochim, 1967). None of these studies have provided information about the special needs of girls and women.

The most recent approach to identification of the spatially superior students is to compile a list of characteristics and behaviors common to those students in both quality and quantity (Tuttle & Becker, 1980). Another innovation in identifying artistically talented students has been to use biographical information (Ellison, Abe, Fox, Coray, & Taylor, 1975). Teacher nominations and interviews and, life history information have been shown to be somewhat valuable for predicting artistic talent. Three common indices for identification of artistic talent have been used. One means is to observe the characteristics of talented students' drawings through the work sample technique; another is to observe various general behavioral characteristics of artistically talented students; and a third is to collect biographical information about artistically talented students. It was the recommendation of Clark and Zimmerman (1983) that a battery of diverse sources of information such as these be used as procedures for identifying artistically talented students.

*Personality Characteristics.* Without proper guidance and encouragement it is highly unlikely that the potentially gifted child will make adequate progress (Gaitskell & Horowitz, 1970). The professions chosen by artistically talented individuals demand extraordinary commitment in terms of willingness to take rejection, to live in poverty, and to be field independent.

Personality characteristics on both standardized tests and observational measures of both male and female artists showed them to be aloof, reserved, introspective, serious, and nonconforming to contemporary social values (Getzels & Csikszentmihalyi, 1976). Their self-sufficiency was high, they preferred to make their own decisions, and they were often felt to be independent, subjective, intense, and imaginative. They were both radical and experimental. Superego strength or conscience scores were low. The stereotype of the unconventional artist seems to have some basis for both males and females, and yet there is a great disparity between the number of female visual artists versus male.

*Gender Differences.* Using the California Psychological Inventory, Barron (1972) studied young artists at the San Francisco Art Institute and at the Rhode Island School of Design. Profiles of both male and female art students supported that they were not interested in making a good impression on other people and were not as well socialized. They also reported a high need to achieve success independently, were more flexible in outlook, and were less cheerful than others. Using the Minnesota Multiphasic Personality Inventory in the same study, male and female art students scored in the pathological ranges on all scales. This could be an indication of their low need for conformity. They were far less rigid, and did not show other signs of overt psychosis. The females were also unconventional, flexible, open, and showed independence. They approached life vigorously. The females were different from the male artists in that they had less flamboyance, seemed more naive, and were more introverted. In comparison with other females, however, they appeared to be adventurous, independent, and very willful.

Upon interviewing the art students, Barron (1972) found out what the test did not reveal. This centered around the degree of intensity with which the students pursued their chosen careers. The main difference came in the intensity of the commitment of the young artists to their work. Almost all of the men said their artwork was their life, was necessary for life, and was their main reason for living; in other words, "without painting I couldn't function" (p. 34). Conversely, only one woman indicated that her work was essential, and the other made comments such as this: "It's half my life, the other half is my future family" (p. 35). The men tended to view their work with passion and zeal, the women with distance and detachment. Barron thus pointed out differences in self-image in the women and that these differences were not indications of the real quality of the men's and women's art work, indicating that the quality of the women's art work was equally high. He wondered why they were not as intense in their pursuit of art as a career, especially because this intensity seemed to be a clue in deducing the reasons for the ultimate successes of male artists. In conclusion, Barron assumed in 1972 that women's creative energies were sapped by having children, and that they could not continue to be creative and still have children. This argument tends to prevail today.

At the Art Institute of Chicago, Getzels and Csikszentmihalyi (1976) administered a battery of tests to 321 sophomore and junior student artists, 152 females and 169 males. They tried to compare the personality characteristics of these students with students who were not studying art. They found that more females than males decided on art as a career before age 10. Getzels and Csikszentmihalyi commented that teachers appraised male students on the basis of their personalities rather than their abilities and perceptual areas, but they appraised the female students on the basis of what perceptual skills they displayed. This may reflect a covert belief that a male artistic student will develop his vocation with time, whereas a female student who does not have an intense vocation to begin with will abandon her aspirations and settle for more traditional pursuits. When gender differences with the two groups were taken into consideration, female artists showed more masculine values than female college students of their age. And the male artists had more effeminate personalities than most male college students. It seems as though artists in this study were more androgynous, tending toward the middle of the continuum on masculinity/femininity.

In the development of Talent Research Project at the University of Chicago, Sloane and Sosniak (1985) studied 12 men and 8 women sculptors. Their research indicated few gender differences in describing the development of these artists, with the exception of the parents' wishes for their children. To a larger extent, the parents wanted the females to be happily married. With regard to gender differences, research has suggested that perhaps the reason few women become successful visual artists might have to do with how intensely they pursue their art, as well as their spatial abilities. Also, faculty attitudes toward female students seem to be important, with the personality characteristics of the males being more valued than the real abilities of the females. Lastly, the expectation that females should get married and have children is advocated and communicated through parental values (Piirto, 1991).

## Kinesthetic Giftedness

*Definition of Kinesthetic Intelligence.* Skilled use of one's body has been important for thousands of years. The Greeks revered the beauty of the human form and sought to develop a body that was graceful and perfect in proportion. Generally speaking, they attempted to seek a harmony between mind and body, with the mind trained to use the body properly and body trained to respond to the power of the mind. Kinesthetic intelligence is the ability to use one's body in highly differentiated and skilled ways, for expressive as well as goal-directed purposes (Gardner, 1983). An additional characteristic is the capacity to skillfully work with objects, both those that utilize fine motor movements and also those that require gross motor movements. In essence, kinesthetic performance cannot come about simply through the exercise of one single ability. It is the combination of these two capacities, control of one's bodily movements and the capacity to handle objects skillfully, that defines the core of bodily intelligence.

*Assessment.* Even with the best psychological testing procedures, the identification of the kinesthetically gifted is not entirely satisfactory. This is particularly so in areas of aptitude testing where tests of specific talent do not effectively predict subsequent achievement. Nevertheless, a child who is manifestly achieving sporting activities at a level well beyond her contemporaries is easily spotted by parents or teachers or coaches. What is not so obvious is whether the manifest achievement is more or less an index of exceptional ability or a temporary acceleration due to advantages of opportunities in adult support or coaching, or even relatively early physical maturation (Kane, 1986). Although precocious achievement of children in sporting activities makes it relatively easy to select some for special additional training, there is no evidence to indicate how successful these essentially subjective methods are for identifying those most likely to succeed at the highest levels of competitive performance.

*Socialization of Females.* In understanding the female gifted in kinesthetic intelligence it is important to trace the typical development of the athletic girl. Typically, a female is rewarded very early in life for being quiet and still, for not being active, and for not climbing or exploring her environment (Roberts, 1984). Often the verbal praise for "being a good girl" is the end result. As a consequence, females learn to become dependent and to be more sedentary. In addition, physical activity is a behavior that tends to be reserved for males. Female styles of play reflect social learning; activities are expressive and not instrumental, are close to mothers, and are allowed less growth of motor skills through climbing, running, jumping, and throwing. Unfortunately, females do not learn, or are not taught, many motor skills at an early age; therefore, during childhood they do not have opportunities or experiences to practice and perfect movement patterns because there is a void in their learning. Not only does this delay motor movement, but it also retards performance. As a result, girls do not have at their disposal the vast repertoire of movement experiences that boys have. Because motor skill learning is predicated on a series of progressive stages of development, failure to learn rhythm entry skills interferes with subsequent learning and places a limit on future performance. If girls do not learn and practice basic motor skill patterns, the potential for performance at later stages is hindered (Boutillier & San Giovanni, 1983).

*Early Socialization Experiences.* Of course, all females do not live a childhood devoid of physical activity. Many young girls play in some games and sports. What may be a consequence of participating in these games? First, most girls can see for themselves that their skill level may not be comparable to that of their male peers. Second, girls are not easily chosen to play on a team, or if so are typically chosen last. Third and most important, their peers often tell them that they are not good or that they don't need to be, because sports are for boys anyway. Two negative outcomes of these early socialization experiences occur: (a) a lack of experience leads to low interest, and (b) lower skills lead to lack of success. As a result a belief system evolves, one that appears to have some validity: Boys are good in sports, girls are not. Unfortunately, the assumption behind this belief system, that girls do not have the innate capacity to execute motor skills very well, is not valid (Kleiber & Hemmer, 1981).

*Socialization.* The role of the mother and father is critical as socializing agents in the development of the kinesthetic gifted female. Although both parents promote sex-typed behaviors, several studies indicate that fathers emphasize sex-typed play more than mothers. For this reason fathers play a more important role in sports socialization than previously believed. Playful children have fathers who roughhouse with them, whereas girls who are highly playful have fathers who practice physical skills with them (Greendorfer, 1979). Fathers also play a role in sex-typing female activities, particularly in choice of sex-appropriate toys or nursery school activities. Fathers of highly feminine daughters encourage sex-appropriate activities more than do fathers of unfeminine girls. Parents may not be fully aware of how their practices undermine the principle of equal treatment (Parke & Suomi, 1980). By the time they reach elementary school age, children have determined for themselves that active sports are masculine and not feminine and they perceive that masculine games have a higher perceived value. Further evidence of this social learning appears in children's ranking of activities. Boys indicate that sports are the most important attribute for popularity, whereas girls indicate that grades are. Also, girls identify "being nice" as most important, while boys identify "to being good in sports" as most important (Buchanan, Blankenbaker, & Cotton, 1976).

Labeling has a particularly powerful effect on children's choice of games and sports (Armstrong, 1982), with boys and girls choosing sports that have been labeled according to their gender.

Family influences have tended to channel the majority of females into activities other than sports and thus perpetuate sexism in sports. However, many women do become interested and involved in sports. Some become world-class athletes and demonstrate superior levels of performance, achievement, and competence. How are the social learning experiences different from the majority of females? What was the nature of the early childhood experiences, and how did the family provide a social milieu that supported a sport involvement? Several studies (Greendorfer, 1974, 1979) reveal that female intercollegiate athletes are raised in families in which one or both parents actively participate in sports. In addition, games and sports are typical family activities, and during an athlete's childhood, parents frequently played with them in these games. Also, most athletes acknowledge that the family first initiated their early interest in and participation in sports. A positive relationship has been found between parental encouragement, parental interests, and female adolescent sport participation. Often, sport is viewed as a family activity. Indirectly, parents encourage sport participation, and these women perceive sport activities as "normal." Because the parents are participants themselves, they also serve as role models and tend to reinforce their daughters' play in sport behaviors (Orlick, 1974).

Other characteristics of childhood patterns were that these athletes enjoyed sports when they were young; that they were good in sports; that they rated their ability above average; and that they placed some value and importance on being good in sports (Kane, 1986). Related to this point, they perceived their parents as placing some importance on their being good in sports. Thus, women who become athletes had a history of early sport participation, were rewarded for their participation, and interpret their social sport experiences as having positive consequences.

*Gender Differences.* Spreitzer, Lewko, and Snyder (1976) found some variation in the types of influences on boys and on girls. Boys who were highly involved in sports were influenced by their father and have a higher value toward sports than those not highly involved. For the girls, those who were highly involved in sports received more influence from each family member, held a higher value toward sports, and perceived themselves to be more skilled then those less actively involved. This is an interesting profile, because it seems that several sources of influence must be present in order for girls to overcome stereotypic socialization experiences.

If one major social system does not provide sufficient influence, then another must have a strong positive impact if sports socialization is to occur. The school is a logical choice because it influences so much of our cognitive as well as social learning and provides a context within which children learn many social competencies. However, research indicates that, for athletes as well as nonathletes, the school plays a minor role in socializing females in sports (Greendorfer, 1977). First of all, despite the implementation of Title IX, the school merely reinforces sport roles learned elsewhere. It does not introduce females to sports, nor does it have a strong impact in teaching them sport skills (Greendorfer, 1977; Greendorfer & Lewko, 1978). This relatively insignificant role of the school represents a major difference between male and female patterns.

The process of socializing women into sports is more complex then originally believed. Unlike males, who receive strong, consistent influences from all major social systems, females must receive most of their influence from the family. Therefore, guidance of gifted female athletes should focus on supporting the family's effort to enhance athletic excellence.

The next most important influence for the female athlete is the coach. It is the shared goal of the coach and the elite athlete to facilitate her physical skill and performance and also have a positive effect on her psychosocial development by participating in competition. To accomplish these two goals a coach is needed to facilitate the athlete's performance in acquiring skills of the sport. The second, and perhaps more ambiguous, goal concerns the extent to which desired behaviors and athletic performance are brought under each athlete's self-control. It is always the athlete and never the coach who engages in the sport act. To achieve these goals, modeling stands as one of the most impressive means for affecting behavior and predictable and controllable ways. Modeling involves the acquisition of new skills and alteration of existing skills through observation of someone else demonstrating those skills. From such modeling the athlete learns not only how to behave, but also what to expect as likely consequences of her behavior.

Another technique presented for coaches' use in developing self-control in athletes exerts tremendous influence on the extent to which any coach can achieve their goals. This development of self-control is in reference to internal rather than external behaviors. Self-control consists of self-observation plus self-regulation. In essence, the athlete becomes her own behavioral scientist, replacing unsystematic observations and control with systematic techniques. The coach should assist gifted athletes in their efforts to benefit from cognitive behavioral modification techniques and develop self-control. External controls guided and directed by the coach at the outset should give way to internal controls as each athlete progresses toward self-control. With a combined effort from the coach and athlete, sport participation for the elite can often fulfill some of the long-term goals of personal psychosocial development.

The attainment of competitive success and enduring life skills in the gifted female athlete is influenced by socialization, personality characteristics, identification of abilities, and developmental issues. Guidance of female athletes should include support for the family's efforts to promote the young woman's identity and abilities as an athlete; the selection of a coach who will work as an active partner; and the encouragement of techniques that will bring about self-control of athletic behavior.

## NURTURANCE OF A SPECIFIC EXTRAORDINARY TALENT

There are some commonalities among talented women with regard to the nurturance of their specific talents. In Bloom's (1985) study of eminent concert pianists, Olympic athletes, and sculptors, stages were identified in which parents, teachers, and others had provided critical assistance in promoting the development of these young people's talents. The first stage of talent development, according to Bloom, is the development of identity. In this stage, usually late childhood and early adolescence, the gifted young person begins to discover an identity in her area of interest; she may be labeled the "class artist" or the "school musician." Throughout adolescence the reinforcement of others and an internal sense of growing confidence in a talent helps the gifted young person to believe in herself as a musician, an athlete, or an artist. It is this stage that seems to pose a problem for gifted girls who are in environments that do not recognize and support their talents. As has been seen for both visual artists and musicians, women seem to be less likely than men to see their creative work in these fields as their central identity.

The second stage of the development of talent, according to Bloom, is the relationship with a mentor. Mentors are critical to the development of specific talent. Mentors may be tutors, coaches, or even a caring and interested adult with some connection with the field of interest of the young person. The mentor not only nurtures the talent but seeks outlets for the young person's creative expression. The mentor provides introductions to other talented people in that area and familiarizes the young person with the nature of the profession that she is about to enter. Mentors are able to acquire recognition for the young person's talent among others in that field. For gifted women, a mentor may be the deciding factor in assuring later equality in salary and status with male peers (Kaufmann, 1980).

The mentor is often the key to the third component in the development of talent: specialized education and training. Often it is the mentor who provides the specialized training; sometimes, however, it is the mentor who identifies precisely the right coach or tutor for that young person's talent. Bloom found that parents of young people with specific extraordinary talents were willing to travel long distances or even move the entire family in order to provide the kind of specialized training that was necessary to the young person's talent.

Finally, extraordinary talent cannot be actualized as products or performances unless the gifted individual is able to resolve conflict that interferes with productivity and maintain an organized and disciplined approach to his or her work. Therefore, the final stage of the nurturance of specific, extraordinary talent is the shaping of a lifestyle in which continuous productivity is the norm.

Therefore the counselor who is working with young women of specific extraordinary talent must attend to the issues of nurturing identity, assisting in the discovery of a mentor, assisting in arranging of specialized training in education, and preparing the young woman for sustained productivity in adulthood. The review of the characteristics of young women with specific extraordinary talent shows that an important difference between males and females in many of these talent areas is the stronger identification of males with their profession. More males than females who are gifted in the arts consider themselves artists (Piirto, 1991); more male than female composers would consider no other work than music; and mathematically gifted girls consider math to be less relevant to their lives and their futures than mathematically gifted boys. Therefore, despite equal talent it may be that males' stronger identification with their work promotes their eventual success.

Second, these descriptions of specifically talented girls and women also make clear the importance of mentoring and specialized education in the development of these talents. Perhaps more than males, these gifted females need role models, particularly in areas in which women are very rare, such as musical composition and theoretical physics.

There is some evidence from the study of specifically talented girls and women that they are less likely to seek special education and specialized training. Verbally precocious girls and mathematically precocious girls are less likely than their male counterparts to participate in summer workshops and to seek further opportunities in gifted education (Fox, 1981). Mentors may choose males more often than females as their proteges (Sandler, 1983).

# CAREER DEVELOPMENT INTERVENTIONS WITH GIFTED GIRLS AND WOMEN

## Problems with Career Development Interventions

Developing career interventions for gifted young women is a difficult and sometimes frustrating endeavor. As many counselors have found, gifted girls may resist efforts to expand their options, raise their aspirations, or change attitudes toward work and relationships (Daniels, Heath, & Enns, 1985; Kerr, 1985; Olshen & Matthews, 1987). There may be good reasons that gifted girls and young women sometimes resist interventions aimed at changing their attitudes toward careers. First of all, there is mounting evidence that girls and women are far more interested in "connectedness" than in achievement (Gilligan, 1985; Belenky, Clinchy, Goldberger, & Tarule, 1986). Gifted girls and women not only are concerned about the impact of careers on personal relationships but are also concerned about the overall societal impact of particular choices of work. The mathematically gifted girl wishes to know not only how being a mathematician will affect her marriage and family choices, but also to what degree math-related careers can help to improve society. Few career development interventions for women or girls address these relationships and social issues. Instead, career development workshops, career counseling, and career education often treat career planning in isolation from lifestyle or relationship planning. Gifted girls and women may simply be unwilling to deal with career planning separately from the planning of other issues important to them and to their lives.

Second, most interventions for gifted girls and women have focused on raising aspirations, changing attitudes, or nurturing particular career choices, rather than attending to the development of identity, purpose, and commitment. The literature on specific talents seems to show that it is these characteristics that define the vocational behavior of eminent individuals. Career development is too often seen as assisting women in the search for appropriate jobs rather than the search for meaning. If, as Holland and Eisenhart (1990) contended, girls and women continue to be persuaded by the peer groups that meaning can only be attained through relationships with men, it is unlikely that career interventions that do not confront this assumption will be effective. Gifted girls and women need to be taught that it may be as satisfying to fall in love with an idea as it is to fall in love with a partner. Gifted girls and women need the opportunity to learn how one might establish one's identity through one's work as well as through one's loving relationships. Finally, girls and women need to understand that they can create meaning through their activities and accomplishments and not merely through the association with people of great accomplishments. Interventions that do not attend to these more profound issues are likely to have only a superficial impact on women's career plans and goals.

In addition to these philosophical problems of career development interventions for women there are frequently structural problems that mitigate their effectiveness. First of all, many interventions that are used with gifted girls and women are simply too brief to have any real impact on a lifetime of socialization for lower status careers. Most career interventions for gifted girls are no more than 1 or 2 hours of a workshop or a brief counseling session. Another frequent problem with career intervention for gifted girls and women is lack of follow-up. Even a brief workshop might be effective if goals that were identified in the workshop were reinforced through further contact with counselors, teachers, or mentors. However, it is unusual for career workshops to be followed by any kind of individual attention. Finally, a structural problem of many career interventions for gifted girls and young women appears in the selection of components of the workshop. Often the major component of workshops for gifted girls is the presentation of a successful woman or a panel of successful women talking about their work and their lives. The intention of such presentations is usually to expose gifted girls to effective role models. However, for modeling to occur it is necessary for the model to be observed being rewarded for her behavior. If successful women spend too much time in their presentations describing the stress and suffering that they have undergone in the attainment of their goals, gifted girls may draw the conclusion that high career aspirations are simply not worth the trouble. Other problems may include the use of inefficient or inappropriate assessment instruments, the use of career education material that is below level or patronizing, and ineffective instruction and guidance by the leaders.

Finally, a major problem for the counselor who wishes to choose effective interventions is the lack of evaluation of those interventions that exist. Few interventions for gifted girls have included an evaluation component; even fewer have been designed and implemented with a comparison or control group. Therefore, conclusions about the effectiveness of these interventions are difficult to draw. Nevertheless it seems important to examine the various interventions that have been developed for gifted girls and women in order to glean those components that seem to be effective in promoting and enhancing self-concept, increasing career aspirations, nurturing the development of purpose, and establishing commitment to career goals.

## Levels of Career Development Interventions

Career interventions for gifted girls and women can be categorized roughly into three levels of intervention (Kerr, 1989). Each of these levels is more sophisticated than the one before because it incorporates more of the strategies and techniques that are associated with lasting and more profound changes in the attitude of gifted girls and young women toward the role of work in their lives. At the first level of intervention, girls are encouraged to explore careers in nontraditional fields such as engineering, computer science, and math, no matter what their actual interests, needs, or values are. They are encouraged to explore high-status occupations and to have high aspirations, no matter what their actual interests might be. They may be discouraged from traditionally feminine occupations. This may be the most common approach to career education for gifted girls.

At the second level of intervention are the kinds of workshops that encourage gifted girls to raise their aspirations within occupations that are congruent with their personalities and needs. Those interventions take into account the need for individual assessment and the need for individualized guidance. These interventions may include "diagnostic-prescriptive" models and some guidance laboratory approaches (Kerr, 1983).

At level three are counseling interventions that are now in the process of being developed (Kerr & Erb, 1991). These are value-based career counseling interventions. This is a comprehensive approach that involves assessment, group counseling, and individual counseling and that takes into account the importance of roles and relationships as well as career goals. The focus of these workshops is the search for meaning rather than the search for a job. The workshop is based on the assumption that encouraging a sense of purpose may be more effective in maintaining high aspirations than simply targeting high-salary, high-prestige occupations. Young women are encouraged to commit themselves to an idea that they value most deeply by entering the occupation that will most likely allow the actualization of this value. In this way deeply held values are used to create career goals that take into account all aspects of women's needs and concerns.

The career development interventions that are described in the next section are for the most part interventions that fall in categories two and three. Although a great many workshops abound in level one, they are not reviewed here.

## Examples of Career Development Interventions

*Changing Awareness and Self-Esteem.*   Olshen and Matthews (1987) describe a study in which the experimenters attempted to increase gifted girls' awareness of conflicts related to being female and gifted and enhancing self-esteem in the process. Fourteen gifted students at a private school for gifted children were included in the study. They were grouped into two sections, Grades 4 through 7 and Grades 8 through 12. As pre- and posttests the girls were given the Piers-Harris Self-Concept Test. A curriculum was designed with the intent of increasing awareness of gender-role stereotypes; illustrating the restrictiveness of gender roles; increasing awareness of direct and indirect sexism in the media; increasing awareness of possible lifestyle choices; and raising consciousness of gender stereotyping in work roles. Twelve weekly 40-minute sessions were planned with each group of girls, including homework assignments. Most of the group meetings centered around discussion of material taken from mass media and other sources that illustrated the ways in which gender bias is transmitted. Girls were also encouraged to reflect on their own feelings about being a girl. Biographies were used as a source of information, with eminent women's biographies being used to raise awareness of women's participation throughout history and leadership positions.

Finally, many structured group exercises were performed that included some aspect of increasing awareness. Self-concept scores for the participants in the group did improve over the course of the workshop. In addition to the scores on the self-concept test, however, the researchers gathered observations of the girls' behavior in the groups. It was observed that the girls in the younger group were more enthusiastic and interested and completed more homework assignments than did the older group. Girls in this group believed that women and girls were sometimes treated badly in society but overall were glad to be girls. They felt better equipped to identify injustice and to work at dealing with it. At the end, all of the girls in this group agreed that girls have choices that they can make about how to live their lives.

The girls in the older group were frequently tardy and complained quite a bit about the groups. Although they called the discussions boring, they animatedly participated in them and frequently had new insights into the roles of women and society. They often did not complete homework assignments. Most of the young women believed that they did need a course like this, but preferred a course in mathematics or computers. There were clear double standards in this group in that all of them desired not to be discriminated against or to be treated as inferior to men; however, they did enjoy other aspects of sex-role stereotyped behaviors, such as being given "the red carpet treatment" by males. Although in the second group there was a great deal of resistance there was also observable development of self-assertion and group cohesion over the course of time. The experimenters noticed that the girls in both groups initially seemed unaware of the natural consequences of their choices "that if they did not want to be limited by double standards, they could not use these standards to their advantage" (Olshen & Matthews, 1987, p. 231). Apparently, by the end of the study the girls had reached some level of awareness of this double standard.

*Changing Attitudes and Course-Taking Behaviors.* At Johns Hopkins University's Study for Mathematically Precocious Youth, Lynn Fox (1976b) developed a program to change junior high gifted girls' attitudes and course-taking behaviors with regard to careers in science and mathematics. The purpose of the program was to create an environment in which girls could be motivated to continue in math and science who might normally drop out of these fields. Twenty-six seventh-grade girls who were gifted in mathematics were selected for this study. A 3-month course in mathematics was taught by women instructors in exclusively all-girls classes. There was an informal structure that stressed small-group and individualized instruction and cooperative rather than competitive activities. In keeping with girls' interests in socially oriented careers, teachers emphasized the ways in which mathematics was related to solving various social problems. Girls were helped through counseling to view themselves as competent in mathematics and to overcome math anxiety. This group of girls was compared to two control groups, one male and one female group attending other mathematics classes. Eighteen of the 26 girls continued to attend the class on a regular basis and 11 of these enrolled in Algebra II the following year. At the end of the first year, 10 girls and none of the boys were accelerated by 1 year, and all of the girls were more advanced in math knowledge than the boys in the control group. Two years later 48% of the girls in the experimental group were accelerated by 1 or more years compared to 90% of the control group girls. Control group boys were accelerated about the same rate as the girls in the experiment.

Therefore the program was successful in helping girls to accelerate their knowledge of mathematics to at least an equal level to that of gifted boys. However, during that same period the math-career interests of these girls rose, but then dropped off. As time went by the gains from the experimental treatment passed, possibly because there was little further encouragement after the class was over to consider careers in mathematics. Therefore, encouraging academic achievement in gifted girls is not enough to promote career aspirations in that area; rather, it is important for continued effort of the sort described here.

Interestingly, although Fox's study was designed well before the publication of the work of Gilligan (1985) and Belenky et al. (1986) on women's cognitive and moral development, the workshop included many features that are in accordance with their contention that girls need a more relationship-oriented and socially focused approach to education and guidance. The all-girl classes, the presence of female role models, the emphasis on the social aspects of math and science, and the emphasis on cooperation rather than competition may all have contributed to the initial success of this experiment. Perhaps if these features were present in continuing guidance interventions for gifted girls, the career aspirations in math and science might also have been maintained.

*Diagnostic-Prescriptive Career Counseling.* Fleming and Hollinger (1979) developed one of the most comprehensive approaches to guiding gifted girls with their project CHOICE: Creating Her Options In Career Exploration. In Hollinger's (1991) summary of characteristics of effective career development strategy for gifted girls, several steps were noted. These include broadening career exploration so that gifted young women do not eliminate occupational choices as inappropriate for their sex or too difficult; helping girls to integrate multiple life roles; and developing essential skills such as objective self-appraisal and critical evaluation of external barriers. All of these components were present in the workshop developed by Fleming and Hollinger in 1979. This diagnostic prescriptive program for talented adolescent young women was created for high school girls in the Cleveland area. Eleventh-grade girls were screened by counselors using a talent inventory and school records. A student questionnaire was used to assess internal barriers that gifted girls might perceive or might be experiencing, such as the fear of success or lack of confidence in goals. Another questionnaire sought information about external barriers such as lack of family support, low parental aspirations, lack of exposure to role models, low financial resources, or sex discrimination. The maturity of each student's career development was also measured, and students were assessed with regard to the degree to which their career ideas had been crystallized and the degree to which these ideas were appropriate.

For each participant a prescriptive plan was developed that indicated possible treatment of or solution to internal or external barriers. Sometimes the strategies were individual and sometimes they were group strategies. Over a 14-week period, a career development experience was provided that included three career information workshops, role-model experiences in which each girl interacted with a role model of her own selection, and 11 group sessions in which a career education curriculum was modified and individualized to meet the needs of every girl in the group. Although immediate evaluation information was not available, the participants have been followed up by the authors in order to discover the degree to which the program was successful in reducing barriers to gifted girls.

*Developing Vocational Purpose and Identity.* The Values Based Career Counseling approach is based on interventions developed at the Nebraska Guidance Laboratory for Gifted and Talented and the Counseling Laboratory for Talent Development at the Belin National Center for Gifted Education. In its original form, it was an intervention intended to raise the career aspirations of rural, adolescent, gifted girls (Kerr, 1983). It was reconceptualized and expanded into an intervention with a much more ambitious goals: to raise aspirations, to specify career goals based on values, to heighten sense of purpose, and to increase confidence in vocational identity. The intervention, called Values Based Career Counseling, was very successful in raising aspirations (Kerr, 1983) and was moderately successful in helping both men and women to set goals (Kerr & Ghrist, 1987) and to increase their self-perceived sense of purpose and confidence in identity (Kerr & Erb, 1991).

Values Based Career Counseling is a three-part intervention including assessment, individual counseling, and group counseling. The three components can be built into a day-long workshop or can be delivered over the course of three separate sessions. Students generally participate in groups of 10 to 12 individuals. In the first session, students are introduced to the idea of values-based career counseling; they are urged to consider making choices based on their most deeply felt needs and values rather than on practical bases alone. Then, in small groups, they are guided through a Perfect Future Day Fantasy (Kerr, 1991b), in which students visualize a perfect working day 10 years in the future, from morning till night. The exercise is processed at length, with a focus on the barriers that the participants see to achieving their perfect day and ways of overcoming those barriers. The values that underlie each student's fantasy are described and discussed. In the second session, students are administered one of the vocational interest tests based on the Holland Themes (Holland, 1985), the Personality Research Form (PRF; Jackson, 1974), and the Rokeach Values Survey (Rokeach, 1982).

In the third session, students meet individually in 75-minute sessions with counselors. Students are asked to state their ideal career goals. The counselors interpret the results of the inventories in such a way as to support students' values-based choices. That is, Holland codes are interpreted first in order to establish general vocational interests; the

PRF scales are interpreted to narrow down occupations within interest areas that are most likely to meet the highest needs as described by the PRF; and finally, the top-ranked values on the Rokeach Values Survey are presented as the ideal arbiters of a career goal. Those career goals that fit the individual's interests and needs and that serve her highest values are encouraged by the counselor. The counselor also presents information about eminent people, describing the process of "falling in love with an idea," and encourages the student to think of a career as a vocation or calling, based on the love of a value or ideal. Because the values-based approach has been effective in helping students to perceive careers as a source of meaning and purpose, it may be a promising intervention for gifted young women. Like other interventions described here, it is relationship oriented; it is brief and powerful; it can be used with all-female dyads; and it focuses on the interpersonal and intrapersonal aspects of career goals, which are most likely to concern gifted women.

## CONCLUSION

All of these interventions are the beginning of a search for ways of counseling gifted girls and women that are uniquely suited to their needs. These techniques must treat gifted girls and women first as individuals of extraordinary intellectual potential, and second, as females with internal and external barriers to the realization of that potential.

The literature that has been reviewed here clearly points to the need for a deeper understanding of the needs of gifted girls and women as well as to the need for effective counseling strategies for this population. Gifted females have different vocational needs at different stages of their development, and those with specific talents may have specialized needs for guidance, an area that remains fairly unexplored.

Although the development of career counseling strategies for gifted girls and women seems difficult and frustrating, some interventions, particularly those that take into account theory and research on women's development, seem to be helpful and effective for this population. Few other endeavors can unlock such potential and make available to society such an extraordinary source of skills as the counseling of gifted girls and women.

## REFERENCES

Armstrong, D. (1982). Psycho-social study of outstanding female athletes. In R. Sands (Ed.), *The world of sociology* (pp. 99–116). Melbourne: Rusden.

Arnold, K., & Denny, T. (1985, April). *The lives of academic achievers: The career aspiration's of male and female high school valedictorians and salutatorians.* Paper presented at the annual meeting of the American Educational Research Association, Chicago, IL.

Ayer, F. C. (1916). *The psychology of drawing.* Baltimore: Warwick & York.

Bachtold, L. M., & Werner, E. E. (1973). Personality characteristics of creative women. *Perceptual Motor Skills, 36,* 311–319.

Bakken, L., Hershey, M., & Miller, P. (1990). Gifted adolescent females' attitudes toward gender equality in educational and intergender relationships. *Roeper Review, 12,* 261–264.

Barron, F. (1972). *Artists in the making.* San Francisco: Seminar Press.

Belenky, M. F., Clinchy, B. M., Goldberger, N. R., & Tarule, J. M. (1986). *Women's ways of knowing: The development of self, voice, and mind.* New York: Basic Books.

Benbow, C. P., & Stanley, J. C. (1983). Sex differences in mathematical reasoning ability: More facts. *Science, 222.*

Beanbow, C. P., & Stanley, J. C. (1984). Gender and the science major: A study of mathematically precocious youth. In M. W. Steinkamp & M. L. Maehr (Eds.), *Women in science* (pp. 165–196). Greenwich, CT: JAI Press.

Betz, N. E., & Hackett, G. (1981). The relationship of career-related self-efficacy expectations to perceived career options in college women and men. *Journal of Counseling Psychology, 28,* 399–410.

Bloom, B. S. (1985). *Developing talent in young people.* New York: Ballantine Books.

Boutillier, M., & San Giovanni, L. (1983). *The sporting woman.* Champaign, IL: Human Kinetics.

Brody, L. E., & Benbow, C. P. (1986). Social and emotional adjustment of adolescents extremely talented in verbal or mathematical reasoning. *Journal of Youth and Adolescence, 15,* 1–18.

Buchanan, H., Blankenbaker, J., & Cotten, D. (1976). Academic and athletic ability as popularity factors in elementary school children. *Research Quarterly, 47,* 320–325.

Card, J. J., Steele, L., & Abeles, R. P. (1980). Sex differences in realization of individual potential for achievement. *Journal of Vocational Behavior, 17,* 1–20.

Clark, G., & Zimmerman, E. (1983). At the age of six, I gave up a magnificent career as a painter: Seventy years of research about identifying students with superior abilities in the visual arts. *Gifted Child Quarterly, 27*(4), 180–184.

Colangelo, N., & Kerr, B. A. (1990). Extreme academic talent: Profiles of perfect scorers. *Journal of Educational Psychology, 82,* 404–410.

Daniels, R. R., Heath, R., and Enns, K. S. (1985). Fostering creative behavior among university women. *Roeper Review, 7*(3), 164–168.

Dolny, C. (1985). University of Toronto Schools' gifted students' career & family plans. *Roeper Review, 7*(3), 160–162.

Eccles, J. (1984). Sex differences in mathematics participation In Advances in motivation and achievement (Vol. 2, pp. 93–137). Greenwich, CT: JAI Press.

Ellis, J. L., & Willinsky, J. M. (1990). *Girls, women, and giftedness.* Monroe, NY: Trillium Press.

Ellison, R., Abe, C., Rox, D., Coray, D., & Taylor, C. (1975). Using biographical information in identifying artistic talent. In W. B. Barke & J. S. Renzulli (Eds.), *Psychology and education of the gifted.* New York: Ironington Publishers.

Fleming, E., & Hollinger C. (1979). *Project Choice: Creating her option in career education.* Cleveland, OH. ERIC Reproduction service No. ED185321.

Fox, L. H. (1976a). Career education for gifted pre-adolescents. *G.C.O., 20*(3), 262–268.

Fox, L. H. (1976b, August). *Changing behaviors and attitudes of gifted girls.* Paper presented at the American Psychological Association, Washington, DC.

Fox, L. H. (1981). Preparing gifted girls for future leadership roles. *G/C/T, 17,* 7–11.

Fox, L. H. (1982). *Verbally precocious youth*. Baltimore: Johns Hopkins University Press.

Fox, L. H., Benbow, C. P., & Perkins, S. (1983). An accelerated mathematics program for girls: A longitudinal evaluation. In C. P. Benbow & J. C. Stanley (Eds.), *Academic precocity* (pp. 221–256). Baltimore: Johns Hopkins University Press.

Fox, L. H., & Cohn, S. J. (1980). Sex differences in development of mathematically precocious talent. In L. H. Fox, L. Brady, & D. Tobin (Eds.), *Women and the mathematical mystique* (pp. 94–111). Baltimore: Johns Hopkins University Press.

Gaitskell, C., & Horowitz, A. (1970). *Children and their art* (2nd ed.). New York: Harcourt Brace.

Frederickson, R. H., & Rothrey, J. W. H, (1972). *Recognizing and assisting multipotential use*. Columbus, OH: Charles Merril.

Gardner, H. (1983). *Frames of mind: The theory of multiple intelligences*. New York: Basic Books.

Getzels, J. W., & Csikszentmihalyi, M. (1976). *The creative vision: A study of problem finding in art*. New York: Wiley.

Gilligan, C. (1985). *In a different voice*. Cambridge, MA: Harvard University Press.

Greenberg Lake Analysis Group & American Association for University Women. (1991). *Shortchanging girls, shortchanging America*. Washington, DC: American Association for University Women.

Greendorfer, S. L. (1974). *The nature of female socialization into sport: A study of selected college woman's sport participation*. Unpublished doctoral dissertation, University of Wisconsin.

Greendorfer, S. L. (1977). Role of socializing agents in female sport involvement. *Research Quarterly, 46*(2), 304–310.

Greendorfer, S. L. (1979). Differences in childhood socialization: Influences of women in sport and women not involved in sport. In M. L. Krotee (Ed.), *The dimension of sport sociology* (pp. 59–72). West Point, NY: Leisure Press.

Helson, R. (1983). Creative mathematicians. In R. Albert (Ed.), *Genius and eminence: The social psychology of creativity and exceptional achievement* (pp. 311–330). London: Pergamon.

Hildreth, G. H. (1966). *Introduction to the gifted*. New York: McGraw-Hill.

Holland, J. L. (1985). *Making vocational choices*. Englewood Cliffs, NJ: Prentice-Hall.

Holland, D. C., & Eisenhart, M. A. (1990). *Educated in romance: Women, achievement, and college culture*. Chicago: University of Chicago Press.

Hollinger, C. L. (1983). Counseling the gifted and talented female adolescent: The relationship between social self-esteem and traits of instrumentality and expressiveness. *Gifted Child Quarterly, 27*(4), 157–161.

Hollinger, C. L. (1985). The stability of self perceptions of instrumental and expressive traits and social self-esteem among gifted and talented female adolescents. *Journal for the Education of the Gifted, 8*(1), 107–126.

Hollinger, C. L. (1986). Career aspirations as a function of Holland personality type among mathematically talented female adolescents. *Journal for the Education of the Gifted, 9*(2), 133–145.

Hollinger, C. L. (1991). Facilitating the career development of gifted young women. *Roeper Review, 13*(3), 135–139.

Hollinger, C. L., & Fleming, E. S. (1985). Social orientation and the social self-esteem of gifted and talented female adolescents. *Journal of Youth and Adolescence, 14*, 389–399.

Hollinger, C. L., & Fleming, E. S. (1988). Gifted and talented young women: Antecedents and correlates of life satisfaction. *Gifted Child Quarterly, 32*(2), 254–261.

Hollingworth, L. (1923). *Special talents and defects*. New York: Macmillan.

Hollingworth, L. S. (1926). *Gifted children: Their nature and nurture*. New York: Macmillan.

Hollingsworth, L. S. (1942). *Children above 180 IQ Stanford-Binet: Origin and development*. Yonkers on Hudson, NY: World Book.

Hyde, J. S. (1981). How large are cognitive gender differences? A meta-analysis. *American Psychologist, 36,* 892–901.

Jackson, D. N. (1974). *The Personality Research Form.* Odessa, FL: Psychological Assessment Resources.

Jacobs, J. E., & Eccles, J. S. (1985, March). Gender differences in math ability: The impact of media reports on parents. *Educational Researcher,* pp. 20–24.

Janos, P. M., & Robinson, N. M. (1985). Psychosocial development in intellectually gifted children. In F. D. Horowitz & M. O'Brien (Eds.), *The gifted and talented: Developmental perspectives.* Washington, DC: American Psychological Association.

Kane, J. E. (1986). Giftedness in sport. In G. R. Gleeson (Ed.), *The growing child in competitive sport* (pp. 185–204). London: British Association of National Coaches Limited.

Karnes, F. A., & Wherry, J. N. (1983). CPQ personality factors of upper elementary gifted students. *Journal of Personality Assessment, 47,* 303–304.

Kaufmann, F. (1981). The 1964–1968 Presidential Scholars: A follow-up study. *Exceptional Children, 48,* 2.

Kerr, B. A. (1983). Raising the career aspirations of gifted girls. *The Vocational Guidance Quarterly, 32,* 37–43.

Kerr, B. A. (1985). *Smart girls, gifted women.* Columbus, OH: Ohio Psychology.

Kerr, B. A. (1989). The career development of gifted girls and women. In J. L. Ellis & J. M. Willinsky (Eds.), *Girls, women, and giftedness.* Toronto, ONT: Trillium Press.

Kerr, B. A. (1991a, August). *A twenty year follow-up of gifted women graduates of an accelerated learning program.* Paper presented at American Psychological Association, San Francisco.

Kerr, B. A. (1991b). *Handbook for counseling the gifted & talented.* Alexandria, VA: American Association for Counseling & Development.

Kerr, B. A., & Colangelo, N. (1988). The college plans of academic talented students. *Journal of Counseling and Development, 66*(9), 366–370.

Kerr, B. A., Colangelo, N., & Gaeth, J. (1988). Gifted adolescents' attitudes toward their giftedness. *Gifted Child Quarterly, 32*(2), 245–248.

Kerr, B. A., & Erb, C. E. (1991). Career counseling with academically talented students: Effects of a value-based intervention. *Journal of Counseling Psychology, 38*(3), 309–314.

Kerr, B. A., & Ghrist, S. (1987). Intervention for multipotentiality: Effects of a career counseling laboratory for high school students. *Journal of Counseling and Development, 56*(8), 366–370.

Kleiber, D., & Hemmer, J. (1981). Sex differences in the relationship of locus of control and recreational sport participation. *Sex Roles, 7,* 801–810.

Kline, B. E., & Kerr, B. A. (1991a). Gender equity: Meeting the special needs of gifted females. *Roeper Review, 13*(3), 115–136.

Kline, B. E., & Kerr, B. A. (1991b). Gender equity issue continued and meeting the special needs of gifted males. *Roeper Review, 13*(4), 171–229.

Lowenfeld, V., & Brittain, W. L. (1964). *Creative and mental growth* (4th ed.). New York: Macmillan.

Manuel, H. T. (1919). *A study of talent in drawing.* Bloomington, IL: Public School Publishing.

Meier, N. (1939). Studies in the psychology of art. *Psychological Monographs, 51,* 5.

Munro, T. (1956). *Art education: Its philosophy and psychology.* New York: Liberal Arts Press.

Noble, K. D. (1989). Counseling gifted women: Becoming the heroes of our own stories. *Journal for the Education of the Gifted, 12*(2), 131–141.

Noble, K. D. (1990). Living out the promise of high potential: perception's of 100 gifted women. In J. L. Ellis & J. M. Willinsky (Eds.), *Girls, women, and giftedness* (pp. 123–140). Monroe, NY: Tirllian Press.

Olshen, S., & Mathews, D. (1987). The disappearance of giftedness in girls: An intervention strategy. *Roeper Review, 9*(4), 251–254.

Orlick, T. (1974). Sport participation: A process of shaping behavior. *Human Factors, 5,* 558–561.

Parke, R., & Suomi, S. (1980). Adult male-infant relationships: Human and non-private evidence. In K. Immelmann, G. Barlow, M. Main, & L. Petrinovitch (Eds.), *Behavioral development: The brelefeld interdisciplinary project.* (pp. 90–96). New York: Cambridge University Press.

Phelps, C. R. (1991). Identity formation in career development for gifted women. *Roeper Review, 13*(3), 140–141.

Piirto, J. (1991). Encouraging creativity and talent in adolescents. In J. Genshaft & M. Bircley (Eds.), *The gifted adolescent: Personal and educational issues.* New York: Teachers College Press.

Reis, S. (1991). The need for clarification in research designed to examine gender differences in achievement and accomplishment. *Roeper Review, 13*(4), 193–197.

Roberts, G. C. (1984). Achievement motivation in children's sport. In J. G. Nicholls (Ed.), *The development of achievement motivation* (pp. 256–279). Greenwich, CT: JAI Press.

Robinson, N. M., & Janos, P. M. (1986). Psychological adjustment in a college-level program of marked academic acceleration. *Journal of Youth & Adolescence, 15,* 51–60.

Rodenstein, J. M., & Glickhauf-Hughes, C. (1979). In N. Colangelo & R. Zaffran (Eds.), *New voices in counseling the gifted* (pp. 398–415). Dubuque, IA: Kendall/Hunt.

Rokeach, M. (1982). *Rokeach Values Inventory.* Sunnyvale, CA: Halgren Press.

Sanborn, M. P. (1974). *Career education of gifted and talented boys and girls.* Madison, WI: Research and Guidance Laboratory, Wisconsin University.

Sandler, B. (1983). *The college campus: A chilly climate for women.* Washington, DC: American Council of Education.

Schwartz, L. L. (1980). Advocacy for the neglected: Females. *Gifted Child Quarterly, 24*(3), 113–117.

Sears, P. S., & Barbee, A. H. (1977). Career and life satisfactions among Terman's gifted women. In J. C. Stanley, W. C. George, & C. H. Solano (Eds.), *The gifted and the creative: A fifty year perspective.* Baltimore MD: Johns Hopkins University Press.

Sells, L. W. (1980). The mathematics filler and the education of women and minorities. In L. H. Fox, L. Brady, & D. Tobin (Eds.), *Women and the mathematical mystique.* Baltimore: Johns Hopkins University Press.

Shuter-Dyson, R. (1985). Musical giftedness. In J. Freeman (Ed.), *The psychology of gifted children* (pp. 159–183). New York: Wiley.

Silverman, L. K. (1986). What happens to the gifted girl? In C. J. Maker (Ed.), *Critical issues in gifted education: Programs for the gifted.* Rockville, MD: Aspen.

Silverman, L. K. (1990). Social and emotional education of the gifted: The discoveries of Leta Hollingworth. *Roeper Review, 12*(3), 171–178.

Sloane, K. D., & Sosnick, L. A. (1985). The development of accomplished sculptors. In B. Broom (Ed.), *The development of talent in young people* (pp. 90–138). New York: Ballantine.

Spreitzer, E., Lewko, J., & Snyder, E. E. (1976). Socialization into sport: An exploratory path analysis. *Research Quarterly, 47,* 238–245.

Subotnik, R. F. (1988). The motivation to experiment: A study of gifted adolescents' attitudes toward scientific research. *Journal for the Education of the Gifted, 11*(2), 19–35.

Terman, L. M. (1925). Mental and physical traits of a thousand gifted children. *In Genetic studies of genius.* Stanford, CA: Stanford University Press.

Terman, L. M., & Merrill, M. A. (1960). *Revised Stanford-Binet scale.* New York: Houghton-Mifflin.

Terman, L. M., & Oden, M. H. (1935). The promise of youth. In *Genetic studies of genius* (Vol. 3). Stanford, CA: Stanford University Press.

Terman, L. M., & Oden, M. H. (1947). The gifted child grows up. In *Genetic studies of genius* (Vol. 4). Stanford, CA: Stanford University Press.

Tobin, D., & Fox, L. (1976). *Career interests and career education: A key to change. Women and the Mathematical Mystique.* Baltimore: Johns Hopkins University Press.

Trollinger, L. M. (1983). Interests, activities, and hobbies of high and low creative women musicians during childhood, adolescent, and college years. *Gifted Child Quarterly, 27*(2), 94–97.

Tuttle, F., & Becker, L. (1980). *Characteristics and identification of gifted and talented students.* Washington, DC: National Education Association.

Wechsler, D. (1974). *Wechsler Intelligence Scale for Children–Revised.* New York: Psychological Corporation.

Weiner, N. C., & Robinson, S. E. (1986). Cognitive ability, personality and gender differences in math achievement of gifted adolescents. *Gifted Child Quarterly, 30*, 83–87.

White, W. L. (1984). *The perceived effects of an early enrichment experience: A forty year follow-up study of the Speyer School experiment for gifted students.* Unpublished doctoral dissertation, University of Connecticut, Storrs.

Yochim, L. D. (1967). *Perceptual growth in creativity.* Scranton, PA: International Textbook.

# ❧ 7 ❧

# Career Counseling for Women in the Sciences and Engineering

Nancy E. Betz
*Ohio State University*

This chapter begins by reviewing data regarding the chronic and serious underrepresentation of women in the sciences and engineering. It then proceeds to a discussion of factors related to this underrepresentation, and concludes with recommendations for counseling and other interventions.

## WHY AN INTEREST IN THE SCIENCES AND ENGINEERING?

Occupational choices in the sciences and engineering are of vital concern not only to counseling psychologists interested in helping individuals utilize their abilities and talents, but to our society, which increasingly faces a severe shortage of trained scientists and engineers (Holden, 1989; Vetter, 1989). Thus, the relative shortage of women pursuing science and engineering (S/E) careers represents not only a loss to individual women but a grave loss to our society (Vetter, 1989; Widnall, 1988). These points are elaborated next.

First, Labor Department projections indicate that in the 1990s the number of science-based jobs will increase by 27%, and the number of jobs requiring significant math background will increase by 36% (Green, 1989). Ironically, though, even in the context of greatly expanding job opportunities, we are witnessing a general decline in the proportions of students selecting science majors (Green, 1989; Holden, 1989), and the problem is especially serious among women and minorities. Based on

237

the most recent (1990) report from the National Science Foundation (NSF), although women constitute 45% of workers, they are only 16% of scientists and engineers (30% of scientists and 4% of engineers). Blacks are 10% of workers but only 2.6% of scientists and engineers (S/Es). Hispanics are 7% of the labor force and 1.8% of S and Es. Native Americans are less than 1% of the labor force and about one-fifth of 1% of S and Es. Asian-Americans are relatively well represented, constituting 2% of the labor force but 5% of S/Es.

Although the underrepresentation of minorities is also a serious problem, this chapter focuses on women per se, some of whom are (of course) also minorities. Where relevant, I mention particular issues for minority women, but in general in may be assumed that situations causing barriers for Anglo women are amplified in effect for minority women (recall the notion of double jeopardy introduced in my opening chapter). For a more complete discussion of barriers to minority women, see Bingham's chapter herein, and for a more extensive discussion of the barriers to minorities in science and engineering, see Betz (1991).

There are three critical points in the "pipeline" at which women are lost to the sciences:

1. The initial choice of careers in the sciences, engineering, and mathematics.
2. The transition from undergraduate degrees in the sciences, where women are considerably better represented than at the graduate level, to the pursuit and attainment of master's and, especially, Phd degrees.
3. Hostile "climates" for token women scientists in academe and elsewhere, which may reduce occupational success and satisfaction and, in some cases, may lead to abandonment of her career.

The discussion to follow reviews the problems and counseling implications of each of these major areas.

## WOMEN IN SCIENCE: THE PROBLEMS

### Barriers to Women's Choices of Science and Engineering Fields

The first stage where women are lost to careers in science and engineering is the initial choice stage, exemplified by choice of a collegiate science (or math or engineering) versus nonscience major. Data shown in Table 7.1 illustrate these losses—of 1,000 male high school students,

**TABLE 7.1**
Number of Males and Females Achieving Each Educational Milestone, for 2,000 Male and 2,000 Female Ninth Graders

|  | Males N (% of parameter above) | Females N (% of row above) |
|---|---|---|
| Sufficient math after ninth grade to pursue science | 1,000 (50%) | 1,000 (50%) |
| Sufficient high school math to pursue science major | 280 (28%) | 220 (22%) |
| Choice of science major in college | 140 (50%) | 44 (20%) |
| Completion of BS | 46 (33%) | 20 (45%) |
| PhD in science or engineering | 5 (11%) | 1 (5%) |

Note. Data from "Educating Scientists and Engineers" by the Office of Technology Assessment, 1988, Washington, DC.

28% obtain enough high school math to be able to pursue a collegiate science major, versus 22% of high school women. Worse, though, is that of those students who have enough math, 50% of males but only 20% of females elect to major in science in college. Because science and engineering educational and career fields are a subset of "male-dominated" or "male-stereotypic" career areas, the forces described in Chapter 1 as fostering females' choices of traditionally female fields and avoidance of nontraditional fields are especially applicable to the understanding of avoidance of science and engineering fields.

Thus, understanding of the barriers covered in Chapter 1, including occupational stereotyping, discrimination in higher education, lack of role models, bias in counseling and interest inventories, and the pernicious effects of null educational environments, is essential for counseling women vis-à-vis science/engineering majors and careers. In the case of science and engineering careers in particular, an expanded discussion of several of these major barriers—that is, a lack of high school math/science background, low math/science self-efficacy expectations, stereotypes about scientists, bias in the use of aptitude test scores, and a lack of "interest" in math/science areas—is also relevant and follows in this section.

## Mathematical Background Versus Talent

The idea of math as a critical filter to career options was discussed in Chapter 1. The work of Sells (1982) vividly illustrated how failure to continue in high school math courses restricts individuals' career options. Another example of the importance of math background comes from a 1976 study by Goldman and Hewitt, who reported that sex differences in Scholastic Aptitude Test (SAT) Math score were the major moderator of sex differences in the likelihood of choosing science-based careers—in essence, students with higher SAT-Math scores were more likely to choose math/science majors, regardless of sex, but because girls had lower math scores than boys, they also chose math/science majors less frequently. Because there is ample evidence that performance on the SAT-Math subtest is closely related to amount of math background, greater math coursework would be predicted to lead not only to better SAT-Math performance in girls but to more frequent selection of science and engineering careers.

Although women have been taking more math in recent years, they are still significantly less likely than young men to have completed the fourth year of high school math, usually a calculus or precalculus course (NSF, 1990). They are also significantly less likely to have taken high school physics, even though their participation in biology and chemistry courses has increased (NSF, 1990). Participation in physics may be particularly important because this is where interests in careers in engineering are often born—high school women often report being tracked away from both physics and computer science courses (Ehrhart & Sandler, 1987; NSF, 1990).

And lack of participation in math/science coursework is not due to a lack of ability—simply put, we as a society are wasting a vast amount of female mathematical talent. Data from a follow-up study of mathematically gifted students were reported by Lubinsky and Humphreys (1990). These were children whose math achievement scores were at or above the 99th percentile in the Project Talent sample, a longitudinal study of 100,000 students in each of four high school grades. Particularly shocking was differences in the percentages of boys versus girls who ultimately obtained various degree levels. For example, 21% of mathematically talented girls stopped with high school diplomas, in contrast to only 9% of mathematically talented high school boys. Almost two thirds of talented boys ended up with at least a master's degree, in comparison to only 30% of girls. Most disturbing was the finding that while 32% of mathematically gifted boys obtained PhDs, only 6% of girls obtained this degree. This is clearly a waste of talent. Similarly, in a study of mathematically precocious youth at Johns Hopkins (Benbow, 1988), 42% of the boys but only 22% of the girls going to graduate school had selected science and engineering majors. Not only are we are losing gifted girls, but even boys who fall into the lower half of the achievement distribution are more likely than are females to continue the study of math and science (Sherman & Fennema, 1978).

Although much has been written about why U.S. females avoid mathematics (for reviews see Betz & Fitzgerald, 1987; Chipman, Brush, & Wilson, 1985; Fennema & Leder, 1990; dramatic evidence for the overwhelmingly sociocultural basis for this avoidance is provided by the fact that U.S. students' math performance lags behind that of other Western countries and Japan, and the gap is large enough that most Japanese girls outscore most U.S. boys (U.S. Department of Education, 1986). Sociocultural bases for differences in math performance are open to educational and counseling interventions.

## Bias in the SAT

There are at least two problems with the use of the SAT in collegiate admissions and the award of scholarships. First, the SAT underpredicts the performance of women in college, including in courses in science and math (Brush, 1991; Rosser, 1989). In essence, this means that if a woman and a man have equal SATs, the woman's college grades will be better. As a specific example, Gross (1988) compared a group of boys and girls who took the same advanced math courses. The girls had lower scores on the SAT-Math subtest, by an average of 33 to 52 points, but earned higher grades in the courses. Thus, schools and scholarship programs emphasizing the SAT over high school grades—for example, the New York State Regents Scholarship program—discriminate against women students. Fortunately, a few top science schools are addressing this discrimination. For example, MIT adjusted its admissions criteria to give greater weight to non-SAT criteria; since doing so, women students are achieving grades equal to those of men even with SAT—Math scores 20 to 25 points lower. And in the classes of graduated students, women had higher cumulative grade-point averages (GPAs) in 11 of 21 majors where both sexes were represented, including mechanical engineering, computer science, and physics (cf. Brush, 1991).

It should also be noted that even these less-than-predictive gender differences on the SAT-Math receive much more publicity than they deserve. Although many studies report statistically significant differences on tests of math aptitude, the practical significance of differences amounting to less than half a standard deviation and accounting for between 1% (math ability) and 4% (visual-spatial ability) of the variance (Hyde, 1981) is questionable. Even more dramatic is that these "statistically significant" differences may be due to males getting one more item correct on the SAT-Math subtest (cf. Matlin, 1987).

Thus, women's lack of participation in science and engineering careers simply cannot be attributed to a gender-related deficit in math ability. Given that women get grades as good with SATs 50 points lower, the effects of small male score advantages are effectively canceled out.

*Stereotypes of Scientists.* Again, choice of careers in science and engineering, like male-dominated career fields more generally, may be adversely affected by occupational sex stereotypes (see Betz & Fitzgerald, 1987, for a review). But there are, in addition, strong stereotypes of scientists that further distance young women from these choices (Brush, 1991; Ruskai, 1989). In the original studies of the perceptions of scientists (e.g., Mead & Metraux, 1957), which, for example, asked the person to "draw a scientist," the scientist was described or drawn as older, male, and White over 90% of the time. Interestingly, he's also drawn wearing glasses 86% of the time and as having facial hair half the time. Scientists, then, are bearded bespectacled White males. Here's a summary of what 35,000 high school students thought about scientists:

### Shared Image

The scientist is a man who wears a white coat and works in a laboratory. He is elderly or middle aged and wears glasses . . . He may be bald. He may wear a beard, may be unshaven and unkempt. He may be stooped and tired. . . . He is surrounded by equipment: test tubes, bunsen burners, flasks, and bottles, a jungle gym of blown glass tubes and weird machines with dials. . . . He spends his days doing experiments. He pours chemicals from one test tube into another. . . . He experiments with plants and animals, cutting them apart, injecting serum into animals. . . .

### Negative Image

The scientist is a brain. He spends his days indoors, sitting in a laboratory, pouring things from one test tube into another. His work is uninteresting, dull, monotonous, tedious, time-consuming. . . . He may live in a cold water flat. . . . His work may be dangerous. Chemicals may explode. He may be hurt by radiation or may die. If he does medical research, he may bring home disease, or may use himself as a guinea pig, or may even accidentally kill someone. . . . He is so involved with his work that he doesn't know what is going on in the world. He has no other interests and neglects his body for his mind. . . . He has no social life, not other intellectual interests, no hobbies or relaxations. He bores his wife. . . . He brings home work and also bugs and creepy things.

Stereotypes today are similar, except that we have coined the term "nerd" to describe this slightly mad, asexual scientist—even though negative, "nerd" itself is not a generic term: we understand it to apply to boys and men (LaFollette, 1988). As Parker (cf. Crowley, 1990) put it, "real men don't do science, real women don't even think about it." Related to the poor images of scientists, and possibly to the lack of any image at all for women scientists, is their almost complete absence from texts (Brush, 1991), even though women have made many important scientific discoveries. In one illuminating study (Roscoe, Peterson, & Voege, 1982), 509 female college students were asked to name the people they most admired. Only three named a scientist, and all three scientists mentioned were male (Cousteau, Einstein, and Edison). Ruskai also documented the damaging effects on women's choices of science of ignoring the many contributions of women scientists. Lips (1992) reported that perceptions of scientists as asocial and beliefs that women could not combine science careers with having a family were negatively related to college women's interest in science careers.

## Self-Efficacy Expectations

Self-efficacy expectations as a barrier to women's choices of nontraditional career fields were discussed in Chapter 1, but they may be particularly important to the understanding of avoidance of mathematics and, therefore, scientific careers.

Hackett and Betz (1981) formulated a self-efficacy model to explain women's underrepresentation in male-dominated career areas. We suggested that women's socialization led to insufficient exposure to sources of information—performance accomplishments, vicarious learning, verbal persuasion and support, and low anxiety—which would lead to the development of strong expectations of efficacy with respect to many traditionally male-dominated career fields, particularly those in the sciences and technology. Low self-efficacy expectations also lead to vicious cycles of avoidance behavior. Assume, for example, a young woman whose low expectations of self-efficacy lead her to avoid math coursework. Avoidance of math courses is detrimental to her ability to perform math, so when she is forced to confront it she naturally performs poorly because she is not well prepared. Her performance suffers, validating her beliefs that she is incompetent in math. At the first sign of failure, she gives up because she has no enduring belief that she can actually succeed. Because she never persists long enough to learn that she can do math, her self-perception of incompetence may be permanent. In contrast, a person with higher efficacy expectations in math would take versus avoid math, be better prepared for math courses and tests, be less anxious in those situations, and persist longer if failure experiences were encountered.

In an early study, Betz and Hackett (1981) showed that females were less self-efficacious with respect to male-dominated than female-dominated careers, and that low self-efficacy was particularly apparent in reference to quantitatively oriented careers. For example, in the sample of 250 college students with equivalent American College Test (ACT) scores, 70% of the men but only 30% of the women reported that they believed they had the ability to complete a degree in engineering. It is probably true that neither 70% nor 30% is probably an accurate estimate of the number of students who could complete an engineering degree—some of the men may have been overestimating their abilities, while many of the women were underestimating theirs. But if an error is to be made, overestimators may try and fail, but underestimators may never try at all, never test their abilities.

Betz and Hackett (1983) measured math self-efficacy, or students' beliefs about their competence to perform math tasks and problems and to get adequate grades in math courses. Not only were predictable and large gender differences reported, with males being much more self-efficacious with respect to math than females, but math self-efficacy was significantly related to the science-relatedness of college major choice (along with math background and Math ACT).

## Vocational Interests

Another major barrier to women's choices of scientific/technical careers is lack of interests in these areas. In both measured and expressed interests, women have tended to score highly in social areas and less highly in scientific and, especially, the technical (Realistic) areas vital to careers in engineering (for a review see Betz, 1991). Because there is absolutely no evidence that social interests are carried on the extra X chromosome (sic) and technical interests on the Y (sic), we must look for environmental bases for gender differences in interest patterns. There is evidence that interests are heritable—Maloney, Bouchard, and Segal's (1991) study of monozygotic and dizygotic twins reared apart led them to estimate that for interests, like personality traits, 45%–50% of the variance can be attributed to heredity. But this kind of heritability is from both parents to children of either sex—it is not sex linked.

The two major culprits leading to gender-stereotypic interest patterns are gender-restrictive interest inventories and gender-based socialization and experiential background (see Betz, 1991; Matlin, 1987). Because Hackett has covered sex restrictiveness in interest inventories in her chapter on assessment herein, I only briefly mention its relevance here.

Sex restrictiveness in interest inventories refers to the existence of differential score patterns depending on the gender of the examinee and, in particular, the fact that these differences guide women and men into gender-stereotypic career fields. For example, on measures of the Holland themes females were overrepresented in Social, Artistic, and Conventional areas, and obtained significantly lower scores than males on Realistic, Investigative, and Enterprising (Gottfredson, Holland, & Gottfredson, 1975; Lunneborg, 1980; Prediger & Hanson, 1976). When these scores are taken to the interpretive guides accompanying interest inventories (such as the Occupations Finder accompanying the Self-Directed Search [SDS]; Holland, 1985), the resulting occupational suggestions tend to reinforce the existing segregation of females and males in our society into traditionally female and traditionally male occupations. High scores on the Social and Conventional themes suggest traditionally female educational and social welfare and office and clerical occupations. In contrast, females' lower scores on the Realistic, Investigative, and Enterprising themes result in less frequent suggestion of traditionally male professions, for example, medicine, engineering, science, and of occupations in management and the skilled trades (Holland, 1985). Thus, socialized patterns of interest lead to interest inventory results that perpetuate females' underrepresentation in male-dominated occupations, especially science and engineering.

Such divergent and sex-stereotypic suggestions of occupational alternatives to males and females were the basis for the criticisms of sex bias and sex restrictiveness in interest inventories, extensively documented and discussed in reports funded by the National Institute of Education (Diamond, 1975; Tittle & Zytowski, 1978). To their credit, test developers have addressed sex restrictiveness by combining the men's and women's forms—for example, the Strong Interest Inventory (SII)—by eliminating sexist language, and by discussing issues of sex-role socialization in interpretive materials (AMEG Commission on Sex Bias in Measurement, 1977). In revisions of the SDS, sexist occupational titles were changed, and items with vastly different endorsement percentages for the two sexes were omitted.

In addition to changes such as those already mentioned, other test developers focused on the use of same-sex norms (as in the Strong Interest Inventory) and sex-balanced item sets, for example, in the Unisex Edition of the ACT-IV (UNIACT) and Vocational Interest Inventory (VII), as means of highlighting areas where nonstereotypical interests have developed. Same-sex normative scores compare a person's scores on basic dimensions of vocational interest, for example, the Holland themes or the Basic Interest scales of the SII, to those of persons of the same sex. Thus, women are compared to other women, and men are compared to other men. The use of same-sex norms increases the likelihood that the background socialization experiences of the comparison sample are more similar to those of the examinee, and this in turn tends to highlight interests that have developed in spite of the limiting effects of sex-role socialization. Sex-balanced inventory scales, for example, measuring the Holland themes, are constructed to include a combination of items reflecting socialization experiences typical of males and experiences typical of females. The desired end result is interest scales on which the sexes obtain similar raw scores. The Unisex Edition of the ACT-IV (UNIACT; Lamb & Prediger, 1981) and the revised version of the Vocational Interest Inventory (VII; Luneborg, 1980,) are based on this strategy of scale construction, and both result in more equivalent distributions of scores across the six Holland themese (UNIACT) or Roe's eight fields (VII) for the two sexes. Thus, on the UNIACT for example, the Realistic scale contains items pertaining to sewing and cooking, that is, content areas more often emphasized in the backgrounds of females, in addition to items more reflective of males' socialization experiences, for example, the skills learned in high school shop courses.

The use of same-sex normative scores and sex-balanced interest scales is intended to increase the probability that females who could potentially be interested in Realistic, Investigative, or Enterprising occupations will obtain interest inventory profiles suggesting those areas. Thus, such methods of constructing and scoring interest inventories are designed to facilitate females' exploration of the full range of occupational alternatives and to minimize the extent to which women continue to be directed toward traditionally female occupations. This has obvious implications for women and science. Better yet, however, would be to enhance women's range of background experiences to include investigative and realistic areas. This and other specific suggestions regarding the interpretation of interest inventories follow in the discussion of counseling implications.

**Barriers in Higher Education**

The barriers discussed so far not only operate to decrease the likelihood that a woman will choose a collegiate science major in the first place, but serve as some of the negative societal messages that, over time, make free choices and persistence in those choices more and more difficult— as discussed by Betz (1989), the cumulative weight of society's messages about women's roles and capabilities, if met by a null educational environment, may eventually crush even the most longstanding of female aspirations. Unfortunately, higher education often provides to women an environment that is at best null, and at worst hostile, and the "chilly climate" for women (Hall & Sandler, 1982, 1984) seems chilliest for women in traditionally male dominated fields, which in higher education are exemplified by the sciences, math, and engineering.

The losses of women to the science/engineering "pipeline" are particularly serious following completion of the BA/BS degree, that is, in the small numbers of women who complete advanced degrees in science and engineering fields. Table 7.1, presented at the beginning of this chapter, shows these losses. Recall that of high school students with sufficient math, 50% of males but only 20% of females choose science majors. Note, however, that female science majors are more likely than males to graduate, and although not shown, they obtain higher collegiate GPAs, including GPAs in science and math courses. Most dramatic, though, is the fact that of those completing the BS degree, 11% of males but only 5% of females complete a PhD in science and engineering. Table 7.2 provides another look at the situation. Note, for example, that the proportion of women graduating with degrees in the physical sciences drops from 30% at the BS level to 17% at the PhD level. For engineering degrees, the percentages are 14.5% at the BS level but only 6.8% at the PhD.

Because women science majors actually get better grades (including grades in science and math courses) in comparison to their male counterparts and, more generally, enter graduate school as well pre-

TABLE 7.2
Proportions of S/E Degrees Awarded to Women, Across Fields and Degree Levels

| Field | Proportion Women | | |
| --- | --- | --- | --- |
| | BS | MS | PhD |
| Sciences | 45.3 | 40.5 | 31.7 |
| Physical | 29.7 | 24.9 | 16.8 |
| Mathematical | 46.5 | 35.2 | 16.2 |
| Computer | 35.8 | 29.9 | 10.9 |
| Environmental | 22.3 | 23.1 | 19.8 |
| Life | 44.0 | 41.4 | 32.9 |
| Psychology | 69.0 | 64.9 | 54.8 |
| Social | 43.4 | 38.9 | 33.1 |
| Engineering | 14.5 | 11.6 | 6.8 |
| Aeronautical/Astronautical | 8.5 | 6.9 | 6.0 |
| Chemical | 24.7 | 15.7 | 9.6 |
| Civil | 13.1 | 10.2 | 5.1 |
| Electrical | 12.0 | 10.0 | 4.3 |
| Industrial | 30.1 | 16.9 | 15.0 |
| Mechanical | 10.3 | 7.7 | 4.3 |
| Other | 16.8 | 13.7 | 8.4 |

Note. From *Women and Minorities in Science and Engineering* by National Science Foundation, 1990, Washington, DC. Proportions reflect BS & PhD degrees earned in 1988 and MS degrees in 1986.

pared academically as the men, we must look to institutional or "climate" factors and the null educational environment to explain the losses of women for graduate programs in science and engineering (note also that these losses result in fewer women available for the academic job market or pipeline, thus perpetuating the token status of academic women scientists and the dearth of women faculty role models for women graduate and undergraduate students).

Research on the institutional climate has documented not only overt discrimination, such as higher admissions requirements for female than male applicants, sex quotas for admission, discrimination in the award of financial aid, and sexual harassment, but more subtle forms as well. A series of review articles prepared under the auspices of the project on the Status and Education of Women of the Association of American Colleges (Hall & Sandler, 1982, 1984; Sandler & Hall, 1986) documents the myriad ways in which the campus climate, both in and out of the classroom, is "chilly" for women students at both the undergraduate and graduate levels. These ways were reviewed for the general case in Chapter 1, but a few studies of women actually enrolled in graduate science/engineering programs provide a clear picture.

In Zappert and Stansbury's (1984) study of women graduate students in science/engineering at Standord, for example, comments such as these were made: "Many times female students were questioned rather than simply accepted when making technical statements, though this didn't generally happen to men." "It was pointed out to me that the only reason I was at Stanford was because I was female and a minority. I was told that I'd never pass qualifying exams. Several time I nearly gave up because of this."

Another set of examples comes from women graduate students and staff at MIT's Laboratory for Computer Science and Artificial Intelligence (MIT Computer Science Female Graduate Students and Staff, 1983). These women noted two major obstacles to their success—beliefs that women's commitments to computer science were not serious, and negative judgements about women's qualifications simply because they were female.

In addition to outright discrimination, the environment may be nonsupportive both in actuality and psychologically. First, most faculty role models in the science and engineering continue to be men. And although we know that most women scientists and engineers report male models and mentors, these women were the ones who succeeded—we need to know more about the women who didn't make it, not just about those who did. The women graduate students at Stanford (Zappert & Stansbury, 1984) reported that one of the hardest battles was being taken on by a mentor and having the kind of close working mentoring relationship that turns a graduate student into an independent scientist and scholar. The fact is that most science and engineering professors are male, and whether it is a conscious process or not, most male professors are more comfortable with and accustomed to male students. Kanter's (1977) research suggested that numerical minorities in work organizations tend to be excluded from informal and discretionary interactions, even if it is not done consciously. In graduate school, discretionary interactions with faculty members include being invited to join his or her research lab, to co-author a paper, and/or to present together at a scientific meeting. Informal interactions include having lunch together, participating in sports (like golf or the department's intramural basketball team), and being introduced by a faculty member to colleagues attending conventions. The women at MIT's Computer Science Lab concluded that the difficulties involved in participating in informal interactions that facilitated both research collaboration and future professional interactions created one of the most serious barriers to success as a scientist (MIT Computer Science Female Graduate Students and Staff, 1983).

Here are two Stanford graduate students in engineering and the physical sciences one female, one male: "Unlike the male students, I don't go hiking with my adviser, I don't eat lunch with my adviser, I don't shoot the bull with him like the guys do," and from a male student "My adviser has gone out of his way time and time again for me—he's always willing to help me with both academic and personal problems— he's an all around great guy!" There are advantages in same-sex or same-race role models. These advantages are greater willingness to work with a same-sex student, greater comfort in the interaction, and the vicarious learning that occurs by virtue of associating with a same-sex person who has already accomplished what you intend to accomplish.

Because women graduate students in science and engineering are often "tokens" (numerical minorities, usually defined as less than 15%), the psychology of tokenism is relevant. First, because tokens look different, they are highly visible—this visibility conveys a vulnerability that can impede behavior and undermine self-confidence (Ehrhart & Sandler, 1987). Token may also feel (often justifiably) that their performance will reflect on their entire sex or race. Again, the resulting anxiety and perfectionism can be debilitating to performance. And being a token is lonely. For women in science and engineering, the most important ingredient becomes the presence of other women students and faculty. Ehrhart and Sandler (1987) have termed this the "comfort factor," where comfort level is probably a direct function of the representation of "like others" in the immediate milieu. Some researchers have postulated a "critical mass" of the token group, below which feelings surrounding tokenism continue to constitute a serious barrier to retention. When the critical mass is reached, there are sufficient opportunities for social support, and the feeling that "there are others in the same boat" can encourage a woman (or minority) to persist. We also need to get more of these students to pursue academic careers so that the composition of faculties, as well as of student bodies, will gradually lose its homogeneous quality.

**The Career Adjustment of Women Scientists**

A final focus of attention for counseling psychologists should be the career adjustment of those women who do enter the job market in science and engineering. The situation for these women, like women students in science and engineering, is likely characterized by the effects of discrimination, harassment, and tokenism. Thus, interventions directed at increasing personal resources and social support and at improving the organizational "climates" for women are vital. Employed women S/Es continue to report "chilly" organizational climates. For example, women physicists report continuing discrimination in the professional and social aspects of their lives (Cook, 1989; Flam, 1991). An article in the *Chronicle of Higher Education* (McDonald, 1991) documented the continuing bias and harassment experienced by women astromers, and the well-publicized resignation from Stanford's Medical School of a renowned, but no less harassed, woman full professor (Barinaga, 1991) illustrates the continuing hostility to women of these work environments.

Although all employed women scientists and engineers are of concern, a group of particular concern is academic women scientists. Generally, women are still badly underrepresented on university faculties—nationally, for example, women constitute only about 20% of tenure-track faculty members, and less than 10% of full professors. And women do not pursue academic careers in proportion to their receipt of PhDs—for example, even though women make up over 50% of PhD recipients in psychology, they are 20% of the faculty members. Women earn 20% of the PhDs in chemistry but are only 4.9% of chemistry faculty. Many science departments have no women faculty at all, and the modal number of women in departments of chemistry nationwide is 1! Academic women in the sciences are almost always tokens, and their environments continue to be hostile, even in the 1990s (Blum, 1991). The problems facing academic women easily deserve chapters and/or books in themselves, but suffice it to say that academic women scientists are double tokens—as women scientists they represent the least well represented disciplines in a profession (academe) that is itself male-dominated. And not only are their survival and success important, but their presence is vitally important in its role-modeling function for women students. If more women were on our science faculties, we might both improve the climate and strengthen the aspirations of women graduate and undergraduate students. (Recall the importance of role models in the self-efficacy model.)

## WOMEN IN SCIENCE: COUNSELING IMPLICATIONS

First, all the recommendations made in Chapter 1 regarding career choice counseling for young women are relevant here—because that chapter focused on the desirability of a general broadening of young women's career options, the discussion of the null environment, self-efficacy theory, and the necessity to help clients combat stereotypes and deal with realistic fears which are all relevant to the restoration of options in science and engineering careers.

Second, interventions need to be broader than simply those accomplished in one-to-one counseling. Because counseling and career psychologists are often in positions where they can propose or design educational or organizational programs and interventions, these provide an excellent opportunity to facilitate broadening experiences and opportunities for women. Such programs are also consistent with the counselor's responsibility to facilitate social change (which includes changes within existing organizational structures), as discussed in the Division 17 Guidelines for Counseling Women (see Fitzgerald & Nutt, 1986). Thus, the suggestions to follow include both individual counseling and educational/organizational interventions.

### Career Choice Counseling

First of all, young women need to be encouraged to continue math and science coursework throughout high school and, ideally, into the collegiate years. Even if they do not end up choosing careers in science or engineering, math background is invaluable for most other career areas, especially at the graduate level. As mentioned earlier, Goldman and Hewitt (1976) reported that higher scores on the SAT-Math subtest was the major explanation of why more men than women pursued science majors. Because math coursework is not only necessary to the pursuit of collegiate science and engineering majors but a major predictor of SAT-Math performance, girls who continue in math will have the option to pursue science and engineering majors in college. This option is important, at least in part because 20% of science and engineering majors did not enter college with that intent (Office of Technology Assessment, 1989).

Part of encouraging women to continue in math may be providing treatment for math anxiety. I recommend that treatment for math anxiety (or other forms of anxiety preventing the pursuit of science and engineering careers, e.g., computer anxiety) be based on a self-efficacy model, with interventions including all four sources of efficacy information: successful performance accomplishments, provision of successful role models in math (preferably female), teaching anxiety management techniques, and providing encouragement and support. A more detailed discussion of the use of self-efficacy theory to guide counseling interventions is provided by Betz (1992).

In addition to encouraging continuation in math/science coursework, counselors should interpret both ability and interest test scores advisedly, recalling the likely effects of experience deficits on scores. Very relevant here is the APA/AERA/NCME (1985) Test Standard originally designed to apply to test use with racial/ethnic minorities: "A test taker's score should not be accepted as a reflection of a lack of ability with respect to the characteristic being tested without alternative explanations for the test taker's inability to perform on that test at that time" (p. 43). An alternative explanation central to gender differences in scores on ability tests and interest inventories is gender-based socialization experiences.

To begin with aptitude test score differences, males have been encouraged to take math, science, and shop courses, and females have been encouraged to take English, home economics, and typing. But tests themselves have worsened the problem through bias in item content and wording. In aptitude tests, for example, predominantly male characters in word problems, sexist language, and sex-biased content have frequently been used (for numerous examples see Betz, 1990; Betz & Fitzgerald, 1987).

In an illuminating example of the effects of content, Betz and Hackett (1983) measured the perceived self-efficacy expectations of college women and men with respect to a variety of math tasks and problems. There were 18 math tasks, 16 math-related college courses, and 18 math problems, for a total of 52 items. As predicted, males reported higher expectations of self-efficacy on 49 of the 52 math-related items. There were only 3 out of 52 items on which females reporter higher expectations of self-efficacy than males: (a) figure out how much material to buy in order to make curtains; (b) estimate your grocery bill in your head as you pick up items; and (c) calculate recipe quantities for a dinner for 41 when the original recipe was for 12 people. Given these data, one wonders what the effects would be of testing math ability, as well as math self-efficacy, using a more balanced set of items. If the sex differences in self-efficacy expectations can be eliminated by asking questions based on content familiar to women, it seems that ability measurement should also be revised. A similar conclusion has been made by Lunneborg and Lunneborg (1986) in their research exploring the experiential bases for the development of spatial ability.

There are several ways to address these issues. First, counselors should be well informed regarding the nature and occurrence of sex bias in ability tests. In an important recent study, Selkow (1984) evaluated the extent of bias and sex-role stereotyping in 74 major tests of ability, personality, and school achievement and readiness. Familiarity with the methods and findings of this study would facilitate informed test use.

Second, it is critical that counselors, when interpreting differential aptitude test scores, for example, mathematics versus verbal ability, remember that gender-role socialization shapes girls and boys differently, that girls are not encouraged to continue taking math, and that girls may need more help in building confidence and reducing anxiety with respect to math. The amount of math taken in high school and college is strongly related to the degree to which educational and career options remain open or closed to the individual. A counselor examining a pattern of aptitude test scores should not overlook alternative explanations for low scores, particularly in the context of overall high ability.

Finally, in interpreting vocational interest inventories, the use of same-sex norms and/or sex-balanced interest inventory scales allows counselors to be alert for areas in which the person has developed interests in spite of sex-role socialization. This approach to interpretation is also consistent with the "opportunity dominance" versus "socialization dominance" approach to interest inventories (Cole & Hansen, 1975). The socialization dominance hypothesis suggests that stereotypic interest patterns are the result of durable gender-role socialization experiences and should not be tampered with. This approach implies that we should take a laissez-faire approach and leave people to go in the directions in which prior socialization experiences have led them. In contrast, the opportunity dominance hypothesis (Cole & Hansen, 1975) suggests that individuals can develop new interests if exposed to new learning experiences and, as a corollary, that we cannot accurately assess the potential for interest development if a person's previous learning experiences and opportunities have been limited in some way, for example, by gender-role socialization.

In other words, attempting to assess interest in science or carpentry or nature or cooking is premature if the person has not been exposed to background experiences in those areas. There seems no good reason why such interests should not be encouraged by suggesting further, or in some cases initial opportunities for exploration. Most counselors would resist the suggestion that it is too late for them as individuals to develop new interests, so it would be inconsistent and unfair to endorse a view of clients, especially those 16 to 22 years old, as irrevocably limited by the shaping of gender-role socialization.

Although there are potentially many ways to facilitate experiences fostering interest in science and engineering, one avenue involves outreach programs to high school students from colleges and universities. As an excellent example, the Women in Science Program at the University of Michigan (Sloat, 1984; Sloat & DeLoughry, 1985), with Women's Educational Equity Act Program (WEEAP) funding, has a program of summer internships in science for high school women. The model program involves the cooperation of women scientists and engineers from both academic and industrial settings. Each student selected, from among any high school women who obtained grades of B or better in their math and science courses, spends 6 weeks working under the mentorship of a woman scientist or engineer, spending 30 hours a week working on a research project. In addition, the program involves weekly lunch meetings with the program staff and with women scientists from other fields, so that students get a broader look at careers in the sciences. The summer ends with a public Student Science Symposium. The students who are returning for their senior year of high school then agree to do workshops and presentations with younger women students, so that they can act as role models for them. Consider the benefits if many more colleges and universities could support programs of this nature, for both women and minority students—initial funding for program development could come from federal, state, and/or university sources, with subsequent support from the local businesses and industries that will stand to gain in the long run.

Other programs could focus on bringing adult minority and women scientists/engineers as guests into the secondary schools, to provide role modeling and information functions but also to challenge stereotypes of scientists—for example, an athletic, stylishly dressed young black scientist, or an engineer who was also married and a mother, would be among the kinds of role models who might be useful. Films, videos, and changes in the media could also be very helpful here—the effectiveness of films, videos, and public service ads featuring women and minority scientists should be studied.

Counselors are advised also to learn something about the many contributions of women to science and to familiarize themselves with books and other resources that might help a young woman seek out women scientist role models, whether current or historical figures.

Articles/books by Ruskai (1989) provided examples of women who have succeeded in the sciences.

Another important focus involves women just beginning college work—we need to make the assumption that it's not too late to encourage students to consider science/engineering majors even in their freshman or sophomore year of college and, based on this assumption, actively develop intervention programs that could assist in this process. Twenty percent of science/engineering majors did not enter college with those plans but selected science/engineering in their freshman or sophomore year (Office of Technology Assessment, 1989). There is always a large pool of undecided students, some of whom have enough ability to pursue science. There is also usually a pool of potential teachers who may be swayed, by good teaching, advising, and support, to consider specializing in high school math and science, including computer science (Carter, 1990). Not only are more secondary school math and science teachers needed, but getting more women (and minorities) to teach high school math and science would add to the presence of role models and the overall lessening of stereotypes.

Finally, counselors need to examine their own attitudes toward women and science and math. Counselors who have underestimated women's potential abilities or are themselves intimidated by math/science/engineering content areas need to expand their awareness of and knowledge about these issues.

To summarize at this point, recommendations regarding additional math background and adherence to an "opportunity dominance" hypothesis do not imply that we should tell women (or men) what to do. However, as discussed by Betz (1989), a major implication of the concept of the null environment for counselors and psychologists is that we have a responsibility to be "options restorers"—to be aware of how sexism and stereotyping reduce the viability or attractiveness of a given career option based solely on gender, and to restore that option to our clients. So-called "free choice" is possible only in the context of viable, attractive options.

## Counseling in Higher Education

Given the "chilly climate" issues discussed in the preceding section, the roles of the counseling psychologist include providing enrichment and support to enable survival and persistence in science/engineering majors and graduate programs. That is, counseling psychologists in higher educational systems may be the only individuals who can counteract the effects of the null educational environment on a young woman. They may be the positive voice enabling her to persist in her nontraditional aspirations in the face of a null or even hostile external environment. Some ideas for doing this follow.

First, counselors should keep track of the young women clients who declare science and engineering majors, possibly inviting them to check in periodically so that encouragement and support can be provided. They should be encouraged to participate in support groups for women science and engineering majors. In order to do this, counselors should be aware of both local and national organizations providing support systems for women students and workers. For example, the Society for Women Engineers has both national and local branches—most university schools of engineering have a local group. Lists of women's science/engineering groups and many other resources can be obtained from the Washington, DC-based Association for Women in Science and are also available from the Women in Science Program at the University of Michigan and, in brief, in Ehrhart and Sandler (1987). The American Association for the Advancement of Science and the National Science Foundation frequently publish information related to women (as well as minorities and handicapped individuals) in the sciences. Counseling psychologists can initiate local outreach programs so that science/ engineering departments develop their own support programs and special courses for women students. Special programs, for example, residence hall floors or even entire halls for women science and engineering majors, research assistantships, and cooperative and summer internship programs can be invaluable.

As far as overtly hostile environments—for example, those involving sexual harassment of students—counselors need to be aware of university grievance procedures and to be able to help the young woman address the problems she faces. Several excellent pamphlets directed at helping students deal with sexual harassment and date rape are published by the Project on the Status of Women, of the Association of American Colleges (AAC).

In addition to the attempts of the counselor to enrich the support system of young women science and engineering majors, attention to personal resources is also important. As an example, the strength of self-efficacy expectations is postulated by Bandura (1986) to be related to the persistence of behavior in the face of obstacles—it is this persistence that is vital to surviving null or even hostile environments. There is, unfortunately, evidence that even gifted women science and engineering graduate students lack strong expectations of self-efficacy—Zappert and Stanbury's (1984) study of male and female graduate students in science and engineering at Stanford showed that the female students underestimated their abilities in math and science and were insecure about their preparedness for graduate school—in spite of comparable and, in some cases, superior test scores and academic records.

Lent, Brown, and Larkin (1984) reported that self-efficacy regarding 15 science and engineering majors was a significant predictor of persistence in those majors 1 year later, over and above the effects of measured ability. They divided students in the Institute of Technology (IT) at the University of Minnesota into high self-efficacy and low self-efficacy groups—100% of the former (high self-efficacy) were enrolled in IT all four quarters following the study, while only about 50% of the low self-efficacy students persisted that long. Note that these were all relatively high ability students, as they had been admitted to a highly selective Institute of Technology. In subsequent studies (1986), Lent, Brown, and Larkin again found that the self-efficacy of high-ability science and engineering majors contributed unique variance to the prediction of grades and persistence in science/engineering majors over and above the effects of ability.

Thus, individual counseling and group programs focusing on the strengthening of individual self-confidence concerning the pursuit of a S/E degree, using the four sources of efficacy information, may be an important buffer to the stress related to a lack of support or overt discrimination.

At the institutional level, we need more and better data collection about retention, especially at the graduate level and disaggregated by gender and minority status. We need disaggregation so that we can see what's happening to minority women, who are in what has been called double jeopardy, that is, being a member of not one but two groups discriminated against by society. Retention research is made difficult by the failure of record-keepers to be able to differentiate drop-outs from "stop-outs," students who are not taking courses but who intend to resume doing so or who are on internship or have finished everything but the dissertation and eventually will finish. The average time from BA to PhD has been steadily increasing—it is now 10.5 years, of which 7 is what is called "registered time" (Tuckman, Coyle, & Bae, 1990). Fortunately, these times are lower in the sciences, ranging from 7 total years in chemistry to about 10 in the earth, atmospheric, and marine sciences. The figure for the social sciences is about 10.5. Such long times to degree make it hard to know who has dropped out, versus "stopped out" (Tuckman et al., 1990).

If the dropouts could be identified, exit interviews could be conducted to determine the reasons for leaving and environmental or personal changes that could have made the difference between retention versus loss of a gifted women (or minority) student.

## Counseling for Career Adjustment

Interventions for academic women scientists could occur through individual counseling and might include the same focus on social support and surviving in hostile climates where one is tokenized that were mentioned in conjunction with students. More effective and reaching more people, however, would be systemic interventions. Betz and Cleveland (1991) designed a model program at Colorado State University, in which both support groups and communication/problem solving involving groups of women science faculty and their department chairs were implemented. Because there tend to be so few women in individual science departments, these interventions need to be instituted at the college level. All the faculty women in a College of the Sciences could constitute the kind of "critical mass" that seems to change a climate from hostile to friendly.

## SUMMARY

Careers in the sciences and engineering are one of the strongest growth areas of the labor market, and at the same time the proportion of White men in the labor market is decreasing markedly. Thus, science/engineering jobs provide an excellent opportunity for women and minorities.

Encouraging women to choose and succeed in careers in science and engineering is important not only from the standpoint of individual actualization of potential, but because society needs women's contributions in these areas.

Individual counseling and support, along with judicious use of interest inventories and aptitude test results, is especially important at the career choice stage, as is attention to the facilitation of broadening experiences and opportunities. Counseling, support groups, and interventions directed at both strengthening individual resources and improving the educational/organizational climate are important for retaining women in undergraduate and graduate science and engineering programs and on academic science and engineering faculties. Women have not only been taught by society that math and science are men's domain, but they are reminded of it every day in environments where they are tokens.

Psychologists and counselors working with women at any or all of these stages should constantly be cognizant of the fact that it may take only one supportive, encouraging voice to enrich a null environment and to counter "society's" detrimental effects on their choices and aspirations. We owe it to women and to society to help women aspire to and succeed in careers in the sciences and engineering.

## REFERENCES

AERA, APA, & NCME (1985). *Standard for educational and psychological testing*. Washington, DC: APA.

AMEG Commission of Sex Bias in Measurement. (1977). A case history of charge: A review of responses to the challenge of sex bias in interest inventories. *Measurement and Evaluation in Guidance, 10*, 148–152.

Bandura, A. (1986). *Social foundations of thought and action*. Englewood Cliffs, NJ: Prentice-Hall.

Barinaga, M. (1991). Sexism charged by Stanford physician. *Science, 252*, 1484.

Benbow, C. P. (1988). Sex differences in mathematical reasoning ability in intellectually talented preadolescents: Their nature, effects and possible causes. *Behavioral and Brain Sciences, 11*, 169–183, 217–232.

Betz, N. E. (1989). The null environment and women's career development. *Counseling Psychologist, 17*, 136–144.

Betz, N. (1990). Contemporary issues in the use of tests in counseling. In C. Watkins & V. Campbell (Eds.), *Testing in counseling practice*. Hillsdale, NJ: Lawrence Erlbaum Associates.

Betz, N. E. (1991). *What stops women and minorities from choosing and completing majors in science and engineering*. Washington, DC: Federation of Behavioral, Psychological, and Cognitive Sciences.

Betz, N. (1992). Counseling uses of career self-efficacy theory. *Career Development Quarterly, 41*, 22–26.

Betz, N., & Cleveland, J. (1991). *Faculty women in a College of National Sciences: Identification of barriers and Possible solutions*. Fort Collins, CO: Office of the Provost, Colorado State University.

Betz, N. E., & Fitzgerald, L. F. (1987). *The career psychology of women*. New York: Academic Press.

Betz, N. E., & Hackett, G. (1981). The relationship of career-related self-efficacy expectations to perceived career options in college women and men. *Journal of Counseling Psychology, 28*, 339–410.

Betz, N. E., & Hackett, G. (1983). The relationship of mathematics self-efficacy expectations to the selection of science-based college majors. *Journal of Vocational Behavior, 23*, 329–345.

Blum, D. E. (1991). Environments still hostile to women in academe, new evidence indicates. *Chronicle of Higher Education, 38*(7), 1–20.

Brush, S. G. (1991). Women in science and engineering. *American Scientist, 79*, 404–419.

Carter, C. (1990). Gender and equity issues in science education. *Proceedings of the First International Conference on the History and Philosophy of Science and Science Education* (Vol. 2). Tallahassee, FL.

Chipman, S. F., Brush, L. R., & Wilson, D. M. (1985). *Women and mathematics: Balancing the equation*. Hillsdale, NJ: Lawrence Erlbaum Associates.

Cole, N. S., & Hansen, G. (1975). Impact of interest inventories on career choice. In E. E. Diamond (Ed.), *Issues of sex bias and sex fairness in career interest measurement* (pp. 10–25). Washington, DC: National Institute of Education.

Cook, G. (1989). Women in physics: Why so few? *American Journal of Physics, 57*, 679.

Crowley, G. (1990). Not just for nerds: Science is now too important to be left to the technicians. *Newsweek, 115,* 52–64.

Diamond, E. E. (1975). Guidelines for the assessment of sex bias and sex fairness in career interest inventories. *Measurement and Evaluation in Guidance, 8,* 7–11.

Ehrhart, J. K., & Sandler, B. R. (1987). *Looking for more than a few good women in traditionally male fields.* Washington, DC: Project on the Status and Education of Women, American Association of Colleges.

Fennema, E., & Leder, G. (Eds.). (1990). *Mathematics and gender.* New York: Teachers College Press.

Fitzgerald, L., & Nutt, R. (1986). The Division 17 principles concerning the counseling/ psychotherapy of women: Rationale and implementation. *Counseling Psychologist, 14,* 180–216.

Flam, F. (1991). Still a "chilly climate" for women? *Science, 252,* 1604–1606.

Goldman, R. D., & Hewitt, B. N. (1976). The scholastic aptitude test "explains" why college men major in science more often than college women. *Journal of Counseling Psychology, 23,* 50–54.

Gottfredson, L., Holland, J. L., & Gottfredson, L. S. (1975). The relation of vocational aspirations and assessments to employment reality. *Journal of Vocational Behavior, 7,* 135–148.

Green, K. C. (1989). A profile of undergraduates in the sciences. *American Scientist, 77,* 475–480.

Gross, S. (1988). *Participation and performance of females and minorities in mathematics. Vol. 1: Findings by gender and racial/ethnic group* (executive summary). Rockville, MD: Montgomery County Public Schools.

Hackett, G., & Betz, N. E. (1981). A self-efficacy approach to the career development of women. *Journal of Vocational Behavior, 18,* 326–339.

Hall, R. M., & Sandler, B. R. (1982). *The classroom climate: A chilly one for women.* Washington, DC: PSEW, AAC.

Hall, R. M., & Sandler, B. R. (1984). *Out of the classroom: A chilly campus climate for women?* Washington, DC: PSEW, AAC.

Holden, C. (1989). Wanted: 675,000 Future scientists and engineers. *Science, 244,* 1536–1537.

Holland, J. L. (1985). *Making Vocational Choices* (2nd ed.). New York: Prentice-Hall.

Hyde, J. (1981). How large are cognitive gender differences? *American Psychologist, 36,* 892–901.

Kanter, R. (1977). *Men and women of the corporation.* New York: Basic Books.

LaFollette, M. C. (1988). Eyes on the stars: Images of women scientists in popular magazines. *Science, Technology, and Human Values, 13,* 262–275.

Lamb, R. R., & Prediger, D. J. (1981). *Technical report for the unisex edition of the ACT Interest Inventory (UNIACT)* Iowa City: American College Testing Program.

Lent, R. W., Brown, S. D., & Larkin, K. C. (1984). Relation of self-efficacy expectations to academic achievement and persistence. *Journal of Counseling Psychology, 31,* 356–362.

Lent, R. W., Brown, S. D., & Larkin, K. C. (1986). Self-efficacy in the prediction of academic success and perceived career options. *Journal of Counseling Psychology, 33,* 265–269.

Lips, H. M., (1992). Gender- and science-related attitudes as predictors of college students' academic choices. *Journal of Vocational Behavior, 40,* 62–81.

Lubinsky, D., & Humphreys, L. G. (1990). A broadly based analysis of mathematical giftedness. *Intelligence, 14,* 327–356.

Lunneborg, P. (1980). Reducing sex bias in interest measurement at the item level. *Journal of Vocational Behavior, 16,* 226–234.

Lunneborg, C. E., & Lunneborg, P. W. (1986). Beyond prediction: The challenge of minority achievement in higher education. *Journal of Multicultural Counseling and Development, X,* 77–84.

Maloney, D. P., Bouchard, T. J., Jr., & Segal, N. L. (1991). A genetic and environmental analysis of the vocational interests of monozygotic and diazgotic twins reared apart. *Journal of Vocational Behavior, 39,* 76–109.

Matlin, M. (1987). *The psychology of women.* New York: Holt, Rinehart & Winston.

McDonald, K. (1991, February 13). Many female astronomers say they face sex harassment and bias. *Chronicle of Higher Education,* pp. All, A15.

Mead, M., & Metraux, R. (1957). Images of the scientists among high school students. *Science, 126,* 384–390.

MIT Computer Science Female Graduate Students and Staff. (1983). *Barriers to equality in academia: Women in computer science at MIT.* Cambridge, MA: Laboratory for Computer Science and Artificial Intelligence.

National Science Foundation. (1990). *Women and minorities in science and engineering.* Washington, DC: Author.

Office of Technology Assessment. (1988). *Educating scientists and engineers.* Washington, DC: Author, Congress of the United States.

Office of Technology Assessment. (1989). *Higher education for science and engineering: A background paper.* Washington, DC: Author, Congress of the United States.

Prediger, D. P., & Hanson, G. R. (1976). Holland's theory of careers applied to men and women: An analysis of implicit assumptions. *Journal of Vocational Behaviour, 8,* 167–164.

Roscoe, B., Peterson, K. L., & Voege, J. M. (1982). Most admired people: Do they exist for college students? *College Student Journal, 16,* 298–302.

Rosser, P. (1989). *The SAT gender gap.* Washington, DC: Center for Women Policy Studies.

Ruskai, M. B. (1989, January). How stereotypes about science affect the participation of women. Talk presented for symposium Women in Physics: Why so few? at APPPS/AAPT, AAAS, San Francisco.

Sandler, B. R., & Hall, R. M. (1986). *The campus climate revisited:Chilly, for women faculty, administrators, and graduate students.* Washington, DC: Association of American Colleges, Project on the Status and Education of Women.

Selkow, P. (1984). *Assessing sex bias in testing.* Westport, CT: Greenwood Press.

Sells, L. (1982). Leverage for equal opportunity through mastery of mathematics. In S. M. Humphreys (Ed.), *Women and minorities in science* (pp. 7–26). Boulder, CO: Westview Press.

Sherman, J., & Fennenea, E. (1978). Sex-related differences in mathematics achievement and related factors: A further study. *Journal of Research in Mathematics Education, 9,* 189–203.

75 Reasons to become a scientist. (1988). *American Scientist, 76,* 450–463.

Sloat, B. F. (1984, April). *Women in science: A university program of intervention, outreach, and research.* Paper presented at Second International Interdisciplinary Congress on Women, Groningen, the Netherlands.

Sloat, B. F., & DeLoughry, C. M. (1985). *Summer internships for women in the sciences: A model program at the University of Michigan.* Ann Arbor: University of Michigan.

Tittle, C., & Tzytowski, D. (1978). Sex fair interest measurement: Research and implications. Washington, DC: National Institute of Education.

Tuckman, H., Coyle, S., & Bae, Y. (1990). *On time to the doctorate.* Washington, DC: National Academic Press.

U.S. Department of Education. (1986). *What works: Research about teaching and learning* Washington, DC: Author.

Vetter, B. M. (1989, May 5). Bad news for women scientists—and the country. *AAAS Observer,* p. 10.

Widnall, S. (1988). AAAS Presidential lecture: Voices from the pipeline. *Science, 241,* 1740–1745.

Zappert, L., & Stansbury, K. (1984). *In the pipeline: A comparative analysis of men and women in graduate programs in science, engineering, and medicine at Stanford University.* Stanford, CA: Stanford University.

# ❈ 8 ❈

# Career Counseling for Women in Management

Joyce E. A. Russell
*University of Tennessee*

Over the past 50 years, the influx of women into the work force and their growing interest in managerial careers has been one of the major developments in American society (Bowen & Hisrich, 1986). In fact, the proportion of women managers more than doubled between 1970 and 1987, increasing from 16% to 38%, and this upward trend of women in managerial positions is expected to continue in the decades ahead (Morrison, White, VanVelsor, & the Center for Creative Leadership, 1987a; Powell, 1988). Given the increasing numbers of women entering managerial positions, researchers and practitioners have examined some of the career-related issues facing women as they move into this traditionally male-dominated occupation. Although male and female managers share some similar experiences in career development, they also encounter some unique issues resulting in different career tactics, plans, and career progression (Powell, 1988).

The present chapter reviews the major issues confronting women in management and discusses strategies and counseling techniques that may provide assistance to women managers. Emphasis is placed on the issues facing women who currently are managers, rather than those aspiring to managerial positions. The reader is referred to other sources (e.g., Rosen, 1982; Russell & Rush, 1987) to review concerns facing the latter group of women. It is assumed that the career issues facing men and women in management differ to some degree, and that the concerns confronting women themselves vary as well. That is, women managers are considered to be a heterogeneous group with respect to their career plans and progress (Fitzgerald & Crites, 1980).

An attempt is made to integrate literature from a variety of disciplines including vocational behavior, counseling psychology, industrial and organizational psychology, and organizational behavior. To date, very few attempts have been made to combine the research from these distinct fields in order to describe career counseling for women in management. For example, researchers in the areas of vocational behavior and counseling psychology have examined career counseling issues and strategies for employed women in general. They have identified relevant theories, barriers, and work–family issues facing women, pertinent counseling strategies, and counselor biases in treating women (Fitzgerald & Crites, 1980). At the same time, researchers in the areas of industrial and organizational psychology and organizational behavior have documented obstacles confronting women managers and assistance strategies, yet with little emphasis on career counseling concerns (Powell, 1988). This chapter attempts to merge this diverse literature in order to discuss career counseling issues for women in management.

## CAREER DEVELOPMENT FOR WOMEN VERSUS
## MEN MANAGERS

In general, most of the research on career development has focused on the issues facing men, assuming that similar issues also confront women (Betz & Fitzgerald, 1987). It is now believed that the career development of women may be different from men's due to differences in attitudes, role expectations, behaviors, and sanctions arising from the socialization process (Borman & Guido-DiBrito, 1986). Gutek and Larwood (1987) argued that a theory for women's career development must be separate from a theory of men's career development because women face unique opportunities and problems. Women and men have different expectations regarding the perceived appropriateness of jobs for them, women face more constraints in the workplace (e.g., gender stereotypes and biases in hiring and promotion decisions), and marital and parental roles have a differential impact on the career progress of women versus men (e.g., women often accommodate to their spouse's careers). Relative to men, women have divergent career perspectives, choices, priorities, and patterns that need to be understood. These discrepancies are further compounded when societal expectations and norms, employment opportunities, marital and parental practices, and organizational policies are considered (Gallos, 1989).

Having a separate theory for women's career development does not, however, mean that women's career achievements are any less important than those of men or that some women do not fit the male model of work and careers. The premise behind a separate theory is that women on the whole face a set of opportunities and problems distinct from those of most men (Morrison et al., 1987a). The career theories for men do not fit many women's lives and development. A separate theory of women's career development should address career preparation, societal opportunities and constraints, and the influence of marriage, pregnancy, and children on career choices (Gutek & Larwood, 1987).

In management positions in particular, Powell (1988) noted that the career development process is unique for men and women managers, although this is diminishing to some degree. Men and women managers face similar management functions and goals, yet the process of reaching those goals differs (Carr-Ruffino, 1985). They may share similar levels of work motivation, yet they make different career choices due to their socialization experiences and the opportunities available to them (Astin, 1984). The career patterns for male and female managers differ. Women managers do not advance as far in the organizational hierarchy as their male counterparts (Stewart & Gudykunst, 1982). Male managers often have more mentors, are more likely to be in line positions, have greater professional status, and occupy higher positions than do women managers (Larwood & Gattiker, 1987). Also, men and women managers have different career tactics and plans. Men are more likely than women to assume personal control for their own careers by developing long-range career plans, whereas women often believe that their superiors will look out for their career progress and opportunities.

Marital and parental factors are likely to lead to differences among male and female managers. Women with families are less likely to pursue careers in management than men with families. Also, married male managers are more likely than female managers to have a stay-at-home spouse who takes care of family responsibilities. Because women who are part of a dual-career couple still handle most of the household activities, having a family appears to pose a greater constraint on a woman's career than on a man's. This is particularly true in a "time-greedy" career such as management.

Some of the differences in career development may be due to generational effects. For example, the career paths of younger male and female managers have been shown to be more similar than the career paths of older male and female managers. Regardless of the reasons for the differences, it is important for career counselors to receive special preparation when working with women managers so that they are able to offer distinctive services to this population (Fitzgerald & Crites, 1979, 1980; Worell, 1980).

## LABOR TRENDS FOR WOMEN'S PARTICIPATION
## IN MANAGEMENT

### Women Entering Management Positions

Management is still a male dominated field (Hammer-Higgins & Atwood, 1989). Almost a decade ago, Caucasian men made up 40.5% of the U.S. population, yet constituted 54.8% of professional and managerial jobs. Women of all races made up 50.9% of the population, yet only 40.7% of professional and managerial jobs (Hines, 1983). Women have, however, made some progress in entering management positions. In 1970, women comprised only 16% of managers, which increased to 26% in 1980 and 39.3% in 1988 (Bureau of the Census, 1990; Powell, 1988).

Not all women are interested in entering management. In many cases, women do not pursue management careers because they perceive barriers to exist. These barriers may be external (e.g., discrimination) or internal (e.g., limited skills) (Russell & Rush, 1987; Terborg, 1977). Some of the reasons why other women have been increasingly entering management careers include changes in cultural norms, federal legislation banning gender discrimination in employment practices, increased opportunities for women to obtain training or advanced education, delays in childbearing, and the women's movement (e.g., consciousness raising) (Hammer-Higgins & Atwood, 1989; Rosen, 1982; White, Crino, & DeSanctis, 1981). Jerdee and Rosen (1976) reported some of the reasons given by a sample of 93 women interested in pursuing a management career. These included achievement and self-realization, money, altruistic motives, expectation of general satisfaction, affiliative opportunities, greater autonomy, and greater job security.

### Women Entering Top Management

Despite the fact that women have been entering management positions in record numbers, relatively few women have made it to top management (Burke & McKeen, 1992; DeVanna, 1987). The greatest number of women managers exists at the lowest levels, followed by the middle levels. One review noted that in 1980, women earned 22.3% of all MBA degrees, yet were still only at the first levels in management positions (White et al., 1981). By 1984, it was reported that 32% of all managers and administrators were women, yet many were in the lowest managerial level with little hope for advancement (Carr-Ruffino, 1985). In fact, in 1984, no women were even viewed as being on the fast track to the top (Fraker, 1984).

A U.S. Department of Labor study conducted in 1985 indicated that only 5% to 7% of middle-level to upper-level corporate managers were women (Hammer-Higgins & Atwood, 1989). Of the Fortune 50 companies, only 1.3% of the corporate officers were women (Morrison et al., 1987a). A 1991 Labor Department report showed that of 94 large employers, women made up 37% of 147,000 employees, but only 17% of the women held any management job, and only 7% of women were at higher levels (e.g., assistant vice president or higher). At the very top positions, a survey conducted in 1986 with Fortune 500 firms revealed that only 2% of senior executives (e.g., vice presidents or above, excluding president and chairperson) were women (Taylor, 1986; Williams, 1988). More recently, it was reported that of the Fortune 1000 firms, only one had a woman CEO, and she shared this responsibility with her husband (Aburdene & Naisbitt, 1992; Roman, Mims, & Jespersen, 1991). Women's underrepresentation in top management is prevalent across a diversity of firms (e.g., technological, engineering, educational, welfare) (Hearn & Parkin, 1988).

Several reasons explain why women make up such a small percent of top management positions. One view is that many women managers have not been in organizations long enough to have entered into the senior management ranks. For example, many women have not yet accumulated the 25 years of work experience necessary to move into senior management, or 35 years of experience needed to sit in the CEO's chair ("For Women," 1992). Human-capital reasons posit that women managers have less education, seniority, training, and experience than their male counterparts (Cox & Harquail, 1991). Other reasons offered include sex discrimination in promotion practices, fewer training opportunities to prepare women to advance, and less interest among women for moving into senior management (Larwood & Gattiker, 1987; Powell, 1988). In addition, women face greater demands regarding family issues (e.g., housework, childcare, marriage), and may experience more career interruptions than male managers (Rothwell, 1986).

## Women Dropping Out of Management Positions

Some researchers have indicated increasing numbers of women dropping out of management. Cotton and Tuttle (1986) noted that gender was more predictive of turnover in managerial than nonmanagerial populations. Thus, the attrition rate for women managers may be uncharacteristically high, although other researchers have suggested that these estimates have been overexaggerated (Burke & McKeen, 1992; Rosin & Korabik, 1991). Morrison et al. (1987a) observed that newspapers regularly carry stories about how women managers are exiting from management. Taylor (1986) suggested that some of the best educated and most highly motivated women have been departing from management. He found that 30% of 1,039 women managers in large corporations dropped out, while only 21% of 4,255 male managers left the firms 10 years after receiving their MBA degrees. In another study, he reported that of the MBA graduates from New York's Pace University between 1976 and 1980, 21% of the women were no longer working full-time in management, compared to 1% of the men. Rosin and Korabik (1990) revealed that 17% of women receiving MBAs in Canada had left organizations (9% became unemployed, 8% became self-employed), and another 25% of the 391 women managers said they were considering quitting their jobs.

Women who leave their current managerial jobs often due so in order to change employers, start their own business, work part-time, work out of their homes, job share, or stay home to be full-time homemakers (Lipovenko, 1987; Maynard, 1988; Schwartz, 1989; Taylor, 1986; Williams, 1988). In the 1980s, according to Census Bureau statistics, the number of women-owned start-up businesses grew at twice the rate of all U.S. business start-ups. The number of self-employed women rose from 2.1 million in 1980 to 2.6 million in 1985 in fields such as consulting, retail sales, educational services, public relations, real estate, and advertising. Rosin and Korabik (1990) reported that 8% of their sample of women managers left organizations to become self-employed. Maynard (1988) found a similar rate (10%) among a sample of women managers. Many of the women managers became entrepreneurs because they desired autonomy and felt stifled by the rigidity of organizations and homogeneity of the management ranks (e.g., primarily all white males) (Taylor, 1986). Others wanted to escape "hostile" corporate America (Garland, 1991; Hunsaker & Hunsaker, 1991; Nelton & Berney, 1987). Frustration, disappointment, and disillusionment with career progress, rather than family concerns, accounted for most of the departures by female managers and professionals (Hardesty & Jacobs, 1986). Some women have changed employers in order to work for a more compatible firm (Nicholson & West, 1988). Few women have actually left corporations solely for family reasons, although when these reasons were cited, they were viewed as temporary. In fact, Rosin and Korabik (1990) noted that women who reported being likely to leave organizations felt this way due to office politics and limited opportunities to progress, rather than marital or family factors. One recent report found that 73% of the women managers who quit large companies moved to another company, while only 7% left to become full-time homemakers (Garland, 1991).

Surprisingly, many of the women who left the management ranks are the ones who were the pioneers in MBA programs a decade ago when only 12.5% of MBAs were women. Because these were the first women managers to try juggling the demands of full-time jobs with family life, their examples may deter other women coming up behind them (Taylor, 1986).

**Future Trends for Women's Management Participation**

Although women are expected to continue to increase their participation in management, their participation rate may remain below 50%. Powell (1988) offered several reasons for this rate, including enormous family constraints and pressures, limited managerial aspirations of women, minimal organizational support for family issues, and discriminatory hiring practices for management positions.

Although it is expected that women will increase their numbers in senior management positions as they move up the ranks, there are several reasons why the present imbalance may continue to exist. These include sex discrimination in hiring for middle and upper management positions, sex discrimination in the development of lower-level managers so that they are unprepared to move up, and less interest among women to move up in management careers (Powell, 1988). Women themselves are not optimistic. In 1985, Sutton and Moore found that despite the existence of more favorable attitudes toward women managers, almost half of the women surveyed stated that women will never be completely accepted as executives in corporate America. In addition, researchers have predicted that no more than a handful of women will reach the senior management level of U.S. Fortune 100 corporations within the next decades due to continuing barriers (Hunsaker & Hunsaker, 1991; Morrison et al., 1987a). Others note that in firms throughout the world, it is unlikely that a critical mass of women in positions of economic power will appear soon. They believe this would require a major restructuring of power in these societies that is not likely to occur soon (Adler & Izraeli, 1988).

## ISSUES AND STRATEGIES FOR COUNSELING WOMEN IN MANAGEMENT

There are a number of factors that counselors should consider when helping women managers cope with the barriers they experience. First, they should be aware of their role and their own stereotypic biases as counselors. In addition, they should be cognizant of the issues and barriers women managers face. They should tailor their counseling efforts to the career phase the woman manager is in (e.g., early career, middle career, late career). Further, they should recognize that women managers are a diverse group, and are confronted with unique experiences that require distinct assistance strategies. For example, women managers comprise reentry women, members of dual-career couples, minorities, token women, and women in international assignments, among others.

Counselors should be committed to understanding women in a societal context, and should use intervention models that are appropriate to this context. They must recognize that women's careers can only be understood in relation to the social structure in which they live (Richardson & Johnson, 1984). The primary counseling focus should be on removing barriers or obstacles to career choice or advancement by examining attitudes of significant others, discrimination in the workplace, and other barriers posed by the social, political, and economic system. Counselors should educate clients about marketplace realities and teach them strategies to overcome or cope with these issues (Brown, Brooks, & Associates, 1990). They should also weigh the benefits and risks associated with providing sex-segregated training. Finally they should be aware of future changes in managers' jobs and in organizations to know which issues and topics to emphasize (e.g., global issues, teamwork).

Although a number of problems confront women and men managers, some issues are unique or more prevalent for women (Powell, 1988). This is because management is still a traditionally male career field. Some of the barriers facing women are similar to those they encounter in other nontraditional careers (e.g., having trouble anticipating obstacles). In most cases, they are better prepared for getting into the job than knowing how to survive in it on a daily basis. As a result, they may become disillusioned and experience lower job satisfaction than expected (Haring-Hidore & Beyard-Tyler, 1984). Prior to providing assistance, counselors need to identify the source of women managers' concerns and the external and internal barriers they perceive to exist (Brown, Brooks, & Associates, 1990; Fitzgerald & Betz, 1983; Powell, 1988; Rosen, Templeton, & Kichline, 1981; Terborg, 1977).

## External Barriers Facing Women Managers and Assistance Strategies

As entrants to a nontraditional career field, women managers may encounter a number of external barriers. In fact, the pressures experienced by women managers appear to be due more to external sources, than internal factors, whereas the opposite is true for male managers

(Davidson & Cooper, 1988). The external factors include discriminatory attitudes and sex-role stereotypes and discriminatory practices in the workplace (e.g., biased treatment, unequal compensation, limited access to training and developmental opportunities, slower advancement and fewer promotion opportunities, backlash, sexual harassment). In addition, women managers may experience social isolation due to tokenism, having few female role models, little contact with subordinates, and limited access to mentoring relationships and informal networks (Hammer-Higgins & Atwood, 1989; Kanter, 1977a).

### Discriminatory Attitudes and Sex-Role Stereotypes

*Women Are Not Suited for Management.* Over the years, researchers have found that women are perceived by others to be unsuited for managerial jobs. This view was initially based on early research efforts to identify characteristics or traits of successful leaders. Because these successes were often taken from military and sports figures who were predominately men, it is not surprising that "feminine" characteristics were not identified (Harragan, 1977; Henning & Jardim, 1977; Rizzo & Mendez, 1991). Management has never been considered to be a female occupation, and women leaders have often been regarded as aberrations (Hearn & Parkin, 1988).

The model of the successful manager in the United States is a masculine one. The effective manager is perceived to be aggressive, competitive, firm, and just. " 'He' is not feminine, soft, yielding, dependent or intuitive in the womanly sense. In fact, the expression of emotion is seen as a feminine weakness that interferes with effective business processes" (McGregor, 1967, p.23). The successful manager is one who possesses characteristics, attitudes, behaviors, and temperament more commonly ascribed to men than to women. This is because men are seen as rational, decisive, assertive, self-sufficient, tough-minded, venturesome, and in control. Women are seen as being too emotional or sentimental, unable to act under pressure, less competent, less independent, less objective, and less logical than men (Basil, 1973; Broverman, Vogel, Broverman, Clarkson, & Rosenkrantz, 1972; Cook & Mendleson, 1984; Schein, 1973, 1975).

In one study, 884 male managers and administrators working in 66 U.S. organizations were asked to evaluate men and women on aptitudes, knowledges, and skills, interests and motivations, temperament, and work habits and attitudes (Rosen & Jerdee, 1978). Overall, women were seen as being better suited to secretarial work than managerial work, and there were more negative perceptions of women than men. In terms of aptitudes, knowledges, and skills, men were rated more favorably than women on understanding the big picture of the organization, approaching problems rationally, getting people to work together, understanding financial matters, sizing up situations accurately, and having more leadership potential. Women were rated more favorably on having clerical aptitude and being good at detail work. Regarding interests and motivations, men were rated higher on liking math, science, and high finance, setting long-range goals, and wanting to get ahead. Women were rated higher on being home-oriented rather than job-oriented, and enjoying doing routine tasks. In terms of temperament, men were evaluated higher on standing up under fire, keeping cool in emergencies, and being independent, self-sufficient, and aggressive. Women were rated higher on crying easily, being sensitive to criticism, being timid rather than forward, being jealous, being too emotional about their jobs, and being sensitive to others' feelings. Finally, regarding work habits and attitudes, women relative to men were perceived as being absent more from work, being more likely to quit, and putting family matters ahead of the job.

Recent studies exploring stereotypes for male and female managers have been consistent with earlier findings. Rizzo and Mendez (1991) reported that male managers were perceived as being unafraid to say what they think, more knowledgeable about the organizational and political system, exerting authority diligently, being concerned about meeting the organization's needs, and rarely losing their tempers. Also, they were seen as having the courage of their convictions and being willing to take a stand on tough issues. Women managers were viewed as being pushy, too emotional if they do not get what they want, manipulative (e.g., using methods other than productivity to move up), and having difficulties overcoming basic nurturing instincts. On the positive side, they were seen as knowing how to balance concerns for productivity with sensitivity.

Garland (1991) cited a recent study conducted by Catalyst, a research firm, which found that nearly half of the human resource managers surveyed thought that women managers had less initiative than men and were less willing to take risks. Women were perceived to be less committed, especially if they were mothers. They were seen as people who would not stay with a firm and would not be willing to relocate. Further, it was reported that men used different management styles than women. Male managers relied on hierarchical, order-and-obey structures, whereas women managers were seen as getting people to work by inspiring them and involving them in decisions. Although this is apparently favorable, the women were actually seen as being indecisive or unwilling to assert themselves.

*Women Managers Are Not Career Committed Due to Family Obligations.* Managers are expected to spend a significant amount of time at work. Often, women managers are viewed as being unable or unwilling to commit the necessary time to be effective managers due to their involvement in their families. Gallos (1989) noted that women are seen as failures if they limit their work time to parent their children or if they refuse to be workaholics. If they are unsure about their home demands and relationships, they appear unfocused or look like they do not have the required inner drive. If they do choose to leave the organization to gain more control over their lives, they may be seen as less career committed or motivated.

Although some organizations have started allowing women managers to work part-time, most firms are resistant to managers working less than 40 hours a week (Rodgers & Rodgers, 1989). In many cases, it is believed that part-timers will not be able to contribute anything useful to the firm. In addition, managers are expected to be employed full time so they can be easily accessible to their subordinates and colleagues. Interestingly, this view ignores the fact that many managers are unavailable anyway due to travel, attendance at meetings, and closed-door policies.

*The Prevalence of Sex-Role Stereotypes.* Despite the passage of equal employment laws and policies, beliefs about sex differences at work and in management have persisted (Powell, 1988; Ruble & Ruble, 1982). Fitzgerald and Betz (1983) noted that attitudes of men and women toward women in management are still negative. Individuals still believe that women are not desirable in management positions, even when they are judged to be competent. In a 15-year follow-up study, Brenner, Tomkiewicz and Schein (1989) found that negative attitudes by male managers for women in management still persisted, although women managers' attitudes had become more favorable.

Other changes in attitudes regarding women in management have been recorded. In a 20-year follow-up study, Sutton and Moore (1985) found that attitudes toward women in management were more favorable. For example, in 1965, 6% of the male executives surveyed strongly opposed women in management and another 41% saw it with disfavor. By 1985, only 5% of the male executives saw having women in management with some disfavor. In addition, in 1965, 90% of the male executives thought a woman had to be exceptional in order to succeed in business, while only 59% said so in 1985. For women, no difference was noted; the proportion remained at 85% at both times. Also, in 1965, 61% of the male executives thought that the business community would never wholly accept women executives. This decreased to 20% in 1985. For women, the differences were not that obvious, changing from 47% in 1965 to 40% in 1985. Finally, from 1965 to 1985, the change in degree of reported comfort with working for a woman manager increased from 27% to 47% for male executives and from 75% to 82% for women executives. Overall, male executives believe things are easier for women now due to affirmative action, equal employment policies, and less overt discrimination. Women executives, on the other hand, do not appear to be as optimistic, perhaps because they have experienced subtle forms of discrimination.

*Accuracy of Sex-Role Stereotypes for Management.* Many researchers have investigated actual similarities and differences between male and female managers to determine the accuracy of sex-role stereotypes. Powell (1988) reported that male managers typically have more managerial experience, are at higher managerial levels, and have higher salaries than female managers. These differences may be partially due to the fact that male managers are generally older than women managers. An American Management Association study found that female managers were more committed to their careers relative to their family or home lives than were male managers, and were found to have higher motivation to manage then male managers (e.g., higher need for achievement and power). Essentially, women managers exhibited a more mature and higher achieving motivational profile than male managers (Chusmir, 1985; Powell, 1988).

In other research, women managers were found to be less open and candid with their colleagues. One reason given was that they experienced more social isolation than their male colleagues (Donnell & Hall, 1980). Women managers were shown to make fewer attempts to influence their subordinates' performance and to use a more limited range of influence strategies (e.g., fewer positive strategies). They generally exhibited less self-confidence than men, which may have been due to the lower expectations others have for their performance. In addition, women managers have been found to be more accessible to their subordinates than male managers and they have more difficulty saying no to others' demands. Their need to be available to others, including their subordinates, may be due to the intense effort they feel to prove themselves in the organization. Women managers may be more available to subordinates because they are perceived to be more caring and less intimidating than their male managers. Or perhaps, subordinates do not want to disturb male managers if they believe their work activities are more important than those of women managers.

Generally, while some differences have been detected between male and female managers, researchers have found that more similarities than differences exist (Fitzgerald & Betz, 1983). Jacklin and Maccoby (1975) found no sex differences in achievement motivation, risk-taking, or task-persistence, and concluded that women were not psychologically handicapped for management, but were hindered by discriminatory personnel practices (e.g., hiring, promotions). More recently, Morrison et al. (1987a) found that male and female managers of comparable positions were similar in terms of personality, intelligence, leading, influencing, and motivating others, analyzing problems, task-orientation with subordinates, and verbal skills. Similarly, Rosen et al. (1981) found that 68 female and 53 male MBA graduates had similar career motivations including a sense of achievement, challenge, money, and independence.

*Dangers of Sex-Role Stereotypes for Women Managers.* Despite the limited support for actual behavioral differences between male and female managers, many individuals still subscribe to the view that effective managers are men. This means that women managers face an obstacle that men do not experience. Fitzgerald and Betz (1983) concluded, after reviewing literature in this area, that "negative and discriminatory attitudes are a major and serious barrier to women's career advancement" (p. 131). Sex-role stereotypes have had negative consequences for women in terms of hiring and promotion practices and in biased treatment on the job (Rosen, 1982; Rosen & Jerdee, 1978). Women are placed in different career paths than men because they are denied access to line positions in management and are segregated in lower level jobs (Larwood, Gutek, & Gattiker, 1984).

Sex-role stereotypes are often used by men and women to affect the decisions they make about others in organizations (Rizzo & Mendez, 1991). Such stereotypes may lead individuals to believe that women managers are unprepared for careers in management. They may allow gender to overshadow women's managerial performance. This is particularly true if the women managers are "tokens" and highly salient to male colleagues. In addition, because of the considerable public scrutiny experienced by women managers, they may try to avoid failures by minimizing risk-taking and continuing to work in lower level positions.

Women managers are not rewarded for using "feminine" behaviors (e.g., warmth, expressiveness), yet at the same time, they are not supposed to exhibit "masculine" behaviors (e.g., aggressiveness). In fact, they often receive social sanctions for stepping out of sex-role expectations (Hammer-Higgins & Atwood, 1989). Consequently, they may hide their emotional, sensitive, and feminine qualities in an effort to copy male colleagues' behavior (Rizzo & Mendez, 1991). If they advance in the organization, they may mask their uniqueness and creativity so that their behavior is not seen as nonrational. Women managers may be underutilized and devalued in the workplace (Ruble & Ruble, 1982). This devaluation may lead them to experience feelings of low self-worth that might affect future behaviors (Bhatnagar, 1988). That is, sex-role stereotypes may serve as self-fulfilling prophecy.

Prevalent beliefs about the level of women's career commitment may undermine their effectiveness in organizations. For example, the Women's Bureau of the U.S. Department of Labor reported in 1971 that there were some widely held falsehoods regarding women's career commitment. Women were believed to be out of the office more than men due to illnesses, unlikely to work as many hours as men, and likely to drop out of the work force sooner than men. Particularly damaging were the beliefs that women took jobs away from men who needed them and that the employment of mothers led to juvenile delinquency (Fitzgerald & Crites, 1980). The implications of these beliefs for the career advancement of women are profound. Women may not receive the proper developmental opportunities or counseling they need from their superiors if it is believed that training women is a waste of resources. In addition, male colleagues may be resentful of women managers if they believe they are taking jobs away from others who need them more. This hostility may further exacerbate the social isolation felt by women managers.

Another factor that impacts on women's success as managers is the belief that subordinates will not want to work for women managers. Managers may deny women managerial positions over concerns that employee morale will suffer (Fitzgerald & Betz, 1983). If subordinates are initially resistant to working for women managers, this may discourage women from continuing in managerial positions or aspiring to higher level positions. Interestingly, Vetter (1983) revealed that most men complaining about women managers have never worked for them. In a study where 75% of the male and female executive respondents had worked for women managers, their evaluations were favorable.

*Strategies for Dealing with Sex-Role Stereotypes.* Because the image of the successful "masculine" manager is pervasive, it may be difficult to completely eliminate. There are, however, some strategies that have been suggested for addressing sex-role stereotypes that individuals hold (Rizzo & Mendez, 1991). These include:

1. Illustrating that there are examples of successful managers who are women.

2. Supporting women entering management to enable them to remain in management.
3. Providing women managers with challenging situations so that they can demonstrate their ability to succeed and their male colleagues can observe them as effective (Catalyst, 1987).
4. Promoting women managers out of lower level positions.
5. Sponsoring organizational workshops to focus on the prevalence and dangers of stereotypes.
6. Moving women managers into male-dominated positions in organizations (e.g., line positions).
7. Giving women reinforcements for making accomplishments in male-dominated areas.
8. Building women's self-confidence by giving them feedback, allowing them to take risks, and offering rewards.

Some firms have implemented some of these strategies for addressing sex-role stereotypes. For example, Lotus Development, Corning, and US West provide value-diversity programs. In day-long workshops, executive of both genders participate in role-playing exercises or discussion groups designed to "search and destroy" stereotypes (Garland, 1991).

### Discrimination in the Workplace

Women managers experience various forms of discrimination in the workplace. These include biased treatment on the job, unequal compensation, limited access to training and development opportunities, slower advancement and fewer promotion opportunities, and sexual harassment (Harriman, 1985). Rosen et al. (1981) noted that 30% of the women managers they surveyed stated that the careers of male managers advanced more rapidly than equally qualified women managers, 49% reported having been a victim of some form of discrimination, and 26% said they had experienced sexual harassment on the job. More recently, Cox and Harquail (1991) reported bias in the allocation of raises and promotions for a sample of male and female managers. The bias was primarily due to systematic gender-related differences in starting salaries, starting job levels, and company seniority.

Obviously, one recommendation to assist women managers with discrimination in the workplace is to eliminate it. This strategy, will take time, however. In the meantime, counselors need to be able to understand the types of discrimination women managers experience to assist them in one-on-one interventions or in workshops. Also, the barriers that women managers are confronted with are important for counselors to be aware of so they can provide sex discrimination counseling to women (i.e., provide women involved in legal suits with information, support, and direction).

*Biased Treatment on the Job.* Women managers experience a number of psychological and economic barriers that keep them in lower level and dead-end jobs that serve to deflate their self-esteem. They may be discriminated against in the allocation of salaries and in hiring and promotion decisions. For example, women typically only earn 60% of what similarly educated male colleagues earn (Hansen, 1978). The 1981 Census statistics revealed that of all women managers, 9.26% earned $25,000 or more, while 45.9% of male managers earned this much (U.S. Department of Commerce, 1983). In addition, the salary gap between male and female managers actually widens as they move up the management hierarchy (Brown, 1988). With respect to hiring practices, Powell (1988) indicated that most studies revealed a preference for hiring male applicants over female applicants. Particularly for demanding managerial positions, there is a reluctance to hire women (Rosen & Jerdee, 1974a, 1974b). In addition, attractive females applying for higher level managerial positions have been shown to be less favorably evaluated than attractive males or unattractive females. This was true for the evaluation of qualifications, hiring recommendations, and suggested starting salaries (Heilman & Saruwatari, 1979).

Rosen and Jerdee (1976) argued that male managers often do not believe that women have the necessary technical and interpersonal skills to be effective in management positions. As a result, men provide women managers with routine assignments, deny them opportunities to attend conferences, exercise great control over them, and allow them little discretion and autonomy. Also, they may provide them with negative or limited feedback and harsher discipline. As a result of these actions, the newly appointed female managers may show evaluation apprehension and increased anxiety, and have rigid perceptions. This may lead to errors, mistakes, or mismanagement. These ineffective behaviors serve to confirm the initial expectations held by the male managers. In effect, a self-fulfilling prophecy may operate.

Over the long term, the condescending treatment and minor rebuffs and put-downs ascribed to women managers may have severe consequences for their effectiveness and their own self-perceptions. If the women managers respond to sex discrimination in a quiet way to avoid being labeled as troublemakers, then they continue to perpetuate males' expectations that they are docile. If they react in an aggressive manner (e.g., threaten litigation), this may lead to retaliation by management.

Interestingly, male managers who use both pleading and threatening appeals are well received, whereas female managers can only use tempered assertive appeals to be well received (Rosen, 1982; Rosen & Jerdee, 1975).

*Limited Access to Training and Developmental Opportunities.* Women managers are discriminated in the access they are given to training and development information and opportunities. They may not be sent to professional conferences, and are usually given less professional information and support (Bolton & Humphreys, 1977; Hammer-Higgins & Atwood, 1989). In addition, women managers receive mixed messages about their worth to the organization. They may be given developmental feedback that they are needed, yet are censored when they perform well, take risks, or threaten male superiority (Wells, 1977). One of the consequences of these behaviors is that women managers may be less prepared to move up into the organization.

*Slower Advancement/Fewer Promotion Opportunities.* Women managers do not experience the rapid promotions typical of their male counterparts. One reason is because they are initially placed into low-status, low-power staff positions with little opportunities for advancement (Gallos, 1989). Or, if they are in line positions, it is usually in departments that are considered to be dead-end areas (e.g., highly routinized jobs such as clerical/staff). Although they may advance in a staff area or low-status line area, they are not on a career path leading to senior management. To move into senior management, they would need to be in positions that are responsible for profits and losses (e.g., marketing, plant management) (Garland, 1991). Male managers, on the other hand, are often placed into upwardly mobile, fast-track, line positions with a more direct route to senior management (Carr-Ruffino, 1985; Hammer-Higgins & Atwood 1989; Terborg, 1977).

Another reason women managers may not advance as quickly as men in organizations is due to discrimination. Individuals subscribing to the belief that women will drop out of the workforce prematurely may not offer women many developmental opportunities. Consequently, women managers may not be adequately prepared to move up into higher levels of management (DiSabatino, 1976). Also, women managers experience discrimination in promotion decisions. As Williams (1988) noted, most men still favor men over equally qualified women for promotions. One reason for this is that men believe they will be more comfortable working with someone like them. When conducting executive searches, top managers often look for individuals similar to themselves (e.g., White males) (Garland, 1991).

Some women may not be promoted as rapidly as men because they are not aggressive in fighting for promotions. Recognizing that women historically have been excluded from higher level, nontraditional managerial positions, they may feel that their efforts may be met with resistance (e.g., the glass ceiling) (Carr-Ruffino, 1985; Rizzo, Mendez, & Brosnan, 1990). The glass ceiling not only denies women access to top positions, but it affects their subsequent career interests, life choices, and commitments (Gallos, 1989).

*Discrimination Due to Backlash.* Equal employment opportunity guidelines and affirmative action policies have been implemented to resolve some of the discrimination experienced by working women. One consequence of these policies, however, has been backlash experienced by women. That is, actions have been taken against women because men believe women have received preferential treatment. Rosen and Jerdee (1979) found in their survey of 884 male managers that the men believed there was favoritism toward women relative to men. Nineteen percent believed that women could get their complaints resolved more easily than men, 26% felt that organizations were forced by law to favor women, and 13% believed that women were given too many breaks. Also, the male managers felt women received better promotion and training opportunities. Fifty percent stated that promotion opportunities were better for women, 23% said there was a greater emphasis on training women, and 10% stated that women received more special opportunities for development. In addition, the male managers were concerned about the amount of power women would get. Twenty-seven percent said they were afraid of women's liberation, 17% stated they thought it would be disastrous if women got too much control of the power, 14% noted that they resented women's attempts to get more power, and 5% stated that women have too much say on organizational policies and decisions. Finally, the male managers had different views about the careers appropriate for men and women. Forty-five percent reported that some jobs should remain men's jobs and others should remain women's jobs, 26% stated that a woman's place is in the home, and 21% said that men should always be the backbone of the firm.

The consequences of attitudes such as these held by male managers is that men may resent women if they believe women have received special treatment. Although they may hire women as managers, they may offer them lower starting salaries and later try to undermine their effectiveness (Rosen & Mericle, 1979). Jacobson and Koch (1977) found that women were rated less favorably if they were seen as hired due to affirmative action policies rather than for their meritorious performance.

Their performance and accomplishments were undervalued by their colleagues and superiors. In essence, backlash can have serious consequences for the career progress of women.

*Sexual Harassment.*  Within the past decade, sexual harassment has been recognized as one of the most pervasive and serious problems facing workers, particularly women (Fitzgerald & Betz, 1983; Gutek, 1985). A 1980 study of 20,000 federal employees noted that 42% of women and 15% of men reported being harassed in the previous 24 months (U.S. Merit Systems Protection Board, 1981). In addition, 10% of the women managers quit their jobs due to sexual harassment (Gutek, Cohen, & Konrad, 1990). This is despite the fact that the Equal Employment Opportunity Commission (EEOC) published guidelines banning sexual harassment as an unlawful act (Powell, 1988).

Women who are managers are not protected from experiencing sexual harassment. In cases where peers or superiors resent the presence of female managers, they may engage in harassing behaviors to further isolate women managers or to make them feel uncomfortable enough to leave (Powell, 1988). In fact, the most common harassers for men and women are peers (65% for women, 76% for men), although superiors are over 2.5 times more common as harassers of women (37%) than of men (14%) (U.S. Merit Systems Protection Board, 1981)

One difficulty women managers experience is that men and women have different views about what constitutes sexual harassment and what should be done about it. At lower levels, male managers are more likely to believe sexual harassment is a real problem facing women than are managers at middle or upper levels of management. This may pose problems for women managers who experience sexual harassment in higher level positions. Male colleagues and superiors may not be sympathetic, assuming that harassment does not exist at higher levels (Collins & Blodgett, 1981).

### Social Isolation

Women managers may experience social isolation in organizations for a number of reasons. If they are one of the only women managers in a group, they may be seen as "tokens" and excluded from informal group activities. In addition, they may have few, if any, female role models to emulate and share experiences with. Also, male managers may experience discomfort working with female colleagues or bosses and may limit their contact with them. Consequently, women managers may have less contact with their peers and subordinates, and less access to informal networks and mentoring relationships.

*Tokenism.* Often, in organizations, among a group of managers, few, if any, are women. Even when an organization has several women managers, they may be located throughout the firm so that there is only one or two per department. As a result, each woman manager stands out in her group and may have difficulty fitting in with her male colleagues. Often, minority employees experience the same phenomenon. If the woman manager is also a member of a minority group that is underrepresented in the department, she may feel the effects of social isolation to an even greater extent.

Women managers who are members of skewed groups (e.g., 85% males, 15% females) may experience even more stress and gender stereotyping than women managers who are members of more balanced groups (e.g., approximately equal numbers of male and females; Kanter, 1977b). This is because tokens are highly visible to others, and face additional performance pressures (i.e., they may be singled out for being female rather than for being successful; Davidson & Cooper, 1988). Also, the differences between tokens and dominants (e.g., White male managers) may become exaggerated by the dominant members in the group. This process is called boundary heightening. The dominant members (e.g., White males) engage in discussions or activities that serve to exclude the token (e.g., woman). For example, they may discuss auto mechanics and playing football in an attempt to let the woman know that she is not one of them. This may be done consciously or unconsciously. In skewed groups, dominant members are more likely to stereotype women tokens. Role encapsulation takes place such that the women's characteristics become distorted or misperceived. They are classified according to their gender even if their personal characteristics are not consistent with the stereotypes. For instance, they may be assigned the role of taking notes in a meeting or getting coffee for male colleagues, or be assigned routine detail tasks (Kanter, 1977b).

Several strategies have been recommended for women to help them cope with their experiences as tokens. First, they need to become indispensable to their groups in some way. For example, they could develop a special area of expertise that is highly valued by the groups. In addition, they need to develop the skills required of successful dominants. These include having a power base, and being perceived as having self-confidence, taking risks, and supporting important group causes (Fairhurst & Snavely, 1983). Counselors should offer token members opportunities to discuss any problems they are experiencing to reduce the amount of social isolation they feel. In addition, they should work with them to develop effective coping strategies.

*Few Female Role Models.* Women managers have few, if any, women above them in organizations to serve as role models. Without effective role models, women managers may be unsure how to address the unique issues they experience (e.g., tokenism, sexual harassment, work–family conflict, social isolation). Even in cases where higher level women managers are available, they may not be able or willing to serve as role models for women below them. For instance, women at higher levels are faced with their own set of difficulties that require an enormous amount of their time and attention. In addition, because there are few women at higher levels in organizations, their behavior is salient to others. Recognizing this, they are often careful about the amount of attention they bestow on their female subordinates relative to their male subordinates to avoid charges of favoritism. Another reason given for why women do not support other women is known as the "queen bee syndrome" (Josefowitz, 1980a, 1980b). This is the tendency for successful women to be hostile and unsupportive of other women's attempts to achieve and advance in the organization. Although some anecdotal literature suggests that this syndrome exists, empirical research has failed to establish it as a common organizational phenomenon (Fitzgerald & Betz, 1983).

*Limited Contact with Subordinates.* Women managers are isolated in the organization due to the limited contact they have with their subordinates. Rosen et al. (1981) reported that women managers had fewer contacts with their subordinates than did male managers. One reason given for why this occurred was that some subordinates were biased toward working for women bosses. Some of the reasons given by men for not wanting to work for women managers include their perceptions that they (a) are lacking in confidence, (b) are lacking in organizational politics, (c) come across too strong, (d) have limited clout, and (e) are only tokens. In addition, male subordinates often express discomfort in knowing how to treat their female superiors (Carr-Ruffino, 1985).

The danger for female managers in having few contacts with their subordinates is that they may lose some of their credibility and power in the eyes of peers and superiors. Subordinates can provide a strong power base for managers, as well as valuable information and feedback. Without this support, female managers may not receive the recognition and information they need to advance in the organization.

*Limited Access to Mentoring Relationships.* Mentoring is considered to be a critical aspect of the professional development and advancement of men and women in organizations (Hunsaker & Hunsaker, 1991). Mentoring serves two primary functions for proteges. Career development functions include sponsoring employees for promotions, helping them learn the ropes and prepare for advancement, offering challenging assignments to develop them, providing exposure and visibility for proteges, coaching them and giving feedback, serving as role models to proteges, and protecting them from damaging experiences. Psychosocial functions offered by mentoring include improving proteges' sense of competence and identity, providing them with psychological support, building their confidence, offering acceptance and confirmation, and providing personal counseling (Kram, 1985).

Mentoring relationships have numerous benefits for individuals and organizations. Generally, proteges are better educated, better paid, less mobile, and more job satisfied (Hunt & Michael, 1983). Also, they earn more money at a younger age, and are more likely to follow a career plan (Borman & Colson, 1984; Roche, 1979). In fact, some firms consider mentoring to be so beneficial that they have established formal mentoring programs for all employees (Lunding, Clements, & Perkins, 1978) or for women and minority employees (Cook, 1979).

Most effective women managers believe that mentors are critical for success (Hunsaker, 1982). More women than men who advance to senior management report having mentors. Phillips (1978) found that two-thirds of over 300 top women executives had at least one mentor, and the majority had two or more mentors. Women are more likely than men to cite "help from above" as one of the essential factors they lacked if they do not reach senior managerial positions (Burke, 1992). Women managers may need mentors even more than men because of the discrimination and work-related obstacles they encounter (Kanter, 1977a). Relative to their male counterparts, women managers typically have more barriers to overcome, less access to inside information, and less relevant training or developmental experiences to help them advance into management. Mentoring relationships provide them with opportunities to demonstrate their career commitment. This is particularly important for women because they are often perceived to be less committed to their careers than are men (Carr-Ruffino, 1985).

In a survey of 85 successful middle and upper level women managers, Hunsaker and Hunsaker (1991) reported that the women respondents found mentors to be helpful by:

1. teaching them how to deal with male counterparts,
2. developing their knowledge of the industry,
3. recommending them for promotions,
4. encouraging them to strive for higher goals,
5. introducing them to corporate politics,
6. providing constructive criticism,
7. advising them on their worth and enhancing their self-confidence,

8. helping them cope with others' resentments and discrimination,
9. pointing out their positive attributes to others,
10. sticking out their own neck to promote the proteges,
11. helping them overcome discouragement,
12. inspiring them to be more creative,
13. keeping their performance visible to senior management, and
14. giving them credit for their work (p. 105).

For women managers, mentoring is especially needed at two stages of their career development. In the early phase, mentoring teaches women the ropes in the organization and shows them how to build their image and become team players. Mentors are needed to provide encouragement, support, and advice, and to make sure that women receive credit for their work (Fitt & Newton, 1981). In later career stages, when women are trying to make it into higher management, mentoring provides them with endorsements to advance (Halcomb, 1980), and helps them gain the respect of their colleagues and superiors (Westoff, 1986). Mentors need to sponsor their proteges to help them move up in the corporation (Fitt & Newton, 1981). In both stages, it is important for women to receive professional and emotional support from their mentors in addition to work-related assistance (Stonewater, Eveslage, & Dingerson, 1990). If women managers experience social isolation from their peers and subordinates, they will need to be able to discuss this with their mentors and learn to cope with it (Hunsaker & Hunsaker, 1991).

Despite the importance of mentoring for women, in general women are less likely than men to be mentors or proteges. They are less likely to be mentors since there are very few women in higher-level positions in organizations. In most cases, men have served as mentors (Missarian, 1982; Roche, 1979). In addition, since women are often excluded from informal organizational networks and often occupy a token status, they are less likely to be chosen as proteges. They have less access to mentors and more difficulty finding a mentor (Burke, 1992; Hunsaker & Hunsaker, 1991). As Epstein (1970) noted, men are less interested in selecting women as proteges because they are perceived to be less capable of fulfilling the duties of a protege (e.g., carrying on the mentor's work, easing the mentor's transition to retirement). Williams (1988) reported that most successful men have had at least one sponsor who suggested them for a promotion, but male mentors have been less likely to take on women. When men have chosen women proteges, they have often done so not to help "promote the proteges' dream" but to show the organization's commitment to promoting women or to develop talent (Fitt & Newton, 1981; Kanter, 1977a).

Those women who do have mentors typically have male mentors. As a result, both experience the difficulties associated with a cross-gender mentoring relationship. For example, the mentor and protege may have to deal with perceptions by peers and others that there is an intimate, sexual component to the relationship (Burke, 1992). This may be particularly salient when the mentor and protege travel together, share meals, or attend social functions together. Their relationship may be subject to gossip or to marital difficulties resulting from the extensive time they spend together (Chusmir & Franks, 1988; Clawson & Kram, 1984; Fitt & Newton, 1981; Westoff, 1986). To circumvent these perceptions, male mentors may avoid working with female proteges or limit their contact with them. This is especially true for the psychosocial functions. Consequently, female proteges may not receive the same kind of support, counseling, and friendship that their male colleagues experience (Burke, 1992).

Another difficulty with cross-gender mentoring relationships is that women managers argue that even with supportive male mentors, men can never fully understand or empathize with the constraints facing a woman in a male-dominated environment. Male mentors may have difficulty counseling their female proteges on how to deal with being a token or being isolated from their peers, or giving them guidance on work-family issues. Thus, male mentors may not be able to fulfill all of the female protege's mentoring needs.

Male mentors and female proteges may fall into the trap of relying on gender stereotypes when working together. Male mentors may foster stereotypical behaviors by overprotecting women or encouraging feelings of dependency among their female proteges (Kram, 1983). Because they are used to seeing women in servant roles, they may have women proteges perform lower level work (Josefowitz, 1980a). Essentially, they may be fearful of challenging them or testing them.

Women managers should be encouraged to develop several less intense mentoring relationships (e.g., sponsors, guides, peer pals) to fulfill mentoring functions. Having multiple mentors may avoid the speculation common to cross-gender relationships, as well as provide women managers with several sources of support (Kram, 1983). Another strategy is for organizations to establish formal mentoring relationships to be sure that each individual is given access to a mentor. For example, at Chubb & Son Inc., a New Jersey insurer, female middle managers are formally assigned to sponsors who are responsible for their career development. Mentors are expected to provide women managers with a variety of developmental opportunities to help them acquire the breadth of experience necessary to advance into senior management (Garland, 1991).

*Limited Access to Informal Networks and Communication Channels.*
Networking involves linkages and communication between people at
vertical and lateral levels. It takes place through grapevines, conferences, workshops, phone calls, parties, mutual friends, and sharing
books, newsletters, and articles (Rizzo, Mendez, & Brosnan, 1990). The
value of networking is that it provides individuals with moral support or
political backing, inside information, and access to those who make
decisions related to advancement. Most successful managers use networks so they can trade information, technical expertise, and advice, as
well as garner support (Kaplan, 1984).

For years, women have expressed their frustration at being excluded
from the informal networks in organizations. The "old boy's network"
has consisted primarily of White male managers who effectively serve to
control the power and resources of the organization. Women managers
have traditionally been denied access to the important informal networks and interactions in organizations (Hendrick, 1981). Rosen et al.
(1981) found that more than 60% of female managers said they had been
excluded by their male colleagues from informal social networks.
Interestingly, when women have had the opportunity to become
integrated into the workplace, they have been perceived as being more
central to interactions and more successful at building informal networks than have men. Women have been shown to be especially
successful at building networks with other women (Brass, 1985).

Exclusion of women managers from informal networks may exist for
a number of reasons. Women may have been boycotted because they
were not considered viable candidates for promotions and equal status
in the organization. Also, they may have been excluded because men
were uncomfortable communicating with women or wanted to maintain
their dominance over women (Kanter, 1977b). In addition, the token
status of many women managers has served to exclude them from
important informal networks (Terborg, 1977). Although White males
may be assumed to have the requisite characteristics to be part of the
managerial circle, women and minorities may not be considered acceptable (i.e., the "cloning effect"). Women may have to pass certain tests
concerning behavior, attitudes, and values before they can be considered acceptable to the group (Rizzo & Mendez, 1991).

The danger of excluding women from important informal networks is
that their career progress may be hindered as they attempt to move up
the corporate ladder. This can be further exacerbated by any childrearing responsibilities or restrictions on job mobility (e.g., spouse's job
offers). In addition, for the organization's welfare, the omission of
women from important networks affects the quality of resources available in those groups (Campbell, 1988).

One of the outcomes of excluding women from "old boy's networks" has been the formation by many women of their own networks. "New girl's networks" have been created in occupational groups, organizational groups, and regional circles. For example, a number of networking groups currently exist for managerial and professional women, including the National Association for Female Executives, Catalyst, the American Society of Professional and Executive Women, and the American Business Women's Association, among others (Hunsaker & Hunsaker, 1991). Women's networks are formally organized to help women learn the importance of building contacts and to develop their networking skills. Also, they focus on career advancement strategies for women. Unfortunately, with very few executive women available, there are few women to serve as role models (DeWine & Casbolt, 1983). Although women's networks are gaining in popularity, there are still some women who do not participate in networking activities. DeWine and Casbolt (1983) found that one-third of the women they studied said they never attended meetings nor met with women outside of the organization for the purpose of networking.

Although networking with other women is an effective strategy to assist executive women, women managers will still need to establish informal networks with male managers if they are to have access to important organizational information and advancement strategies. Also, they need to make sure they develop contacts with individuals in positions of authority who have information and high status (e.g., usually males).

## Internal Barriers Facing Women Managers and Assistance Strategies

Women managers may have difficulties advancing in management due to some internal barriers they perceive. They may believe they lack the necessary skills to be successful in management, that they will not be suited to the work, or that they will not have the self-confidence needed. They may think that they will be intimidated by men and that they will have to be too competitive or will have to outperform men. They may encounter a number of work–family issues and conflicts. For example, they may feel they do not have enough support from significant others for working in a nontraditional career. In fact, women face tremendous social and peer pressure to select traditional careers (Hollenbeck, 1985; Morrison, White, & VanVelsor, 1987). In addition, they may have concerns over childcare issues, experience role conflict and overload, and feel that they have to sacrifice their careers for their marital or parental responsibilities.

The barriers that women perceive to exist may be reinforced by their families, communities, and society. In their socialization experiences, women are often confronted with norms regarding appropriate behaviors for themselves. These norms and expectations influence their attitudes, perceptions, and subsequent behaviors. In effect, the internal barriers perceived by women and reinforced by others may bar women from maintaining a career in management or advancing into higher management.

### Perceptions Regarding Skills and Career Goals

Rosen et al. (1981) reported that almost 50% of the women they surveyed said that compared to their male peers they lacked skills in organizational politics. Women managers often avoid office politics and power and seem to be less interested in the inner workings of organizations, the authority hierarchy and chain of command, and power sources. This may be because they have traditionally been excluded from the informal power networks. Also, women managers often concentrate almost exclusively on their own job performance, rather than trying to build alliances and garnering power for themselves. In group meetings, they may give in to the requests of others, especially when they are in male-dominated groups (Carr-Ruffino, 1985).

Women managers may lack confidence in their abilities to handle financial matters, work on projects requiring math or technical skills, or situations requiring problem-solving and decision-making skills (Carr-Ruffino, 1985). Relative to men, women managers may experience greater fear of failure, lower self-esteem, and more sex-role conflict (Borman & Guido-DiBrito, 1986; Cochran & Warren, 1976). For example, women managers may fear being too successful in their careers if they believe it will make them less attractive to men or if it will cause marital difficulties (e.g., if they become more successful than their spouses; Carr-Ruffino, 1985).

Women managers often do not actively manage their career goals to the extent that their male colleagues do. Rosen et al. (1981) found that women managers reported that they had fuzzy career goals. They had a tendency to suppress their ambitions and goals, while expecting their superiors to acknowledge their achievements and direct their career progress. Often, women are more reticent to talk about their abilities and achievements with the people who should be kept informed (e.g., superiors). Male managers, on the other hand, are usually more proactive in planning their own career progress and letting others know of their accomplishments (Carr-Ruffino, 1985). Recently, Callanan and Greenhaus (1990) found that women managers and professionals reported being more undecided about their long-term career goals than their male counter-parts. They speculated that women may anticipate extensive work–fa-mily conflict, which makes it difficult for them to plan their career goals and aspirations. Catalyst (1990) also noted that most CEOs and human resource directors believe that women in their firms were less prepared than men in terms of initiative and career commitment.

*Assisting Women Managers to Enhance Their Skills and Career Goals.* All successful managers need to develop personal and interpersonal skills in order to be effective. Practitioners should assist women man-agers to refine their skills by becoming more powerful, logical, and analytical when solving problems, and being more entrepreneurial and taking greater risks. In addition, women managers need to be encour-aged to be more confident and assertive about stating their own needs and refusing to back down even if the immediate response is not receptive. Further, counselors can encourage women to stop others from engaging in demeaning behaviors toward them (e.g., interrupting them when they talk, excluding them from decision making). In addition, counselors can help women managers develop stronger sup-port systems and networks and share their expertise with other women (Carr-Ruffino, 1985).

Women managers need to develop clearer career goals and objectives and construct action plans to implement their goals. When preparing career goals and plans, they need to take into consideration other im-portant life goals (e.g., family, personal) so that they can balance these roles and resolve any role conflicts (Carr-Ruffino, 1985). To assist women, counselors need to help them to understand their attitudes toward career planning and help them establish goals, set priorities, and develop action plans. In addition, they can help them to enhance their financial, political, and technical skills and build their self-esteem so that they are more comfortable using these skills. If the women managers are averse to taking risks, counselors must provide them with support and encourage them to get additional assistance (e.g., role models, mentors, support groups). Also, counselors should advise women to obtain career-related information, performance feedback, and challenging job assignments from their superiors. As Callanan and Greenhaus (1990) noted, career management assistance is crucial for reducing fears and anxieties and improving self-confidence among managers and professionals.

### Work–Family Issues

Many women managers who combine a demanding career and a family encounter a variety of problems and conflicts (Gray, 1980). They may be faced with practical problems (e.g., limited time) or career restrictions resulting from excessive work commitments (limited time) and the primacy of their husbands' careers. Also, they may experience psychological problems such as limited support from others, concerns over home and childcare, psychological burnout and role conflicts (Burke & McKeen, 1992).

*Excessive Work Commitments and Limited Time.* Due to the large time commitment involved in a managerial career, many women managers feel unable to devote much time to their personal lives. One survey reported that in 1986, 75% of all male managers were married, while only 58% of female managers were married (Powell, 1988). Another study found similar results from the MBAs graduating from Columbia between 1969 and 1972. Only 58% of the women managers were married, while 73% of the male managers were married (Taylor, 1986). In top management, a 1982 survey revealed that 52% of female senior executives had never married or were widowed, separated, or divorced, and 61% did not have children. A similar study of male executives in 1979 found that only 5% were unmarried and only 3% had no children (Powell, 1988). More recently, Schwartz (1989) reported that 90% of executive men have children by age 40, whereas only 35% of executive women do.

Organizations often demand that managers work long hours, travel extensively, and relocate frequently. They assume that managers are solely dedicated to their careers and do not have other major life demands placed on them (e.g., home and childcare). This is more true for male rather than female managers. Men at the executive levels of corporations often have wives who are traditional homemakers and who provide a support system at home. Women at the same level may be unmarried or have working spouses. For these women, a full-time caretaker of the home or children typically does not exist. Thus, for women managers, the rigorous demands of a managerial career may pose undue hardships on them because they bear the primary responsibilities for child and home care (Ogintz, 1983). Women managers may have difficulties competing with male peers who have fewer family and housekeeping burdens. Women may put in fewer hours at work due to family commitments resulting in less visibility, and consequently they may be less likely to be included in formal and informal networks. Also, they may choose different managerial positions than their male peers in order to provide more flexibility for the demands imposed by childcare, eldercare, and home maintenance (Gray, 1980). Unfortunately, these career choices may be out of the mainstream for fast-track career promotions.

*The Primacy of the Husband's Career.* Often, women only pursue their careers fully if their husbands' self-esteem is not threatened (Lopate, 1971). They feel that their husbands must be able to cope with them being equally or more successful than their husbands are (Bernard, 1975). For managerial or professional women of dual-career couples, this may be difficult. One study illustrated that for every $1,000 increase in the women's earnings, her chances of a divorce increased by 2% (Parker, Peltier, & Wolleat, 1981).

In many dual-career couples, the husband's career is considered to be the most important one when decisions are made regarding opportunities for advancement. In a study of dual-career couples, 66% of the men and 75% of the women described themselves as believing in egalitarian marriages, yet they stated that the wife's career would be sacrificed for the husband's when necessary (Foster, Wallston, & Berger, 1980). Among male and female graduate students in traditionally male career fields (e.g., business, law, medicine), when asked what they expected to be doing in 2, 5, and 10 years, women expected to make greater accommodations to their marriage and family than the men did (Shann, 1983). One of the consequences of these views is that some women managers may have to turn down promotion opportunities or geographic moves if their husband's career will not benefit (Wallston, Foster, & Berger, 1978). In fact, one study noted that 79% of the women had moved at least once for their husbands' careers, whereas only 2% reported that their husbands had moved primarily for the benefit of the wives' careers (Deitch & Sanderson, 1987). This poses particular difficulties for women managers as they try to advance in the management hierarchy. Another problem is that organizations may show more concern for their male managers' careers if they believe them to be more important. If they expect women managers to make career sacrifices for the sake of their families, they may perceive them to be less committed to the organization. Consequently, they may make fewer efforts to retain or advance them in the organization (Rosen & Jerdee, 1974a, 1974b).

*Limited Support by Significant Others.* Women managers often express concern that they have limited support for a nontraditional career from their significant others (e.g., spouse, husband's colleagues, in-laws, parents, friends, married professionals) (Borman & Guido-DiBrito, 1986). They perceive that others disapprove of the time they spend away from their home and childcare responsibilities. As a result of these concerns, women managers expend considerable energy worrying about others' attitudes (Darley, 1976). These fears may be legitimate since as Etzion (1987) noted, women managers who experienced success and self-fulfillment on the job were also more likely to experience failure and dissatisfaction in their personal lives.

*Concerns over Home and Childcare.* Despite the increasing amount of home and childcare assistance provided by husbands, women still assume the primary responsibilities for home and childcare. One study reported that working mothers log in a total work week of 84 hours between the home and job, compared to 72 hours for working fathers, and 50 hours for married employed men and women who are childless (Burden & Googins, 1986). Recently, another study found that working mothers spend about 80 hours on the job and on childcare and household chores, whereas working fathers average about 50 hours per week (Barnett & Rivers, 1992). Many individuals believe that employed women work the equivalent of two jobs (Betz & Fitzgerald, 1987).

Because women have the primary responsibility for home and child care, they experience a number of concerns. Often, they report difficulties finding time for household tasks and locating high-quality affordable childcare. They experience guilt over leaving their children for their careers, and they have trouble taking time off work to care for sick children. Women managers in particular experience difficulties due to heavy demands required of managerial jobs. Given the extensive time commitments and pressures, women managers must be able to work in a relatively uninterrupted fashion if they are to advance (Carr-Ruffino, 1985). This means it is imperative that reliable childcare assistance be available. Few organizations have embraced the idea of providing childcare assistance and many are resistant to allowing managers to work part time to accommodate their personal lives (Zeitz & Dusky, 1988).

*Role Conflict and Overload.* Women managers encounter a number of conflicts between their roles. These include difficulties between being a wife, mother, homekeeper, and career person. Often, the roles of wife and mother require the use of nurturing, emotional, people-oriented behaviors, whereas a managerial role necessitates using assertive, rational, task-oriented behaviors. Conflicts may arise for them if they are unable to employ these different types of behaviors or if they use behaviors inappropriate to the particular role (Loerch, Russell, & Rush, 1989). For example, they may encounter difficulties being feminine and tough as managers. In addition, they may experience social sanctions and a lack of support or disapproval from significant others and society (Rapoport & Rapoport, 1971). The conflicts may result in anxiety, stress, fatigue, emotional depletion, and guilt (Gray, 1979; Johnson & Johnson, 1977; Sekaran, 1983, 1985). Women managers who are part of a dual-career couple report tremendous strain dealing with sick children, day care, changing jobs, relocation, and housework (Williams, 1988). Role overload is common because women managers typically add their work role on top of their family roles without decreasing their involvement in their family activities (Betz & Fitzgerald, 1987). This has come to be known as the "superwoman" syndrome.

*Assisting Women Managers to Deal with Work–Family Issues.* Counselors can provide assistance to help women managers cope with work–family issues and conflict. Most interventions focus on helping women managers achieve a balance in their lives. They may be taught how to negotiate with others at home or at work regarding hours, projects, benefits, and obligations (Gallos, 1989). Family and marital role counseling may be useful to clarify expectations that women and their significant others have regarding their roles and responsibilities. In addition, women managers who are single mothers may find counseling beneficial for addressing unique issues they face such as financial stress, loneliness, single parenting, developing new relationships, autonomy, and legal issues.

Counselors need to provide women managers with strategies for coping with role conflict. These include eliminating unsupportive relationships, limiting obligations taken on, redefining involvements, manipulating schedules to accommodate demands, delegating tasks and roles, and seeking support and assistance from others (Epstein, 1970; Gray, 1980). Hall (1972) suggested three coping strategies for use: Type I coping or structural role redefinition (i.e., changing the expectations of others to reduce the number of obligations); Type II personal role redefinition (i.e., changing your own perceptions of your role demands); and Type III reactive role behavior (i.e., attempting to meet all role demands and please everyone). He reported a positive relationship between using Type I and II coping strategies and satisfaction, and a negative relationship between using the Type III coping strategy and satisfaction. Gray (1979) further examined the relationship between Hall's coping strategies and satisfaction. She sampled 232 married professionals and found strong positive associations between satisfaction and the strategies of having family members share household tasks, reducing standards within roles, and considering personal interests important. Strategies that were weakly positively related to satisfaction included having family members help resolve role conflicts, and organizing and scheduling activities carefully. Strategies negatively related to satisfaction included having overlapping roles, keeping roles totally separate, attempting to meet the expectations of all, eliminating entire roles, and not having any conscious strategies for dealing with role conflicts. In general, factors such as flexibility, avoiding competition with one's spouse, gaining emotional support of significant others, and having a strong will to succeed were related to a woman's satisfaction.

*Organizational Strategies to Deal with Work–Family Issues.* Hall (1989) argued that senior executives need to reexamine their assumptions about what constitutes a "good" executive, a "good" career, and a "good" parent in today's times. Also, he stated that firms should examine the effectiveness of their executive succession systems for advancing women into higher management. Finally, he recommended that top managers establish a task force to examine work–family issues throughout the organization. The task force should be charged with developing recommendations that top managers can implement.

A recent Families and Work report has shown that efforts to provide work–family assistance by organizations is haphazard and piecemeal. Assistance from the government has also been scant (Miller & Tsiantar, 1991). In fact, it has been reported that the United States does less than most industrialized nations to accommodate working mothers (Taylor, 1986; Williams, 1988). Some organizations have, however, started offering a number of programs for relieving some of the work–family conflicts and difficulties experienced by women. Companies such as Hewlett-Packard, IBM, Quaker Oats Co., NCNB, Johnson & Johnson, Stride Rite, Wegmans Food Markets, John Hancock, Skaden Arps, Aetna, Corning, Bank of America, Pacific Telesis Group, and Levi Strauss offer a variety of programs to assist women, including alternative career paths, extended leaves, childcare facilities, flexible work time, part-time work, intergenerational day care, and flexible work places (Keller, 1989; Miller & Tsiantar, 1991; Sekaran, 1989). Many of these organizations have found the programs to be beneficial in retaining women, improving morale and productivity, and reducing turnover rates (Burke & McKeen, 1992; Miller & Tsiantar, 1991).

One recently proposed strategy for addressing work–family conflict for women managers has been called the "mommy track." Schwartz (1989) argued that women managers who primarily want careers should be differentiated in organizations from women managers who want both careers and families. She suggested that career-primary women (i.e., women who are willing to set aside family considerations), should be treated like their male counterparts. As high-potential candidates, they should be identified early and provided with developmental opportunities to help them advance into the highest levels in the organization. Career-and-family women, on the other hand, should be assisted so that they can effectively work in less demanding jobs such as middle management positions. They should be helped in planning for and managing their maternity leaves, allowed flexibility in their careers (e.g., part-time work, job sharing), and helped to find high-quality childcare. These women managers would leave the fast track and opt for a path that offers them more time to care for their families. Organizations would provide alternative career paths, extended leaves of absence, flexible scheduling, flexitime, job sharing, and telecommuting as options to women who select the mommy track (Ehrlich, 1989). In this way, organizations would be able to retain effective managers, while at the same time reducing the conflict experienced by working mothers.

Since Schwartz's (1989) article was released, the mommy track has generated considerable controversy. Some opponents contend that Schwartz's views reinforce prejudices of male executives that women are not really committed to careers. They fear that male executives will have a ready excuse for denying women promotional opportunities, will treat them as second-class citizens, and will continue to believe that it is a bad investment to groom working mothers for top management jobs (Castro, 1989; Hall, 1989). In addition, they argue that the mommy track perpetuates the existing masculine culture where women are required to "fit in" rather than forcing the firm's culture to change. Also, the mommy track continues to place the burden of childcare on women, rather than on both parents, and assumes that no women in senior management will want to have children (Lewin, 1989). Opponents further argue that managerial women should not have to choose between having a career and a family, especially because men are not typically faced with that choice (Castro, 1989). Also, if a choice is to be made then women themselves should make their own decisions about what tracks they want to be on, rather than having top management make those decisions. Further, a woman should not be forced to make a decision early in her career and then have to stay in one track for her entire work career (Mack, 1990).

## Barriers and Counseling Strategies for Women at Varying Career Stages and Management Levels

Women managers may experience unique barriers as a function of their level or managerial rank (Jerdee & Rosen, 1976; Rosen, 1982). Figure 8.1 illustrates some of the barriers faced by women as they move up the organizational hierarchy. These barriers are important to identify because they have implications for the counseling strategies and assistance that may be effective for women in different career stages and at different management levels.

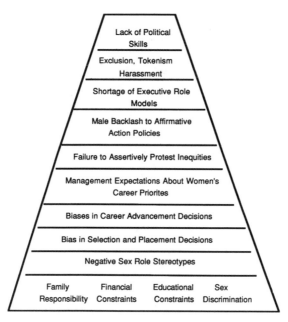

FIG. 8.1. Women's career ladders: Some broken steps. Note "Career Progress of Women: Getting in and Staying in," by B. Rosen (1982), in H. J. Bernardin (Ed.), *Women in the work force*, New York: Praeger, p. 97. Copyright 1982 by Greenwood Publishing Group, Inc. Reprinted with permission.

## Women During Early Career (Aspiring to or Entering Management)

**Barriers.** In a study of 93 women aspiring to managerial careers, Jerdee and Rosen (1976) revealed a number of obstacles perceived by women. These included family and lifestyle considerations (e.g. finances, time and energy demands, husband's career, children, relocation), training, experience, and health requirements of the career, sex discrimination or lack of opportunities, and age (e.g., too old to start a new career). More recently, Powell (1988) noted that women still view management as a masculine career field and are still somewhat tentative in their plans to enter into management.

Women who do enter managerial positions have been advised to think about a career in management as if they are "going to a foreign country for an extended stay" (Hennig & Jardim, 1977). They face some unique hurdles. Some of these include:

1. Being assigned jobs that are not initially challenging.
2. Being rewarded for conforming to standards rather than being creative, leading to feelings of frustration and discontent.

3. Receiving few formal performance appraisals or poorly conducted appraisals making them confused about the required performance standards and how they can improve.
4. Holding unrealistically high expectations about the degree to which they will be able to apply their new skills in the "real world."
5. Being placed in low-visibility or "safe" positions (e.g., personnel, public relations) with few opportunities to make decisions relating to corporate policy or affecting the bottom line (Chusmir & Franks, 1988).
6. Being excluded from informal networks, leading to feelings of isolation and limited control.
7. Being bypassed for promotions to more influential positions.
8. Being seen as a threat to higher-level superiors who may have less education (Hunsaker & Hunsaker, 1991).

*Strategies.* For women who are aspiring to a managerial career, counselors can work with them to determine their career maturity levels, vocational preferences, attitudes about family–work conflict, and sex-role self-concepts. A variety of interventions can be used, including structured exercises for career and life planning, group counseling, career homework assignments, and one-on-one counseling to explore educational and vocational options (Kimbrough, 1981). Workshops may be useful to help women determine a life line, clarify roles, assess vocational interests, and express their feelings regarding working in a managerial career (Cochran & Warren, 1976).

Counselors can use similar interventions with women who are trying to enter into management. They can encourage them to participate in career planning workshops and self-assessments in order to identify their career interests and abilities and desires for career growth. Also, they can assist them in formulating their short- and long-term career plans and developing specific action plans with goals and timetables (Hunsaker & Hunsaker, 1991; Vetter, 1975). Other programs that may be particularly beneficial for these women include more flexible academic programs (e.g., work-study programs, part-time and evening professional programs) and counseling for career development and placement.

During the early career period, some women experience a considerable amount of stress due to family and career issues and conflicts (Gallos, 1989). They may be seeking to find the proper balance between their various roles while receiving pressures from work or family for greater involvement. Counselors can provide special advising to address work–family questions and conflicts. In addition, they can prepare women for anticipating the difficulties they may experience in a male-dominated field. For example, Milwid (1983) noted that few professional women had given much thought to the dynamics of working with men. Few expected any difficulties, yet most experienced psychological stress during the first 2 years. She recommended that counselors offer a variety of interventions to support young professional women in male-dominated fields. For example, counselors could help women managers develop support groups and networks to discuss issues such as developing interpersonal power and handling office politics, preventing and dealing with sexual harassment, avoiding being stereotyped, working with others, becoming visible to top management, reducing stress, being assertive, and taking risks (Hammer-Higgins & Atwood, 1989; Milwid, 1983).

One counseling intervention that may be useful for assisting women managers during the early career period is *The Management Game* (Hammer-Higgins & Atwood, 1989). This is a model developed to sensitize counselors and clients to the many barriers faced by women who choose nontraditional careers. As a simulation, it includes internal and external barriers. The major purpose of the game is to increase awareness and information, although some coping strategies are built into it. The goal is to prepare women for some of the barriers and issues they may face in a career in management. Some of the topics that are discussed include work–family conflict, expectations from others about work–family issues, maternal guilt, forming women's networks, sex-role stereotypes, pay equity, spouse support, sexual harassment, limited skills, job performance feedback, informal networks, mentoring, child care, ineffective working relationships, limited training opportunities, and the queen bee syndrome.

### Women During Midcareer or Middle-Level Management

***Barriers.*** Morrison et al. (1987a) noted that women may be seduced into thinking they have made it in the business world because they experience fewer difficulties in getting into management today than they have in years past. These same women, however, often become disillusioned when they confront barriers as they try to move up into higher management. Although male and female managers share many similar situations, they still work in different executive environments (Morrison et al., 1987a). Women have only a small range of behaviors considered acceptable for them. They have to use some of the behaviors considered appropriate for men and some of those considered appropriate for women. They cannot use too many gender-specific behaviors or they may be viewed as being too masculine (e.g., abrasive) or feminine (e.g., too emotional). Also, women managers have to pass through more hoops and work harder than their male counterparts, and usually for fewer rewards and recognition (Morrison et al., 1987a).

Some of the barriers women face as they move up into higher management include the following:

1. Limited access to important opportunities (e.g., overseas assignments, mainstream jobs.
2. Reduced support for women due to the cutbacks required by organizations to remain competitive (Hellwig, 1985).
3. Limited support among male colleagues and higher level executives.
4. Difficulties balancing work and family lives due to the excessive time commitments required of higher level managerial positions.
5. Hostility from younger men who resent women for "creating" stress for them (e.g., making men take on more home and child care) (Sutton & Moore, 1985).
6. Few female role models.
7. Less support from higher level women than expected because these women are fearful of appearing biased (Miller, Labovitz, & Fry, 1975).
8. Denial by some women that problems exist.
9. Having little room to make mistakes due to their salient status as tokens.
10. Discrimination (Rizzo et al., 1990).
11. Having to prove themselves to their male peers.
12. The glass ceiling (Bunker, 1988; Morrison et al., 1987a).

*Strategies.* As some women move into middle-management positions, counselors need to assist them to reassess their lives in terms of their involvement in work, family, and personal roles. Hennig and Jardim (1977) found that the women managers in their study who had achieved professional success had a new strategy at midlife. They put their careers on hold and reassessed their personal lives. For the first time, some of these women closely examined their intimate relationships.

A decade later, Hardesty and Jacobs (1986) found similar results. Women measured their success by more than their professional success. For some women managers, a reassessment led to feelings of frustration, emptiness, exhaustion, disillusionment, and a sense of personal failure when they realized the personal and interpersonal costs of their professional successes. For these women, having power, status, titles, and money was not enough. They also wanted fair treatment and compensation, and opportunities to be themselves at work and to be closer to people around them. When they were unable to find this, they reassessed their life and career priorities and made major career shifts (e.g., self-employment) (Rogan, 1984a, 1984b).

Women in middle management comprise a diverse group. Some women may have made personal sacrifices (e.g., not getting married or having children) in order to move into management. These women may question whether it was worth it. Other women may have grown children by this time and have more independence in their lives (Gallos, 1989). Older women whose husbands have retired may have more time to devote to their own careers because they no longer have to provide the support for their husbands' careers.

Counselors serve an important role in assisting women in middle management to understand their life roles and involvements, and in making effective career changes when necessary. Life-span developmental counseling is necessary to help women manage their multiple roles. Counselors must encourage their clients to spend some time thinking about their roles and potential role strains, and make them aware that a constant reassessment of changing needs may be necessary. At a minimum, they should help them develop skills in setting realistic goals and clarifying values, managing time effectively, being assertive, and negotiating with others. Further, they should help women evaluate their options and develop effective coping strategies (Gray, 1980).

Interestingly, there is more advice and assistance available to help women enter management or nontraditional careers than to help them survive once on board. Counselors need to offer support to women, particularly during the middle career period. One of the reasons why counseling is so critical during this period is that some women report lower job satisfaction. Often this is due to ineffective working relationships they have with male peers, superiors, and subordinates (Gruneberg, 1979). They may experience sexual harassment, lack of cooperation from other workers, isolation, and limited faith in their abilities (Haring-Hidore & Beyard-Tyler, 1984).

Women who are successful in their careers may be dissatisfied due to psychological factors, family or social issues, developmental changes, or skill deficits (Fee-Fulkerson, 1988). Psychological factors include burnout, poor tolerance of stress, depression, anxiety, role strain, sex-role conflict, poor self-esteem, conflicts of interest, inadequate training for career advancement, poor interpersonal skills, and unrealistic goals and expectations. Family or social issues related to lower satisfaction include a lack of family support, insufficient free time, desires to have children or develop intimate relationships, financial difficulties, and unfulfilled expectations of family members. Women in nontraditional careers may experience developmental changes due to family members' deaths, midlife crisis, or their children leaving home. Skill deficits related to dissatisfaction include difficulties relating to superiors and peers and inaccurate assessment of skills.

Personal counseling is needed to assist women managers in coping with dissatisfaction, depression, anxiety, poor self-esteem or confidence, and career-related issues. Career counselors can prepare women for understanding these issues and learning how to cope with them. They can use cognitive restructuring techniques to enable women to develop new ways of viewing themselves and other women (Kahn, 1988). Cognitive career counseling might be beneficial for enabling them to eliminate roadblocks they have to reaching their career goals (e.g., having unrealistic expectations, experiencing burnout). Additionally, counselors can focus on consciousness raising, building a support system, and providing role models (Hansen, 1978). During this period, women managers may need to be empowered so that they have feelings of control and self-efficacy, and can think independently and resist organizational pressures to conform (Rizzo & Mendez, 1991).

Counselors can work with women to help them take proactive career actions such as career planning, setting goals, seeking mentors and membership in informal networks, obtaining career-related information, and developing needed skills and education (Hunsaker & Hunsaker, 1991; Powell, 1988). They can employ behavioral and psychological skills training to address women managers' deficits in stress and time management, and enhance their skills in assertiveness and interpersonal communication. If the women managers decide to leave their career field, counselors can provide grief counseling to help them discuss their loss (e.g., opportunities, dreams, relationships). If they decide to continue in their current job, counselors can help them develop negotiation skills to use with their employer to try to make their current job or work relationships more satisfying.

## Women Advancing into Top Management

**Barriers.** One reason why corporate America is seen as hostile to women managers is the "glass ceiling." The glass ceiling is an invisible barrier of stereotypes and subtle discrimination constructed by corporate leaders to block women from breaking through to the top managerial ranks (Bunker, 1988; Schwartz, 1989). There is considerable evidence that it exists in large firms (Morrison & Von Glinow, 1990). Also, the U.S. Labor Department presented a report that indicated that in a

18-month study of promotion practices in firms, entrenched attitudes (e.g., glass ceiling) prevented women from moving up the corporate ladder ("Labor's Martin," 1991).

One of the major reasons women have difficulties moving up into top management is because of others' perceptions of their ability. Although they may have the necessary education and skills to move up, women are not often perceived to have the political savvy required of senior managers. In many cases, women do not have the power they need because they lack political clout and powerful mentors or sponsors. Top executives may be fearful of giving women too much power because women are seen as different and less predictable (Blum & Smith, 1988).

In addition, women are not viewed as upwardly mobile, as being able to command adequate resources for their units, or as having significant influence in decision making. Often, they use different types of power than men. For example, women may try to show their power by being nurturing and supportive (McClelland, 1975). Their male colleagues, however, may not view this as being powerful. Often women are placed in jobs that further aggravate the situation. For example, they may be denied access to challenging assignments or put in situations where they are neither expected nor encouraged to take risks or where their authority or positional power is undermined by their superiors (Burke & McKeen, 1992). If the women themselves feel insecure about their authority and communicate this insecurity to their subordinates, their subordinates may in turn resist their authority. Consequently, this perpetuates a self-sustaining cycle that discounts woman managers' abilities (Carr-Ruffino, 1985; Wiley, 1987).

Women perceive a number of barriers to exist in top management positions that may explain their disenchantment and increasing drop-out rates. Women believe that it is harder for women than men to advance. They observe that men hold the most important jobs, and that it is unlikely that they will be able to move beyond the level of vice president. They feel stuck in less challenging jobs (e.g., purchasing, public relations, personnel) (Hunsaker & Hunsaker, 1991). Because they see few women being promoted for their efforts, the costs are perceived as being too great and the rewards too few (Hammer-Higgins & Atwood, 1989). In fact, research indicates that women managers have needed more assets and fewer liabilities than men (Burke & McKeen, 1992). Women are aware of the fact that they are not paid as well as their male counterparts (e.g., usually women receive $6,400–$9,000 less than men, and $2,200 less when work experience and job type are considered). In fact, some women experience salary discrimination because they "have a husband who works" (Williams, 1988, p. 134). Mid-level women managers report being disillusioned with corporate cultures.

They work in highly competitive, cutthroat environments where they need to be assertive yet not abrasive. Many successful women managers have reported encountering biases in their careers. Their expectations are not realized, which frustrates them. In addition, they face considerable work–family demands if they are married or have children.

*Strategies.* Counselors must recognize that the organizational climate in top management is not the same for men and women managers. Counselors need to help women managers develop the skills needed to break the glass ceiling (e.g., political savvy). For example, women managers generally have to earn their power, while male managers are initially ascribed more power due to their gender (Stechert, 1986). As such, women need to demonstrate to higher-ups that they are involved in important decisions, and are proficient at office politics (e.g., gaining support, developing a power base).

Some strategies that women managers can be taught for increasing power include being proactive in career planning, being exceptionally competent, acquiring needed resources and information, developing credibility among peers, developing connections with people who have power, taking risks, and being able to take criticism and implement suggestions (Carr-Ruffino, 1985; Haskell, 1985). In addition, women managers need to be taught how to use several different influence strategies, including reason, friendliness, bargaining, assertiveness, coalition building, appeals to higher authorities, and sanctions (Kipnis & Schmidt, 1982). Generally, women managers moving up into middle and upper level management have primarily used institutional sanctions for influencing others rather than persuasive strategies, yet persuasive strategies may be more effective (Kipnis & Cosentino, 1969). It may be that women need to build up their confidence in using a variety of influence strategies before they can be expected to do so with any frequency (Rizzo et al., 1990).

## North American Women in International Management Assignments

Recently, as more firms from the United States and Canada have globally expanded their businesses, more research has focused on what this has meant for women managers. Researchers (e.g., Adler, 1986, 1988) have described the barriers and issues of concern facing women in international management assignments, and have offered recommendations to enhance the effectiveness of women in these positions.

Adler (1984) noted that North American companies have sent 32 times as many male as female managers overseas. She offered several reasons for the limited number of women sent on international assignments. These include the myths that women do not want to be international managers and that foreigners are prejudiced against expatriate women managers. In one survey, Adler (1984) found that 54% of the vice presidents from 60 multinational firms were hesitant to send women overseas. This was due to the fact that 70% believed that women would be reluctant to accept such assignments, and that 73% felt that foreigners were prejudiced against women managers.

Surveys with women managers indicate that their interest in international work is similar to that of males (Adler, 1986). In addition, in a survey of 52 women who worked in 61 Asian management assignments, 97% stated that the experience had been a success. Objective criteria mirrored these findings (Adler, 1988). Interestingly, 42% of the women reported that being a female served more as an advantage than a disadvantage and only 20% found it to be primarily a disadvantage. The primary advantages included receiving greater attention and more confidential information from foreign clients due to the women managers' high visibility and good interpersonal skills. In addition, they reported being perceived as extraordinary (i.e., foreign clients expected them to be superstars if the company sent them). The primary disadvantages cited for being a female expatriate manager were due to the perceptions and treatment received by the home country rather than the foreign country. Many women reported difficulty in receiving the assignment due to stereotypes and discrimination. Others reported discrimination in the types of assignments and latitude they were given relative to their male peers (e.g., being given shorter assignments, limited travel, less prestigious assignments, being restricted to working solely with internal company employees rather than foreign clients). Some difficulties were noted for working with foreign clients such as being initially perceived without credibility.

For women in international managerial assignments to be effective, several recommendations are offered. First, counselors need to be aware of their own biases in supporting women's interest and entry in international assignments. They need to encourage women's interest in these assignments by making sure they are not perpetuating the popular myths that keep women out of these assignments (e.g., that women will not want the assignments, that foreigners will not accept them). Also, they need to help women anticipate unique problems they may encounter (e.g., credibility problems) as well as similar problems faced by most women managers (e.g., work–family conflict). In addition, practitioners will need to ensure that female expatriates receive the support of their expatriate male peers. These peers may need to help women managers initially gain respect from their foreign clients who are not used to working with female managers (Adler, 1988).

## Global Issues for Women Managers

Women comprise over 50% of the world's population, yet in no country do they constitute close to half of the corporate managers. Although the number of women managers has increased over the last decades, their numbers are substantially below those for men. In addition, the higher the rank within the organization, the fewer the women found there. This pattern of unequal representation of women prevails in countries throughout the world, although there are differences in women's prospects for entry and promotion in management positions (Adler & Izraeli, 1988). According to a survey of 420 firms in nine Western European countries (e.g., Belgium, France, Germany, Italy, the Netherlands, Portugal, Spain, Switzerland, United Kingdom), only 49% of the firms had ever employed a women manager. Of the remaining 51%, 15% stated they would never consider promoting a woman into management. The firms with the most women managers included the United Kingdom (83% of the firms), France (74%), and Portugal (67%). These figures may be misleading, however, because in each of the countries only a small fraction of the total number of managers is women (8%, 9%, 13%, respectively). Italy reported the fewest number of companies (12%) having women managers, and firms in Germany, Italy, and the Netherlands reported no women in top management. In addition, most firms surveyed did not have any programs implemented to increase women's participation rates into management positions (Management Centre Europe, 1982).

*Similarities.* Despite the differences among countries in culture, level of technological and economic development, and availability of resources (e.g., human, material), similar factors affect women's participation rates in management and their career patterns. Women managers worldwide share a number of barriers. These barriers are structural (e.g., legal restrictions, cultural sanctions, social norms, stereotypes, discrimination, historical policies, corporate obstacles, educational barriers) and psychological (e.g., difficulties coping with role expectations and conflict, lack of political skills, disinterest in pursuing management careers) (Adler & Izraeli, 1988, Chan, 1988). In most countries, if not all, management is considered to be a masculine career field and is heavily dominated by men, especially at the senior levels. (Carney & O'Reilly, 1987; Davidson & Cooper, 1987). Even in countries (e.g., Indonesia) where women are more highly educated than men, women are underrepresented in management positions (Crockett, 1988). Women managers are typically located in less powerful, lower paid, and lower status positions than their male counterparts (Chan, 1988; Hearn & Parkin, 1988). Across countries, they experience credibility problems, blocked mobility, discrimination, and stereotypes. These stereotypes were found to be pervasive across most countries (e.g., France, Canada, Japan, Singapore, Indonesia, United States). They include the beliefs that successful managers have masculine attributes (Crockett, 1988), that women do not have the commitment and involvement required of careers in management and that they value their family lives more than their careers (Antal & Krebsbach-Gnath, 1988; Crockett, 1988; Symons, 1988), that married women or mothers are unsuitable for jobs requiring frequent travel or long hours, that men are emotionally more stable than women and are intellectually superior (Crockett, 1988), and that others will not want to work for women managers (Chan, 1988). Women managers in various countries also experience similar isolation and loneliness in management positions, especially at higher levels. They share similar feelings of having limited authority and poor career prospects (Chan, 1988). In many countries (e.g., Fiji), successful women managers are viewed as deviants (Renshaw, 1988). Work–family role conflict exists for women managers in most countries (Andrew, Coderre, & Denis, 1988). In fact, given the time-intensive nature of managerial positions, in most countries where women are managers, they are less likely than men to be married or parents.

*Differences.* Across countries there are differences in the proportion of women in management and their prospects for entry and promotion into management. These variations may be due to differences in fundamental assumptions about women's role in management. In some countries (e.g., the United States), women managers are expected to assimilate into the corporate culture, and effectiveness is measured against male norms. Essentially, there is one best way to manage. In other countries (e.g., France, Sweden), the underlying assumption is that there are multiple effective ways to manage. Women managers are expected to be different from male managers, and organizations attempt to set up conditions that enable women and men to make unique, equally important contributions (Adler & Izraeli, 1988).

Differences among women managers worldwide also exist due to varying cultural traditions and social norms, level and form of economic development, social policies, access to education, and organizational processes (Adler & Izraeli, 1988). *Cultural traditions and social norms* may dictate women's participation rates in management. For example, the social norm in Japan due to the paternalistic system indicates that for women to achieve senior management positions, they must be the appropriate age and unmarried (Steinhoff & Tanaka, 1988). In other countries (e.g., Fiji, Indonesia), women born into elite classes are ascribed leadership positions (Crockett, 1988; Renshaw, 1988). In countries where the roles of women as wife and mother are central (e.g., Israel), women are discouraged from becoming managers (Izraeli, 1988). *Economic developments* affect women's access and opportunities in management positions. For example, Singapore's rapid economic growth in the 1980s led to an increase in women's participation rates in management. However, women were still concentrated in traditional functions (e.g., personnel, administrative services, public relations, consumer affairs) and in lower and middle management positions (Chan, 1988). *Social policies* (e.g., legislation, allocation of resources) that differ across countries have also impacted on women's participation in management. Some countries such as the United States have policies (e.g., Affirmative Action) that actively promote women's participation into management (Brown, 1988). Others (e.g., Singapore, South Africa) have governmental policies that discourage women's labor-force participation (Chan, 1988; Erwee, 1988). Women's *access to education* differs across countries, which affects their subsequent selection and advancement in management positions. For example, in the United States, Canada, and Israel, women are often recruited directly from universities for management positions, whereas in the United Kingdom, a university degree is less important. *Organizational processes* differ for women in various countries. For example, in some countries (e.g., Japan), women are excluded from geographic transfers, which are critical to advancement into senior-level management positions (Steinhoff & Tanaka, 1988).

*Assistance Strategies.* Various strategies have been utilized to assist women managers in different cultures. Mentoring and sponsorship have been considered critical for women managers, although the degree to which women managers enjoy these activities has varied. For example, women managers in the United States and Canada receive more sponsorship than in France (Symons, 1988). Similar social policies across countries serve to encourage or discourage women's participation and survival in management careers. These include the availability of childcare, parental leave, and flexible working arrangements. For example, in Germany, childcare is government subsidized, although in most German schools children have half-day schedules, making it difficult for women managers to combine their parental and work roles (Antal & Krebsbach-Gnath, 1988). Across countries, formal education is considered to be an important criterion for women's participation and advancement in management. In addition, in most countries women managers in the public sector fare better than they do in the private sector, perhaps due to specified criteria and public control (Adler & Izraeli, 1988).

Career counselors need to recognize the similarities and differences among women managers of various cultures if they are to provide relevant assistance. In most cases, women will need to receive education and training to build their self-confidence and develop their political and networking skills. Across countries, women managers have reported a need for support from counselors, practitioners, family members, peers, superiors, and subordinates (Renshaw, 1988).

## Segregated Training for Women in Management

One of the issues that has come under increasing debate is the degree to which training women for management careers should be conducted separately from the training provided to men. Harriman (1985) noted substantial disagreement regarding the most desirable approach for training women for managerial careers. Most practitioners conclude that if separate training is given to women managers, it should be offered in addition to the sex-integrated training they receive, not in place of it, and it should be voluntary (Rizzo & Mendez, 1991).

*Reasons for Sex-Segregated Training.* Many reasons have been offered for providing training for women managers separately from that provided to male managers. Some researchers (e.g., Larwood, Wood, & Inderlied, 1978) suggest that due to socialization experiences, women react differently in situations where men are present. Most management development programs are heavily dominated by men so that women are considered as "outsiders" or tokens. As a result, women may have to deal with sex-role stereotypes. For example, women may be assigned stereotypically feminine roles in group activities and simulations (e.g., personnel functions) and may not get opportunities to practice and develop skills in stereotypically male functions (e.g., finance, production) (Hartnett & Novarra, 1980). When men are present, some women tend to revert to the comfortable established pattern of deferring to men for advice and leadership. With a class of assertive men, outspoken women may be easily intimidated into silence or may not be able to speak as honestly as they would like (Larwood et al., 1978).

Women may gain some benefits from participating in sex-segregated classes. They may be able to establish a network of female peers by sharing their experiences with other competent women. Also, they are given the opportunity to observe effective female role models, and can participate in stereotype-free career planning (Hartnett & Novarra, 1980). For example, they may have opportunities to discuss some of the unique issues they experience in management (e.g., discrimination, harassment, tokenism, social isolation, stereotyping). Classes may be needed for women to gain additional skills in areas they are less exposed to, including building self-esteem, learning new behaviors for managing interpersonal conflict, developing leadership and team-building skills, and enhancing political skills and influence strategies (Heinen, Mc-Glauchlin, Legeros, & Freeman, 1975). In some organizations (e.g., Capital Cities, ABC) women have been sent to additional financial and management training to build their self-confidence and the confidence of their male peers toward them (Williams, 1988). In addition, women can receive help with career planning, and learn the perceptions, strategies, and behavioral skills needed to fit into the corporate arena (White et al., 1981). While all of these skills may be needed for some male managers, they are considered critical for women managers.

*Reasons Against Sex-Segregated Training.* Some researchers and practitioners express concern that the sex-segregated training that women managers receive will end up being the only training they receive. Also, they argue that having separate training courses assumes that women have unique problems that cannot be resolved through traditional developmental programs (White et al., 1981). Others argue that separate training still places the primary burden on women rather than organizations to change the status quo. Women have to overcome the effects of role socialization by learning how to be assertive, plan careers, make a commitment to work, and manage their own time. In other words, these programs assume that organizations cannot be changed and that women bear the sole responsibility for adapting to the existing organizational climate (White et al., 1981). Kanter (1977a) suggested that this is an ineffective strategy because it is the organizational structure, rather than the behaviors of women, that should be altered.

If women have difficulties asserting themselves with men, it is argued that using sex-segregated training will not assist women in developing these skills. At some point they will have to interact with male managers (Larwood et al., 1978). In addition, the programs may perpetuate the stereotypes about occupational and personality differences between men and women managers (Bolton & Humphreys, 1977; Shockley & Staley, 1980). Sex-segregated training assumes that women managers are a homogenous group with respect to their skills or training needs (Albrecht, 1978), and that they are very different from male managers. There are, however, probably more similarities than differences between women and men managers (Bolton & Humphreys, 1977). Segregated training may in fact facilitate sexism or lead to perceived sex differences where none had existed or may magnify differences that otherwise would not have had serious detrimental consequences. Also, men may be perceived as having had managerial training, whereas women may be perceived as having had remedial training. That perception may occur if women attend "women only" classes prior to attending management development programs.

## ORGANIZATIONAL EFFORTS TO ASSIST WOMEN MANAGERS

This chapter has described strategies counselors can use to help women adjust or fit into existing organizational cultures. Recently, some firms have started implementing support programs for women managers. In some cases, the firms have developed programs to help women fit into the prevalent corporate cultures, whereas in other situations, the organizations have attempted to change their own structures to better accommodate the needs of women managers (Burke & McKeen, 1992). Many believe that organizations will have to become more flexible in addressing issues of concern to women, especially since 67% of the future work-force growth is expected to come from women (Johnston & Packer, 1987; Solomon, 1989). One goal of many corporate efforts is to make women feel that they are a significant part of the organization, because currently many women managers report that they are not made to feel important in the companies they work for (Ciabattari, 1986). In addition, many firms are becoming more concerned with losing highly skilled women managers to competitors (Trost, 1989).

Recently, increasingly more firms have became "women friendly" by implementing programs to assist women managers. To date, these strategies have primarily been adopted by large, progressive companies (Russell, 1991). These organizations have provided special training for women managers addressing intrapersonal, interpersonal, and technical areas. Often the focus is on improving communication and assertiveness skills, enhancing goal setting, building confidence, and developing greater expertise in substantive topics (e.g., finances, problem analysis, planning and decision making, leadership, team dynamics) (Gomez-Mejia & Balkin, 1980).

Other strategies that organizations have used to assist women managers have included offering career planning services (e.g., personal counseling, workshops, managerial coaching, job postings) and developmental programs (e.g., assessment centers, job rotation, additional training opportunities, formal mentoring programs). Also, work–family issues have been addressed through workshops that focus on work–family conflicts, and through offering leave for childcare, flexible work arrangements, relaxed organizational policies on travel and transfers, childcare support, and childcare referral systems. These strategies are briefly reviewed here; the reader is referred to other sources (e.g., Russell, 1991; Zeitz & Dusky, 1988) for a more detailed discussion.

## Career Planning Assistance

Some organizations have provided career planning programs to assist women managers. For example, Gulf Oil initiated a program that included assessment, individual advising, and a career planning workshop. The issues for the workshop discussion consisted of career versus family life issues, strategies for making and implementing educational and career plans, goal setting, decision making, identification of organizational career resources and opportunities, communication skills, and relevant academic programs at nearby schools. Prior to participating in the program, 85% of the women stated that their career plans were unfocused. After completion of the program, 76% said their plans were firmly focused (Fort & Cordisco, 1981).

## Training and Developmental Opportunities

Some firms (e.g., Capital Cities, ABC) have found that their women managers are predominately liberal arts graduates who need additional financial and management training. As a result, they have enrolled them in management development programs (e.g., Smith Management program at Smith College). Other firms (e.g., Merck, Corning, Gannett) have provided training courses for women managers to make them better equipped, more confident, and more competitive for higher-level managerial positions (Williams, 1988).

## Work–Family Assistance

Some organizations have reduced childcare burdens by providing childcare aid or centers. For example, in 1985 the Conference Board estimated that 2,500 companies (e.g., DuPont, IBM, Campbell Soup) provided some form of childcare aid. This increased from 600 companies providing aid in 1982 (Bernstein, 1986). Also, more organizations have started offering maternity leave (Morrison et al., 1987a). Other firms (e.g., Hewlett-Packard, Eastman Kodak, Aetna Life and Casualty, General Motors, Mellon Bank) have initiated assistance for dual-career couples in the form of flexible work arrangements such as job sharing, part-time employment, and flexitime (Taylor, 1986). At Touche Ross, mothers who want to stay on the partnership track are able to alter their workweek to 4 days a week to allow them time with their children. Rather than having an organization-wide policy, individuals are able to negotiate the issue with their respective superiors. It takes these women 10–12 years to reach the partner level, compared to 8–10 years for individuals working full-time. Similarly, at Peat Marwick Mitchell, managers are allowed to take a lighter client load and less than a 40-hour work week for up to 2–3 years. Pacific Bell and Mountain Bell have programs where managers can work at home on computer terminals, and at Mutual Life Insurance Company, individuals are able to work some of their hours at home. Other companies offer relaxed job transfer and travel plans or paternity and maternity leaves (e.g., Proctor & Gamble, Lotus Development, General Foods, Gannett) (Taylor, 1986). A few firms (e.g., Johnson & Johnson) offer support for elder care (Carr-Ruffino, 1985; Hansen, 1978; Rodgers & Rodgers, 1989).

One strategy that has been suggested by managerial women themselves, which has not yet been implemented, is the idea of changing the way organizations define productivity. Currently, the tendency for many firms is to measure productivity by the number of hours worked by an individual, yet this assumes that individuals are always working efficiently. It is likely, however, that managers may work late evenings or on weekends because they are not very efficient (Rodgers & Rodgers, 1989). Unfortunately, using hours or quantity measures rather than efficiency or quality measures may penalize women managers who are productive yet cannot put in numerous hours due to family constraints.

### Addressing Discrimination and Advancing Women

Some companies (e.g., Merck, Mead Corporation) have sponsored workshops to change the attitudes of male executives toward women and affirmative action (Wessel, 1986). Other firms (e.g., Corning, Merck, Gannett Company) have started tying managers' bonuses to their success at meeting equal employment opportunity or upward mobility goals (Pave, 1986). For example, Merck raised the proportion of women among their top 85 executives from 3.5% in 1983 to 11.8% in 1988. Corning had a similar goal, and by 1988 women made up 3% of the senior executive positions, 3% of middle management, and 17% of lower management jobs (Williams, 1988).

Another suggestion for advancing women into senior management, which may be particularly beneficial for working mothers, is to change seniority systems. Currently, in some organizations, individuals are promoted more rapidly if they work the later shifts (afternoon, evening). Unfortunately, these shifts pose hardships on parents. If these policies were changed, parents, particularly mothers, might have better opportunities for being promoted (Rodgers & Rodgers, 1989).

Recently, firms have started offering training programs for diversity awareness to reduce sex discrimination (Powell, 1988; Russell, 1991). A discussion of gender stereotypes helps individuals identify their own biases in order to avoid hindering or socially isolating women managers. Other firms (e.g., Xerox) have tried to form a mass of women in significant jobs so that they will have female colleagues. This would ensure that they are not tokens in the organization where each one is isolated and scrutinized. Some women executives believe having female colleagues would be beneficial for women managers (Morrison et al, 1987b). Another strategy adopted by some companies (e.g., AT&T, Prudential, DuPont, General Public Utilities) to address discrimination is to have strong policies on sexual harassment and well-established grievance procedures to reduce and deal with cases of sexual harassment (Powell, 1988; Rapp, 1982).

## DIRECTIONS FOR FUTURE RESEARCH AND PRACTICE

### State of the Research

Counseling interventions for women in management have not been clearly defined nor have they been widely researched (Hammer-Higgins & Atwood, 1989). In the last few decades, the focus has primarily been on having counselors educate women on the barriers to career achievement and the strategies to overcome those barriers (Gray, 1980; Hammer-Higgins & Atwood, 1989). Much of the research on women in management was conducted in the 1970s and 1980s. Topics of concern included identifying barriers such as discrimination issues and sex role stereotyping. Many self-help books were written to assist women in becoming better managers or to move into management (e.g., Carr-Ruffino, 1985). In addition, numerous resources were created to help women managers network, gain information, and get support and counseling. National support groups were formed and magazines (e.g., *Executive Female, Savvy, Working Woman*) were published to provide advice to women managers and professionals.

Today, some subscribe to the belief that less research on women managers is needed because most of the problems they face have been solved. Others contend that research is needed more today than ever before because discrimination and barriers still exist for women, although they are much more subtle and difficult to detect. More innovative research methodologies may be necessary to tease out the difficulties and dilemmas confronting women managers.

Although a considerable amount of research has been conducted on issues, barriers, and concerns facing women in management, very little research has specifically focused on career counseling strategies that may prove useful to this population. In fact, research on women in management and on career counseling has not overlapped to any great extent. This is unfortunate because research is clearly needed to identify the types of counseling that can assist women managers.

## Directions for Future Research and Practice

Researchers need to identify why some women may not be entering MBA programs or management careers, and why others are dropping out. Exit interviews with women leaving management positions may prove useful in identifying barriers and strategies needed to maintain a managerial career. With their findings, counselors may be better able to assist women in entering or surviving in careers in management. For example, some types of coping strategies or counseling techniques may prove useful as women enter management careers. Other strategies may be more beneficial to help women managers survive once they are in a management career (Haring-Hidore & Beyard-Tyler, 1984). Longitudinal research is needed to uncover the differences in the issues confronting women as they move through their careers.

Research that examines the types of barriers that exist for women at varying levels of management or at varying stages in their careers is needed. Up to now, much of the research has assumed that women managers are a homogenous group, sharing similar problems. Researchers need to identify the unique issues that may be applicable to various managerial women in order to recommend effective counseling for each subgroup (Russell & Rush, 1987). For example, women in higher level management positions may face different pressures from male peers than women who are in lower level management.

It seems important to investigate the issues confronting women managers who comprise different career patterns. Any number of classification systems could be used, including Super's (1957) system, which identifies women according to the centrality of their work-force participation and homemaking, or Zytowski's (1969) career patterns for women, which classify women by the time of their career entry (early, late) and participation (low, high). It would be interesting to see the issues and barriers facing women in management who vary with respect to their participation (pattern) in their career and home lives. We might expect women who enter management careers after raising their children to experience different concerns than women entering management as single women or new wives or mothers.

It would be meaningful to see the similarities and differences in the feelings experienced by men and women managers in various career stages (e.g., maintenance). For example, during middle career, if both male and female managers experience low self-esteem, is it for the same reasons? Her feelings may be due to sex-role issues and discrimination, whereas his may be due to career plateauing. Even among women or men themselves, their feelings may exist for different reasons. Clearly, the underlying rationale for their concerns and perceptions must be identified before appropriate counseling can be provided.

Research is needed that identifies the unique issues facing different subgroups of women managers, such as minorities, reentry women, and dual-career couples. For some of these women (e.g., African-American women managers), it seems important to examine how the double effects of tokenism may serve to isolate them, and what counseling they may need. Also, issues and assistance may differ for women managers who work in varying sizes and types of organizations (e.g., manufacturing vs. services, private vs. public sector, profit vs. nonprofit). In addition, research with women managers of a broader, more global nature is needed. Research should include issues confronting U.S. women managers in international assignments as well as women managers of other cultures. For example, what is the role of ascribed versus achieved status in defining women's participation and career patterns in management? The recent book edited by Adler and Izraeli (1988) is an important step in this direction.

Although women managers should be the target population for much of the research called for, the attitudes and behaviors of men should also be investigated. This includes men in their work and home roles (e.g., spouses, fathers, peers, superiors, subordinates). It is important to further understand men's perceptions of women managers and to determine the amount and type of support they provide to women managers. Researchers should try to discern to what degree men are aware of the barriers facing women, and what their role is in contributing to or minimizing some of the problems.

Research is needed that examines the relative effectiveness of women managers and the nature of the contributions they make to organizations (Adler & Izraeli, 1988). In addition, very little research has evaluated the relative effectiveness of interventions used to assist women managers, despite the fact that this research is critical (Rosen, 1982). Research is needed that examines the relative importance of various assistance strategies (e.g., mentoring, coping strategies, individual counseling) and to determine when each strategy is most effective. It is important to see how these strategies address problems of low job satisfaction, low self-esteem, feelings of powerlessness in dealing with inequities, organizational commitment, etc. Researchers should examine the financial and psychological costs associated with various programs, the necessary refinements to maximize benefits and reduce negative features, and any unintentional negative consequences such programs may have on managers. Finally, research is needed to determine the effectiveness of both individual strategies employed by women managers and organizational strategies adopted by firms for dealing with the issues and concerns facing women managers.

## CONCLUSIONS

Women managers continue to experience a number of external and internal barriers that hinder their effectiveness in organizations. Although some progress has been made in remediating these difficulties, in some cases the problems have simply become more subtle and difficult to detect. Career counselors must recognize that women managers comprise a diverse group. Across management levels and career phases, they report unique concerns and require different types of assistance. Even within levels and phases, they may confront varying barriers due to their marital and parental status as well as their age, race, and personality characteristics.

Counselors need to recognize that organizations are not static, thus the skills needed for women managers are constantly changing. Today, organizations are much more competitive and operate in a global, changing environment. Successful managers, regardless of gender, need to develop skills to demonstrate the contribution they can make to the organization as a whole. This means they need to be more innovative and proactive about change. Some of the personal skills required include taking a broader perspective, being more creative, advocating a vision for the firm, and being persistent about their ideas. Some of the interpersonal skills required include coalition building, using teams and participative management, and empowering peers and subordinates (Kanter, 1983, 1986). Many researchers believe that women already possess the characteristics needed for future organizations. For example, many women have the interpersonal and transformational leadership skills considered critical in the increasingly service-driven market place (Aburdene & Naisbitt, 1992; Catalyst, 1987; Rizzo & Mendez, 1991). Counselors and practitioners need to encourage women to use these skills and at the same time urge organizations to more fully appreciate the unique contributions women managers can make.

A variety of career counseling efforts are needed to assist women managers in dealing with the issues they face in organizations. Some of these include career planning workshops and self-assessments, cognitive career counseling, and individual and group counseling. At the same time, organizations must adopt more innovative techniques and interventions to alter their structure to meet the needs of women managers. The future will continue to require change at both the individual level (e.g., woman manager) and organizational level to address the issues confronting women managers. For example, women managers will probably have to continue to learn how to "fit into" the male managerial model. Likewise, organizations will need to continue to offer them assistance (e.g., counseling) to help them assimilate into the corporate culture. However, organizations will also need to make greater strides in altering their organizational structures (e.g., offering flexible work arrangements, childcare) to enable women managers to provide the unique contributions they are capable of making. That is, organizations will need to recognize that "there are many equally valid, yet different ways to manage" (Adler & Izraeli, 1988, p. 6). Future research will be needed to determine the relative effectiveness of these approaches for assisting women as they enter, survive, and advance in management careers in the decades ahead.

## ACKNOWLEDGMENTS

I thank Lynn B. Curtis, Lillian T. Eby, Aaron T. Fausz, and Tammy Allen Sitver for their extensive and timely library assistance and support. I also appreciate the considerable support provided by Michael C. Rush.

## REFERENCES

Aburdene, P., & Naisbitt, J. (1992). *Megatrends for women.* New York: Villard Books.

Adler, N. J. (1984). Women in management: Where are they? *California Management Review, 26*(4), 78–89.

Adler, N. J. (1986). Do MBAs want international careers? *International Journal of Intercultural Relations, 10*(3), 277–300.

Adler, N. J. (1988). Pacific Basin managers: A Gaijin, not a woman. In N. J. Adler & D. N. Izraeli (Eds.), *Women in management worldwide* (pp. 226–249). Armonk, NY: M. E. Sharpe.

Adler, J. J., & Izraeli, D. N. (Eds.). (1988). *Women in management worldwide.* Armonk, NY: M. E. Sharpe.

Albrecht, M. (1978). Women, resistance to promotion and self-directed growth. *Human Resource Management, 17*(1), 12–17.

Andrew, C., Coderre, C., & Denis, A. (1988). Women in management: The Canadian experience. In N. J. Adler & D. N. Israeli (Eds.), *Women in management worldwide* (pp. 250–264). Armonk, NY: M. E. Sharpe.

Antal, A. B.; & Krebsbach-Gnath, C. (1988). Women in management: Unused resources in the Federal Republic of Germany. In N. J. Adler & D. N. Izraeli (Eds.), *Women in management worldwide* (pp. 141–156). Armonk, NY: M. E. Sharpe.

Astin, H. S. (1984). The meaning of work in women's lives: A sociopsychological model of career choice and work behavior. *Counseling Psychologist, 12,* 117–126.

Barnett, R. C., & Rivers, C. (1992, February). The myth of the miserable working woman. *Working Woman,* pp. 62–65, 83, 88.

Basil, D. C. (1973). *Women in management.* New York: McGraw-Hill.

Bernard, J. (1975). *The future of motherhood.* New York: Penguin Books.

Bernstein, A. (1986, October 6). Business starts tailoring itself to suit working women. *Business Week,* p. 51.

Betz, N. E., & Fitzgerald, L. F. (1987). *The career psychology of women.* Orlando, FL: Academic Press.

Bhatnagar, D. (1988). Professional women in organizations: New paradigms for research and action. *Sex Roles, 18*(5,6), 343–355.

Blum, L., & Smith, V. (1988). Women's mobility in the corporation: A critique of the politics of optimism. *Journal of Women in Culture and Society, 13*(3), 528–545.

Bolton, E., & Humphreys, L. (1977). A training model for women—An androgynous approach. *Personnel Journal, 56*(5), 230–244.

Borman, C. A., & Colson, S. (1984). Mentoring: An effective career guidance technique. *Vocational Guidance Journal, 3,* 192–197.

Borman, C. A., & Guido-DiBrito, F. (1986). The career development of women: Helping Cinderella lose her complex. *Journal of Career Development, 12*(3), 250–261.

Bowen, D. D., & Hisrich, R. D. (1986). The female entrepreneur: A career development perspective. *Academy of Management Review, 11*(2), 393–407.

Brass, D. J. (1985). Men's and women's networks: A study of interaction patterns and influence in an organization. *Academy of Management Journal, 28*(2), 327–343.

Brenner, O. C., Tomkiewicz, J., & Schein, V. E. (1989). The relationships between sex role stereotypes and requisite management characteristics revisited. *Academy of Management Journal, 32,* 662–669.

Broverman, I. K., Vogel, S. R., Broverman, D. M., Clarkson, F. E., & Rosenkrantz, P. S. (1972). Sex role stereotypes: A current appraisal. *Journal of Social Issues, 28*(2), 59–78.

Brown, D., Brooks, L., & Associates (Eds.). (1990). *Career choice and development: Applying contemporary theories to practice* (2nd ed., pp. 455–505). San Francisco: Jossey-Bass.

Brown, L. K. (1988). Female managers in the United States and in Europe: Corporate boards, M. B. A. credentials, and the image/illusion of progress. In N. J. Adler & D. N. Izraeli (Eds.), *Women in management worldwide* (pp. 265–274). Armonk, NY: M. E. Sharpe.

Bunker, K. A., (1988). Cinderella doesn't live here anymore. *Issues & Observations,* Spring, 1–6.

Burden, D., & Googins, B. (1986). *Boston University balancing jobs and homelife study.* Boston University School of Social Work.

Bureau of the Census. (1990). *Statistical abstracts of the United States, 1990.* Washington, DC: U.S. Department of Commerce.

Burke, R. J. (1992). Mentoring in organizations. *Women in Management, 2*(3), 8.

Burke, R. J., & McKeen, C. A. (1992). Women in management. In C. L. Cooper & I. T. Robertson (Eds.), *International Review of industrial and organizational psychology* (pp. 245–283). New York: Wiley.

Callanan, G. A., & Greenhaus, J. H. (1990). The career indecision of managers and professionals: Development of a scale and test of a model. *Journal of Vocational Behavior, 37,* 79–103.

Campbell, K. E. (1988). Gender differences in job-related networks. *Work and Occupations*, 15(2), 179–200.

Carney, L. S., & O'Reilly, C. G. (1987). Barriers and constraints to the recruitment and mobility of female managers in the Japanese labor force. *Human Resource Management*, 26, 193–216.

Carr-Ruffino, N. (1985). *The promotable woman: Becoming a successful manager* (rev. ed.). Belmont, CA: Wadsworth.

Castro, J. (1989, March 27). Rolling along the mommy track. *Time*, p. 72.

Catalyst. (1987). A matter of personal ability, not gender. *Management Solutions*, 32(11), 38–45.

Catalyst. (1990). *Women in corporate management: Results of a Catalyst Survey*. New York: Author.

Chan, A. (1988). Women managers in Singapore: Citizens for tomorrow's economy. In N. J. Adler & D. N. Izraeli (Eds.), *Women in management worldwide* (pp. 54–73). Armonk, NY: M. E. Sharpe.

Chusmir, L. H. (1985). Motivation of managers: Is gender a factor? *Psychology of Women Quarterly*, 9, 153–159.

Chusmir, L. H., & Franks, V. (1988). Stress and the woman manager. *Training & Development Journal*, 42(10), 66–70.

Ciabattari, J. (1986, October). The biggest mistake top managers make. *Working Women*, p. 48.

Clawson, J. G., & Kram, K. E. (1984). Managing cross-gender mentoring. *Business Horizons*, 27(3), 22–32.

Cochran, D. J., & Warren, P. M. (1976). Career counseling for women: A workshop format. *School Counselor*, 24(2), 123–127.

Collins, E. G. C., & Blodgett, T. B. (1981). Sexual harassment, some see it, some won't. *Harvard Business Review*, 59(2), 76–95.

Cook, M. (1979). Is the mentor relationship primarily a male experience? *Personnel Administrator*, 24(11), 82–86.

Cook, S. H., & Mendelson, J. L. (1984). The power wielders: Men and/or women managers. *Industrial Management*, 26(2), 22–27.

Cotton, J. L., & Tuttle, J. M. (1986). Employee turnover: A meta-analysis and review with implications for research. *Academy of Management Review*, 11, 55–70.

Cox, T. H., & Harquail, C. V. (1991). Career paths and career success in the early career stages of male and female MBAs. *Journal of Vocational Behavior*, 39, 54–75.

Crockett, V. R. (1988). Women in management in Indonesia. In N. J. Adler & D. N. Izraeli (Eds.), *Women in management worldwide* (pp. 74–102). Armonk, NY: M. E. Sharpe.

Darley, S. A. (1976). Big-time careers for the little women: A dual-role dilemma. *Journal of Social Issues*, 75, 37–40.

Davidson, M. J., & Cooper, C. L. (1987). Female managers in Britain- A comparative perspective. *Human Resource Management*, 26, 217–242.

Davidson, M. J., & Cooper, C. L. (1988). The pressures on women managers. *Management Decision*, 25, 57–63.

Deitch, C. H., & Sanderson, S. W. (1987). Geographic constraints on married women's careers. *Work and Occupations*, 14, 616–634.

De Vanna, M. A. (1987). Women in management: Progress and promise. *Human Resource Management*, 26, 409–481.

DeWine, S., & Casbolt, D. (1983). Networking: External communication systems for female organizational members. *Journal of Business Communication*, 20(2), 57–67.

DiSabatino, M. (1976). Psychological factors inhibiting women's occupational aspirations and vocational choices: Implications for counseling. *Vocational Guidance Quarterly*, 25(1), 43–49.

Donnell, S. M., & Hall, J. (1980). Men and women as managers: A significant case of no significant difference. *Organizational Dynamics, 8*, 60–77.

Ehrlich, E. (1989, March 20). The mommy track. *Business Week*, pp. 126–134.

Epstein, C. F. (1970). Encountering the male establishment: Sex-status limits on women's careers in the professions. *American Journal of Sociology, 75*, 965–982.

Erwee, R. (1988). South African women: Changing career patterns. In N. J. Adler & D. N. Izraeli (Eds.), *Women in management worldwide* (pp. 213–225). Armonk, NY: M. E. Sharpe.

Etzion, D. (1987). Burning out in management: A comparison of women and men in matched organizational positions, *Israel Social Science Research, 5*, 147–163.

Fairhurst, G. T., & Snavely, B. K. (1983). Majority and token minority group relationships: Power acquisition and communication. *Academy of Management Review, 8*, 292–300.

Fee-Fulkerson, K. (1988). Changing canoes in white water: Counseling women successful in careers they dislike. *Journal of Career Development, 14*(4), 249–258.

Fitt, L., & Newton, D. (1981). When the mentor is a man and the protege is a woman. *Harvard Business Review, 59*(2), 56–60.

Fitzgerald, L. F., & Betz, N. E. (1983). Issues in the vocational psychology of women. In W. B. Walsh & S. H. Osipow (Eds.), *Handbook of vocational psychology* (Vol. I, pp. 83–159). Hillsdale, NJ: Lawrence Erlbaum Associates.

Fitzgerald, L. F., & Crites, J. O. (1979). Career counseling for women. *Counseling Psychologist, 8*(1), 33–34.

Fitzgerald, L. F., & Crites, J. O. (1980). Toward a career psychology of women: What do we know? What do we need to know? *Journal of Counseling Psychology, 27*(1), 44–62.

For women, senior management jobs are in sight. (1992, January). *Women in Management, 2*(3), 2.

Fort, M. K., & Cordisco, J. H. (1981). Career development for women in industry. *Training and Development Journal, 35*(2), 62–64.

Foster, M., Wallston, B., & Berger, M. (1980). Feminist orientation and job-seeking behavior among dual-career couples. *Sex Roles, 6*(1), 59–65.

Fraker, S. (1984, April 16). Why women aren't getting to the top. *Fortune*, pp. 40–45.

Gallos, J. V. (1989). Exploring women's development: Implications for career theory, practice, and research. In M. B. Arthur, D. T. Hall, & B. S. Lawrence (Eds.), *Handbook of career theory* (pp. 110–132). New York: Cambridge University Press.

Garland, S. B. (1991, September 2). How to keep women managers on the corporate ladder. *Business Week*, p. 64.

Gomez-Mejia, L., & Balkin, D. (1980). Can internal management training programs narrow the male-female gap in managerial skills? *Personnel Administrator, 25*(5), 77–83.

Gray, J. D. (1979). Role conflicts and coping strategies in married professional women. Doctoral dissertation, University of Pennsylvania. *Dissertation Abstracts International*, 1980, 40, 3781-A. (University Microfilms No. 7928135)

Gray, J. D. (1980). Counseling women who want both a profession and a family. *Personnel and Guidance Journal, 59*(1), 43–46.

Gruneberg, M. (1979). *Understanding job satisfaction*. New York: Wiley.

Gutek, B. A. (1985) *Sex and the workplace*. San Francisco: Jossey-Bass.

Gutek, B. A., Cohen, A. G., & Konrad, A. M. (1990), Predicting social-sexual behavior at work: A contact hypothesis. *Academy of Management Journal, 33*, 560–577.

Gutek, B. A., & Larwood, L. (Eds.). (1987). *Women's career development*. Newbury Park: Sage.

Halcomb, R. (1980, February). Mentors and the successful woman. *Across the Board*, pp. 13–18.

Hall, D. T. (1972). A model of coping with role conflict: The role behavior of college educated women. *Administrative Science Quarterly, 17*, 471–486.

Hall, D. T. (1989). Moving beyond the "Mommy Track": An organization change approach. *Personnel, 66*(12), 23–29.

Hammer-Higgins, P., & Atwood, V. A. (1989). The Management Game: An educational intervention for counseling women with nontraditional career goals. *Career Development Quarterly, 38*(1), 6–23.

Hansen, L. S. (1978). Promoting female growth through a career development curriculum. In L. S. Hansan & R. S. Rapoza (Eds.), *Career development and counseling of women* (pp. 425–442). Springfield, IL: Charles C. Thomas.

Hardesty, S., & Jacobs, N. (1986). *Success and betrayal.* New York: Franklin Watts.

Haring-Hidore, M. & Beyard-Tyler, K. (1984). Counseling and research on nontraditional careers: A caveat. *Vocational Guidance Quarterly, 33*(2), 113–119.

Harragan, B. L. (1977). *Games mother never taught you.* New York: Rawson Associates.

Harriman, A. (1985). *Women/men/management.* Westport, CT: Praeger.

Hartnett, O., & Novarra, V. (1980). Single sex management training and a woman's touch. *Personnel Management, 12*(3), 33–35.

Haskell, J. R. (1985). Women blocked by corporate politics. *Management World, 14*(9), 12–15.

Hearn, J., & Parkin, P. W. (1988). Women, men, and leadership: A critical review of assumptions, practices, and change in industrialized nations. In N. J. Adler & D. N. Izraeli (Eds.), *Women in management worldwide* (pp. 17–40). Armonk, NY: M. E. Sharpe.

Heilman, M. E., & Saruwatari, L. R. (1979). When beauty is beastly: The effects of appearance and sex on evaluations of job applicants for managerial and nonmanagerial jobs. *Organizational Behavior and Human Performance, 23,* 360–372.

Heinen, J. S., McGlauchlin, D., Legeros, C., & Freeman, J. (1975). Developing the woman manager. *Personnel Journal, 54*(5), 282–286, 297.

Hellwig, B. (1985, April). The breakthrough generation: 73 women ready to run corporate America. *Working Woman,* pp. 99, 148.

Hendrick, S. S. (1981, October 8). Why women don't succeed. *National Business Employment Weekly,* pp. 9–11.

Hennig, M., & Jardim, A. (1977). *The managerial woman.* Garden City, NY: Anchor Press/Doubleday.

Hines, W. (1983, May 4). White men reap good jobs. *Bryan-College Station Eagle,* pp. 1, 11A.

Hollenbeck, K. (1985). *Education and employment: A handbook to promote sex equity.* Pueblo, CO: Pueblo Community College.

Hunsaker, J. S. (1982, August). *The mentor relationship: Fact or fiction.* Paper presented at the annual meeting of the Academy of Management, New York.

Hunsaker, J., & Hunsaker, P. (1991). *Strategies and skills for managerial women.* Cincinnati, OH: South-Western.

Hunt, D., & Michael, C. (1983). Mentorship: A career training and development tool. *Academy of Management Review, 8,* 474–485.

Izraeli, D. N. (1988). Women's movement into management in Israel. In N. J. Adler & D. N. Izraeli (Eds.), *Women in management worldwide* (pp. 186–212). Armonk, NY: M. E. Sharpe.

Jacklin, C. N., & Maccoby, E. E. (1975). Sex differences and their implications for management. In F. Gordon & M. Strober (Eds.), *Bringing women into management* (pp. 23–38). New York: McGraw-Hill.

Jacobson, M. B., & Koch, W. (1977). Women as leaders: Performance evaluations as a function of method of leader selection. *Organization Behavior and Human Performance, 20,* 149–157.

Jerdee, T. H., & Rosen, B. (1976, September). *Factors influencing the career commitment of women.* Paper presented at the annual meeting of the American Psychological Association, Washington, DC.

Johnson, C. L., & Johnson, F. A. (1977). Attitudes toward parenting dual-career families. *American Journal of Psychiatry, 134,* 391–395.

Johnston, W., & Packer, A. (1987). *Workforce 2000: Work and workers for the twenty-first century.* Indianapolis: Hudson Institute.

Josefowitz, N. (1980a). Management men and women: Closed vs. open doors. *Harvard Business Review, 58*(5), 56, 58, 62.

Josefowitz, N. (1980b). *Paths to power: A woman's guide from first job to top executive.* Reading, MA: Addison-Wesley.

Kahn, S. E. (1988). Feminism and career counseling with women. *Journal of Career Development, 14*(4), 242–248.

Kanter, R. M. (1977a). *Men and women of the corporation.* New York: Basic Books.

Kanter, R. M. (1977b). Some effects of proportions on group life: Skewed sex ratios and responses to token women. *American Journal of Sociology, 82*(5) 965–990.

Kanter, R. M. (1983). *The change masters: Innovation & entrepreneurship in the American corporation.* New York: Simon & Schuster.

Kanter, R. M. (1986). Mastering change: The skills we need. In L. L. Moore (Ed.), *Not as far as you think: The realities of working women* (pp. 181–194). Lexington, MA: D. C. Heath.

Kaplan, R. (1984). Trade routes: The managers' network of relationships. *Organizational Dynamics, 12*(4), 37–52.

Keller, A. (1989, March 20). The mommy track. *Business Week,* pp. 126–134.

Kimbrough, F. H. (1981). *Effects of a group career/life planning counseling model on the sex role and career self-concept of female undergraduates.* Unpublished doctoral dissertation. Texas A & M. *Dissertation Abstracts International, 42* (3), 291-A. (University Microfilms No. 8118274)

Kipnis, D., & Cosentino, J. (1969). Use of leadership powers in industry. *Journal of Applied Research, 53,* 460–466.

Kipnis, D., & Schmidt, S. (1982). *Respondent's guide to the profiles of organizational influence strategies.* San Diego: University Associates.

Kram, K. (1983). Phases of the mentor relationship. *Academy of Management Journal, 26,* 608–625.

Kram, K. E. (1985). *Mentoring at work: Developmental relationships in organizational life.* Glenview, IL: Scott, Foresman.

Labor's Martin is out to break the glass ceiling. (1991, August 9). *Wall Street Journal,* pp. B1, B6.

Larwood, L., & Gattiker, U. E. (1987). A comparison of career paths used by successful women and men. In B. A. Gutek & L. Larwood (Eds.), *Women's career development* (pp. 129–156). Newbury Park, CA: Sage.

Larwood, L., Gutek, B., & Gattiker, U. E. (1984). Perspectives on institutional discrimination and resistance to change. *Group and Organization Studies, 9,* 333–352.

Larwood, L., Wood, M. M., & Inderlied, S. D. (1978). Training women for management: New problems, new solutions. *Academy of Management Review, 3*(3), 584–593.

Lewin, T. (1989, March 12). Managers or mommies. *Knoxville News-Sentinel,* p. F1.

Lipovenko, D. (1987, Feb. 26). Mom's choosing nursery over career. *Globe and Mail Report on Business Magazine,* B1–B2.

Loerch, K. J., Russell, J. E. A., & Rush, M. C. (1989). The relationship among family domain variables and work-family conflict for men and women. *Journal of Vocational Behavior, 35,* 288–308.

Lopate, C. (1971). Marriage and medicine. In A. Theodore (Ed.), *The professional woman.* New York: Schenkman Publishing.

Lunding, F. L., Clements, G. L., & Perkins, D. S. (1978). Everyone who makes it has a mentor. *Harvard Business Review, 56*(4), 89–101.

Mack, T. (1990). Mommy tracks making waves in the workplace. *Networker, 8*(3), p. 2.

Management Centre Europe. (1982). An upward climb for women in Europe (Executive Report). Summarized in An upward climb for career women in Europe. *Management Review, 71*(9), 56–57.

Maynard, R. (1988, January 15). Thanks, but no thanks. *Globe and Mail Report on Business Magazine*, 26–34.

McClelland, D. (1975). *The inner experience*. New York: Irvington.

McGregor, D. (1967). *The professional manager*. New York: McGraw-Hill.

Miller, A., & Tsiantar, D. (1991, November 25). Mommy tracks. *Newsweek*, pp. 48–49.

Miller, J., Labovitz, S., & Fry, L. (1975). Inquires in the organizational experiences of women and men. *Social Forces, 54*, 365–381.

Milwid, B. (1983). Breaking in: Experiences in male-dominated professions. *Women & Therapy, 2*(2/3), 67–79.

Missarian, A. (1982). *The corporate connection: Why executive women need mentors to reach the top*. Englewood Cliffs, NJ: Spectrum.

Morrison, A. M., & Von Glinow, M. A. (1990). Women and minorities in management. *American Psychologist, 45*, 200–208.

Morrison A. M., & White, R. P., VanVelsor, E. (1987, August). Executive women: Substance plus style. *Psychology Today*, pp. 18–26.

Morrison, A. M., White, R. P., VanVelsor, E., & the Center for Creative Leadership. (1987a). *Breaking the glass ceiling: Can women reach the top of America's largest corporations?* Reading, MA: Addison-Wesley.

Morrison, A. M., White, R. P., VanVelsor, E., & the Center for Creative Leadership. (1987b, June). Women with promise: Who succeeds, who fails? *Working Woman*, pp. 79–82.

Nelton, S., & Berney, K. (1987, May). Women: The second wave. *Nation's Business*, pp. 18–22.

Nicholson, N., & West, M. (1988). *Managerial job change: Men and women in transition*. New York: Cambridge University Press.

Ogintz, E. (1983, December 18). Career mothers outnumber housewives. *Bryan-College Station Eagle*, pp. 1A, 12A.

Parker, M., Peltier, S., & Wolleat, P. (1981). Understanding dual career couples. *The Personnel and Guidance Journal, 60*(1), 14–18.

Pave, I. (1986, June 23). A woman's place is at GE, Federal Express, P&G . . . *Business Week*, pp. 75–76.

Phillips, L. L. (1978, October 23). Women finally get mentors of their own. *Business Week*, pp. 74–80.

Powell, G. N. (1988). *Women & men in management*. Newbury Park, CA: Sage.

Rapoport, R., & Rapoport, R. N. (1971). *Dual-career families*. Baltimore, MD: Penguin Books.

Rapp, E. (1992, February). Dangerous liaisons. *Working Woman*, pp. 56–61.

Renshaw, J. R. (1988). Women in management in the Pacific Islands: Exploring Pacific stereotypes. In N. J. Adler & D. N. Izraeli (Eds.), *Women in management worldwide* (pp. 122–140). Armonk, NY: M. E. Sharpe.

Richardson, M. S., & Johnson, M. (1984). Counseling women. In S. D. Brown & R. W. Lent (Eds.), *The handbook of counseling psychology* (pp. 832–877). New York: Wiley.

Rizzo, A. M., & Mendez, C. (1991). *The integration of women in management: A guide for human resources and management development specialists*. New York: Quorum Books.

Rizzo, A. M., Mendez, C., & Brosnan, D. (1990). Critical theory and communication dysfunction: The case of sexually ambiguous behavior. *Administration and Society, 21*(4).

Roche, G. R. (1979). Much ado about mentors. *Harvard Business Review, 57*(1), 14–15, 20–28.

Rodgers, F. S., & Rodgers, C. (1989). Business and the facts of family life. *Harvard Business Review, 67*(6), 121–129.

Rogan, H. (1984a, October 25). Top women executives find path to power is strewn with hurdles. *Wall Street Journal*, pp. 35, 44.

Rogan, H. (1984b, October 30). Executive women find it difficult to balance demands of job, home. *Wall Street Journal*, pp. 33, 55.

Roman, M., Mims, R., & Jespersen, F. (1991, November 25). A portrait of the boss. *Business Week*, pp. 180–184.

Rosen, B. (1982). Career progress of women: Getting in and staying in. In H. J. Bernardin (Ed.), *Women in the work force* (pp. 70–99). New York: Praeger.

Rosen, B., & Jerdee, T. H. (1974a). Effects of applicant's sex and difficulty of job on evaluations of candidates for managerial positions. *Journal of Applied Psychology, 59,* 511–512.

Rosen, B., & Jerdee, T. H. (1974b). Sex stereotyping in the executive suite. *Harvard Business Review, 52,* 45–58.

Rosen, B., & Jerdee, T. H. (1975). Effects of employee's sex and threatening versus pleading appeals on managerial evaluations of grievances. *Journal of Applied Psychology, 60,* 442–445.

Rosen, B., & Jerdee, T. H. (1976). *Becoming aware.* Chicago: Science Research Associates.

Rosen, B., & Jerdee, T. H. (1978). Perceived sex differences in managerially relevant behavior. *Sex Roles, 4,* 837–843.

Rosen, B., & Jerdee, T. H. (1979). Identifying and coping with "backlash" to affirmative action plans. *Business Horizons, 22,* 15–20.

Rosen, B., & Mericle, M. (1979). Influence of strong versus weak fair employment policies and applicant's sex on selection decisions and salary recommendations in a management simulation. *Journal of Applied Psychology, 64,* 435–439.

Rosen, B., Templeton, M. E., & Kichline, K. (1981). Early career experiences of women in management. *Business Horizons, 24,* 26–29.

Rosin, H. M., & Korabik, K. (1990). Marital and family correlates of women managers' attrition from organizations. *Journal of Vocational Behavior, 37,* 104–120.

Rosin, H. M., & Korabik, K. (1991). Workplace variables, affective responses, and intention to leave among women managers. *Journal of Occupational Psychology, 64,* 317–330.

Rothwell, S. (1986). Manpower matters: Women's career developments. *Journal of General Management, 11,* 88–93.

Ruble, D. N., & Ruble, T. N. (1982). Sex stereotypes. In A. G. Miller (Ed.), *In the eye of the beholder* (pp. 188–252). New York: Praeger.

Russell, J. E. A. (1991). Career development interventions in organizations. *Journal of Vocational Behavior, 38,* 237–287.

Russell, J. E. A., & Rush, M. C. (1987). A comparative study of age-related variation in women's views of a career in management. *Journal of Vocational Behavior, 30,* 280–294.

Schein, V. E. (1973). The relationship between sex role stereotypes and requisite management characteristics. *Journal of Applied Psychology, 57,* 95–100.

Schein, V. A. (1975). Relationship between sex role stereotypes and requisite management characteristics among female managers. *Journal of Applied Psychology, 60,* 340–344.

Schwartz, F. N. (1989). Management women and the new facts of life. *Harvard Business Review, 67*(1), 65–76.

Sekaran, U. (1983). Factors influencing the quality of life in dual-career families. *Journal of Occupational Psychology, 58*(2), 161–174.

Sekaran, U. (1985). The paths to mental health: An exploratory study of husbands and wives in dual-career families. *Journal of Occupational Psychology,* 129–137.

Sekaran, U. (1989). Understanding the dynamics of self-concept of members in dual-career families. *Human Relations,* 97–116.

Shann, M. (1983). Career plans of men and women in gender dominant professions. *Journal of Vocational Behavior, 22,* 343–356.

Shockley, P., & Staley, C. (1980). Women in management training programs: What they think about key issues. *Public Personnel Management Journal, 9,* 214–224.

Solomon, J. (1989, November 7). Firms grapple with language barriers. *Wall Street Journal,* pp. B1, B4.

Stechert, K. B. (1986). *Sweet success: How to understand the men in your business life and win with your own rules.*. New York: Macmillan.

Steinhoff, P. G., & Tanaka, K. (1988). Women managers in Japan. In N. J. Adler & D. N. Izraeli (Eds.), *Women in management worldwide* (pp. 103–121). Armonk, NY: M. E. Sharpe.

Stewart, L., & Gudykunst, W. B. (1982). Differential factors influencing the hierarchical level and number of promotions of males and females within the organization. *Academy of Management Journal, 25,* 586–597.

Stonewater, B. B., Eveslage, S. A., & Dingerson, M. R. (1990). Gender differences in career helping relationships. *Career Development Quarterly, 39* (1), 72–85.

Super, D. E. (1957). *The psychology of careers.* New York: Harper and Row.

Sutton, C. D., & Moore, K. K. (1985). Executive women—20 years later. *Harvard Business Review, 63*(5), 42–66.

Symons, G. L. (1988). Women's occupational careers in business: Managers and entrepreneurs in France and in Canada. In N. J. Adler & D. N. Izraeli (Eds.), *Women in management worldwide* (pp. 41–53). Armonk, NY: M. E. Sharpe.

Taylor, A., III. (1986, August 18). Why women managers are bailing out. *Fortune,* pp. 16–23.

Terborg, J. R. (1977). Women in management: A research review. *Journal of Applied Psychology, 62*(6), 647–664.

Trost, C. (1989, November 22). New approach forced by shifts in population. *Wall Street Journal,* pp. B1, B4.

U.S. Department of Commerce, Bureau of the Census (1983). *Money income of households, families and persons in the United States: 1981,* Series P-60, No. 137, pp. 176–181.

U.S. Merit Systems Protection Board (USMSPB). (1981). *Sexual harassment in the Federal workforce: Is it a problem?* Washington, DC: Government Printing Office.

Vetter, L. (1975). The majority minority: American women and careers. In J. S. Picou & R. E. Campbell (Eds.), *Career behavior of special groups* (pp. 224–240). Columbus, OH: Charles E. Merrill.

Vetter, L. (1983). Career counseling for women. *Counseling Psychologist, 4*(1), 54–67.

Wallston, B. S., Foster, M. A., & Berger, M. (1978). I will follow him: Myth, reality, or forced choice—Job seeking experiences of dual-career couples. *Psychology of Women Quarterly, 3,* 9–21.

Wells, T. (1977). Up the management ladder. In E. I. Rawlings & D. K. Carter (Eds.), *Psychotherapy for women: Treatment toward equality* (pp. 221–249). Springfield, IL: Charles C. Thomas.

Westoff, L. A. (1986, October). Mentor or lover. *Working Woman,* pp. 116–119.

Wessel, D. (1986, March 24). The last angry men. *Wall Street Journal,* p. 20D.

White, M. C., Crino, M. D., & DeSanctis, G. L. (1981). A critical review of female performance, performance training and organizational initiatives designed to aid women in the work-role environment. *Personnel Psychology, 34*(2), 227–249.

Wiley, K. W. (1987, June). Up against the ceiling. *Savvy,* pp. 51–52, 71.

Williams, M. J. (1988, September 12). Women beat the corporate game. *Fortune,* pp. 128–138.

Worell, J. (1980). New directions in counseling women. *Personnel and Guidance Journal, 58*(7), 477–484.

Zeit, B., & Dusky, L. (1988). *The best companies for women.* New York: Simon & Schuster.

Zytowski, D. G. (1969). Toward a theory of career development for women. *Personnel and Guidance Journal, 47*(7), 660–664.

# ❧ 9 ❧

# Women and Work:
# Theory Encounters Reality

Louise F. Fitzgerald
James Rounds
*University of Illinois at Champaign-Urbana*

Work has become an integral part of women's lives. In 1993, most women in the United States worked outside the home—including the majority of those with small children—a fact that is generally considered one of the most significant social phenomena of the 20th century. This virtual revolution in women's work behavior has produced an equally dramatic shift in the literature devoted to examining and understanding such behavior. On the eve of the 1970s, Crites eliminated women from consideration in his classic *Vocational Psychology* with the remark that the literature was too disparate to warrant review (Crites, 1969); shortly thereafter, Bill Bingham and his co-worker found that career counselors typically knew little about the realities of women and work, believing that women were rarely discriminated against and that there must be something wrong with a woman who held a "man's" job (Bingham & House, 1973a, 1973b). Less than 25 years later, the journals are filled with articles on women and work, at least two major books have appeared (Betz & Fitzgerald, 1987; Nieva & Gutek, 1981), and chapters and topical reviews abound (see, for example, Betz, in press; Fitzgerald & Betz, 1983; Fitzgerald & Weitzman, 1992; and Gutek & Larwood, 1987, to name a few). Each year, the authors of the *Journal of Vocational Behavior* (*JVB*) annual review note the continuing popularity and heuristic value of the topic and, as we ourselves found in 1989, it is clearly one of the most active areas of research in vocational psychology (Fitzgerald & Rounds, 1989).

As Betz and Fitzgerald (1987) noted, the majority of this work has focused on women's career choices, including the question of why and under what conditions they choose to work at all. As occupational involvement became more common for women, the focus began to shift to the nature and degree of their career orientation itself, studying for example the degree to which choices were traditional or nontraditional, or whether the woman could be classified as a "pioneer" or an "innovator" (Almquist, 1974; Rossi, 1965; Tangri, 1972). A variation of this work involved examination of the degree to which a choice involved a science versus nonscience focus (Goldman & Hewitt, 1976), science being historically an atypical pursuit for women.

Contemporary studies, although considerably more sophisticated, continue to focus on the content and nature of women's choices (Fassinger, 1985, 1990), and the overwhelming majority of interventions that have been reported are designed to facilitate the choice process or expand the options that women consider (see Hammer-Higgins & Atwood, 1989, and portions of Brooks & Haring-Hidore, 1988, for rare exceptions). Relatively little attention has been paid to adult women actually in the workforce, that is, to women's work adjustment, despite the fact that the great majority of vocational behavior takes place during the years after a choice is made and implemented.

An examination of the literature here is instructive. In the last decade, the *Journal of Vocational Behavior* has published an average of three studies per year that could reasonably be classified as focusing on women's vocational adjustment (this out of the 40 or so empirical articles that appear each year); the *Journal of Counseling Psychology* has published seven, only one of which is an intervention study (West, Horan & Games, 1984). Although these papers examine a wide range of topics (e.g., success, satisfaction, attrition, mentoring and so forth), by far the most common topics are the work–family interface (e.g., Beutell & Greenhaus, 1982; Granrose, 1984; Ralston & Flanagan, 1985), occupational stress (Higgins, 1986; Vredenburgh & Trenkhaus, 1983; and others), or a combination of the two (e.g., Anderson-Kulman & Paludi, 1986; McLaughlin, Cormier, & Cormier, 1988).

Magazines designed for women themselves, however, focus on a broad range of topics such as strategies for career advancement, managerial skills, decision making, and a host of practical issues from handling co-worker relationships to evaluating the wisdom of a mid-life career change. The importance of such topics to women is reflected in the circulation figures for magazines such as *Working Woman*, and the popularity of books with titles such as *Games Mother Never Taught You* and *The Managerial Woman*. Even highly traditional periodicals such as *Glamour* and *Mademoiselle*, historically dedicated to issues of fashion and beauty, currently devote considerable monthly space to career-related issues, features, and problems. Clearly, women themselves are seriously interested in issues of vocational adjustment, even if vocational psychologists and career counselors apparently are not.

The relative neglect of this topic may have much to do with the fact that as women were moving into the workforce, counseling psychologists were moving away from their historical interest in vocational behavior (Fitzgerald & Osipow, 1986, 1988); those who remain are generally located in colleges and universities – as are their subjects and clients, the undergraduate students who populate university counseling centers, career development classes, and journal pages. A focus on the process and problems of career choice, issues with which such individuals are highly concerned, becomes both understandable and to some degree inevitable.

We suspect, however, that the neglect of work adjustment issues that characterizes the contemporary career counseling literature is more than a matter of convenience and demographics. Rather, it seems to us that part of the problem has to do with the ways that theorists have structured our understanding of the work adjustment process; in particular, such attempts have sought to provide nomothetic description at the highest level of generality and in so doing ignored variables important mainly to particular groups of individuals (in this case, women). In addition, general models of work adjustment (e.g., Crites, 1976; Dawis & Lofquist, 1984; Lofquist & Dawis, 1969) have arisen in the context of an intellectual tradition that has typically dichotomized the concerns of work and family, thus vitiating their usefulness for women for whom these domains are generally closely connected (Fitzgerald & Weitzman, 1992; Richardson, 1981). Attempts to address issues more specific to women, although important, are typically narrow and atheoretical and fail to link themselves to more general models of work adjustment. The work on coping with multiple roles is illustrative here (see, for example, early work by Hall, 1972a, 1972b, as well as Beutell & Greenhaus, 1982; Gray, 1980; Johnson & Johnson, 1977; McLaughlin et al., 1988). The result is the absence of any systematic framework for understanding women's work behavior that is both theoretically grounded and parsimonious, yet sufficiently comprehensive to account for the complex realities of women's lives. Lacking such a framework, research efforts – where they exist at all – are both partial and ad hoc; applications, absent a framework to apply, are for all intents and purposes nonexistent.

This chapter represents an attempt to provide such a framework, within the general context of the theory of work adjustment (TWA; Dawis & Lofquist, 1984; Lofquist & Dawis, 1969, 1991), arguably the most empirically powerful model of the work adjustment process so far available. We begin with a description of the theory, highlighting its strengths and the research it has generated, and then proceed to provide a critique from the perspective of the career psychology of women. We then attempt to demonstrate how the theory could be expanded to account more adequately for women's vocational adjustment, and conclude with a discussion of practical ways in which such an expanded formulation could be applied in counseling adult working women.

## THEORY OF WORK ADJUSTMENT

The theory of work adjustment (TWA)—introduced in 1964 (Dawis, England, & Lofquist) and revised in 1969 (Lofquist & Dawis) and 1984 (Dawis & Lofquist)—is one of the few career development theories that focuses on the prediction and process of adult career adjustment rather than solely on occupational choice. It uses a person–environment perspective (Osipow, 1990) to explain how an individual or environment adapts to the ongoing transactions between them. Although most applicable to adult career adjustment and counseling (Lofquist & Dawis, 1991; Rounds & Tracey, 1990), its core concepts have also been applied to rehabilitation (Dawis, 1987) and to many areas of industrial and organizational psychology such as selection, training, work motivation, and ergonomic design (Hesketh & Dawis, 1991).

The theory has two conceptual components: a prediction model and a process model. The prediction model describes the characteristics of the person and environment that are important for understanding work adjustment; the process model, on the other hand, describes how individuals achieve adjustment to work. Overall, both components are integrated and formally presented in the form of 17 propositions, which have also been translated into a systems conceptualization of the dynamics of work adjustment (Dawis & Lofquist, 1978).

Because the theory is very elaborate, attempting to describe all aspects of work adjustment, we describe here only those concepts that are central to the prediction and process of work adjustment. We urge readers to seek out primary sources cited in the text to develop a more complete understanding of the theory as a whole.

### Prediction of Work Adjustment: Central Components

Central to TWA is the concept of *correspondence* between the person and the environment (P–E). The P–E correspondence, viewed as reciprocal and complementary, can be described as a balanced and harmonious interrelationship between the individual and her environment. When applied to work, correspondence involves the relationship between what the individual worker brings to the work environment and what that environment has to offer in return. Typically, the worker brings certain types of knowledge, competencies, skills, and abilities to her job or occupation, which in return provides certain rewards (e.g., wages, opportunities, working conditions, and so forth). Work environments can be either broadly (e.g., career or occupation) or narrowly conceived (i.e., job); typically, they are defined fairly narrowly to include working conditions, benefits, relations with co-workers and superiors, and the challenge of day-to-day work tasks.

Both the individual and the work environment have certain minimal requirements that must be fulfilled if their relationship is to continue. Employees, for example, expect that if they perform well, they should receive certain benefits such as increased pay and opportunities for advancement; the work environment, on the other hand, requires a minimally acceptable level of performance and productivity if the individual is to remain in her job. Therefore, Dawis and Lofquist (1984) define correspondence as "the individual fulfilling the requirements of the work environment and the work environment fulfilling the requirements of the individual" (p. 54). Work adjustment itself is defined as "the continuous and dynamic process by which the individual seeks to achieve and maintain correspondence with the work environment" (p. 55).

The process of work adjustment begins the first day on the job, with the worker attempting to meet whatever expectations are required for adequate performance. At the same time, she also begins to experience the rewards of her work. In the course of this day-by-day encounter with the world-of-work, two types of appraisals occur: (a) her supervisor or boss evaluates her performance and productivity (i.e., her satisfactoriness), and (b) she herself evaluates the quality and types of work outcomes (rewards) she experiences (i.e., her satisfaction). Thus, *satisfactoriness* (more generally referred to in the literature as *vocational success*) can be thought of as how satisfied the work environment (employer) is with the individual, and *satisfaction* as the individual's appraisal of whether the work environment fulfills her requirements.

Satisfactoriness and satisfaction are key indicators of the correspondence between the individual and work environment: They are important for determining *tenure*, that is, whether and for how long the worker stays in the work environment or, conversely, decides to leave. Workers whose important needs go unmet by the job are predicted to be dissatisfied and to leave; those who fail to meet performance requirements theoretically should be judged unsatisfactory and be dismissed. The reverse is, of course, also true. Tenure is thus the ultimate criterion variable in TWA; vocationally adjusted workers will remain on the job, demonstrating both successful job performance and positive affective reactions to work.

This formulation implies, then, that specific worker characteristics are critical to the prediction of both satisfaction and satisfactoriness; such characteristics are termed the *work personality*, which is generally conceived as including (though not limited to) values and abilities. Similarly, the work environment is described along commensurate dimensions of reinforcers (rewards) and ability requirements. Figure 9.1 shows the relations among the principle concepts (correspondence, individual's work personality, work environment, satisfaction, satisfactoriness, and tenure).

### The Process of Work Adjustment

In 1984, Dawis and Lofquist formally introduced a process component into their theory of work adjustment. Recognizing that the work personality and work environment change over time and that correspondence is therefore an ongoing process, they suggested that individual differences exist in the amount of discorrespondence (mismatches) that employees will tolerate before they leave the work environment, and they hypothesized *adjustment style dimensions* to explain the process of work adjustment. Adjustment styles are behaviors directed toward achieving or maintaining P–E correspondence; within the framework of the theory, they are thought to moderate the relationship between (a) satisfaction and value-reward correspondence and (b) ability-requirement correspondence. The four adjustment styles are flexibility, activeness, reactiveness, and perseverance.

*Flexibility* is defined as the level of discorrespondence an individual will tolerate before she acts to either improve her fit with the work environment or leave it altogether; in a sense, it can be thought of as a sort of psychological "reaction time." It is considered an indicator of the minimal correspondence necessary for satisfaction and determines when the adjustment modes of activeness and reactiveness are used. For example, if a computer programmer who values working alone and autonomy is promoted to the position of system analyst (typically a position of supervision), a flexible individual may tolerate the increased interaction with other computer programmers and remain relatively satisfied with her job. A less flexible person may not tolerate the dissatisfaction as well, and would attempt to seek a better adjustment or leave the organization.

If she attempts to change the discorrespondence, our fictional analyst may do so either (or both) actively or reactively. *Activeness* is a mode of coping with discorrespondence through actively attempting to change

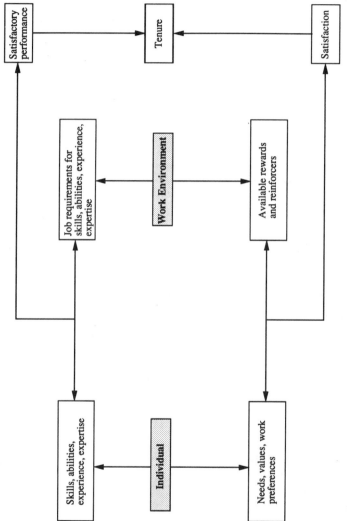

**FIG. 9.1.** Representation of the theory of work adjustment's prediction model. (Based on the work of Lofquist & Dawis, 1991, p. 82.)

the work environment to better fit one's values; *reactiveness*, on the other hand, involves acting on the self to change the expression of the work personality (e.g., values) to improve adjustment. An active system analyst, for example, may restructure her work to deemphasize supervisory tasks by giving more responsibility and autonomy to the programmers she supervises. The reactive analyst, on the other hand, may reconceptualize the situation (e.g., it will get better, or I can learn to like this role) so as to better endure the new situation. The active and reactive modes are independent dimensions, and individuals can thus use both concurrently to improve correspondence.

Finally, *perseverance* is tolerance of discorrespondence with the environment before the individual leaves; it is indicated by the length of time in a discorrespondent situation. Some individuals will make multiple attempts to achieve correspondence and can tolerate dissatisfaction for a long period of time. Others will make a few attempts and if not successful will leave the work situation at that point.

### Research on the Theory of Work Adjustment

A considerable number of studies, now numbering over 250, have been conducted on the construct, measures, and propositions of the Theory of Work Adjustment, many conducted by members of the Work Adjustment Project at the Department of Psychology at the University of Minnesota.

A unique feature of the Minnesota studies is that their measures were developed and the theory revised based on data from an unusually diverse sample of research participants. The participants in the early Minnesota studies in the 1960s and early 1970s were primarily rehabilitation clients from the Division of Vocational Rehabilitation, and employees (both skilled and unskilled) of companies in Minneapolis and St. Paul. In the mid 1970s through the 1980s, however, participants were also drawn from the Vocational Assessment Clinic, which serves adults in the Twin Cities and surrounding counties. The initial clinic clientele were primarily reentry women, but as the 1980s approached, clients began to include a large percentage of managerial and professional individuals, both women and men.

Much of the research on the Theory of Work Adjustment has concerned the measurement model, that is, the methods and instrumentation of the theory's constructs. Early efforts focused on the development of measures of the central constructs for research and counseling purposes. These studies led to the development of:

1. The Minnesota Importance Questionnaire (MIQ; Gay, Weiss, Hendel, Dawis, & Lofquist, 1971; Rounds, Henly, Dawis,

2

Lofquist, & Weiss, 1981), to assess an individual's work values and vocational needs.

2. The Minnesota Job Description Questionnaire (MJDQ; Borgen, Weiss, Tinsely, Dawis, & Lofquist, 1968), to yield occupational reinforcer (reward) patterns.
3. The Minnesota Satisfaction Questionnaire (MSQ; Weiss, Dawis, England, & Lofquist, 1967), to assess job satisfaction.

The Minnesota Occupational Classification System III (MOCS III; Dawis, Dohm, Lofquist, Chartrand, & Due, 1987) was developed using reinforcer (reward) patterns and ability requirement patterns to group the approximately 1,800 occupations from the Dictionary of Occupational Titles (U.S. Department of Labor, 1965, 1977). The MOCS III contains a wealth of information about occupations including ratings of prestige, interest, temperaments, physical demands, aptitude patterns, reward patterns, and worker functions.

Although measures have thus been developed for the central constructs in the prediction model, the Work Adjustment Project has yet to develop standard measures for the four adjustment styles of flexibility, activeness, reactiveness, and perseverance. Dawis and Lofquist (1984) have suggested that biographical information can be used to assess an individual's standing on these dimensions and have developed an experimental form, the Minnesota Adjustment Style Checklist (Lofquist & Dawis, 1991), that counselors can use to describe the adjustment style of a client. Counselors, on the basis of biographical information, interview data, and inference, estimate the likelihood that a client would engage in various activities (e.g., "ask for a transfer to other duties") and describe a client on an adjective checklist. These activities and adjectives are scored for the adjustment styles of flexibility, activeness, and reactiveness. On the environment side, occupations in the MOCS III have been rated on flexibility, an estimate of occupational tolerance for discorrespondence typically found in a given occupation. The measures for the prediction and process models have been reprinted in Dawis and Lofquist (1984) and Lofquist and Dawis (1991) and are available from Vocational Psychology Research, Department of Psychology, University of Minnesota.

As with other research in this area (e.g., Bokemeier & Lacy, 1986; Harris & Earle, 1986; Mottaz, 1986; Zalesny & Farace, 1988), most of the studies generated by TWA have found a notable lack of sex differences in the relevant constructs. For example, research on perceptions of reward patterns suggests that men and women view the reinforcing characteristics of occupations very similarly (e.g., Flint, 1980). The picture with respect to work values is comparable. The MIQ (used to assess work values within the framework of TWA) is an ipsative measure and thus does not generate norms in the general sense, making it inappropriate to examine the level of MIQ scale scores for sex differences; however, structural studies of the MIQ (for a review, see Dawis & Lofquist, 1984; Gay et al., 1971; Lofquist & Dawis, 1978) have shown that women and men have a parallel organization of vocational needs and work values, indicating that they respond similarly to work value statements. Betz and Fitzgerald (1987), reviewing the existing literature in this area, noted that men and women appear to be very similar with respect to work values and needs, despite multiple hypotheses to the contrary.

Large sex differences have been found, however, in the life history correlates of such vocational needs and work values. In a study of 290 female adults, Rounds, Dawis, and Lofquist (1979) showed that biographical information predicted MIQ scores, but that the prediction equations did not generalize to an adult male sample. It seems that the development of needs and values derives from different experiences for the two sexes, suggesting that counselors need to be knowledgeable of the differential experiences that shape women's work values.

With respect to ability-requirement correspondence (Proposition II), the theory states, in part, that, satisfactoriness (i.e., job performance and productivity) is determined by the match between the individual's abilities and the ability requirements of the work environment. Ability has generally been operationalized by the General Aptitude Test Battery (GATB), and the theory has relied on the evidence gathered by the U.S. Department of Labor studies on the GATB (see Hartigan & Wigdor, 1989), as well as the well-documented findings that abilities are related to supervisor ratings (e.g., Ghiselli, 1966). Most of the evidence available suggests that sex differences in cognitive abilities are either nonexistent or trivial, with the possible exception of some forms of spatial ability (Ackerman & Humphreys, 1990; Caplan, MacPherson, & Tobin, 1985; Hyde, 1981; Hyde & Linn, 1988).

Finally, Proposition III of the theory states that satisfaction with work is a function of the correspondence between an individual's work values and the reinforcers (rewards) of the work environment. Of the 17 formal propositions in the theory, Proposition III has received the most research attention. With few exceptions, research studies (e.g., Betz, 1969; Elizur & Tziner, 1977; Lichter, 1980; Rounds, 1990; Rounds, Dawis, & Lofquist, 1987; Salazar, 1981) have lent strong support to Proposition III.

The first study (Betz, 1969) to explicitly test Proposition III studied women in the occupations of cashier, checker marker, and sales clerk. Betz reported significant correlations between job satisfaction and the correspondence of work values and occupational rewards, ranging from .32 to .45. Lichter (1980) studied men and women clients ($N = 223$) 1 to 2 years after they received vocational assessment and counseling. Correlations between job satisfaction and correspondence showed with one exception a similar pattern for women and men: (a) $r = .39$ for women under age 30; (b) $r = .24$ for women age 30 and over; (c) $r = .41$ for men under 30; and (d) $r = .41$ for males age 30 and over. For the women 30 and over a smaller than expected correspondence–satisfaction relationship was found. In comparison, Rounds et al. (1987) studied a sample of women and men both with a median age of 30 years and reported a similar pattern of correspondence–satisfaction relationships for women ($r = .52$) and men ($r = .55$) 1 year after vocational assessment. In summary, there seem to be few sex differences in the research results reported for Proposition III.

## CRITIQUE AND EVALUATION

Taken on its own terms, the theory of work adjustment has proven to be both heuristically powerful and practically useful. Its measures, most notably the MIQ and MSQ, are widely used in both research and practice, and a large body of research supports their general framework. As with most other vocational behavior theories, however, its contents, although applicable to the experience of women workers, are of necessity incomplete, based as they are on the behavior and experiences of the male population. And, as the preeminent proponent of the individual differences approach extant today, it focuses purposely and solely on individual characteristics, excluding the influence of structural or cultural influences in determining the shape of individuals' working lives. Even the environment—of necessity an equal determinant in any P–E interaction theory—is conceptualized solely in terms of its match with a parallel set of psychological variables. Elegantly symmetric, TWA is essentially a closed system (see Hesketh & Dawis, 1991, for a different perspective).

Fitzgerald and Betz (1992) presented a strong critique of vocational behavior theory, arguing that the literature lacks any systematic explanation of the role of structural and cultural factors in shaping individuals' work-related behavior despite the fact that such factors can be shown to influence most of the major constructs that have been proposed. Arguing for the importance of contextual variables (i.e., gender, race, ethnicity, class, and sexual orientation), they noted that each is related to various cultural and structural factors that affect

vocational behavior in important, systematic, and predictable ways—yet
are generally absent from the major theories of vocational behavior.

Of particular relevance to this chapter is their discussion of the factors
that have been shown to influence women's working lives. According to
Fitzgerald and Betz, women's vocational development is affected in
specific and predictable ways by a variety of structural factors (e.g.,
discrimination, a null educational environment, sexual harassment, and
the interface between home and work) as well as by cultural constraints
(primarily sex role socialization and the dictates of the "motherhood
mandate" [Russo, 1979]). Each of these factors is hypothesized to
moderate important theoretical relationships predicted by the major
theories of career development. Possibly the most obvious example is
that of sex-role socialization, which has been shown to affect career
choice in a variety of ways, most notably in the inhibition of math- and
science-related interests and the consistent underutilization of abilities
by highly talented women.

These structural and cultural factors appear in Table 9.1, along with
the relationships between each factor and specific theoretical criteria and
the process or mechanism through which each is thought to exert its
influence. Examination of Table 9.1 reveals that the most critical influences on women's work adjustment are exerted by sexual harassment

**TABLE 9.1**
**Structural and Cultural Effects of Gender on Women's Vocational Behavior**

| Factor | Process | Criterion |
|---|---|---|
| Structural | | |
| Discrimination | Inhibition of ability/requirement match | Satisfactoriness |
|  |  | Realism |
| Null environment | Inhibition of ability/requirement match | Satisfactoriness |
|  | Truncation of range of interests | Realism |
| Sexual harassment | Job loss; job change; educational loss; | Tenure |
|  | change of educational field | Satisfaction |
|  |  | Congruence |
|  |  | Self-efficacy |
|  |  | Self-concept |
| Home–work | Inhibition of ability/ | Realism |
| interface | requirement match | Satisfactoriness |
|  |  | Satisfaction (?) |
|  |  | Work-force participation |
| Cultural | | |
| Sex-role socialization | Inhibition of interest/field match | Congruence |
|  |  | Satisfaction |
|  | Inhibition/facilitation of ability | |
|  | /requirement match | Satisfactoriness |
|  |  | Realism |

Note. From Fitzgerald and Betz (1992).

and what Fitzgerald and Betz (1992) refer to as the work–family interface—that is, the problems and processes associated with handling the competing temporal and psychological demands of these two major life arenas. Our critique and examples are organized around these two factors.

In the following pages, we attempt to demonstrate that TWA—as presently conceived and operationalized—cannot adequately explain important influences on women's working lives. Our brief examples are exactly that, and we encourage readers to consult the major sources in the career psychology of women for a more thorough treatment.

## INTERFACE BETWEEN HOME AND WORK

Discussions of the connections between home and work in women's lives have dominated the vocational behavior literature since the serious study of women and work began in the 1970s. As noted in our introduction, it is by far the most common focus in studies of women's vocational adjustment (see Richardson, 1981, for an early theoretical paper, and Betz & Fitzgerald, 1987, and Fitzgerald & Weitzman, 1992, for reviews). In the popular arena, magazines such as *Working Mother* derive their considerable popularity from women's concern with successfully combining their work lives with their family responsibilities.

Studies such as those of Baber and Monaghan (1988) consistently' show that young women are determined to "have it all" (i.e., combine career and family), despite data showing they still receive scant cooperation and assistance in doing so (Nock & Kingston, 1988; Presser, 1988) and often experience considerable stress as a result. Indeed, the difficulties imposed by current cultural arrangements (e.g., lack of adequate childcare, inadequate or nonexistent family leave policies) constitute not only a central dilemma in the lives of women themselves but can arguably be considered a national crisis (National Research Council; Ferber, O'Farrell, & Allen, 1991). Their specific impact on women's vocational adjustment can be seen in a variety of studies, including those by the Catalyst Career and Family Center (1981) demonstrating that women cite family considerations as the most important factor in their job relocation decisions, whereas men give first priority to "job for self."

Despite this large body of data indicating that the interface between work and family considerations is critical to women's vocational satisfaction, such considerations are largely absent from theoretical statements concerning women's vocational adjustment. A recent volume devoted to counseling within the framework of TWA (Lofquist & Dawis,

1991) indexes neither women, nor gender, nor sex differences, the only reference to home–work issues being embedded in the comment, "Because individuals interact with a number of main environments, it is important to identify the salience of environments in terms of both frequency of problems and importance to the individual" (p. 38). This seems to us to be an insufficient articulation of what is arguably the most salient issue in women's vocational adjustment.

## EFFECTS OF SEXUAL HARASSMENT ON WORK ADJUSTMENT

Although only recently reaching public and scholarly awareness as an important issue, sexual harassment has been a problem for as long as women have worked outside the home (Burlarzik, 1978). Extrapolation from government studies suggests that over 15,000 women leave federal employment annually as a result of harassment; figures from random samples of employed women show comparable percentages (Gutek, 1985), and studies of college women confirm that the phenomenon is not limited to the post-job-entry years (Fitzgerald et al., 1988).

Completely absent from both popular and scholarly discussions less than a decade ago, the issue of sexual harassment has been recently highlighted by several dramatic events on the national scene (e.g., the Clarence Thomas Senate confirmation hearings, the Navy sexual harassment scandal); more formally, research shows that approximately 50% of female employees experience some form of this problem at some point during their working lives (Fitzgerald, 1993; Fitzgerald & Ormerod, in press). In one study of outcomes, Coles (1986) demonstrated that 50% of women who filed complaints with a state enforcement agency were fired and another 25% resigned due to the pressures associated with the complaint or the harassment itself; in addition, harassment has been tentatively linked to a variety of other negative outcomes including decreased morale, absenteeism, decreased job performance and satisfaction, and a spectrum of serious psychological and health-related problems (Fitzgerald, 1993; Gutek & Koss, 1993; Koss, 1990). The problem appears particularly severe in certain fields (science, the blue-collar trades, and other nontraditional areas) where women are routinely "driven out" (see Fitzgerald & Ormerod, in press; Fitzgerald & Shullman, 1993, for a discussion). In the face of such data, assertions that vocational success is solely a function of the ability/requirement match are difficult to maintain.

## Summary

In a recent paper, Krumboltz (1992) remarked that theories are by intention distorted oversimplifications that ignore certain complexities for the purpose of highlighting what are thought to be more central issues. Thus it is with the theory of work adjustment, which for nearly 30 years has focused on those particular aspects of the person (worker) and the environment (job, occupation) that appeared most salient to the prediction and explanation of work adjustment.

During the course of those three decades, however, the composition of the work force has changed dramatically, its ranks now encompassing half the adult female population—women whose work situation, goals and problems cannot be easily accounted for by the theory as it stands. As we have suggested here, research and theory that do not attend to these issues will inevitably fail to account for substantial, systematic, and predictable variance in women's vocational behavior. For counselors, the issues are equally salient and certainly more pressing on a day-to-day basis. We turn now to some specific proposals concerning how TWA might be revised to account for factors (mostly) specific to women's vocational adjustment and propose some general guidelines for applying those revisions in counseling women.

## A MODEST PROPOSAL

We have two suggestions concerning how the theory of work adjustment could be expanded to take into account issues of the work–family interface and sexual harassment, suggestions that mostly have to do with Proposition III (i.e., that satisfaction is a function of the fit between worker values and job rewards). The first (and easiest to implement) involves broadening our idea of what constitutes the traditional domain of work values and occupational rewards. Recall that the theory of work adjustment, as previously discussed, has a theoretical framework, 17 propositions, and a measurement model, with specific measures to assess the constructs imbedded in the 17 propositions. Our first proposal, then, involves revising the contents of the measurement model; the second, a modest revision of the framework of the theory, involves incorporating environmental barriers as a variable (possibly as a formal proposition) to moderate the relationship between value-reward correspondence and work adjustment (satisfaction) and between satisfactoriness and tenure. Our suggestions are in the spirit of recent attempts (Osipow, 1990; Savickas & Lent, 1992) to develop a unified theory of career development. We elaborate on these proposals in the context of Proposition III—that is, that correspondence between work values and the occupational rewards predicts job satisfaction.

## Expansion of the TWA Measurement Model

Traditionally, researchers evaluating Proposition III of the theory of work adjustment have utilized the measurement model proposed by Dawis and Lofquist (1984). This model typically includes the Minnesota Importance Questionnaire to assess vocational needs and work values, Occupational Reinforcer Patterns to represent the work rewards of occupations, and the Minnesota Satisfaction Questionnaire to assess job satisfaction. Each of these measures assesses, from the perspective of either the individual or the organization, the 20 work outcomes shown in Table 9.2. The dimensions are referred to as *work values* when an individual estimates how important they are as outcomes for her ideal occupation, and as *occupational reinforcers* (rewards, also known as job perceptions) when speaking of how well they describe an occupation. The Work Adjustment Project has developed Occupational Reinforcer Patterns (ORPs; Stewart et al., 1986) for approximately 200 occupations.

TABLE 9.2
**List of Work Outcomes from the Theory of Work Adjustment's Measurement Model**

*Ability utilization* Make use of their individual abilities.
*Achievement* Get a feeling of accomplishment.
*Activity* Are busy all the time.
*Advancement* Have opportunities for advancement.
*Authority* Tell other workers what to do.
*Company policies and practices* Have a company that administers its policies fairly.
*Compensation* Are paid well in comparison with other workers.
*Co-workers* Have co-workers who are easy to make friends with.
*Creativity* Try out their own ideas.
*Independence* Do their work alone.
*Moral values* Do work without feeling that it is morally wrong.
*Recognition* Receive recognition for the work they do.
*Responsibility* Make decisions on their own.
*Security* Have steady employment.
*Social service* Have work where they do things for other people.
*Social status* Have a position of "somebody" in the community.
*Supervision–human relations* Have bosses who back up their workers (with top management).
*Supervision–technical* Have bosses who train their workers well.
*Variety* Have something different to do every day.
*Working conditions* Have good working conditions.

*Note.* Statements are from the Minnesota Job Description Questionnaire. (Based on the work of Lofquist & Dawis, 1991, p. 82.)

These ORPs are based on supervisors' or employees' ratings and are used in the prediction model where an individual's work values are matched with each of the ORPs and an estimate of the likelihood of satisfaction is given for each of the 200 occupations. Finally, the MSQ is used by an individual to rate how satisfied she is with the 20 work outcomes, this rating constituting the main criterion variable for Proposition III.

Our first proposal begins with the recognition that this measurement model suggested by Dawis and Lofquist is not necessary to the TWA, itself, but is rather one of many such models that could be proposed to assess the central constructs of the theory of work adjustment; that is, latent traits such as vocational needs and work values can be measured by many different kinds of need and value statements or measures (see Dawis, 1991, for a listing of established measures).

The advantage of using the Minnesota measures, of course, is that they provide empirically derived estimates of an individual's likely satisfaction in numerous occupations, estimates that have great practical value for career counseling. Specifically, counselors using the MIQ are provided with a computerized profile matching the client's work values with patterns of rewards that have been empirically determined to characterize particular occupations. In the context of the present discussion, a critical question is whether these dimensions adequately encompass important work outcomes for working women; in particular, does the current list represent the salient issues of the work–family interface and does it address the phenomena of sexual harassment?

Review of Table 9.2 suggests that none of the 20 work-related outcomes directly assess a large category of issues that are important for working women with families. Missing from the list are variables such as convenient and flexible hours of work, or benefits (e.g., leave for a sick child) that are important for working women. (Parenthetically, we note that work outcomes that facilitate the work–family interface are increasingly important to men as well; nothing that we say here should be taken to imply that we believe that it is necessary or appropriate for only women—or all women—to be concerned with work–family issues.) Similarly, it would seem that none of the dimensions could be interpreted to represent any of a variety of issues involving sexual harassment.

Although our criticisms are directed at the Minnesota taxonomy, a close reading of the literature on work outcomes reveals a more generic problem with the lists of work outcomes available in the vocational literature. In a review of taxonomies of work outcomes, Campbell and Pritchard (1976) addressed two problems that directly pertain to the current discussion: specificity and comprehensiveness.

First, they concluded that although the Minnesota taxonomy is the most thorough and specific list of outcomes available, even it may not be specific enough. For example, the list includes compensation, but "compensation" as such is too broad a category to be optimally useful. It would seem more appropriate to break compensation into the categories of pay (i.e., wages) and benefits (e.g., parental leave for a sick child, work-site childcare). In turn, job benefits could be partitioned into pension plan, vacation time, family leave, work-site childcare, etc.

Another example is "company policies and practices." It is possible to broadly interpret this variable to assess the extent that guidelines on sexual harassment are implemented in the work place, but this is not an obvious interpretation; once again, a more specific set of outcomes seems to be called for. It is an empirical question, of course, whether more specific categories would possess discriminability (Campbell & Pritchard 1976), but it would seem likely that a more precise list of job outcomes could lead to more accurate information and assessment.

In addition to such problems of specificity, Campbell and Prichard (1976) also concluded that available lists may not be fully representative or comprehensive. They noted, "One disturbing element of this litera-ture is the tendency for everyone to borrow everyone else's items. The content is thus rather self-perpetuating" (p. 103). Very few studies have tried to define and systematically sample the overall domain of possible job outcomes. Many of the current taxonomies of job outcomes were developed during the 1950s and 1960s on limited employee samples (e.g., Herzberg, Mausner, & Snyderman, 1959) or reviews of the literature (e.g., Vroom, 1964), and more recent attempts at classification (e.g., Billings & Cornelius, 1980; Elizur, 1984; Quinn & Cobb, 1971; Ronen, Kraut, Lingoes, & Aranya, 1979; Zytowski, 1970) have relied on the outcomes from previous measures and taxonomies. In fact, many of the current work outcomes can be directly traced to the pioneering work of Hoppock (1935) on job satisfaction. In the years since these work outcomes and taxonomies were conceptualized the work force has changed radically; certainly, concerns about family–work interface and sexual harassment are far more prevalent.

We suggest that a more complete sampling of the job outcome domain needs to be pursued. Campbell and Pritchard (1976) recommended that future studies stratify such sampling according to jobs (e.g., job func-tion, job prestige, etc.) and individual (e.g., sex, age, education, etc.). The goals of such studies should be to generate lists of outcomes using structured interview and free recall procedures. We expect such studies will produce work outcomes pertaining to work–family interface and sexual harassment and other concerns of working women that have not yet been acknowledged in the current taxonomies.

Meanwhile, research on Proposition III should expand examination of job outcomes to include those that best represent such concerns. We envision such research taking a form similar to Hesketh, McLachlan, and Gardner's (in press) recent work. They studied work preferences and job perceptions of 170 bank personnel (83 women and 87 men) and included items from Gottfredson's (1981) concept of occupational social space (i.e., Holland's RIASEC themes, preferred sex type of work performed, and preferred power level of occupations), as well as work value statements from Pryor's (1983) Work Aspect Preference Scale. Although they did not examine the issues we highlight here, their research demonstrates the feasibility of expanding the measurement model to include work outcomes that traditionally have been left out of studies of the theory of work adjustment.

## Expansion of the Theoretical Framework

Simple expansion of the contents of the measurement model is a relatively straightforward matter in the case of work–family variables; however, it is unclear whether certain forms of sexual harassment and discrimination can be easily conceptualized within the framework of work outcomes. Such variables—whether framed in the context of work values (how important to you), job perceptions (how characteristic of the job), or satisfaction (how satisfied are you)—are usually stated in a form that is conducive to one's welfare according to normative standards, in other words, in a positive direction. For sexual harassment, which is a negative behavior or event, work outcome statements would need to be framed as a case of *nonoccurrence*, for example, "the work place is free of sexual harassment," or captured in a broader frame of reference "supervisors create an environment of mutual respect."

The most obvious examples of work outcome statements pertaining directly to sexual harassment are awkward, present obvious demand characteristics, and may be objectionable to many women, suggesting that attempting to account for the effects of sexual harassment through specific work outcomes may not be feasible. On the other hand, more broadly stated work outcomes (e.g., "supervisors create an environment of mutual respect") may be insufficient to account for the effects of sexual harassment. Nevertheless, the use of broadly stated work outcomes to capture the effects of sexual harassment on job satisfaction is an empirical question that should be pursued.

If such an approach fails to account for the effects of sexual harassment on job satisfaction, then a modest theoretical revision may be called for. Sexual harassment could be hypothesized as a class of variables, generally termed environmental barriers, that moderate the correspondence-satisfaction link. Such a revision would call for the inclusion of measures of sexual harassment (e.g., Fitzgerald et al., 1988) in studies of the link between work outcomes and job satisfaction. Alternatively, assessment could focus on perceptions of the work environment; Hulin, Fitzgerald, and Drasgow (1992) have developed a measure of perceived organizational tolerance of sexual harassment based on procedures developed by Naylor, Prichard, and Ilgen (1980) to operationalize their theory of organizational climate.

Whatever measurement approach is taken, future research should examine the effects of sexual harassment as a moderator of the relationship between value-reward correspondence and satisfaction, as well as between satisfactoriness and tenure. Our proposals for expanding and revising the TWA model are depicted graphically in Fig. 9.2.

## IMPLICATIONS FOR COUNSELING: SOME OBSERVATIONS

Given our belief that theory should precede applications (else, what does one apply?), we have chosen to focus our discussion on possible

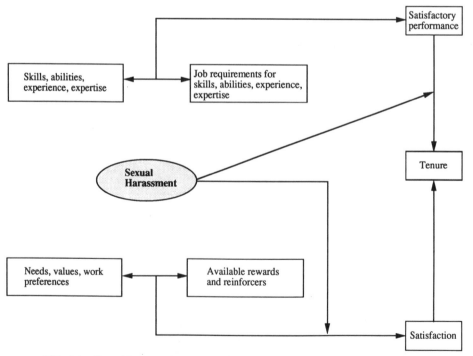

FIG. 9.2. Sexual harassment as a moderator variable of the relationship between value-reward correspondence and satisfaction and between satisfactoriness and tenure.

revisions and expansion of the TWA theoretical framework that we believe will result in a more comprehensive model. Thus, a detailed explication of relevant counseling procedures must await another forum. Still, we believe the foregoing analysis has some direct practical implications for those who counsel women—implications that lead us to offer the following observations.

We begin by recalling Johnson's (1987) distinction between knowing *that* and knowing *how*—and note that the importance of the former seems often subordinated to the latter. As previously discussed, an enormous body of literature on women and work has accumulated in the past 25 years; a working knowledge of this literature would seem to us prerequisite for those who practice in this area. It is our belief that the most effective counselors are sophisticated consumers of the theoretical and research literature; in an area such as the present one, where knowledge is expanding at such a rapid rate, this observation seems even more salient than is generally the case.

It also seems reasonable to suggest that male counselors will need to make more self-conscious and extensive efforts to prepare themselves adequately, as they by definition lack the experiential base of their female colleagues. Experiences both inside and outside the workplace shape vocational behavior. A woman's recollection of life experiences not only contributes valuable information toward making career decisions and plans, but also helps her to clarify aspects of her self—particularly vocational needs, work values, skills, and other vocational behaviors. It is important to realize that there are qualitative differences between women and men in the relationship of previous experience and vocational behavior, and in some cases the relationships are diametrically different (for examples see Rounds et al., 1979). Thus, it is of critical importance to the counseling process that counselors have a knowledge base of the kinds of experiential factors related to vocational behavior for women and how they are related to central components of work adjustment—needs, values, skills, and abilities.

If experience is thought to be the best teacher, it most likely also makes the best counselor. We do not suggest that men cannot understand or work with issues such as home–career conflict, discrimination, or even sexual harassment; it is likely, however, that it will be a much more challenging process, affectively as well as cognitively. In this vein, we note that much helpful guidance is available in professional guidelines on counseling women (e.g., Fitzgerald & Nutt, 1986) as well as similar sources.

With respect to "knowing how," we would argue strongly that a thorough assessment based on a theory of both vocational behavior and counseling is the sine qua non of effective career counseling. It has been fashionable to satirize trait-and-factor career counseling, an assessment-based counseling model, since Crites (1980) made his famous comment concerning "three interviews and a cloud of dust" (for a recent example see Krumboltz, 1992). Rounds and Tracey (1990), however, have described how trait-and-factor career counseling has evolved to person-environment (P–E) fit counseling. Their counseling model, compatible with the theory of work adjustment or any other P–E transaction and interactional model, involves applying the P–E fit premise of trait-and-factor counseling to the client–counselor interaction itself using current conceptions of problem solving, information processing, and decision making.

Although we have taken a critical perspective on the theory of work adjustment, the theory and measures have much to offer in informing and facilitating the counseling process with women. The model itself (and our modest revision) can be used to provide the client with a perspective on her work situation. The focus on work values and what the job offers can help clients identify aspects of the job that lead to satisfaction and dissatisfaction. Discussions of adjustment modes can be used to assist the client to understand both how she typically responds to stressful work situations and the wide array of options she has to cope with dissatisfaction on the job. Foremost, the theory of work adjustment informs a thorough assessment process (see Lofquist & Dawis, 1991, for a complete assessment model). Although it is possible and often desirable to supplement traditional procedures with assessment of developmental issues, life-stage concerns, and so forth, the assessment of abilities, interests, and work values and the ability to "work through" this information with the client remains the prerequisite core of the myriad procedures that go by the rubric "career counseling." But, as we have argued, the theory of work adjustment and its measurement model do not seem to capture two major sources of dissatisfaction with the workplace for many women—work–family interface and sexual harassment. We simply urge counselors to be aware of such facets of the workplace and to intervene when necessary to influence their clients' work adjustment.

## CONCLUSION

We have argued that the theory of work adjustment from the perspective of career psychology of women is not sufficiently comprehensive to account for effects of the work–family interface and sexual harassment on the work adjustment process. From our analysis, we concluded that types of work values and reinforcers in the Minnesota taxonomy are neither specific enough not sufficiently inclusive to represent any of a variety of issues involving work–family interface and sexual harassment. In the case of work–family variables, we suggested a simple remedy—expansion of the contents of the measurement model that assess work values and reinforcers. In the case of sexual harassment, we proposed the hypothesis that sexual harassment moderates the relationship between value-reward correspondence and satisfaction and the relationship between satisfactoriness and tenure. The proposed revision of the theory of work adjustment theoretical framework to account for the effects of sexual harassment on the work adjustment process awaits further examination and investigation.

In closing, we remind readers of our earlier caution that these examples are just that; the ways in which women's lives and experiences differ from those of men are currently many and profound. We urge both theorists and counselors to reflect on and explore these issues as we attempt to construct a fuller understanding of women's vocational adjustment.

## REFERENCES

Ackerman, P. L., & Humphreys, L. G. (1990). Individual differences theory in industrial and organizational psychology. In M. D. Dunnette & L. M. Hough (Eds.), *Handbook of industrial and organizational psychology* (2nd ed., Vol. 1, pp. 63–130). Palo Alto, CA: Consulting Psychologists Press.

Almquist, E. M. (1974). Sex differences in occupational choice: The case for college women. *Journal of Vocational Behavior, 5,* 13–21.

Anderson-Kulman, R. E., & Paludi, M. (1986). Working mothers and the family context: Predicting positive coping. *Journal of Vocational Behavior, 28,* 241–253.

Baber, K. M., & Monaghan, P. (1988). College women's career and motherhood expectations. *Sex Roles, 19,* 189–203.

Betz, E. L. (1969). Need reinforcer correspondence as a predictor of job satisfaction. *Personnel and Guidance Journal, 47,* 878–883.

Betz, N. E. (in press). Women's career development. In F. Denmark & M. Paludi (Eds.), *Handbook of the psychology of women.* New York: Greenwood Press.

Betz, N. E., & Fitzgerald, L. F. (1987). *The career psychology of women.* New York: Academic Press.

Beutell, N. J., & Greenhaus, J. H. (1982). Inter-role conflict among married women: The influence of husband and wife characteristics on conflict and coping behavior. *Journal of Vocational Behavior, 21,* 99–110.

Billings, B. S., & Cornelius, III, E. T. (1980). Dimensions of work outcomes: A multidimensional scaling approach. *Personnel Psychology, 33,* 151–162.

Bingham, W. C., & House, E. W. (1973a). Counselors view women and work: Accuracy of information. *Vocational Guidance Quarterly, 21,* 262–268.

Bingham, W. C., & House, E. W. (1973b). Counselor's attitudes towards women and work. *Vocational Guidance Quarterly, 22,* 16–32.

Bokemeier, J. L., & Lacy, W. B. (1986). Job values, rewards, and work conditions as factors in job satisfaction among men and women. *Sociological Quarterly, 28,* 189–204.

Borgen, F. H., Weiss, D. J., Tinsley, H. E. A., Dawis, R. V., & Lofquist, L. H. (1968). The measurement of occupational reinforcer patterns. *Minnesota Studies in Vocational Rehabilitation, 25.*

Brooks, L., & Haring-Hidore, M. (1988). Career interventions with women. *Journal of Career Development, 14*(4).

Bularzik, M. (1978). Sexual harassment at the workplace: Historical notes. *Radical America, 12,* 25–43.

Campbell, J. P., & Pritchard, R. D. (1976). Motivational theory in industrial and organizational psychology. In M. D. Dunnette (Ed.), *Handbook of industrial and organizational psychology* (pp. 63–130). Chicago: Rand McNally.

Caplan, P. J., MacPherson, G. M., & Tobin, P. (1985). Do sex-related differences in spatial abilities exist? *American Psychologist, 40,* 786–799.

Catalyst Career and, Family Center. (1981). *Corporations and two-career families: Directions for the future.* New York: Author.

Chartrand, J. M. (1991). The evolution of trait-and-factor career counseling: A person × environment fit approach. *Journal of Counseling and Development, 69,* 518–524.

Coles, F. S. (1986). Forced to quit: Sexual harassment complaints and agency response. *Sex Roles, 14,* 81–95

Crites, J. O. (1969). *Vocational psychology.* New York: McGraw-Hill.

Crites, J. O. (1976). A comprehensive model of career development in early adulthood. *Journal of Vocational Behavior, 9,* 105–118.

Crites, J. O. (1980). *Career counseling: models, methods and materials.* New York: McGraw-Hill.

Dawis, R. V. (1992, April). *Career choice and development theory and the theory of work adjustment.* Paper presented at Convergence in Theories of Career Choice and Development conference, East Lansing, MI.

Dawis, R. V. (1987). The Minnesota theory of work adjustment. In B. Bolton (Ed.), *Handbook of measurement and evaluation in rehabilitation.* London: Paul H. Brooks.

Dawis, R. V. (1991). Vocational interests, values, and preferences. In M. D. Dunnette & L. M. Hough (Eds.), *Handbook of industrial and organizational psychology* (2nd ed., Vol. 2, pp. 833–872). Palo Alto, CA: Consulting Psychologists Press.

Dawis, R. V., Dohm, T. E., Lofquist, L. H., Chartrand, J. M., & Due, A. M. (1987). *Minnesota occupational classification system III.* Minneapolis: Department of Psychology, University of Minnesota, Vocational Psychology Research.

Dawis, R. V., England, G. W., & Lofquist, L. H. (1964). A theory of work adjustment (a revision). *Minnesota Studies in Vocational Rehabilitation, 15.*

Dawis, R. V., & Lofquist, L. H. (1978). A note on the dynamics of work adjustment. *Journal of Vocational Behavior, 12,* 76–79.

Dawis, R. V., & Lofquist, L. (1984). *A psychological theory of work adjustment.* Minneapolis: University of Minnesota Press.

Elizur, D. (1984). Facets of work values: A structural analysis of work outcomes. *Journal of Applied Psychology, 69,* 379–389.

Elizur, D., & Tziner, A. (1977). Vocational needs, job rewards, and satisfaction: A canonical analysis. *Journal of Vocational Behavior, 10,* 205–211.

Fassinger, R. E. (1985). A causal model of career choice in college women. *Journal of Vocational Behavior, 27,* 123–153.

Fassinger, R. E. (1990). Causal models of career choice in two samples of college women. *Journal of Vocational Behavior, 36,* 225–248.

Ferber, M., O'Farrell, B., & Allen, L. (1991). *Work and family: Policies for a changing workforce.* Washington, DC: National Academy Press.

Fitzgerald, L. F. (1993). *The last great open secret: Sexual harassment of women in the workplace and academia.* Washington, DC: Federation of Behavioral, Psychological and Cognitive Science.

Fitzgerald, L. F., & Betz, N. E. (1992, April). *Career development in cultural context: The role of gender, race, class and sexual orientation.* Paper presented at Convergence in Theories of Career Choice and Development conference, East Lansing, MI.

Fitzgerald, L. F., & Betz, N. E. (1983). Issues in the vocational psychology of women. In W. B. Walsh & S. H. Osipow (Eds.), *Handbook of vocational psychology* (Vol. I, pp. 83–160). Hillsdale, NJ: Lawrence Erlbaum Associates.

Fitzgerald, L. F., & Nutt, R. L. (1986). Principles concerning the counseling/psychotherapy of women: Rationale and implementation. *The Counseling Psychologist, 14,* 180–216.

Fitzgerald, L. F., & Ormerod, A. J. (in press). Breaking silence: The sexual harassment of women in academia and the workplace. In F. Denmark and M. Paludi (Eds.), *Handbook of the psychology of women.* New York: Greenwood Press.

Fitzgerald, L. F., & Osipow, S. H. (1986). An occupational analysis of counseling psychology: How special is the speciality? *American Psychologist, 41,* 535–544.

Fitzgerald, L. F., & Osipow, S. H. (1988). We have seen the future but is it us: Vocational aspirations of counseling psychology graduate students. *Professional Psychology, 19,* 575–583.

Fitzgerald, L. F., & Rounds, J. B. (1989). Vocational behavior, 1988: A critical analysis. *Journal of Vocational Behavior, 35,* 105–163.

Fitzgerald, L. F., & Shullman, S. L. (1993). Sexual harassment: A research analysis and agenda for the 1990's. *Journal of Vocational Behavior, 42,* 5–27.

Fitzgerald, L. F., Shullman, S. L., Bailey, N., Richards, M., Swecker, J., Gold, Y., Ormerod, A. J., & Weitzman, L. M. (1988). The incidence and dimensions of sexual harassment in academia and the workplace. *Journal of Vocational Behavior, 32,* 152–175.

Fitzgerald, L. F., & Weitzman, L. M. (1992). Women's career development: Theory and practice from a feminist perspective. In Z. Leibowitz & D. Lea (Eds.), *Adult career development: Concepts, issues and practices* (2nd ed., pp. 124–160). Arlington, VA: AACD

Flint, P. L. (1980). *Sex-differences in the perceptions of occupational reinforcers.* Unpublished doctoral dissertation, University of Minnesota, Minneapolis.

Gay, E. G., Weiss, D. J., Hendel, D. D., Dawis, R. V., & Lofquist, L. H. (1971). Manual for the Minnesota Importance Questionnaire. *Minnesota Studies in Vocational Rehabilitation, 28.*

Ghiselli, E. E. (1966). *The validity of occupational aptitude tests.* New York: Wiley.

Goldman, R. D., & Hewitt, B. N. (1976). The scholastic aptitude test "explains" why college men major in science more often than college women. *Journal of Counseling Psychology, 23,* 50–54.

Gottfredson, L. S. (1981). Circumscription and compromise: A developmental theory of occupational aspirations [Monograph]. *Journal of Counseling Psychology, 28,* 545–579.

Granrose, C. S. (1984). A Fishbein–Azjen model of intention to work following childbirth. *Journal of Vocational Behavior, 25,* 359–372.

Gray, J. D. (1980). Counseling women who want both a profession and a family. *Personnel and Guidance Journal, 59,* 43–45.

Gutek, B. A. (1985). *Sex and the workplace.* San Francisco: Jossey-Bass.

Gutek, B. A., & Koss, M. P. (1993). Changed women and changed organizations: Consequences of and coping with sexual harassment. *Journal of Vocational Behavior, 42,* 28–48.

Gutek, B. A., & Larwood, L. (Eds.). (1987). *Women's career development.* Newbury Park, CA: Sage Publications.

Hall, D. T. (1972a). A model of coping with role conflict: The role behavior of college educated women. *Administrative Science Quarterly, 17,* 471–489.

Hall, D. T. (1972b). Role and identity processes in the lives of married women. Unpublished paper. Quoted in O'Leary, V. E. (1977). *Toward understanding women.* Monterey, CA: Brooks/Cole.

Hammer-Higgins, P., & Atwood, V. A. (1989). The Management Game: An educational intervention for counseling women with nontraditional career goals. *Career Development Quarterly, 38,* 6–24.

Harris, C. T., & Earle, J. R. (1986). Gender and work values: Survey findings from a working-class sample. *Sex roles, 15*, 487–494.

Hartigan, J. A., & Wigdor, A. K. (Eds.). (1989). *Fairness in employment testing: Validity generalization, minority issues, and the General Aptitude Test Battery.* Washington, DC: National Academy Press.

Herzberg, F., Mausner, B., & Snyderman, B. B. (1959). *The motivation to work* (2nd ed.). New York: Wiley.

Hesketh, B., & Dawis, R. (1991). The Minnesota Theory of Work Adjustment: A conceptual framework. In B. Hesketh & A. Adams (Eds.), *Psychological perspectives on occupational health and rehabilitation* (pp. 1–16). Sydney: Harcourt Brace Jovanovich.

Hesketh, B., McLachlan, K., Gardner, D. (in press). Work adjustment theory: An empirical test using a fuzzy rating scale. *Journal of Vocational Behavior.*

Higgins, N. C. (1986). Occupational stress and working women: The effectiveness of two stress reduction programs. *Journal of Vocational Behavior, 29*, 66–78.

Hoppock, R. (1935). *Job satisfaction.* New York: Harper and Row.

Hulin, C., Fitzgerald, L. F., & Drasgow, F. (1992). *Organizational Tolerance of Sexual Harassment Inventory.* Unpublished scale, Department of Psychology, University of Illinois, Champaign.

Hyde, J. S. (1981). How large are cognitive gender differences? A meta-analysis using $w^2$ and $d$. *American Psychologist, 36*, 892–901.

Hyde, J. S. & Linn, M. (1988). Gender differences in verbal ability: A meta-analysis. *Psychological Bulletin, 104*, 53–69.

Johnson, S. D. (1987). Knowing that versus knowing how: Toward achieving expertise through multicultural training for counseling. *Counseling Psychologist, 15*, 320–331.

Johnson, C. L., & Johnson, F. A. (1977). Attitudes toward parenting in dual-career families. *American Journal of Psychiatry, 134*, 391–395.

Koss, M. P. (1990). Changed lives. In M. Paludi (Ed.), *Ivory power: Sexual harassment in academia* (pp. 73–92). Albany, NY: SUNY Press.

Krumboltz, J. (1992, April). *Integrating career development theories.* Paper at Convergence in Theories of Career Choice and Development Conference, East Lansing, MI.

Lichter, D. J. (1980). *The prediction of job satisfaction as an outcome of career counseling.* Unpublished doctoral dissertation, University of Minnesota, Minneapolis.

Lofquist, L. H., & Dawis, R. V. (1969). *Adjustment to work.* New York: Appleton-Century-Crofts.

Lofquist, L. H., & Dawis, R. V. (1978). Values as second-order needs in the theory of work adjustment. *Journal of Vocational Behavior, 12*, 12–19.

Lofquist, L. H., & Dawis, R. V. (1991). *Essentials of person-environment correspondence counseling.* Minneapolis: University of Minnesota Press.

McLaughlin, M., Cormier, L. S., & Cormier, W. H. (1988). Relation between coping strategies and distress, stress, and marital adjustment of multiple role women. *Journal of Counseling Psychology, 35*, 187–193.

Mottaz, C. (1986). Gender differences in work satisfaction, work-related rewards and values, and the determinants of work satisfaction. *Human Relations, 39*, 359–378.

Naylor, J. C., Pritchard, R. D., & Ilgen, D. R. (1980). *A theory of behavior in organizations.* New York: Academic Press.

Nieva, V. F., & Gutek, B. A. (1981). *Women and work: A psychological perspective.* New York: Praeger.

Nock, S. L., & Kingston, P. W. (1988). Time with children: The impact of couples' worktime commitments. *Social Forces, 67*, 59–85.

Osipow, S. H. (1990). Convergence in theories of career choice and development: Review and prospect. *Journal of Vocational Behavior, 36*, 122–131.

Presser, H. (1988). Shift work and child care among young dual earner parents. *Journal of Marriage and the Family, 50*, 133–148.

Pryor, R. G. L. (1983). *Manual for the Work Aspect Preference Scale*. Melbourne: Australian Council for Educational Research.

Quinn, R., & Cobb, W. (1971). *What workers want*: Factor analysis of importance ratings of job facets. Ann Arbor, MI: Institute for Social Research.

Ralston, D. A., & Flanagan, M. F. (1985). The effects of flextime on absenteeism and turnover for male and female employees. *Journal of Vocational Behavior, 26*, 206–217.

Richardson, M. S. (1981). Occupational and family roles: A neglected intersection. *Counseling Psychologist, 9*, 13–23.

Ronen, S., Kraut, A. L., Lingoes, J. C., & Aranya, N. (1979). A nonmetric scaling approach to taxonomies fo employee work motivation. *Multivariate Behavioral Research, 14*, 387–401.

Rossi, A. S. (1965). Women in science: Why so few? *Science, 148*, 1196–1202.

Rounds, J. B. (1990). The comparative and combined utility of work value and interest data in career counseling with adults. *Journal of Vocational Behavior, 37*, 32–45.

Rounds, J. B., Jr., Dawis, R. V., & Lofquist, L. H. (1979). Life history correlates of vocational needs for a female adult sample. *Journal of Counseling Psychology, 26*, 487–496.

Rounds, J. B., Jr., Dawis, R. V., & Lofquist, L. H. (1987). Measurement of person-environment fit and prediction of satisfaction in the theory of work adjustment. *Journal of Vocational Behavior, 31*, 297–318.

Rounds, J. B., Jr., Henly, G. A., Dawis, R. V., Lofquist, L. H., & Weiss, D. J. (1981). *Manual for the Minnesota Importance Questionnaire*. Minneapolis: Department of Psychology, University of Minnesota, Vocational Psychology Research.

Rounds, J. B., & Tracey, T. J. (1990). From trait-and-factor to person-environment fit counseling: Theory and process. In W. B. Walsh & S. H. Osipow (Eds.), *Career counseling: Contemporary topics in vocational psychology* (pp. 1–44). Hillsdale, NJ: Lawrence Erlbaum Associates.

Russo, N. F. (1979). The motherhood mandate. *Journal of Social Issues, 32*, 143–153.

Salazar, R. C. (1981). *The prediction of satisfaction and satisfactoriness for counselor training graduates*. Unpublished doctoral dissertation, University of Minnesota.

Savickas, M. L., & Lent, R. W. (Chairs). (1992, April). *Conference on convergence in theories of career choice and development*. East Lansing, MI.

Stewart, E. S., Greenstein, S. M., Holt, N. C, Henly, G. A., Engdahl, B. E., Dawis, R. V., Lofquist, L. H., & Weiss, D. J. (1986). *Occupational reinforcer patterns*. Minneapolis: Vocational Psychology Research, Department of Psychology, University of Minnesota.

Tangri, S. S. (1972). Determinants of occupational role innovation among college women. *Journal of Social Issues, 28*, 177–199.

U.S. Department of Labor. (1965). *Dictionary of occupational titles* (3rd ed.). Washington DC: U.S. Government Printing Office.

U.S. Department of Labor. (1977). *Dictionary of occupational titles* (4th ed.). Washington DC: United States Government Printing Office.

Vredenburgh, D. J., & Trenkhaus, R. J. (1983). An analysis of role stress among hospital nurses. *Journal of Vocational Behavior, 22*, 82–95.

Vroom, V. H. (1964). *Work and motivation*. New York: Wiley.

Weiss, D. J., Dawis, R. V., England, G. W., & Lofquist, L. H. (1967). Manual for the Minnesota Satisfaction Questionnaire. *Minnesota Studies in Vocational Rehabilitation, 22*.

West, D. J., Jr., Horan, J. J., & Games, P. A. (1984). Component analysis of occupational stress innoculation applied to registered nurses in an acute care hospital setting. *Journal of Counseling Psychology, 31*, 209–218.

Zalesny, M. D., & Farace, R. V. (1988). Job function, sex, and environment as correlates of work perceptions and attitudes. *Journal of Applied Social Psychology, 18*, 179–202.

Zytowski, D. G. (1970). The concept of work values. *Vocational Guidance Quarterly, 18*, 176–186.

# ❧ 10 ❧

## Contemporary Developments in Women's Career Counseling: Themes of the Past, Puzzles for the Future

Lenore W. Harmon
*University of Illinois at Urbana-Champaign*

Naomi M. Meara
*University of Notre Dame*

Current discussion related to women's career counseling as exemplified in this volume contains themes that are familiar as well as puzzles that need to be solved if we expect continued progress in the field of women's career counseling. We set forth some of these themes followed by some of these puzzles, in order to highlight essential conflicts that we believe continue to impede women's achievement in the world of work.

First, a note on what we, the editors, authors, and readers of this book, are trying to accomplish. Counseling women is thoughtful serious business conducted by competent professionals of both genders. As demonstrated in the preceding chapters, those who engage in it and those who support it possess an impressive collective desire to "do it right." In attempting to implement this desire it is easy to lose sight of the fact that counseling is an interactive process that goes on between two people who are each growing and changing in their understanding of the human condition themselves, and of each other. Both the counselor and the client are in the midst of developmental processes that affect each of them and their relationship. Sometimes our clients are in stages of personal understanding that we can recognize from our own experience. At other times, they are forging into new territory that we have not experienced as a part of our personal or professional lives or the life of our collective culture. Because this arena is fraught with uncertainty, and because men and women are intimately involved in the issues related to career counseling and family life for women, perhaps we need to recognize that a more attainable goal may be to conduct career counseling with women "better" rather than "right." Setting a goal of "doing it better" acknowledges our commitment to our clients, and our understanding that both we and our clients are in the midst of growth processes that make it difficult to determine whether or not we are doing the "best" or the "right" things in our practice. What we can expect of ourselves is that we do "our best" at the time, recognizing that "our best" is an evolving construct. It changes with our knowledge, experiences, and the expectations and opportunities presented by our society.

## THEMES OF THE PAST

One of the major themes enunciated by those who have advocated changes in career counseling for women in our society since the 1970s has been that women's choices have been constricted by what has been traditionally feminine. Betz (this volume) showed that although women are working in greater numbers these days, their choices still seem disproportionately limited to low-status, low-pay, sex-segregated jobs. A theme that has been articulated more recently is that as women have gained opportunities in the workplace, for the most part they are still bearing the major responsibilities in childrearing, elder care, family entertaining, and household management. Betz characterized this situation as the "excessive demand for multiple roles"; elsewhere (Meara & Harmon, 1989), we have labeled this phenomenon as an unintended result or disappointment of the feminist movement of the 1970s. This excessive demand for multiple roles characterizes the lives of women across status, ethnicity and class. It effects (a) middle-class professionals, (b) single parents, and (c) the poor alike. For example, Russell (this volume) listed a number of barriers to women in managerial careers that have to do with actual or expected family responsibilities. She noted that one way that women have been able to make inroads in management careers is to delay childbearing. As Betz (this volume) pointed out, being single or childless is a facilitator in women's career development. Kerr (this volume) informed us that the "best and the brightest" girls are not pursing their intellectual interests in school in the same fashion as the "best and the brightest boys." In addition, she reminded us that although gifted college women now tend to make nontraditional career choices, these choices seem to be made with little understanding of the way of life associated with such careers. The underlying assumption in the chapters of this book seems to be that childrearing and family responsibilities are inevitably assigned to females. It is women who are primarily burdened by society's need to produce and socialize children. In fact, if they are not present in the home, many men do not even feel the need to support their children financially, let alone contribute to their care or education. (cf. e.g., Ehrenreich, 1984; Pleck, 1987). The assumption that females are responsible for family matters is a sad one for men, women, and their children. As early as 1972, the US. Commission on Population growth and the American Future recognized that for women to work outside the home in greater numbers, "some redefinition of the family roles of men and women would be required." They noted "both husband and wife would share more equally in both economic and domestic functions" (United States Commission, 1972, p. 153). The chapters in this volume seem to indicate that we have given up on trying to reach the goal of equal and equitable distribution of family responsibilities. It is interesting to speculate on why this is so and how it relates to the fact that working or career women have made less progress than one would expect in the world of work.

## PUZZLES FOR THE FUTURE

We review several puzzles that may contribute to this lack of progress. For purposes of discussion we have categorized the first set as puzzles related to social issues affecting clients. This set includes: (a) gender relationships and the distribution of power, (b) the definition of accomplishment in contemporary life, and (c) the ambiguity of having it all. A second set of puzzles relates to our own professional behavior, and includes: (a) individual help versus policymaking, and (b) the unevenness of practice and science. Finally, we present a puzzle that affects both counselors and clients; we have labeled that puzzle as the cognitive–affective gap, that is, the discrepancies between what makes cognitive sense and the affective reactions we have with respect to women's career development. We believe progress toward equality and justice for those who work will be limited and marginal until the issues implicit in these puzzles are recognized and addressed. They need to be resolved by both women and men in such a way that the organizations and institutions they create and sustain are fundamentally changed.

### Puzzles Related to Social Issues Facing Clients

*Gender Relationships and the Distribution of Power.* Very simply, gender is a relational construct; men and women define masculinity or femininity in the context of the other gender (cf. Kimmel, 1987). Traditionally, women and men have had intimate private mutual relationships and commitments that are very different from what one experiences or from what is appropriate in the world of work. The world of work, for example, is often hierarchically arranged, with individuals being responsible for providing guidance, instruction, or management for those "below" them and being held accountable for these activities to those "above" them. Typically in public life men have more power than women. On the other hand, individual male–female couples work out power-sharing accommodations in their private lives with less formal structure and more complex patterns than one finds in the world of work. The resulting organizational structure may be very ambiguous and very unique. The question of who has more power in specific relationships is not always easy to answer. Obviously, these private relationships to which men and women are accustomed do not provide a very useful model for working out gender relationships in the world of work. The difficulties in working out relationships in the world of work arise in two major ways. First, when women enter the work force in positions traditionally considered the prerogative of male workers, either they must accommodate to the informal structures men have established or the men must change these structures (cf. e.g., Fine, 1986; Kanter, 1977). Incidentally, the reverse is true when men enter a female-dominated occupation. Second, women and men are confronted with learning ways of relating to each other that are not romantic or sexual. Often the informal structures of communicating (e.g., sports talk or jokes involving sexual innuendo) are uninteresting or offensive to women. When women enter into what men consider to be their territory or work arena, men experience a loss of freedom and power. Often they cannot behave as they are accustomed to behaving; the "rules of the club" or the mores of male bonding are altered. In addition, men who are married to career women, in particular if the couple has children, often find themselves facing the same feelings of loss of control as well as the realities of having to assume more responsibilities at home. They are expected to communicate in new ways and negotiate more about domestic obligations. In some ways they must give up power or free time more than men whose wives work full-time in the home.

Comparisons are often made between the feminist movement and the struggles of other groups, such as African-Americans or Hispanics, who have been discriminated against or are less powerful in our individualistic Eurocentric society. While there is a certain validity in these comparisons as there are similarities in the experiences and efforts of oppressed groups, there is also a sense in which gender relationships, and the distribution of power that surrounds them, are different from other power struggles. Although a less powerful group may be forced to work out its identity in relation to a more powerful or dominant group, gender relationships are unique in that the more powerful, at least in their private lives, must build mutually satisfying and at least marginally equitable relationships with the less powerful. It is not surprising that as one moves away from male-dominated Eurocentric values to other cultural perspectives, some groups (e.g., lesbians [cf. Gilbert, Hallett, & Elridge, this volume] and African cultures [cf. Bingham & Ward, this volume]) seem to have found this particular problem easier to solve.

When power is unequally distributed, the less powerful typically accommodate more than the more powerful. Although men may believe that they and the institutions they dominate have accommodated fully (either willingly or through legal sanctions) to women's initiative or presence in the workplace, women tend to believe that they have had to accommodate more in both their personal and professional lives. Policies are not in place that allow women to easily fulfill the responsibilities society has set for them at home and at the same time have equal opportunity at work. Until power is more equitably distributed, this will most likely continue to be the case. For women and men in the workplace, then, a gender-dependent power problem exists apart from the customary power problems that are present in organizations where individuals are competing for recognition, advancement, and salary increases. Until men are willing to relinquish more power or women are willingly to insist more forcefully they should have power or, more simply, seize it, the problem will exist.

The reluctance to solve this complicated puzzle is not easily overcome, as solutions involve confronting the ways men and women define themselves with respect to their gender, and the ways they gain support, security, and happiness in their intimate relationships with the other gender (Westkott, 1986).

*Definition of Accomplishment in Contemporary Life.* Success is subjectively defined, and does not have the same meaning for everyone; however, today in the United States the ethic of individual achievement has clearly superseded the ethic of community contribution. Our society often characterizes achievement as attaining high status, being independent, amassing more and more material possessions, and having an apparently happy and successful family. We are often taught, in our work life at least, to expect and to strive for greater and greater achievement, and to work for common goals only when such actions serve our individual purposes. This philosophy or set of values presents us with another puzzle to be solved in our society. It is clear that for women to achieve, according to this philosophy, requires arrangements that limit the potential of men to (a) achieve at work and (b) be part of a household where the majority of the management and childcare responsibilities are attended to by women. It may be that the only resolution is to redefine the situation in a way that allows for everyone to win, or at least so that achievement in the world of work is not a zero-sum game where for every winner there is a loser. Such a solution may be more appealing to women than to men. If women are the winners over men, it can threaten women's traditional status in the sense that they lose security or status in the culture if they are less nuturant and if they provide less care for men and their children. On the other hand, having everyone win is not typically the way male-dominated organizations or contests are organized; for example, everyone seems dissatisfied when a football game ends in a tie. For men, then, having others share accomplishments would seem to be a loss of power and to violate the implicit if not explicit rule of competition, "may the best man win."

*The Ambiguity of Having It All.*   An expression that is often used by feminists and others in contemporary life is "having it all." This is taken to mean the privileges and enjoyments of a satisfying intimate relationship, children, and an intrinsically engaging successful career. Betz (this volume) concluded that women deserve to "have it all." Hackett and Lonberg (this volume) noted that the roles we play "work out differently for men and women," and we would add that "having it all" also generally works out differently for men and women.

Before addressing those differences, however, it may be worth examining the concept itself. First of all, we might address the question of "Who has it all?"; the answer would have to be, "Very few persons, if any, do; but if there are any they are likely to be men." To assume that it is possible to "have it all" implies unlimited resources with respect to (a) time and energy, (b) money, and (c) power over others at work and home. Many men who have substantial resources in these arenas may not believe they have it all or even that they have what they want, but rather see what they have as an excessive burden to provide financially in order to sustain a rather affluent lifestyle. Yet what they have is seen by others, especially women, as considerable privilege. Because of their work demands, they are excused from other responsibilities, so while the demand may be great it is more unidimensional, whereas for women the demand is multidimensional. Their career demands are the same, yet the family demands are greater. Many women see what they have gained as more responsibilities, not greater privilege. So the concept of having it all is probably illusive for most, and it certainly means different outcomes for men and women. Maybe no one can "have it all" if men and women are to have equal opportunity to the levels of achievement they want, at home and work. Although both men and women in our society may "deserve to have it all," that may be an unreasonable expectation from a life that is confined to a 24-hour day. This puzzle, like the contemporary definition of success, may require some reforming and rethinking of our values before it can be solved. For one thing, expectations for success in the world of work need to be reevaluated, as they are predicated on the model of a full-time caretaker/household manager and a full-time wage earner. To alter of our views of "having it all" will take major changes in the current structures with respect to how our society makes its policies, sets its priorities, and conducts its business.

## Puzzles Related to the Professional Behavior of Counseling Psychologists

The puzzles articulated thus far must certainly be solved if women are to make continued progress in the world of work and achieve satisfying lifestyles. However, the reader must also recognize that it is not easy to suggest solutions in which counseling psychologists or other career counselors can participate. In fact, we find more puzzles when we look at our own behaviors and history of help-giving, rather than readily apparent solutions.

*Individual Help Versus Policymaking.* This puzzle centers on the feminist agenda for counseling women and making policies that will ease their burdens and enhance their lives. The particular focus has to do with the tension between providing individual help versus creating major social changes and is exemplified in the expression "the personal is political." For example, as counselors we attempt to help solve power problems that women confront in the world of work on a case-by-case basis. This seems true for other issues as well.

For all of our rhetoric about outreach, prevention, and developmental concerns, the practice of counseling psychology is devoted mostly to individual one-to-one or small-group remedial experiences. Consequently, we seldom, if ever, see our practice, or for that matter our research missions, as having to do with policymaking. Primarily, we help individuals become aware of the social, interpersonal, and intrapersonal realities of their lives and assist them in building on strengths and finding remedies for dissatisfactions. When we deal with the socially constructed realities of our clients lives, the work of counseling focuses on awareness of the milieu and how to cope with its various aspects. This seems particularly true when we are working with women clients who are balancing career and family responsibilities. In their private lives counseling psychologists may work toward social change, or in their writings they may exhort its necessity if women are to have equal status in the world of work, but in general our research and practice is devoted to the individual. Although this may be appropriate to our training and expertise, there remains a question as to how successful the individual approach can be without major policy changes in parental leave, daycare, child support laws, and the like.

It would seem that career counselors are engaged in an enterprise that treats social problems as individual problems and can only be reactive to those problems. This puzzle can only be resolved if we find a way to make a professional impact on policy. As noted in a recent *New York Times* series on "The Good Mother," "around the country, a fundamental debate is going on: whether the new realities of mothers and work, which reflect deep economic and social trends, warrant revising the social contract between government businesses and families" (Barringer, 1992, p. 1). Counseling psychology is notably absent from this debate in both its science and practice.

*The Unevenness of Practice and Science.* It seems to us that our science is the most likely avenue for counseling psychology to make a contribution to policy. Unfortunately, since World War II we have seen a bifurcation of science and practice, and often organized psychology contributes to that bifurcation, to the detriment of the scientist-practitioner model and those specialties of psychology (e.g., counseling and organizational) whose disciplines are built on that perspective (Meara, 1990). Often in social science, experimentally designed empirical inquiry that meets the criterion of internal validity can be only marginally useful for practice or for informing policy. In addition, researching good practice with a goal of maximizing external validity or doing descriptive studies that might inform policy can result in messy science. Indeed, in counseling psychology the worlds of science and practice can be seen as two different cultures with different salient values (cf. Meara & Schmidt, 1991). Those who are interested in career counseling for women seem to be swimming against this tide in an attempt to integrate science and practice. A considerable body of work (e.g., in this volume and in the *Journal of Vocational Behavior* and the *Journal of Counseling Psychology*) considers both the scientific and applied aspects of career counseling with women. Much of this literature also demonstrates awareness of the practical issues facing women in their everyday work and family lives; that is, the literature is sensitive to such things as gender constraints and multicultural issues. It also acknowledges developments in theory, research, and practice. That being said, however, it seems to us that feminist ideas for practice tend to be much more explicit than those for science or theory development. In addition, as useful and logical as these practice suggestions may be, in general they are not particularly theory driven, nor empirically derived or evaluated.

The chapters in this volume provide examples and reviews of quality work that contribute to and promote the scientist-practitioner model; yet, as Brooks and Forrest (this volume) pointed out, more of the feminist critique has "filtered into" practice than into science. One explanation for this could be that a majority of clients and their professional counselors are women who readily understand issues that confront women in work and family life. On the other hand, in academic psychology experimental designs are more highly valued than more naturalistic field studies; yet the latter paradigms may be most appropriate for studying issues that are salient for women in the world of work. The senior leadership of academe may see both the feminist research agenda and methodologies for furthering it as limited, if not inappropriate. Investigators in academic departments who are interested in such research are often less powerful or of lower status, and few are willing or able to risk tenure, promotion, or salary increases.

This state of affairs presents problems for scientist-practitioners, as the feminist agenda for practice or policy will not prevail without the science to validate it. For example, the barriers and facilitators discussed by Betz and Russell (this volume) are part of the experience of most professional women and in that sense are considered by them to be valid. With the possible exception of the mathematics filter, however, the data are correlational and the phenomena have not been researched using the type of design that would allow causal inference. It becomes difficult therefore to make a case for barriers to women's career achievement scientifically, particularly, when one may be trying to make the case to those who oppose a feminist perspective. Hackett and Lonberg (this volume) have recalled for an exploration of the sociocultural premises of counselors that influence assessment. More broadly, there is a need for greater scientific exploration of the sociocultural premises of families, neighborhoods, and schools as they influence career choice.

The most important bond between science and practice is often theory. Here again it seems to us that practitioners are more willing to accept and apply feminist theory to their work than researchers are to use it as a basis for formulating important scientific questions, perhaps because those questions call for designs that are difficult to implement or logical inferences that may violate the canons of the hypotheticodeductive method. In addition, often our theory does not seem to represent the experiences of women. For example, Fitzgerald and Rounds (this volume) pointed out that one of our basic theories of vocational behavior, the theory of work adjustment, which describes work values, and reinforcers, does not relate these to home life and its demands, although it could be modified to do so.

We believe that the puzzle of how to make our science inform and support our practice must be resolved. Further, not surprisingly, we believe the best resolution of the situation is that the scientist-practitioner model prevail, and that advances in science and practice from a feminist perspective occur more evenly. This will not only enhance the quality and relevance of our scholarship and enable us to better serve women and men, but also it will make our agenda more credible to others who do not share our values. In addition, such a route clearly illustrates the point, central to the feminist argument, that science is not value free. This is particularly true of social science, whether the underlying philosophy be logical positivism, feminism, or any other perspective. Unfortunately, here we come face to face with the "pecking order" in psychology. In this case we must face the fact that counseling psychology is low in prestige among psychological disciplines and occupies a place vis-à-vis such specialities as social, quantitative, or cognitive psychology (which are higher in prestige) quite analogous to the power differential between men and women in our society. See the article "The Counselor is a Woman" (Farson, 1954) for a further extension of this analogy.

The consequence of this power differential is that we are in somewhat the same position as our women clients in that we exist in a professional subculture where our work is not as highly valued as other types of research. Our attempts to rearrange our subculture to better accomodate our needs to do work that satisfies us, and addresses research questions of interest, is met with resistance from those who consider it their prerogative to define good science. Thus, we find ourselves facing the need to solve similar puzzles about how to influence our professional society as women face about how to influence society in general. This is important because it affects our ability to make our scientific findings available to inform social policy. The solutions are not apparent or easy. Again, it would seem that we need to reframe the issues in some way that will allow for everyone to achieve satisfaction. That such a reformulation is not easy is well known to counseling psychologists and others who have tried to advance the interests of the scientist-practitioner or other applied training programs in academic psychology departments.

## THE GAP BETWEEN COGNITION AND AFFECT

It is interesting to speculate on why more has not changed for the better for women. Women have entered the work force and have proven their worth. To do so they have assumed greater responsibilities at work, but they have had to either add roles or sacrifice roles in exchange for these achievements. Our speculations about why more has not changed for the better are presented in the form of our final puzzle. As noted above, this puzzle affects both counselors and clients. We call this puzzle the *cognitive-affective gap*. By that we mean the discrepancies that confront women and men, professionals and clients alike, between what makes cognitive sense about women deserving equal opportunities at work and the affective reactions we have when women are extraordinarily successful outside the home or when we contemplate large numbers of them with significant achievements and high status. An example of this was the concern expressed several years ago (Grady, 1987; Howard, 1987) when women began entering psychology graduate school in record numbers. The term often used was the feminization of psychology, and it was seen by some as a negative prospect; for one reason, when women dominate in an occupation, the pay and the prestige of that occupation are usually lowered. A common reaction toward highly successful women, and many report experiencing such reactions from colleagues, is to attribute their accomplishments to affirmative action or perhaps hard work, but seldom to overall excellence or ability. In addition, women who are successful in their careers are often discounted or devalued by others in other areas of their lives; for example, they are not feminine, or good mothers, or pleasant people.

Although many of the authors represented in this volume have recognized internal and structural barriers that are related to woman's lack of power, they have not addressed the issues of why women have not seized the power they lack. Nor has there been much attention to the fact that even men, who are sympathetic to these issues, in particular with regard to their working daughters, have not relinquished more power or assisted women as a group in achieving it. We continue to see that women clients are ambivalent about seizing the opportunities that exist for them, and that articulate, upwardly mobile, career-oriented college women resist the label "feminist." The gender scheme of men and women (see Bem, 1983), in terms of what they see as appropriate for their gender with respect to relinquishing or seizing power, may be operating here.

In addition, it is clear that a large part of mainstream psychology is leery of work in women's career development and counseling; that is, it is skittish about the contents of the previous chapters (a) implementing the feminist critique in science and practice, (b) instilling better cross-cultural preparation in training programs, (c) reducing bias in assessment, and (d) considering what we have to learn from other cultures and lifestyles. It seems that we have not processed our affect or the emotional concomitants of solving or attempting to solve these puzzles or problems that face women in the world of work.

Cognitively, psychologists and others believe, equity and equality of opportunity make sense, but affectively they are frightening, because they imply societal changes we can't control, changes whose logical and/or ultimate conclusions are unforeseeable. While change is usually frightening, gender role change is exceedingly affect laden. Although affect has always been part of career choice, it has become particularly salient when we look at the career choices of women and the career dilemmas of an individual woman client. The significance of affect for scientists, practitioners, policymakers, and clients needs to be a more focused part of our work with regard to women and careers. Until it is, the science and practice of career counseling for women will be incomplete. In the broader sense, society's abilities to make coherent policies with respect to work and family will be limited if not incapacitated. The negative affect that accompanies change is shared by professionals, clients, and citizens alike.

## CONCLUSIONS

We have come full circle. Perhaps we are just as afraid of change as those we seek to help and thus cannot help them to explore the outer limits of what actually taking power over their lives would entail for themselves, their partners, and their children. As counselors we know that we must be aware of our own affective issues before we can help others. Perhaps awareness of our own fears is the first step. As scientists, we know that bias clouds both our result and its useful application. In this highly personal and potentially painful process of confronting affect and bias, we need to remember that we are in the midst of growth and change just as our clients are. We must ask of ourselves that we "do better" so that we improve our science, assist our clients, and encourage our society to become gender fair. We must do so, however, within the context of the complexities that confront women and men at home and work, and the resulting ambiguity that keeps us from knowing whether we are "doing it right" and keeps us frightened about "doing it wrong."

## REFERENCES

Barringer, F. (1992, October 7). In family-leave debate, a profound ambivalence. The good mother: Searching for a policy. *New York Times*, pp. A1–A13.

Bem, S. L. (1983). Gender scheme theory and implications for child development: Raising gender-aschematic children in a gender-schematic society. *Signs: Journal of Women in Culture and Society, 8*, 598–616.

Ehrenreich, B. (1984, May 20). A feminist view of the new man. *New York Sunday Magazine*, pp. 36–39.

Farson, R. E. (1954). The counselor is a woman. *Journal of Counseling Psychology, 1*, 221–224.

Fine, G. D. (1987). One of the boys: Women in male dominated settings. In M. S. Kimmel (Ed.), *Changing men: New directions in research on men and masculinity* (pp. 131–147). Newbury Park, CA: Sage.

Grady, K. (1987, May). Sinister overtones. *APA Monitor*, p. 40.

Howard, A. (1987, May). The pendulum swings. *APA Monitor*, p. 40.

Kanter, R. M. (1977). *Men and women of the corporation*. New York: Basic Books.

Kimmel, M. S. (Ed.). (1987). *Changing men: New directions in research on men and masculinity*. Newbury, CA: Sage.

Meara, N. M. (1990). Science, practice and politics. *Counseling Psychologist, 18*, 144–167.

Meara, N. M., & Harmon. L. W. (1989). In the beginning: Accomplishments and disappointments of the Division 17 committee on women. *Counseling Psychologist, 17*, 314–331.

Meara, N. M., & Schmidt, L. D. (1991). Researching the counseling process. In C. E. Watkins & L. J. Schneider (Eds.), *Research in counseling* (pp. 237–259). Hillsdale, NJ: Lawrence Erlbaum Associates.

Pleck, J. H. (1987). The contemporary man. In M. Scher, M. Stevens, G. Good, & G. A. Eichenfield (Eds.), *Handbook of counseling and psychotherapy with men* (pp. 16–27). Newbury Park, CA: Sage.

United States Commission on Population Growth and the American Future. (1972). *Population and the American future: The report of the commission on population growth and the American future*. New York: New American Library.

Westkott, M. (1986). *The feminist legacy of Karen Horney*. New Haven, CT: Yale University Press.

# Author Index

# Subject Index